THE WAR ECONOMY OF THE UNITED STATES

D1026874

BOOKS BY SEYMOUR MELMAN

Dynamic Factors in Industrial Productivity
Inspection for Disarmament (Editor)
Decision-Making and Productivity
The Peace Race
No Place to Hide (Editor)
Disarmament: Its Politics and Economics (Editor)
Our Depleted Society
In the Name of America (Editor)
Industrial Efficiency Under Managerial vs. Cooperative Decision-Making
Conversion of Industry from a Military to Civilian Economy: A Series (Editor)
Pentagon Capitalism

SEYMOUR MELMAN, editor

THE WAR ECONOMY OF THE UNITED STATES
Readings on military industry and economy

St. Martin's Press
New York

AFFILIATED PUBLISHERS: Macmillan & Company, Limited, London—also at Bombay, Calcutta, Madras and Melbourne; The Macmillan Company of Canada, Limited, Toronto.

PREFACE

In the main, neither the propositions nor the data presented in this volume are present in the principal textbooks that are available for introductory courses in economics. Industrial management texts too do not identify or analyze the managerial characteristics of the military-oriented firm as distinct from the autonomous firm that serves civilian markets.

War economy and its implications for micro- and macroeconomics are relatively neglected by economists. This neglect is at once a reason for the preparation of this volume and an implied admonition to textbook writers. I would like nothing more than to retire from the task of supplementing textbooks with respect to the characteristics and effects of military economy.

This collection is organized in sections that portray, first, the characteristics of the military-industrial firm; second, the nature of its impact on the economy as a whole; and, finally, the problem of conversion from military to civilian economy.

In the research preparation for this volume I was ably helped by my assistant, Stephen Tencer, and by Miss Ruth Cheney. I am indebted to Miss Elaine Yaede of St. Martin's Press for her work in clearing permissions on these materials.

Seymour Melman
Columbia University

CONTENTS

RELEVANT TOPICS IN ECONOMICS

1. From Private to Pentagon Capitalism *Entrepreneurship, Growth*
    Seymour Melman   1

I. The Scale of Military Economy

2. World Military Expenditures, 1969 *The World Market*
    U.S. Arms Control and Disarmament
    Agency   9

3. The War Machine Under Nixon *Growth*
    I. F. Stone   22

4. Arms Sales and Foreign Policy *Foreign Trade*
    U.S. Senate, Committee on Foreign
    Relations   34

5. The Worried Taypayer's Guide to
    the Defense Budget   *Determinants of Growth*
    Richard J. Barnet   44

6. Cost and Status of Major Weapons
    Systems   50 *Market Forecast*

7. Toward a Permanent War Economy? *Long-Range Market Forecast*
    Walter J. Oakes   53

II. The Military-Industrial Firm

8. A Theory of the Military-Industrial
    Firm   *The Economizing Problem*
    John Francis Gorgol   60

9. Firms Without Enterprise *Monopoly, Monopsony*
    Seymour Melman   71

10. Free Enterprise and National
    Defense   *Government Controls and Regulation*
    Jack Raymond   76

11. The Economics of Military
    Procurement
    Joint Economic Committee,   *Market Organization and Price*
    U.S. Congress   85

12. Defense Waste and the Industrial
    Engineer   *Productivity*
    A. E. Fitzgerald   101

13. Weapons Systems: A Story of
    Failure   *Product Quality*
    Bernard D. Nossiter   106

III. Economic Consequences of Military Industry
For the Economy as a Whole

14. **The Defense Sector: An Evaluation
    of Its Economic and Social Impact**   *The Mixed Economy*
    Arthur F. Burns   111

15. **Profits Without Productivity**   *Employment and Comparative Advantage*
    Seymour Melman   122

16. **Federal Science, an Economic Drag,
    Not Propellant**   *Research, Development and Growth*
    Amitai Etzioni   132

17. **The Balance of Military Payments
    Among States**   *Regional Input-Output*
    James R. Anderson   137

18. **Who Decides Technology?**   *Technology*
    Seymour Melman   147

19. **The Price of War**   *Opportunity Cost*
    Bruce M. Russett   152

20. **What the Vietnam War Has Cost**   *Money, Gold, Inflation*
    Terence McCarthy   160

21. **Vietnam, the 200-Year Mortgage**   *Public Debt, Social Cost*
    James L. Clayton   169

22. **American Dollar in Jeopardy**   *Money and Gold*
    Terence McCarthy   173

23. **Statement to the U.S. Senate,
    Committee on Foreign Relations**   *Social Cost, Inflation, and International*
    Louis B. Lundborg, Bank of   *Disequilibrium*
    America   175

24. **The Garrison Society**   *Changing Functions of Government*
    Vernon K. Dibble   179

25. **Whither California**   *Scarce Resource Allocation*
    Martin Gellen   187

IV. Convertibility of Military Industry
to Civilian Economy

26. **Characteristics of the Industrial
    Conversion Problem**   *Scarce Resource Allocation, High*
    Seymour Melman   201   *Employment Equilibrium*

27. **U.S. Industrial Economy Unprepared for Peace**
Seymour Melman 207

Imperfections in Adjustment of Resource Uses

28. **Arms Firms See Postwar Spurt**
Bernard D. Nossiter 209

Oligopoly and Changes in Market Demand

29. **Conversion and the Import Problem**
John E. Ullmann 215

Comparative Advantage

30. **Economic and Social Consequences of Disarmament,**
United Nations 225

Resource Allocation

31. **Economic Report of the President, 1969 / Illustrative New Programs** 229

Opportunity Cost

32. **Impact of Deep Cuts in Defense**
U.S. News and World Report 231

Imperfections in Labor Markets

33. **How to Give Up the Economy of Death and Keep Prosperity**
Richard J. Barnet 234

Employment and Investment

34. **Non-Violent Economics: Next Task for Mankind**
E. F. Schumacher 240

Utility-Maximizing

Bibliography 243

Index 245

1. From Private to Pentagon Capitalism

Seymour Melman

The military-industrial firm and the effects of its operations have changed the internal economics of the firm (microeconomics) and have altered key features of industrial capitalism as a whole (macroeconomics). The extent of these effects is linked to the scale of military-serving industry.

Military industry in 1970 employed about 3 million persons on work directly traceable to the Department of Defense. In addition, 3.4 million men and women served in the uniformed armed forces and about one million civilians were employed by the Department of Defense, mostly on military bases engaged in research, development, testing, prototype manufacture and supporting activities, and base maintenance. All told, about 22,000 enterprises have been linked to the Department of Defense as performers of contracted work.

The tacit assumption has been that the firms serving the Department of Defense are like other enterprises. What has proceeded almost unnoticed is that since 1945 there has been a 25-year experience in which a new type of enterprise has been created that is basically different in many operating characteristics from the entrepreneurial firm of industrial capitalism. The combined effect of this network of enterprises has modified the economy as a whole because of the character and the size of military expenditures.

The autonomous capitalist firm has operated to extend the decision-power of its management, using cost minimization and profit accumulation as major instrumental measures. This extension has been characteristically measured in terms of percentage of a market, percent of capital investment, or change in the proportion of employees in a given industry. For this exten-

sion of decision-power, profitability has been calculated and accumulated as a vital source of fresh capital for investment. Thus, during the last half century, firms have become increasingly self-financed, relying increasingly on themselves for accumulation of capital for further investment. (Profit levels can vary substantially as a function of decisions by managements on allocating various fixed costs. Thereby the magnitude of profit in a given period is diminished as an autonomous indicator of management's operations.)

The character of the military-industrial firm is functionally defined by the way its management participates in decision-making. Managing includes decisions on what products to produce; how to accumulate capital; how to design and organize production; the quantity of the product; the price to be charged; and the mode of distribution of the product. Together, these functions constitute management. The autonomy of the private firm rests on the fact that the final veto power over these decisions is in the hands of its own management. This central characteristic has been altered in the military-industrial firm.

From 1946 on, industrial firms were increasingly linked with military research institutes and with the Department of Defense in conformity with a policy regulation issued by the then Chief of Staff of the United States Army, General Dwight D. Eisenhower. (See text in Appendix A of my book, *Pentagon Capitalism*, McGraw-Hill, 1970.) Following that policy memorandum, the Pentagon arranged durable connections between nominally private firms, nominally private research laboratories (profit, university, and other nonprofit), and the military establishment. Through this period, the Department of Defense proceeded to act in ways that are characteristic of a large, monopolistic buyer — intervening in the internal affairs of the supplying firms to suit the convenience of the monopoly buyer.

Such activity by a monopoly buyer has been noted, for example, as characterizing the relations of large automotive firms to parts suppliers, or the relation of department stores or mail-order houses to suppliers of products, very often under brand names selected by the buyer. Following the Eisenhower policy that effectively founded the market network, which he later named the "military-industrial complex," the main elements of managerial decision-making within the Pentagon-serving private firm were increasingly subject to regulatory stipulations of the official *Armed Services Procurement Regulations.* (Since the monopolist buyer was also the Federal Government, there was the inevitable infusion of government-citizen relations into the buyer-seller pattern.)

After 1961, an organizational transformation was effected under the direction of Robert McNamara which changed the relation of the military-industrial firms to the Department of Defense customer. Robert McNamara established, under the Office of the Secretary of Defense, a central administrative office, functionally similar to the type of unit that has operated in central-office-controlled, multi-division, major manufacturing firms.

With the establishment of this central office, whose nature and effects I detailed in *Pentagon Capitalism,* the relation of the military-industrial firms to the single customer shifted from one of, primarily, seller to buyer towards that of submanagement to top management. The Office of the Secretary of Defense, through its component institutions, took on the function of a top management formulating policy in relation to the nominally autonomous contracting firms. This relationship was enforced through a formal, nation-wide network of administrative offices, which supplemented the administrative organization that had previously existed and reported to the several armed services. The key element here was the concentration of control in new institutions, like the Defense Supply Agency set up by McNamara. The impact of the long-term regulatory process, plus the sharp change to formally centralized control in the new state management, induced a qualitative change in the character of military-industrial enterprise:

Final decision-power over the main components of managerial control was vested in the new state management apparatus.

The military-industrial firm became a functionally dependent subdivision. Decisions on products were formally rendered by the top management in the Department of Defense. Only the most minor decisions on product characteristics were left to the individual firm. The government-based management provided capital, not only by making available land, buildings, or machinery, but also by guaranteeing loans obtained from private sources. The extension of the scope and intensity of the state management's control proceeded in every sort of decision-making: on how to produce, on quantity, price, and shipment. The net effect was to establish the state management as the holder of the final decision-power and also to limit the scope of decision left to the managements of the defense contractors, the subdivisions of the state management.

Within industrial capitalism, subfirms frequently operate under central office control. In the military-industrial system, however, the central office is located in the executive branch of the Federal Government. It is unprecedented in size, and so is the number of submanagements. By 1968, the Department of Defense industrial system supplied $44 billions of goods and services. This exceeded the combined net sales (in billions) of General Motors ($22.8), General Electric ($8.4), U.S. Steel ($4.6), and DuPont ($3.4). Altogether, this constitutes a form of state capitalism operating under the Department of Defense — hence the designation "Pentagon Capitalism."

The military-industrial enterprise is not an industrial capitalist firm. It is not an autonomous entity, being under final control of the Pentagon's state management. Internally, it differs from the entrepreneurial business that is the model unit of industrial capitalism as illustrated by the role of profit and cost minimization.

Profit and loss statements are computed in military industry and a profit category is shown. However, this profit is not a reward for entrepreneurial risk-taking, the conventional justification for the profit accruing to the management or owners of the micro-economic unit of industrial capitalism. Risk of the ordinary sort is eliminated under conditions of assured (by contract) price and quantity of goods to be delivered to the Department of Defense. There may be residual "risk" of not getting further business, but that is another matter. Moreover, profits for a subunit can be readily regulated by the state management which is inclined to regard "profits" of its subunits as a cost to the top controllers.

Within the new military-industrial enterprise, the self-correcting mechanisms that characterize the private firm are altered, if not dissolved. When major managerial functions are poorly performed in the ordinary firm, it is the entrepreneurial obligation, then, to correct the malfunction. In the military-industrial firm, this may not be feasible insofar as final decision-making is in the hands of the state management. Thus unusually high costs, or problems in the design of the product, or problems in acquiring sufficient capital, are not, in a military-industrial enterprise, necessarily autonomously actionable problems for that management.

In the firm of private capitalism, high costs become important pressures for modification of industrial practice. For unduly high cost, as against the cost of alternative methods, can translate into competitive disadvantage and limited profits: hence, limited options for further capital investment; hence, limited options for further production decision-making by the management. Therefore, the manager of the classic industrial firm is moved to act to minimize costs. This is operative except in those circumstances where managements, either singly or in concert with others, restrict market competition and shift cost increases to price, while maintaining an acceptable profit margin for all. However, it is ordinarily understood that the latter practice is an alteration of the more characteristic cost-minimizing calculus of the private firm. In the military-industrial firm, cost increases or unusually high costs are dealt with mainly by raising price. The record

shows that, on the average, the final price of major weapons systems has been about 3.2 times the initial estimate.

Finally, the conventional firm can move among markets when it finds that its products are not well accepted. No options of this sort exist for the military-industrial firm. For the Department of Defense is the market and the firm may not sell to anyone else except with permission of the Department of Defense—as, for example, to a politically allied foreign military establishment.

These modifications in the self-correcting mechanisms of the classic business firm substantially alter the characteristics of that model entity, distinguishing the military-industrial firm and its controlling state management from the private and autonomous entrepreneurial enterprise.

The operation of the military-industrial firms produces a series of unique effects for the economy as a whole. These include distortions of measured growth and opportunity cost in terms of depleted industries, services, and occupations. From 1945 to 1970, $1,100 billions were expended by the U.S. Government for military purposes. This exceeds the 1967 value of all business and residential structures in place on the surface of the United States. However, the prime effects of the military-industrial activity are owed to its economic-functional nature.

Ordinarily, in national income accounting, all money-valued goods and services are included in the category Gross National Product. However, because of the character and size of military economic activity, it is important to make an economic-functional differentiation between economic growth that is productive and economic growth that is parasitic.

Productive growth includes goods and services that are used as part of the level of living or can be used for further production of whatever sort. Parasitic economic growth refers to goods and services that are not part of the level of living, or cannot be used for further production. Plainly, military goods and services are overwhelmingly in the latter class.

Each year, from 1960 to 1970, 8 to 10 percent of the U.S. Gross National Product has been used for the military. Thereby, the men and women who did the work were paid, but their products were, upon completion, withdrawn from market exchange. Whatever worth may be attributed to military products on other than economic-functional grounds, it is apparent that you cannot live in, wear, or ride an intercontinental missile or an antipersonnel bomb. Neither can such products be used for further production. What seemed a small portion, 10 percent or less, of each year's GNP accumulated to an immense sum from 1945 to 1970.

The full cost to a society of parasitic economic growth is two-fold: First, there is the value of the man-hours, materials and whatever goes into making nonproductive goods or services; second, there is the economic use-value that is lost for level of living or for further production (as against possible *military* use-value). Such economic use-value is ordinarily equivalent to the price paid for making nonproductive (or productive) goods. *Therefore the social cost of parasitic economic growth is that of the resources used up directly plus the productive use-value foregone, or double the price nominally paid.* Thus, the $1,100 billion military outlay by the United States from 1945 to 1970 actually cost the nation $2,200 billion, or the value of total reproducible wealth of the nation (excluding only the land).

A collateral effect of sustained parasitic economic activity in the United States has been to jeopardize the international and the domestic value of the dollar. For the payments made to people for parasitic economic growth are made for goods and services that are not purchasable thereafter. These payments for such goods and services are not "sterili:ed" economically and are used as claims on those goods that do reach the marketplace. There is no gainsaying the importance of military economic activity as a cause of price instability in today's American society. The 20 percent drop in the purchasing power of the dollar from 1964 to 1970 places its future value in doubt. This means, of course, that the value of money income, savings, insurance, and pension funds was diminished by a similar amount; that is, the drop in the value of the dollar saw a corresponding destruction of capital.

The value of the dollar, relative to other currencies, is critically affected by another mechanism. In 1950, the United States Treasury possessed $24 billions in gold bullion. By August, 1970, this had diminished to $11.8 billions. The reason for the diminution, despite a sustained favorable balance of trade, was due primarily to the heavy overseas outlays for military and allied purposes during the period 1950 to 1970. The net result was an accumulation of dollars abroad that was not used for purchases from the American economy. Some of these dollars were presented to the U.S. Treasury for redemption in gold. As against $11.8 billions in gold bullion held by the Treasury in August 1970, there were $42 billions of short-term claims by foreigners against the United States reported by American banks. It is plausible to expect that if foreign claimants on United States gold were to attempt massive cashing in of their short-term claims this country would embargo the shipment of gold abroad. The world monetary system would collapse.

A kindred process led to the decline in the international exchange value of the British pound. Thus, the Gross National Product of England rose, year by year, after the Second World War, and the stock of durable goods and wealth in British society also rose. However, the short-term assets, primarily precious metal and hard currencies, available to finally redeem claims on the pound held abroad were in short supply. The visible unlikelihood of Britain meeting her short-term obligations at the then prevailing parity for sterling caused a run on sterling sufficient to bring about the very devaluation which had been feared.

It is significant that the annual portion of GNP used for parasitic economic growth is not an average, homogeneous 8 to 10 percent of U.S. goods and services. For the military-related institutions and military industry have been using more than half of the nation's technical research talent. Since a missile designer cannot be designing railroad equipment or civilian electronics at the same time, the country has had more missiles but less railroad equipment, civilian electronics, and kindred goods.

Only insofar as we understand the consequence of applying half and more of the country's technical research talent to parasitic economic growth can we explain what is otherwise an anomaly: the appearance of technological and economic depletion in many sectors of American industry and services — together with a growth in GNP. Principal industries that are deteriorating include steel, house-building, ship-building, and machinery production of many classes. Deterioration or grossly unsatisfactory performance in services include the telephone and postal systems, the supply of electricity (notably in the Northeastern states during the last period) and the performance of medical services.

In 1967, 40.7 percent of the young men examined by Selective Service for military induction were rejected on grounds of physical or educational incapacity. This means that the American economy, with a GNP in excess of one trillion dollars a year in 1970, has been short-changing the young men and women of this society in education and health care. That is inexplicable except as we appreciate that $1,100 billion was expended for military and related parasitic purposes over 25 years, and the quality of the manpower was concentrated in military and allied work.

"Opportunity cost," the value of something foregone, is one way of assessing the value of goods or services. In the present case, what has been the opportunity cost to American society of expending $1,100 billion for military purposes? Consider that over a period of 20 years this meant a foregone expenditure of $50 billion a year for alternative purposes.

The ordinary use of money as a unit of economic measurement leads to a pervasive misreading of the effects of military and allied spending as the dominant share of the Federal Government's budgets. There is nothing in the nature of money that limits its rapid expansion, at will.

Unlike money, which can be swiftly created, manpower, especially skilled manpower, is finite in quantity and requires a long time for expansion. Therefore, the using up of major portions of research, engineering, and other skilled heads and hands for the military represents an allocation of resources that cannot be fully measured in money terms. Thus the unavailability of skilled people for many civilian industries and services produces deterioration that is not reasonably expressed in money units. As the number of physicians per 100,000 citizens in the U.S. fell from 105 in 1950 to 97 in 1967, available medical care diminished. What is the money-value of the fact that the United States ranks 18th among nations in infant mortality rate?

The period 1950–1970 is marked by the transfer of production by an unknown but large number of American firms from U.S. to foreign locations. This is usually charged to high American wage rates. However, what counts competitively is not the wage per hour but the unit labor cost. With appropriate mechanization and organization of work, a high hourly wage can be translated into products with a low unit labor cost. But this requires the application of skilled technical talent and fresh capital. To the degree that these indispensible elements have been so heavily preempted for military uses, many American managements have chosen the less onerous course of switching from production in the United States to buying abroad.

Perhaps even more important than depletion of industries is the depletion of occupations and regions in the economy. Depleted occupations refer, for example, to an unknown but large number of engineers who functioned for many years on behalf of the military, and thereby acquired a trained incapacity for functioning in a civilian industrial environment. Depleted regions refer to states, cities, and counties which have had a preponderance of military industry and related activity, especially during the decade 1960–1970. By 1970, a slowdown in the rate of military-industrial expenditures, notably in research and development, created depressed areas in regions like the suburbs of Los Angeles, the San Francisco Bay area, Seattle, eastern Long Island, and the area around Route 128 in Boston.

The opportunity cost of the military system includes the inability of the United States to provide for economic development at home for the 30 million Americans who need it. Economic underdevelopment normally is understood to mean high infant mortality rate and limited life span, a high incidence of certain epidemic diseases, and limited education and, hence, limited productivity and income. The process that alters this condition is called economic development. It requires investment in human capital and in physical productive facilities.

In the United States, a process of economic development would require an outlay of about $50,000 for a family unit of four. Considering 30 million possible candidates for economic development, about 60 percent of them white and 40 percent black, the requirement for 7.5 million "equivalent family units" would entail an expenditure of $375 billions over a period of, say, 10 years, or $37.5 billions per year. That sum, it should be noted, compares with estimates of the full annual cost of the Vietnam war at its peak. Obviously, expenditures of $37.5 billions per year for economic development are not conceivable while military budgets use up $70 to $80 billions per year.

The prime limits on the capability of the United States economy are most critically defined in terms of the availability and the use of skilled manpower. To accomplish an economic development process requires an investment of skilled manpower in the work of enhancing the human capital and productive skills of persons who are economically underdeveloped. The same consideration constrains American participation in economic development in other areas of the world.

What has been foregone by the United States owing to the operation of the military economy can be gauged in yet another way. Included in this volume are estimates of what might be expended in America under condition of substantially diminished priority to military activity. The Council of Economic Advisors, in its Report to the President, 1969, itemized expenditures in several spheres of public responsibility totalling $39.7 billions of annual expenditures. The agenda is the familiar one of undercapitalized areas in American society: education, health, nutrition, community service, jobs and manpower, social security, quality of environment, and so forth.

Another set of estimates specifying alternatives to military activity was calculated in 1964 by the Senate Subcommittee on Employment and Manpower. Their agenda of costs for meeting a backlog of national needs in housing, urban renewal, mass transit, highways, pollution control, and the like involved financing of $43 to $53 billions per year for 10 years, then $31 to $41 billions per year for another decade. In my volume, *Our Depleted Society* (New York: Dell Books, 1965; Chapter 10), I called attention to an agenda of public responsibility activities involving outlays of $65 billions per year over an extended period of time.

In each of these estimates, it is useful to translate the possible outlay into man-years of equivalent activity. Thus, applying a factor of, say, $8000 a year as the average cost of one man-year, it is apparent that the possible agendas of public responsibility investments, alternative to the military, involve outlays that would require 6 to 8 million man-years.

The officially budgeted costs of the war in Vietnam include the incremental costs as distinguished from an estimate of the total costs of that war. Thus for 1967, $20 billions; for 1968, $26 billions; for 1969, $29 billions; and for 1970, it is estimated at $23 billions. In 1962, in my book *The Peace Race* (Ballantine and George Braziller) I calculated the total cost of economic development for the populations of Africa, Asia, and Latin America. My reckoning indicated that an annual capital investment of $22 billions was the cost, world-wide, for accelerating an economic development process.

Evidently, the incremental military costs — by themselves — to the United States for the war in Vietnam, from 1967 to 1970, used up a capital sum approximately equal to what I calculated would be required for accelerating economic development in Asia, Africa and Latin America.

For the United States, the policy issue involved in changing from a military-priority economy is not restricted to having the present military force or having none at all, having a military security system of the present sort as against no military security at all. In fact, many alternatives are conceivable in place of the military security goal of preparing to fight 2½ wars at once that dominated U.S. policy in the 1960's. For example, the United States could conceivably define its foreign policies so as to require a military security force to operate a plausible nuclear deterrent; to guard the shores of the United States; and to have a capability for participating in international peace-keeping. The total manpower required to operate such a force, including supporting staffs and functions, would comprise about one million men, and the cost of operation would be about one-third of the 1970 military budget of $75 billions. A military security concept of this sort opens up the possibility of alternative uses of about $50 billions a year of money and manpower now employed for military and related purposes.

The state management that controls the military-industrial system has applied its considerable influence to counter legislative and other kinds of preparations for conversion of military-industrial employees and facilities to civilian work. By Septem-

ber 1970, Senator Abraham Ribicoff summarized the results of an inquiry by his Subcommittee on Executive Reorganization into the status of capability for conversion to civilian economy among military-industrial firms:

In general, the responses indicated that private industry is not interested in initiating any major attempts at meeting critical public needs. Most industries have no plans or projects designed to apply their resources to civilian problems. Furthermore, they indicated an unwillingness to initate such actions without a firm commitment from the Government that their efforts will quickly reap the financial rewards to which they are accustomed. Otherwise, they appear eager to pursue greater defense contracts or stick to proven commercial products within the private sector. . . . After carefully examining the letters as a whole, we found that the need for serious thought and action on conversion has largely been disregarded by most of the business community.

For the business units of industrial capitalism, the development of military industry has meant a transformation from the autonomous entrepreneurial firm to the military-industrial enterprise functioning under a state management. For the economy as a whole, the formalization of Pentagon capitalism and the outlays on its behalf have involved parasitic growth on a large scale and at a large opportunity cost. The economy and society as a whole bear the unknown cost of an array of depleted industries, occupations, and industrial areas, and the cost of sustaining an economically underdeveloped population of 30 million among 200 million Americans.

✳   ✳   ✳

Key characteristics of the military industrial firm and the military industrial system as a whole are stated in the following propositions. The numbers after each statement identify the relevant readings in this volume.

PROPOSITION 1   The military-industrial firm in not autonomous. *(1, 8, 9, 10, 25)*

PROPOSITION 2   The military-industrial firm is controlled by a state management. *(1, 8, 10, 14, 18, 25)*

PROPOSITION 3   The military-industrial firm does not minimize cost. *(1, 8, 9, 11, 12, 25)*

PROPOSITION 4   The military-industrial firm is not a profit maximizing entity. *(1, 8, 10, 12)*

PROPOSITION 5   The state management is a new concentration of industrial control. *(1, 3, 6, 10, 14, 24)*

PROPOSITION 6   Gross National Product is composed of productive and parasitic growth. *(1, 14, 16, 18)*

PROPOSITION 7 Economically parasitic output produces price inflation. *(14, 20, 23)*

PROPOSITION 8 Foreign military spending endangers the value of the dollar. *(1, 20, 22, 23)*

PROPOSITION 9 The cost of the military system entails a large opportunity cost for American society. *(1, 2, 5, 14, 15, 16, 17, 19, 20, 21, 24)*

PROPOSITION 10 The military-industrial firms, as a group, lack flexibility for conversion to civilian work. *(25 through 33)*

I. THE SCALE OF MILITARY ECONOMY

2. World Military Expenditures, 1969
United States Arms Control and Disarmament Agency

HIGHLIGHTS OF THE DATA

World military spending continued to rise in 1969, although at a somewhat slower pace than in the 3 years preceding. The total reached a record $200 billion, up 44 per cent since 1964, when ACDA compiled the first estimates of global military spending based on national data for 120 countries.[1]

During this period, military outlays in current dollars have grown from $139 billion in 1964, $143 billion in 1965, $160 billion in 1966, $181 billion in 1967, to an estimated $191 billion in 1968 and $200 billion in 1969.

Over the 6-year period this means that more than $1 trillion ($1,000,000,000,000) has been spent for arms and armed forces. What an expenditure of this magnitude means is clearer when it is measured against available economic resources. This sum exceeds the value of all the goods and services produced in the United States in the past year. It is more than 2 years' income for the world's 93 developing countries, in which over 2.5 billion people live. Larger than any civilian programs financed by public funds, the world's military budget in this period took as much public money as was spent by all governments on all forms of public education and health care.

From *World Military Expenditures, 1969, and Related Data for 120 Countries,* Economics Bureau, U.S. Arms Control and Disarmament Agency, Washington, D.C. 20451.

The most recent figures indicate that the advanced industrial nations continue to dominate world outlays (Chart 1). Of the $200 billion estimated to have been spent in 1969, the NATO countries accounted for $108 billion, or 54 per cent, the Warsaw Pact countries for $63 billion, or 32 per cent. U.S. expenditures in 1969, which do not yet reflect the budget cuts made during the year, are estimated at $82 billion of the NATO total. Soviet expenditures are roughly estimated at $56 billion of the Warsaw Pact total.

In both 1968 and 1969, however, the military expenditures of countries outside the two major blocs represented an increasing proportion of world outlays. Military budgets of these countries appeared to be growing at a rate more than twice that of the world total, reflecting an accelerated arms race among the developing countries. The upward spiral of arms budgets in the poorer countries was one of the most striking—and disturbing—aspects of the latest trends in world military spending.

The trend of military expenditures

Between 1965 and 1967, world military spending in current prices soared upward at the rate of 13 percent a year. Preliminary data now available for 1968 and 1969 suggest that the year-to-year increase has since slowed down. Outlays of the NATO and Warsaw Pact countries were still rising in 1969, but less rapidly. In the remaining countries, while national trends are spotty, the expansion of military budgets still averaged close to 10 per cent a year. For the world as a whole, the increase has been 5 per cent a year since 1967.

This more recent trend is encouraging in several respects. The rise is not only smaller than in the mid-sixties but also slightly less than the average annual rise since World War II. If the pattern of the last 2 years continues, it will mean some reduc-

Chart 1

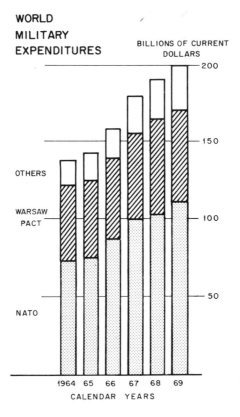

WORLD
MILITARY
EXPENDITURES

BILLIONS OF CURRENT
DOLLARS

OTHERS

WARSAW PACT

NATO

CALENDAR YEARS

Military Expenditures (billion dollars)

	1964	1965	1966	1967	1968 (Est.)	1969 (Est.)
World.	*139*	*143*	*160*	*181*	*191*	*200*
NATO	73	74	86	100	105	108
Warsaw Pact	49	51	54	57	60	63
Other.	17	18	20	24	26	29

tion in the ratio of military spending to world income.

On the other hand, it will take more than a diminished rate of increase to lessen significantly the heavy economic burden of world military expenditures. If recent spending patterns continue, the nations of the world by the end of the 1970's will be devoting more than $300 billion a year to defense. Over the decade they would have spent for this one purpose alone an amount virtually equivalent to the present tangible wealth of the United States—all the land, homes, factories, highways, minerals, and other real assets.

Comparisons with economic growth

Over the period of the survey, there has been a more erratic trend in military spending than in world product although in both cases the trend has been consistently upward. The annual rise in military spending, in current prices, has been as low as 3 per cent and as high as 13 per cent, averaging

7 per cent since 1964. Meanwhile, the value of world product has expanded at a fairly steady 8 to 10 per cent.

In real terms, the economic improvement in the past 6 years has been considerably less than the change in the dollar value of world GNP would indicate. Population has gone up by 2 per cent, prices by 4 per cent yearly. These two factors reduce the actual increase in real product per capita to less than 3 per cent a year, or a total of 14 per cent over the 6 years. This is appreciably less than the 20 per cent increase in military expenditures adjusted for price changes (Chart 2).

Several generalizations can be made from these comparisons:

1. The world's economic standard of living in real terms has improved relatively little during the past 6 years.

2. The diversion of resources to military purposes has expanded in step with the world's capacity to produce.

3. Part of the growth dividend since 1964 has been dissipated in higher military expenditures, rather than contributing to the improvement of living standards.

4. Per capita, the burden of military spending has grown larger over the 6-year period. (And it is in the poorer countries that this increase in burden has been greatest, as the charts and discussion which follow reveal.)

Trends in developing and developed countries

National and regional differences in the trend of military expenditures are so extreme that generalizations based on global figures are sometimes misleading. . . . A small percentage of the world population influences world GNP. . . . Half the world's people produce a share of the world product equivalent to that represented by military expenditures.

Illustrative of the significant differences in national figures are averages for two groupings of countries which are identified in this report as developing and developed. The countries designated as developing represent about three-fourths of the world population but only one-sixth of the GNP and about 11 per cent of all military spending. As a result, their changes have less effect on the world aggregates than do changes in the developed countries. . . . The world indexes for military expenditures and GNP tend to be close to the showing of developed countries. However, the relative expansion of military expenditures in de-

Chart 2

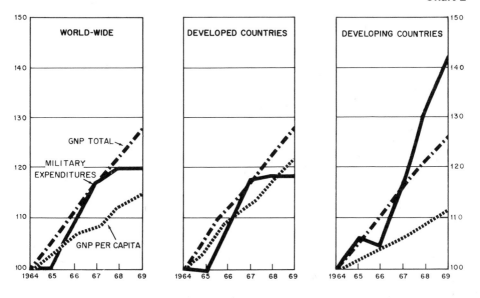

veloping countries has been *twice* that of the developed countries.

In current prices the average annual increase was 15 per cent in developing and 7 per cent in developed countries between 1964 and 1969, while the average increase in GNP was 10 per cent yearly in developing and 9 per cent in developed countries.

Two factors increased much more sharply in developing than in developed countries: prices and population. Both of these cut back the relative economic gains in the poorer countries, and widened the gap between the developing and developed parts of the world. When price and population changes are allowed for, the annual increase in per capita GNP in developing countries was only 2 per cent, bringing them to an average income level of $180 per person in 1969. (Developed countries had a per capita GNP gain of 4 per cent yearly, after price adjustment, bringing their per capita income to an average of $2,332.)

Against this showing, the upward spiral in military spending in the developing countries was particularly striking. Preliminary estimates indicate that in real terms, that is, after price adjustment, their military expenditures rose at an average rate of 7 per cent a year between 1964 and 1969. With GNP per capita growing at the rate of only 2 per cent a year, these populations were bearing a heavy and mounting burden to support military expansion.

In a forthcoming report on trends in military spending since 1950, ACDA will review evidence on the relationships between military spending and development progress. Indications are that in developing countries, where resources are tight, increases in military expenditures tend to mean lower growth rates unless they are subsidized through foreign sources.

Since 1964, developing countries have failed to increase their share of the world product. This has stayed at about one-sixth of the total, a minor share considering that they have almost three-fourths of the world's population (Chart 3), and that this proportion has grown in recent years. Military spending of the developing countries held at 11 per cent of the world total until the sharper upswing of the last 2 years. If

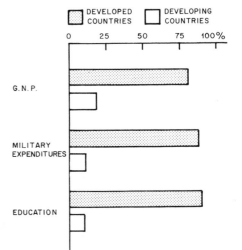

Chart 3

SHARE OF WORLD TOTAL IN 1967

this more recent trend should continue, the developing countries may increase their share of world military power but risk shrinking even further their modest share of world economic power.

Relative burden

The basic table for 1967 . . . provides two statistical indicators that are useful in gaging the relative burden of military expenditures and the ability of an economy to support its military effort. The most commonly used indicator for these purposes, the ratio of military spending to GNP, is inadequate if used alone, and may be misleading. A major weakness of this ratio is that it fails to take account of the population

Chart 4

Relative Burden of Military Expenditures

GROSS NATIONAL PRODUCT PER CAPITA

MILITARY EXPENDITURES AS % OF GNP	UNDER 100	100–199	200–299	300–499	500–999	1000–1999	2000–2999	OVER 3000
OVER 10%	Laos	United Arab Republic, Vietnam, North, Vietnam, Republic of	China, Republic of, Iraq, Jordan, Korea, North, Syrian Arab Republic	Saudi Arabia		Israel		United States, Kuwait
5–10%	Burma, Somali Republic	Cambodia, China, Mainland	Albania, Iran	Mongolia, Portugal	Cuba	Poland, USSR	France, United Kingdom	Sweden
2–5%	Chad, Congo, Kinshasa, Dahomey, Ethiopia, Guinea, Haiti, India, Uganda, Upper Volta	Bolivia, Cameroon, Congo, Brazzaville, Korea, Republic of, Mauritania, Morocco, Pakistan, Sudan, Thailand, Yemen	Algeria, Dominican Republic, Ecuador, Ghana, Paraguay	Malaysia, Turkey, Yugoslavia	Bulgaria, Chile, Greece, Libya, Romania, Spain, South Africa, Republic of, Venezuela	Austria, Czechoslovakia, Finland, Germany, East, Italy, Netherlands	Australia, Belgium, Canada, Denmark, Germany, West, Norway, Switzerland	
1–2%	Afghanistan, Indonesia, Mali, Niger, Tanzania	Central African Republic, Ceylon, Kenya, Malagasy Republic, Nigeria, Philippines, Togo	Colombia, El Salvador, Guatemala, Honduras, Ivory Coast, Liberia, Rhodesia, Southern, Senegal, Tunisia, Zambia	Brazil, Gabon, Guyana, Nicaragua	Argentina, Cyprus, Lebanon, Uruguay	Hungary, Ireland	Luxembourg, New Zealand	
UNDER 1%	Malawi, Nepal	Sierra Leone		Costa Rica, Peru	Jamaica, Mexico, Panama, Trinidad & Tobago	Japan		Iceland

Table 1.—Military expenditures and related data: 1967
[Amounts in current dollars][1]

REGION, GROUP, AND COUNTRY	MILITARY EXPENDITURES (mil. dol.)	GROSS NATIONAL PRODUCT (mil. dol.)	RELATIVE BURDEN		OTHER PUBLIC EXPENDITURES		FOREIGN ECONOMIC AID[4]		ARMED FORCES		
			MILITARY EXPENDITURE (% of GNP)	GNP (dollars per capita)	PUBLIC EDUCATION[2] (mil. dol.)	PUBLIC HEALTH[3] (mil. dol.)	RECEIVED (mil. dol.)	GIVEN (mil. dol.)	ARMED FORCES (thous.)	POPULATION (thous.)	FORCES (per thous. pop.)
A. Summary											
World total	180,682	2,481,743	[5]7.3	722	127,869	59,803	7,244	8,079	21,576	3,434,967	6
Developed	160,364	2,054,440	7.8	2,151	114,677	54,131	—	7,927	10,314	955,113	11
Developing	20,318	427,303	4.8	172	13,192	5,672	7,244	107	11,262	2,479,854	5
North America*	77,301	850,900	9.1	3,875	46,566	19,622	—	4,341	3,503	219,559	16
Europe	83,187	1,111,700	[5]7.5	1,553	62,859	34,713	491	3,169	7,996	715,662	11
Developed	80,357	1,044,000	7.7	1,733	61,197	33,776	—	3,111	6,445	602,424	11
Developing	2,830	67,700	4.2	598	1,662	937	491	58	1,551	113,238	14
Latin America**	2,468	110,039	2.2	433	3,195	1,921	1,291	—	944	254,200	4
Far East	10,950	244,686	4.5	203	9,487	1,609	1,235	424	6,268	1,206,977	5
Developed	1,076	115,660	.9	1,158	5,332	162	—	375	246	99,920	2
Developing	9,874	129,026	7.7	117	4,155	1,447	1,235	49	6,022	1,107,057	5
South Asia**	2,015	61,309	3.3	91	1,831	262	2,105	—	1,660	673,912	2
Near East**	2,440	27,687	8.8	310	1,240	680	320	—	737	89,202	8
Africa	1,061	44,622	2.4	171	1,576	464	1,297	—	375	260,978	1
Developed	370	13,080	2.8	698	467	39	—	—	27	18,733	1
Developing	691	31,542	2.2	130	1,109	425	1,297	—	348	242,245	1
Oceania*	1,260	30,800	4.1	2,128	1,115	492	—	145	93	14,477	6
B. By Country											
World total	180,682	2,481,743	[5]7.3	722	127,869	59,803	7,244	8,079	21,576	3,434,967	6
North America	77,301	850,900	9.1	3,875	46,566	19,662	—	4,341	3,503	219,559	16
United States	75,484	793,500	9.5	3,985	42,435	18,000	—	4,130	3,400	199,118	17
Canada	1,817	57,400	3.2	2,808	4,131	1,662	—	211	103	20,441	5
Europe	83,187	1,111,700	[5]7.5	1,553	62,859	34,713	491	3,169	7,996	715,662	11
NATO, European	23,054	501,000	4.6	1,686	21,101	6,021	250	2,593	2,937	297,193	10

	C1	C2	C3	C4	C5	C6	C7	C8	C9	C10	C11
Belgium*	569	19,500	2.9	2,035	913	39	—	77	102	9,581	11
Denmark*	326	12,200	2.7	2,521	767	411	—	22	47	4,839	10
France*	5,856	115,900	5.1	2,323	4,219	394	—	873	520	49,890	10
Germany, West*	5,349	121,000	4.4	2,097	4,235	1,561	37	634	460	57,699	8
Greece	313	7,000	4.5	803	164	50	NA	NA	159	8,716	18
Iceland*	—	600	—	3,000	22	8	—	286	—	200	—
Italy*	2,175	67,000	3.2	1,280	2,539	415	NA	NA	[7]425	52,334	8
Luxembourg*	8	700	1.2	2,090	35	10	—	88	1	335	29
Netherlands*	884	22,700	3.9	1,802	1,435	+241	—	11	130	12,597	10
Norway*	294	8,300	3.5	2,193	470	139	—	58	35	3,784	9
Portugal	333	4,600	7.2	487	67	41	—	—	149	9,440	16
Turkey	511	10,600	4.8	324	313	121	214	—	480	32,710	15
United Kingdom*	6,436	110,900	5.8	2,014	5,922	2,961	—	542	429	55,068	8
NATO total	100,355	1,351,900	7.4	2,616	67,667	20,555	250	6,934	6,440	516,752	12
Warsaw Pact	57,070	512,600	8(7–8)	1,492	37,567	26,639	—	+456	4,267	335,601	13
Bulgaria	260	8,200	3.2	987	316	194			150	8,309	18
Czechoslovakia*	1,340	26,300	5.1	1,839	1,107	1,091			225	14,305	16
Germany, East**	890	28,800	3.1	1,780	1,236	+1,117			127	16,001	8
Hungary*	290	12,600	2.3	1,234	529	339		+116	102	10,212	10
Poland*	1,680	33,900	5.0	1,061	1,576	1,424			270	31,944	8
Romania*	610	18,800	3.2	975	923	600			173	19,287	9
Soviet Union*	52,000	384,000	8(8–9)	1,630	+31,880	21,874		+340	3,220	235,543	14
Other European	3,063	98,100	3.0	1,184	4,191	2,053	241	120	792	82,868	10
Albania	+69	+700	9 9.9	356	68	12	NA	—	38	1,965	19
Austria*	144	10,600	1.4	1,447	434	298	NA	58	47	7,323	6
Finland*	148	7,100	2.1	1,522	434	234	NA	NA	[7]45	4,664	10
Ireland*	39	3,200	1.2	1,104	131	36	NA	NA	10	2,899	3
Spain	948	26,900	3.0	837	371	+301	157	—	[7]335	32,140	10
Sweden*	945	23,900	4.0	3,037	1,718	672	—	50	65	7,869	8
Switzerland*	374	16,000	2.3	2,645	672	282	—	13	12	6,050	2
Yugoslavia*	396	9,700	4.1	487	363	218	84	—	240	19,958	12
Latin America	2,468	110,039	2.1	433	3,195	1,921	1,291	—	944	254,200	4
Argentina	271	14,945	1.8	649	752	42	85	—	[7]144	23,031	6
Bolivia	15	712	2.3	164	27	+27	31	—	20	4,337	3
Brazil	940	29,743	3.2	347	276	+675	283	—	[7]225	85,655	5
Chile	115	5,426	2.5	605	279	134	141	—	[7]46	8,970	5
Colombia	85	5,534	1.7	288	136	43	146	—	[7]55	19,191	3
Costa Rica	—	671	—	421	28	61	22	—	—	1,594	—
Cuba*	[7]380	+5,400	97.0	622	302	+150	1	—	[7]200	8,033	25
Dominican Republic	31	1,068	2.9	275	24	+24	67	—	19	3,889	5
Ecuador*	27	1,350	2.0	249	31	14	34	—	17	5,429	3
El Salvador	10	882	1.2	286	25	12	16	—	6	3,082	9
Guatemala	16	1,416	1.2	288	28	11	21	—	9	4,913	2
Guyana	2	+230	9 1.0	338	11	6	NA	—	1	680	1
Haiti	7	300	2.4	65	4	3	3	—	5	4,581	1

See footnotes at end of table.

Table 1.—Military expenditures and related data: 1967—Continued
[Amounts in current dollars]¹

B. By Country—Continued

REGION, GROUP, AND COUNTRY	MILITARY EXPENDITURES (mil. dol.)	GROSS NATIONAL PRODUCT (mil. dol.)	RELATIVE BURDEN		OTHER PUBLIC EXPENDITURES				ARMED FORCES		
			MILITARY EXPENDITURE (% of GNP)	GNP (dollars per capita)	PUBLIC EDUCATION² (mil. dol.)	PUBLIC HEALTH³ (mil. dol.)	FOREIGN ECONOMIC AID⁴ RECEIVED (mil. dol.)	GIVEN (mil. dol.)	ARMED FORCES (thous.)	POPULATION (thous.)	FORCES (per thous. pop.)
Honduras	8	577	1.3	236	16	6	13	—	5	2,445	20
Jamaica	5	994	.5	530	26	16	24	—	2	1,876	1
Mexico	168	24,112	.7	528	596	265	161	—	70	45,671	2
Nicaragua	10	641	1.6	360	10	17	19	—	6	1,783	3
Panama	1	773	.1	582	25	13	24	—	—	1,329	—
Paraguay	10	477	2.0	221	7	2	22	—	13	2,161	6
Peru	134	3,974	3.4	321	191	70	80	—	50	12,385	4
Trinidad & Tobago	3	816	.3	808	23	18	5	—	1	1,030	1
Uruguay	28	1,483	1.8	533	55	+27	10	—	12	2,783	4
Venezuela	202	8,515	2.4	910	323	285	82	—	⁷38	9,352	4
Far East	10,950	244,686	4.5	203	9,487	1,690	1,235	424	6,268	1,206,977	6
Burma	103	1,803	5.7	70	45	19	11	—	137	25,811	5
Cambodia	57	962	5.9	150	42	9	14	—	⁷48	6,415	7
China, Mainland	+7,000	+85,000	⁹8.2	108	+2,975	+1,148	—	+49	2,700	789,000	4
China, Republic of	415	3,602	11.5	263	103	9	92	—	⁷600	13,700	44
Indonesia	+172	+9,600	⁹1.8	87	+97	23	255	—	340	110,079	3
Japan*	+1,076	115,660	.9	1,158	5,332	+162	NA	375	246	99,920	2
Korea, North	+600	+3,000	20.0	236	+93	+17	NA	—	368	12,700	29
Korea, Republic of	184	4,612	4.0	155	157	29	270	—	612	29,784	21
Laos	35	194	17.8	70	6	18	74	—	65	2,770	23
Malaysia	123	3,176	3.9	315	129	59	(±)	—	⁷44	10,071	4
Mongolia	+25	+500	⁹5.0	427	+5	+1	NA	—	23	1,170	12
Philippines	108	6,519	1.7	188	188	34	127	—	⁷47	34,656	1
Thailand	133	5,078	2.6	149	145	28	68	—	126	34,008	4
Vietnam, North	+500	+2,000	⁹25.0	100	+136	+36	NA	—	447	20,100	22
Vietnam, Republic of	419	2,980	14.1	177	34	17	450	—	⁷465	16,973	27
South Asia	2,015	61,309	3.3	91	1,831	262	2,105	—	1,660	673,912	2
Afghanistan	16	1,340	1.1	85	15	2	41	—	75	15,751	5
Ceylon	15	1,800	1.8	154	81	39	49	—	10	11,701	1
India	1,486	43,650	3.4	85	1,571	188	1,447	—	⁷1,200	514,200	2
Nepal	6	794	.8	76	5	+10	14	—	15	10,500	1
Pakistan	492	13,725	3.6	113	159	23	553	—	360	121,760	3
Near East	2,440	27,687	8.8	310	1,240	680	320	—	737	89,202	8

Country											
Cyprus	9	469	1.9	764	12	4	6	—	1	614	2
Iran	418	7,495	5.6	285	184	113	82	—	180	26,284	7
Iraq	268	2,240	12.0	265	126	22	14	—	[7]84	8,440	10
Israel	428	4,005	10.7	1,501	292	38	85	—	[7]80	2,669	30
Jordan	77	575	13.4	286	22	4	50	—	50	2,013	25
Kuwait	55	1,860	6.4	3,577	64	35	12	—	6	520	12
Lebanon	40	1,700	2.4	633	42	15	8	—	12	2,685	4
Saudi Arabia	341	2,000	17.1	444	146	+45	-12	—	[7]54	4,500	12
Syrian Arab Republic	†125	1,130	11.1	203	50	66	20	—	[7]64	5,570	11
Yemen	†13	†520	[9]2.5	104	3	+44	2	—	6	5,000	1
United Arab Republic	666	5,693	11.7	184	299	+294	51	—	[7]200	30,907	6
Africa	1,061	44,622	2.4	171	1,576	464	1,297	—	375	260,968	1
Algeria	100	3,000	3.3	242	144	+12	103	—	58	12,380	5
Cameroon	18	775	2.4	142	19	10	41	—	[7]6	5,470	1
Central African Republic	+3	+190	[9]1.6	130	7	+3	21	—	1	1,459	2
Chad	+8	+270	[9]3.0	79	9	3	21	—	1	3,410	‡
Congo, Brazzaville	+6	+125	[9]4.8	145	4	+2	22	—	2	860	2
Congo, Kinshasa	4	1,332	2.7	80	48	+24	96	—	31	16,585	2
Dahomey	37	+180	[9]2.2	72	8	+5	20	—	2	2,505	1
Ethiopia	+3	1,551	[9]2.4	66	22	+48	32	—	43	23,457	2
Gabon	37	+180	1.7	380	12	5	15	—	1	473	2
Ghana	+3	1,734	2.3	213	70	3	72	—	15	8,143	2
Guinea	39	310	4.5	83	17	+7	11	—	5	3,735	1
Ivory Coast	14	1,071	1.6	267	51	+8	41	—	4	4,010	‡
Kenya	17	1,181	1.3	119	47	+20	61	—	3	9,928	4
Liberia	15	240	1.3	216	6	3	45	—	4	1,110	5
Libya	3	1,580	1.9	909	51	+3	4	—	8	1,738	1
Malagasy Republic	30	730	1.7	118	44	12	47	—	4	6,200	‡
Malawi	12	217	.8	52	12	3	30	—	1	4,150	4
Mali	5	333	1.5	70	18	9	18	—	4	4,760	5
Mauritania	+6	+155	[9]3.9	141	9	2	9	—	1	1,100	1
Morocco	75	2,660	2.8	188	101	+28	76	—	[7]58	14,140	4
Niger	+3	+280	[9]1.1	79	5	+8	59	—	1	3,546	‡
Nigeria	89	5,340	1.7	107	117	+85	84	—	20	50,055	‡
Rhodesia, South	19	1,074	1.8	237	20	14	-4	—		4,530	1
Senegal	+15	790	[9]1.9	215	28	+8	52	—	4	3,670	1
Sierra Leone	8	380	.8	156	13	+5	8	—	5	2,439	‡
Somali Republic	—	132	6.1	50	2	3	16	—	2	2,645	1
South Africa Republic	—	13,080	2.8	698	467	+39	NA	—	27	18,733	1
Sudan	370	1,554	[9]3.2	108	61	+30	21	—	18	14,355	1
Tanzania	+50	[10]858	1.4	[10]73	28	8	37	—	4	12,173	‡
Togo	12	205	1.3	119	4	2	16	—	1	1,724	1
Tunisia	3	954	1.5	209	49	20	110	—	[7]23	4,560	5
Uganda	14	734	2.0	93	19	+15	22	—	6	7,934	1
Upper Volta	15	253	[9]2.0	50	6	4	20	—	1	5,054	‡
Zambia	+5	1,174	1.8	297	58	13	70	—	3	3,947	1
Oceania	1,260	30,800	4.1	2,128	1,115	492	—	145	93	14,477	6
Australia*	1,155	25,200	4.6	2,145	890	290	—	145	80	11,751	7
New Zealand*	105	5,600	1.9	2,054	225	202	—	NA	13	2,726	5

See footnotes at end of table.

*Developed countries.   **Developing countries.   NA Not available.   †Rough ACDA estimate.   ‡Less than one-half unit.   —None or not applicable.

[1]For most countries, conversion into U.S. dollars is at official par value exchange rates as rounded by AID (see Notes on Data).

[2]Estimates for 1967 based on data for 1966 or earlier (see Notes on Data).

[3]Most entries are estimates for 1967 based on data for earlier years, some entries are rough projections (see Notes on Data).

[4]Economic aid given by communist countries is included in the world total of aid received but is not distributed by individual recipient countries or regions.

[5]Military expenditures and GNP are not fully comparable due to the use of different dollar conversion rates for the two variables in the Warsaw Pact countries (see footnote 8). Using the more valid ratios shown for these countries in parentheses, the ratio for the world would be 6 to 7 percent and for Europe, 5 to 6 percent.

[6]Includes West Berlin.

[7]Includes paramilitary as well as regular forces.

[8]The implied relationship between dollar amounts of GNP and military expenditures (or other variable) is not entirely valid for Warsaw Pact countries due to the use of noncomparable conversion rates for particular sectors. Military expenditures as a percent of GNP would be about as shown in parentheses when measured in national currencies and at factor cost rather than at market prices.

[9]Since either or both military expenditures and GNP estimates are approximations, the resulting ratio should be viewed with particular caution.

[10]Tanganyika only.

factor and therefore of the level of economic strength as represented by per capita income. To offset this weakness, per capita GNP in each country is shown next to the ratio figure in Table 1. Countries with low per capita incomes are more likely to have greater and more urgent resource scarcities. In these countries military spending competes directly with both consumption and the investment necessary for growth.

Chart 4 summarizes the relative standing of the 120 countries in the survey, taking account of all three relevant factors, military expenditures, GNP, and population. The chart shows where each of the countries stands in per capita GNP and in the ratio of military spending to GNP. Countries with the heaviest defense burden in terms of these two criteria appear in the upper left portion of the chart; countries with the lightest in the lower right portion.

This scatter diagram shows that the economic impact of military spending is extremely uneven throughout the world. The highest spenders relative to GNP are all poor countries in terms of their per capita income. In the first tier—with expenditures exceeding 10 per cent of GNP —there are 11 countries, all of them developing; nine of the countries spending over 10 per cent of GNP on military programs have per capita income of less than $300 a year. In the second tier—spending 5 to 10 per cent of GNP for defense—10 of the 15 countries are classed as developing.

Proportionately more developing than developed countries fall in the high burden categories. At the same time, proportionately more developing than developed countries are also in the low end of the scale (the two lowest tiers of the chart). African and Latin American countries in general show up with the lowest ratios of defense to GNP. The very diverse pattern in relative burden suggests the importance of further study in depth of the impact of military expenditures on the pace and quality of growth, particularly among the newer nations.

Other public expenditures

In the world as a whole, no other single activity of government attracts as much

public financing as military preparedness. Available budget data indicate that in many countries defense accounts for a fourth or more of all expenditures of central governments.

Next to defense the largest single outlay that most governments make is for education. World expenditures on education are estimated to have reached $128 billion in 1967 (Chart 5). Like military spending, this appeared to represent a new record total. However, it was still only two-thirds as large as military expenditures in that year. Considering the rapid growth in the school-age population, education expenditures had not changed appreciably per pu-

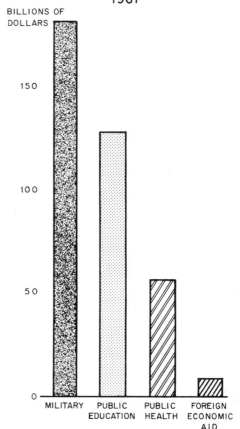

Chart 5

WORLD MILITARY AND
OTHER PUBLIC EXPENDITURES
1967

BILLIONS OF
DOLLARS

150

100

50

0

MILITARY   PUBLIC   PUBLIC   FOREIGN
EDUCATION   HEALTH   ECONOMIC
AID

pil. World population between the ages of 5 to 19 is estimated at 1.1 billion. This indicates a world average expenditure for public education of less than $120 per school-age child.

For all publicly supported health care, governments paid out an estimated $60 billion in 1967, or one-third as much as for defense. For the world population, public health expenditures averaged $17 per person.

One other major budget category for which data are available for global comparisons is foreign economic assistance. For the donors this amounted to $8 billion in 1967. Aid given averaged $9 per capita in the developed countries. Economic aid receipts, when divided among the larger populations in the developing world, amounted to about $3 per person for the receiving countries. . . .

Developed countries in 1967 had a per capita GNP average 12 times that of developing countries. The contrasts were even more extreme in the major categories of public expenditure. Military spending and government outlays for education and health in the richer countries, on a per capita basis, were 20 to 25 times larger than in the developing countries.

In dollar amounts, GNP and expenditures in the major budget categories which are tabulated in this survey compared as follows in 1967 on a per capita basis:

expenditures are somewhat affected by differences in the emphasis given to public as compared to private financing. Country comparisons in particular must be made cautiously because of this factor. Communist countries tend to support all education and health care through the public budget while others do so through varying proportions of public and private funds. In the United States, for example, private expenditures account for about one-fifth of all spending on education and for almost two-thirds of all spending on health care.

Manpower

The latest figures show an increase not only in expenditures but in manpower devoted to defense. The world total for the armed forces in 1967 was estimated at close to 22 million. In the years immediately prior to 1967, the figure has generally held to 20 million or slightly above.

About half of the increase of 1.4 million men between 1966 and 1967 represents accounting adjustments to cover those paramilitary forces which play a significant military role. Included in this paramilitary component are units of armed police, carabinieri, and national guard. These paramilitary units are judged capable of making a significant contribution to regular armed forces strength and are generally funded from the central defense budget.

In proportion to population, armed forces

	GNP	MILITARY	EDUCATION	HEALTH
World.	722	53	37	17
Developed.	2,151	168	120	57
Developing	172	8	5	2

Chart 6 shows how dramatic these expenditure differences are even on a regional basis. North America's per capita spending dwarfs all others. Europe's is next, followed by Oceania's. In contrast to these three regions, the most that other areas spent on education was $14 a year per capita and on public health $8 per capita. South Asia had the lowest spending levels of any region, not only on defense but on public education and health as well; education expenditures averaged out to $2.70 and health to $0.40 per person per year.

All comparisons of education and health

are largest in North America and Europe and lowest in Africa and South Asia. Worldwide, military forces represent 0.6 per cent of the population, with an average of 1.1 per cent in developed countries and 0.5 per cent in developing.

Estimates by U.N. experts in 1962 indicated that for every 100 men in the armed forces there might be in addition over 150 people engaged in productive activities directly or indirectly related to the military. This would mean that in 1967 an estimated 55 million people were either in the armed forces or employed in manufacturing and

Chart 6

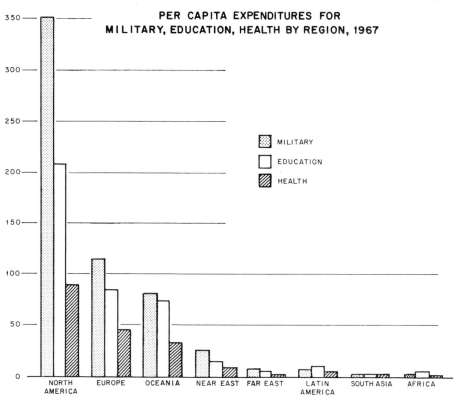

PER CAPITA EXPENDITURES FOR
MILITARY, EDUCATION, HEALTH BY REGION, 1967

other support functions for the forces, a number equalling the total population of the United Kingdom, or the entire labor force of the United Kingdom, West Germany, and Sweden combined.

DEFINITIONS OF TERMS

Gross national product (GNP) represents an economy's total output of goods and services, valued at current market prices paid by the ultimate consumer. Methods of conversion to U.S. dollars are outlined in the Notes on Data.

Military expenditures are current and capital expenditures to meet the needs of the armed forces, including: Expenditures of national defense agencies for military programs; expenditures for the military components of such mixed activities as atomic energy, space, and research and development; military assistance to foreign countries; and expenditures on paramili-

tary forces where they contribute substantially to a country's military capabilities.

Foreign economic aid received by developing countries comprises official bilateral grants and loans (gross of repayments) disbursed by Development Assistance Committee (DAC) countries and net aid received from multilateral agencies. (Aid received from Communist countries is shown in the world total but is not included in country or regional totals). *Aid given* by DAC countries includes official bilateral aid and net contributions to multilateral agencies. Aid given by Communist countries represents deliveries to all non-Communist developing countries, and excludes intra-Communist aid. Aid from private sources and military assistance are excluded.

Public education expenditures include current and capital expenditures for preschool, primary, secondary and university-level education. Wherever possible, expenditures by all levels of government are covered. Private spending is not included.

Public health expenditures represent current expenditures by all levels of government for the provision of medical services. Public health capital outlays are excluded here since they are not consistently available. Private spending is also excluded.

Armed forces refer to military personnel actually on duty, including paramilitary forces where these forces contribute substantially to a country's military capabilities. Reserve forces are excluded.

Developing countries, 93 in number, are the countries listed under Latin America, the Far East except Japan,

South Asia and the Near East, and Africa except the Republic of South Africa, and also include, in Europe, Albania, Bulgaria, Greece, Portugal, Spain, Turkey and Yugoslavia.

Developed countries, 27 in number, are all countries listed under North America, Oceania, European NATO except Greece, Portugal and Turkey, the Warsaw Pact except Bulgaria, and include Austria, Ireland, Finland, Sweden, Switzerland, Japan and South Africa.

---

[1]Since 1967, most of the increase in military spending has resulted from price inflation. In terms of constant prices, 1969 expenditures were 3 percent above 1967 and only fractionally higher than in 1968.

Growth

3. The War Machine under Nixon

I.F. Stone

In government the budget is the message. Washington's heart is where the tax dollar goes. When President Nixon finally, and very tardily, presented his first budget proposals in mid-April in a mini-State of the Union message, he said "Peace has been the first priority." But the figures showed that the first concern of the new Administration, as of the last, was still the care and feeding of the war machine.

Only Nixon's style had changed. "Sufficiency" rather than "superiority" in nuclear armaments remained the new watchword. But in practice it was difficult to tell them apart. Administrations change, but the Pentagon remains at the head of the table. Nixon's semantics recalled John F. Kennedy's eight years earlier. The Eisenhower Administration had waged battle for four years against the bomber gap and the missile gap with the slogan of "sufficiency." "Only when our arms are sufficient beyond

---

Reprinted with permission from *The New York Review of Books.* Copyright © 1969, I. F. Stone.

doubt," was Kennedy's elegant riposte in his Inaugural, signaling a new spiral upward in the arms race, "can we be certain without doubt that they will never be employed." The rhetoric was fresh but the idea was no different from John Foster Dulles's "position of strength." This is the *plus ça change* of American government and diplomacy. It emerged intact after Nixon's first three months in office, too.

At a press conference four days after his budget message, Nixon said again that "sufficiency" in weaponry was "all that is necessary." But a moment later he was clearly equating it with nuclear superiority. He said he didn't want "the diplomatic credibility" of a future President in a crisis like that over Cuba's missiles "impaired because the United States was in a second-class or inferior position." A press corps obsessed with the latest plane incident off North Korea did not pause to consider the implications. Was "diplomatic credibility" to be measured in megatons? Were we preparing again to play a thermonuclear game of "chicken," to see who would blink first at the prospect of instant incineration? Was this not the diplomacy of brinkmanship and the strategy of permanent arms race?

No correspondent asked these questions, and Nixon did not spell out the inferences.

His tone was softer, his language more opaque, than that of the campaign, but the essential "security gap" theme had not changed. The main emphasis of Nixon's first months in office, the main idea he tried to sell the country, turned out to be that it was in mortal peril of a Soviet first-strike capacity. The new administration sought to overcome a mounting wave of opposition to the ABM and to the military generally, by ringing the bells of panic.

True, the Secretary of State often seemed to deny the perils the Secretary of Defense painted. Which was the party line? It was indicative that when visiting editors were given a press kit on the ABM April 7, with a covering letter on White House stationery, signed by Herbert G. Klein as Nixon's "Director of Communications," the only thing new in that kit, the only news it contained, *and the one bit on which nobody commented,* was the "document" the Administration had chosen as the first item. It was a reproduction of a column in which Joseph Alsop three days earlier had exuberantly portrayed the "grim" (a favorite Alsop word) dangers of a first strike from Laird's new monster, the Soviet SS-9. The leading journalistic Pied Piper of the Bomber Gap and the Missile Gap had been enlisted by the new Administration to help it to propagate a new Gap. If the White House stationery and the Klein signature were not enough to make Alsop's nightmare official doctrine, the reproduction of the column carried at the bottom of the page this imprimatur, "Prepared under the direction of the Republican National Committee, 1625 Eye St. N.W., Washington, D.C." The candor was dazzling.

The Budget Bureau fact sheets which accompanied Nixon's spending proposals sought to create the impression that on the military budget, as on so much else, Nixon in power was reversing the course set by Nixon on campaign. "Military and military assistance programs account for $1.1 billion (27%) of the $4.0 billion outlay reduction [for fiscal 1970]," said one fact sheet, "and $3.0 billion (55%) of the cut in budget authority." But, as we shall see, while the cuts in domestic civilian programs proved

all too real, those in the military budget were either dubious or deferrals.

There was in the Nixon budget one complete and dramatic about-face—on the FB-111. Six months earlier, just before the election, at Fort Worth, where General Dynamics was building this new strategic bomber, Nixon had promised to make the F-111 "one of the foundations of our air supremacy." Now it was put permanently on the shelf. Procurement of the bomber was cut back sharply for fiscal 1969, which ends June 30, and abandoned altogether for fiscal 1970. Only the F-111D, the Air Force fighter version of this plane, was to stay in production a while longer.

Thus *finis* was soon to be written to the career of the multi-purpose, multi-service plane originally known as the TFX, one of McNamara's most costly misjudgments. But on this, as on almost every other item of apparent economy in the Nixon-Laird revisions of the Pentagon's budget, the few hundred millions saved in fiscal 1969 and 1970 were linked to commitments which would cost literally billions more in the decade ahead. Every short step back hid another leap forward in expenditures.

The TFX was McNamara's effort to stall off the drive of the bomber generals to commit the country to an entirely new manned bomber in the missile age. He gave them the FB-111, the bomber version of the TFX, instead. Laird reduced FB-111 procurement in fiscal 1969 by $107 million and eliminated altogether the planned outlay of $321 million in fiscal 1970. But he then added $23 million for fiscal 1970 to speed "full scale engineering" of the new intercontinental bomber AMSA (Advanced Manned Strategic Aircraft) for which the Air Force and the aviation industry have been lobbying for years. "The FB-111," Laird told the Senate Armed Services Committee March 15, in an echo of the lobby's arguments, "will not meet the requirements of a true intercontinental bomber and the cost per unit has reached a point where an AMSA must be considered to fill the void."

It will be quite a void. The cost overruns, which had more than doubled the price of the FB-111, now became the excuse for going ahead with a far more expensive bomber. The net saving of $405 million in fiscal 1969 and 1970 ($107 plus $321 minus $23 million) will commit the country to a new plane which Senator Proxmire told the Senate April 22 will cost at least $24 billion during the next decade. Such illusory economies place heavy first mortgages on the future in favor of the military and at the expense of social needs.

Even so, there was hidden in the F-111 cutback a $200 million consolation prize for General Dynamics. The formal budget document[1] carried an increase of $155.7 million for "Production of F-111D at minimum sustaining rate related to FB-111 cancellation." I was puzzled by this reference to a "sustaining rate." What was being "sustained"—military needs or General Dynamics?

I found a fuller explanation when *Aviation Week & Space Technology* arrived for May 5. It said the revised Nixon procurement plans for General Dynamics F-111D provided $599.8 million for aircraft "plus $56 million for advance procurement and $71.4 million to cover excess costs generated in fiscal 1968." It said the total of $727.2 million "represented a sharp increase over original fiscal 1970 plans of $518 million." Indeed this is an increase, though *Aviation Week* did not say so, of $209.2 million rather than the $155.7 specified in the budget message.

The increase had been approved by Deputy Defense Secretary David Packard —a director of General Dynamics until his Pentagon appointment—to counterbalance a cut of $320.9 million in the FB-111 program. It would "enable General Dynamics to retain its present production facilities." Not only did thirteen of these fighter planes crash in their twenty-six months of operations[2] but Senator Curtis of Kansas, in a comprehensive Senate speech last October 3, said they were not maneuverable enough as fighters. They are effective only as tactical bombers against enemy forces like those in Vietnam, which have no air cover of their own. Yet the government was not cutting back on its original plan to buy 331 of these F-111D's.

This is only one of many examples in the budget of how easily the Nixon Admin-istration finds millions for such dubious military purposes but not for urgent social needs. The $200 million consolation for General Dynamics is the same amount— a very inadequate amount—Nixon set aside in his budget message for riot-devastated cities. Nixon got a lot of publicity out of his order to give this urban program priority, but it didn't have enough priority to be a $200 million addition to the budget. It was just deducted from the meager amounts already available for other urban purposes.

II

Those who still look for the "shape" of the Nixon Administration are bound to remain bewildered. Shape is another word for policy, and policy requires the substitution of decision for drift. The campaign promised decision from one direction, the right. The situation requires decision from another direction, which might be called the left. Nixon turns out to take his stand— though that is too strong a word—in the middle of makeshift compromises. Whether on electoral reform or tax reform or poverty, feeble and inadequate half-measures are the rule. This shapelessness is the shape of the new Administration.

Hand-to-mouth decisions are standard in all governments, and inertia is basic in politics as in physics. But drift is only safe in quiet waters; to let inertia have its way in stormy seas is to risk disaster. Richard Nixon in the Sixties is beginning to resemble Calvin Coolidge in the Twenties, when the country kept cool with Cal, just before going over the brink with the stock market crash and the Great Depression.

To let inertia reign in the American government is also to let the military dominate. The sheer size of the military establishment, its vast propaganda resources and its powerful allies in every business, locality, and labor union affected by the billions it spends every year, gives it momentum sufficient to roll over every other department and branch of the government. In the absence of a strong hand and hard choices in the White House, the Pentagon inevitably makes the decisions. If nothing else, it makes them by default.

But there is more than default, and more

than meets the eye, in the military budget. The readiest source of campaign funds and political support for nomination and election as President lies in the military-industrial complex. It is also the most skillfully hidden source. I suspect that the 1968 campaign, like the 1960, was preceded by deals which called for a buildup in military procurement. This would help to account for the steep increase in appropriations by the Kennedy Administration despite its discovery on taking office that the "missile gap" did not exist.[3]

The two plums the military-industrial complex most wanted on the eve of the 1968 campaign were the ABM and AMSA, a new advanced strategic bomber. In 1966 the Armed Services Committees of both houses recommended extra funds to speed both projects. A Congress still comatose on military matters dutifully voted the money. But McNamara refused to spend it. Johnson made two moves during the following year which cleared the way for both projects. In September 1967 he forced McNamara to swallow the bitter pill of advocating a "thin" ABM system in which the Secretary of Defense clearly disbelieved. Two months later Johnson made the surprise announcement—as much a surprise to McNamara as to the press— that he was shifting the redoubtable Pentagon chief to the World Bank. That cleared the way for AMSA, too, and with both projects it also cleared the way for the 1968 campaign.

As late as January 1968, in his last posture statement as Secretary of Defense, McNamara was still fighting a rear-guard action against AMSA. He argued that the principal problem lay in the growing sophistication of Soviet air defenses. "Repeated examination of this problem," he told Congress, "has convinced us that what is important here is not a new aircraft but rather new weapons and penetration devices."

AMSA began to inch forward when Clifford replaced McNamara. In Clifford's first posture statement last January, he struck a new note when he declared the FB-111 would be too small to carry the new weapons and penetration devices McNamara had in mind. One wishes one knew more about this, since it seems unlikely

that McNamara would have overlooked so simple a point. While Clifford said "we are still uncertain whether a new intercontinental bomber will be needed in the 1970's," he more than doubled the research and development funds for AMSA, increasing them from $30 million in fiscal 1969 to $77 million in fiscal 1970, "to keep the program moving."

The Nixon-Laird revisions two months later went further. They not only added $23 million more for AMSA but authorized the Air Force to move into the engineering phase, the last stage in R and D before procurement. "Now, after a very careful review," Laird told the Senate Armed Services Committee March 27, "we have decided to cut off the FB-111 program . . . and concentrate our efforts on the development of a new strategic bomber, AMSA." General Dynamics, which lost out when Nixon phased out FB-111, will be one of the bidders on AMSA.

ABM and AMS together could spell $100 billion in electronic and aviation contracts in the years ahead. AMSA itself may prove a bigger gamble and a far more costly error than the TFX. *Space/Aeronautics* for January published a special issue plotting future trends in strategic warfare. It pointed out some of the pitfalls which may lie ahead for AMSA. About eight years elapse between concept definition and actual production in developing a new bomber. But Pentagon intelligence has never been able to come up with estimates of enemy threat valid for more than two or three years. "Thus," this Conover-Mast publication for the aerospace industry concluded, "there is no way of telling, the critics of AMSA claim, whether we would be committing ourselves to a system we really need or to what will end up as an immensely costly mistake."

The survey admitted that AMSA would be "less vulnerable than the B-52 and perform better," but added philosophically that "in a nuclear exchange time is too important an element for bombers to have any real effect." In other words even the fastest bomber may have no targets left after the far swifter missile exchange is over. One firm intelligence forecast emerged from the survey. "If AMSA is built," *Space/Aeronautics* said, "it will probably be our last strategic bomber. Once the present generation of Air Force commanders is gone, the top-level manpower will not be there to produce the sort of pressure that has kept AMSA alive for so long." Once the bomber admirals are dead, the clamor for a new bomber will die out, too. But the last fly-by will cost plenty.

III

AMSA is only one of many new military projects hidden in the new 1970 budget which will add billions to the future costs of government. "The present inflationary surge, already in its fourth year," Nixon said in his April 14 message, "represents a national self-indulgence we cannot afford any longer." But the principal beneficiaries of that indulgence are the military and their suppliers. And they seem to be exempt from anti-inflationary measures.

Fully to appreciate what the military is getting one has to begin with a disclosure made in the Budget Bureau's presentation of Nixon's budget revisions. Nixon had to squeeze $7.3 billion out of the normal civilian and welfare activities of the government in fiscal 1969 (which ends June 30 of this year) in order to meet the expenditure ceilings imposed by Congress when it enacted the 10 per cent surplus income tax. This reduction over and above Johnson's budget for FY 1969 was made necessary by certain "uncontrollable" items. An example is the interest on the public debt which rose by $300 million. But the biggest uncontrollable item, ten times that much, or $3 billion, was an increase in Vietnam war costs over and above those originally estimated by Johnson.

So all sorts of civilian services during the current fiscal year have had to be pared to meet the unexpected increase in the cost of the Vietnam war. Now let us couple this revelation about the 1969 budget with a basic decision made by Johnson in the 1970 budget. In that budget Johnson for the first time, on the basis of his decision to end the bombing of the North, which was very costly, and perhaps in expectation of less combat on the ground in the South,[4] forecast the first sharp cutback in Vietnam

war costs. This was estimated as a saving of $3.5 billion during fiscal 1970.

This was to be the country's first "peace dividend." But instead of applying this $3.5 billion in the 1970 budget to starved civilian and welfare services, or to reduction of the deficit, Johnson added this $3.5 billion *and $600 million more* to the money available for the Pentagon to spend on procurement and activities other than those connected with the Vietnam war. *The total increase in the non-Vietnamese military budget as projected by Johnson was $4.1 billion more, even though he estimated the Vietnam war was going to cost $3.5 billion less.*[5] In his April 14 message, Nixon said of our domestic needs, "what we are able to do will depend in large measure on the prospects for an early end to the war in Vietnam." The Johnson 1970 budget projected the first slowdown but proposed to use the savings entirely for military expansion. Nixon went along with that decision.

From the Pentagon's point of view there could not have been a smoother transition than the shift from Johnson to Nixon. Nixon revised Johnson's social and welfare programs downward but left his military budget essentially untouched. It read like the handiwork of the Johnson who was the ally of the military and the armament industries as chairman of the Senate Preparedness subcommittee during the Fifties. Johnson's last defense budget was not only the highest ever sent Congress—$81.5 billion as compared with the World War II peak of $80 billion in fiscal 1945—but laid the basis for a huge expansion in spending during future years. It gave the go-ahead signal to a wide variety of projects the armed services had long desired.

Nixon had campaigned on a "security gap" but Johnson left few if any gaps to fill. "The number of new programs spread through the new defense budget," *Space/ Aeronautics* commented in its February issue, "is astounding in comparison with the lean years from fiscal 1965 to 1969." Among them were $400 million for "major developmental activity on no fewer than six new aircraft" and—biggest item of all —an increase of $1.64 billion to a total of $2.85 billion for the Navy's surface ship and submarine building program. Arms research and development was boosted $850 million to a total of $5.6 billion, including work on such new monsters as missiles which can be hidden on the ocean floor.

This farewell budget also put Nixon in a bind. As *Space/Aeronautics* pointed out in that same editorial, if Nixon tried to cut back appreciably on the Johnson budget, he would open himself to "security gap" charges. On the other hand "if he doesn't defer or cancel at least some of them, and if the war in Vietnam cannot be brought to an honorable close some time next year, he will face a crushing arms bill in fiscal 1971, when many of these starts begin to demand more money." That was the risk Nixon and Laird preferred to take.

IV

Nixon claims to have cut $4 billion from 1970 outlays, and taken $1.1 billion, or 27 per cent, from the military. Critics have protested that he took $3 from civilian needs for every $1 he took from the military. But even this is illusory.

From another point of view, even if we accept the Nixon cuts at face value, the military will have $3 billion more in fiscal 1970 for non-Vietnamese war purposes than it had in fiscal 1969. We have seen that Johnson budgeted a $3.5 billion cut in Vietnam war costs for fiscal 1970 and then added $4.1 billion to the military budget for projects unconnected with the Vietnam war. If you deduct Nixon's $1.1 billion from that $4.1 billion, the Pentagon is still ahead by $3 billion.[6] If Nixon had applied the whole projected saving of $3.5 billion on Vietnam to civilian use or deficit reduction, the fiscal 1970 total for national defense would have been reduced to $97,499 million. All Nixon did was to *cut the Johnson increase* by a fourth.

Even this may turn out to be—at least in part—a familiar bit of flimflam. Since Johnson began to bomb the North in 1965 and take over the combat war in the South, almost every annual budget has underestimated Vietnamese war costs. These have had to be covered later in the fiscal year by supplemental appropriations. The under-estimate in fiscal 1969, as we have

seen, was $3 billion. The fiscal 1970 budget is running true to form.

The biggest "economy" item in the Nixon military budget is $1,083.4 million, which is attributed to "reduced estimates of ammunition consumption rates."[7] Just how much of the estimated $1.1 billion "saving" in outlays for fiscal 1970 will be the result of lower consumption of ammunition in Vietnam was not made clear. The $1,083.4 million is given as a net reduction of obligational authority in fiscal 1969 and 1970. It is one of the three main items in that $3 billion cut in obligational authority for fiscal 1970 which make it possible for the new Administration to claim that 55 per cent of the total cut in obligational authority for 1970 ($5.5 billion) came from the military. Obligational authority is not necessarily or entirely translated into actual outlays during the fiscal year in which it is granted.

This projected cut in the rate of ammunition consumption is in addition to Johnson's projected cut of $3.5 billion in Vietnam war costs. Though Laird does not blush easily, even he seems to have been embarrassed by this particular "economy." "To be perfectly frank," said Laird, who rarely is, when he first broached this item to the House Armed Services Committee on March 27, "I think the ammunition consumption rates for Southeast Asia are based on rather optimistic assumptions, particularly in view of the current Têt offensive." Yet, under pressure from the White House to show more economy, the optimism rose sharply in the next four days. The following table shows the change in estimated savings for ammunition and its transportation in millions of dollars in those four days:

	March 27	April 1
Ground Munitions	−$380	−$460
Ammo. Transport	−34.4	−34.4
Air Munitions	−417.9	−511.9
Ship Gun Ammo.	−47.1	−77.1
Total Cuts	879.4	1,103.4

These figures are for total obligational authority for fiscal years 1969 and 1970. Perhaps the Administration hesitated to make public its actual outlay estimates for these two years, since they may easily turn out to be higher rather than lower, and may have to be met later in the year by a supplemental appropriation. Between March 27 and April 1 Laird boosted the estimated reduction in total military outlays for FY 1970 from "about $500 million" to $1,113 million. Most of the increased "economy" seems to have come from this ammunition item.

There are several indications in the official presentations themselves which lead one to think Laird was right to be queasy. The original 1970 budget projected consumption of 105,000 tons a month in ground munitions through December 1970. Actual consumption in January was given as 96,000 tons, but that was before the recent enemy offensive got under way. The consumption of ammunition must have risen sharply with the fighting in February, March, and April, but when I asked the Pentagon for the monthly figures since January, I was told they could not be given out. "We can only say," an official spokesman told me, "that the Secretary's projections are being borne out." If that is true our troops must have been meeting enemy attacks with switch knives.

Another indication—how I love tracking down these liars!—appears in what we know about the volume of bombs dropped on South Vietnam and Laos since we stopped bombing the North. The Pentagon's own figures on total tonnages dropped show little change. Total tonnages dropped in September and October last year, before the bombing of the North stopped, were almost 240,000. Total tonnage dropped in January and February of this year, when it was dropped only on Laos and South Vietnam, was more than 245,000. There was an increase of 5,000 tons. That increase makes the estimate of a saving of more than a half billion dollars in air munitions for fiscal 1969 and 1970 look very phony indeed.

Laird himself said consumption of air munitions was rising. On March 27 he told the House Armed Services Committee that while consumption had been estimated at 110,000 tons per month for the twenty-four months from January 1969 to December 1970—that doesn't sound like much *de-*escalation ahead, at least in the air!—"actual consumption is now running at about 129,000 tons per month." Yet he projected a saving of $42.5 million on air munitions in fiscal 1969 and $375.4 in fiscal 1970. When he got back to the committee four days later, he placed actual consumption even higher, at 130,000 tons a month, but also projected higher savings! Now he was to save $89.5 million on air munitions in fiscal 1969, or twice the figure four days earlier, and $442 million for fiscal 1970, an increase of $47 million over the earlier estimate. Yet Laird said he saw "no indication that consumption will decline by very much during the next twelve to eighteen months." How then were expenditures on air ammunition to be lower than expected when the tonnage of bombs dropped was running higher than expected? Non-Euclidean geometry is not half so exotic as Pentagon arithmetic.

The ammunition figures for Vietnam are stupendous. The original Johnson-Clifford 1970 budget in January projected the cost of ammunition in Vietnam during fiscal 1970 at $5.2 billion. This expenditure of shot and shell over Vietnam is two-and-a-half times the total 1970 revised Nixon budget of $2 billion for the Office of Economic Opportunity (down $132 million), and more than twice the revised elementary and secondary education outlay for 1970 which he set at $2.3 billion (down another $100 million).

V

After this razzle-dazzle on ammunition, the next largest item of military saving in the Nixon-Laird budget revisions is the ABM. Let us return to the formal document sent Congress by the President. There on page 17[8] are given "principal changes in 1970 budget authority resulting from 1969 and 1970 Defense program changes." The second largest of these is $994 million for "Reorientation of the anti-ballistic missile program to the new Safeguard system." This and the ammunition item make up almost $2.1 billion of that $3 billion cut in military obligational authority on which the new Administration commends itself.

A businessman in financial difficulties who thought up such savings for his stockholders would soon be in jail for embezzlement. The "reorientation" of Sentinel into Safeguard may reduce spending in fiscal 1970 but only by adding at least $1.5 billion and possibly $5.5 billion more in the next few years. This is an expensive rebaptism or, better, if we consider the phallic significance of these monsters, re-circumcision. Nixon had an easy way out of the ABM fight if he wanted one. He could have announced that like Eisenhower he had decided to keep the ABM in research and development until he was sure it would not be obsolete before it was deployed.

If he had been a little more daring, and a little less beholden to the military-industrial complex, he might have cut billions[9] from the military budget immediately by offering a freeze on all new deployment of strategic defensive and offensive missiles if the Russians did likewise as a preparation for strategic arms negotiations. This would not only save at least $5 or $6 billion in the new fiscal year but ensure our present nuclear superiority and fully guarantee against first strike nightmares.[10]

Nixon chose instead a tricky stretch-out. This offered some reductions in the new fiscal year, as compared with Johnson's ABM proposal, but at the expense of higher costs later. This ingenious compromise made it possible to offer an apparent saving to the taxpayer *and* larger eventual orders to the electronics and missile industries. This not only fulfilled the Administration's promise of New Directions but enabled it to move in opposite directions at the same time. Johnson's Sentinel was estimated to cost $5.5 billion; Nixon's Safeguard, variously from $6.7 to $7 billion, or $1.5 billion more. This may prove another official underestimate. An authoritative service which covers all developing major weapons and aerospace systems for industrial and governmental subscribers places the total cost of Safeguard much higher.

This is DMS, Inc. (Defense Marketing Service), a ten-year-old service now a part of McGraw-Hill. I had never heard of it until an anonymous reader sent me a re-production of its report on Nixon's Safeguard. I checked with its Washington office by telephone and was given permission to quote it. Its detailed analysis places the total cost of the system at $11 billion and ends by warning that "in a program as complex as Safeguard, historical experience indicates costs in the long run are likely to be considerably higher." When Senator Cooper put the DMS analysis into the *Congressional Record* May 8, he noted that it did not include "about $1 billion AEC warhead costs." This would bring the total cost of Nixon's Safeguard past $12 billion.

Since the ABM authorization will soon be before Congress and this defense marketing service is known only to a restricted circle, we give its computations here:

Perimeter Acquisition Radar (PAR) $560
   PAR unit cost is estimated at $80 million; will be installed at 7 sites

Missile Site Radar (MSR) $1,500
   MSR unit cost is estimated at $125 million; will be installed at 12 sites

Spartan Missiles $1,050
   Unit cost of Spartan when deployed is estimated to be $3 million; DMS believes there will be 350 missiles installed

Sprint Missiles $560
   Unit cost is estimated at $800,000; DMS believes 700 missiles will be deployed with a greater number at Minuteman sites than at other sites

Data Processing Subsystem $1,500
   Includes new generation computer, memory banks, displays, tapes and discs plus an extensive amount of software

Command, Control and $500
Communications Subsystem

Warheads $210
   Figure assumes 1050 warheads at a cost of $200,000 each. AEC funds are used for development and production

Construction $2,100
   Figure assumes construction costs will average $300 million annually through 1975

Total Investment for 12 Sites $7,980
Research and Development $2,400
   Figure assumes R&D costs of $350 million per year through 1975. Does not

include the $150 million per year which will support work on new radars and interceptors

Operations and Maintenance $700
Figure based on an average operation cost of $100 million annually through 1975

Total Safeguard Cost $11,080
Through 1975
Assumes no cost overruns

The DMS report notes that we have already spent $4.5 billion on the ABM from fiscal 1956 when the Army started the Nike Zeus program, through fiscal 1968, and that the research efforts which made Nike-Zeus obsolete before it could be deployed are still going on, at a cost of $350 to $500 million annually. "A number of new concepts as well as hardware," the report said, "are currently under investigation." These threaten Safeguard with obsolescence too. "Preliminary research," DMS said, "has pointed the way toward the following types of advances": One was radars of much higher frequency so the interception "would be made with either a much smaller nuclear warhead or even a conventional high explosive charge." Another was a new third stage for Spartan so the missile could fly out at greater ranges and "maneuver through a cloud of decoys to find and destroy the real warhead." A third—most expensive of all—was "defensive missiles carried either in ships or large aircraft deployed closer to the enemy's launching sites."

We give these details to show that in embarking on the ABM we are embarking on a wholly new sector of the arms race with a high rate of obsolescence to gladden the hearts of the electronics companies and of A.T.&T., whose Western Electric has long been the main contractor. The reader should note that the three advances cited in the DMS report are relatively simple and foreseeable developments. All kinds of "far-out" possibilities are also being investigated. The secret hope which lies behind all this Rube Goldberg hardware is that some day somebody will turn up a perfect ABM defense and thus enable the possessor to rule the world because a power so armed

can threaten a first strike, knowing it will be immune to retaliation.

The most candid expression of this viewpoint was made by Senator Russell during the defense appropriations hearings in May of last year. "I have often said," Senator Russell observed, "that I feel that the first country to deploy an effective ABM system and an effective ASW [anti-submarine warfare] system is going to control the world militarily."[11] This control of the world, however, may be on a somewhat reduced basis. Six months later, during the Senate's secret session on the ABM (November 1, 1968), Senator Russell admitted, "there is no system ever devised which will afford complete protection against any multiple firing of ballistic missiles . . . we will have no absolutely foolproof defense, I do not care how much money we spend on one, or what we do." Senator Clark replied that casualties would be so high as to destroy civilization "and if there are a few people living in caves after that, it does not make much difference." To which Russell made his now famous rejoinder, "If we have to start over again with another Adam and Eve, I want them to be Americans and not Russians." (*Congressional Record*, E9644, November 1, 1968.) Thus we would at last achieve an unchallengeable Pax Americana! And thus the ABM turns out to be another variant of the military's unquenchable dream of an Ultimate Weapon, to leap some day like a jackpot from a slot machine if only they go on pouring money into R and D.

VI

I would ask the reader's indulgence for one more foray into the labyrinthine depths of the Pentagon budget. Deeper knowledge of these recesses is necessary if we are ever to hunt down and slay the dragon. I want to deal with the next largest source of the Nixon military "economies." These involve deferrals of expenditures amounting to about $480 million. Most critical comment has been content to note that mere deferral of spending is not real economy, since what is saved in fiscal 1970 will be spent later. There is a more important point to be made. These deferrals, if closely examined, provide additional proof of how recklessly and wastefully the Pentagon dashes into production before full testing and evaluation have been completed, before it knows, in other words, that these expensive weapons will work. We will see how much pressure it takes to make the Pentagon admit this elementary error.

To grasp the full significance of these so-called "economies" of Nixon and Laird we must see them against the background of revelations by two Senators, one the leading pillar of the military in the Senate establishment, Senator Russell; the other, a former Secretary of and long-time spokesman for the Air Force, who has turned against the military-industrial establishment, Senator Symington.

During the secret debate on the ABM last November 1, Russell told the Senate one of the "most serious mistakes" he had ever made as Chairman of the Armed Services Committee, which passes on all military requests for authorization, and as chairman of the Senate subcommittee, which passes on all defense appropriations, "was in allotting vast sums to the Navy for missile frigates before we knew we had a missile that would work on them." He said "we built missile frigates, we built missile destroyers and missile escort ships" on the basis of "unqualified" testimony of "everyone in the Department of Defense and in the Navy" that effective missiles were being developed. "It probably cost the taxpayers," Russell said, "$1 billion, because they have had to rebuild those missiles three times."

A more comprehensive statement of the same kind was made to the Senate by Symington on March 7 of this year. He put a table into the *Congressional Record* (at page S2464 that day) which showed how much had been spent on missiles in the past sixteen years which were no longer deployed, or never had been deployed, because of obsolescence. The total was fantastic. Symington gave the names, the expenditures, and the life-span of each missile. The total cost of those no longer deployed was $18.9 billion and the cost of those which were abandoned as obsolete or unworkable *before* deployment was $4.2 billion. The total was $23 billion. Imagine what those wasted billions could have done for our blighted cities!

Symington's table was introduced to underscore his point—buttressed by past testimony from McNamara—that the ABM would soon be another monument to this kind of expensive obsolescence. Another inference to be drawn from this table is how many billions might have been saved if the Pentagon had not rushed so quickly into these miscarriages. Behind the glamorous names which flashed through the appropriations hearings and the ads in the aeronautical and military trade journals—Navaho, Snark, Dove, Triton, and even Plato (what did he do to deserve *this* honor?)—lies an untold story of beguiling missile salesmanship and drunken-sailor procurement methods. It might be worth billions in future savings if a Congressional investigating committee really dug up the full story and its lessons.

The need for such an investigation becomes plain if one examines the funny thing which happened to SRAM (acronym for short-range attack missile) on Secretary Laird's way to and from the budget forum on Capitol Hill between March 27, his first appearance before the House Armed Services Committee, and his second appearance on April 1, just four days later. SRAM is one of the new missiles which have been under development. It is supposed to be mounted on a bomber so it can be rocketed into enemy territory from a position more than a hundred miles away from the enemy's defense perimeter. The idea is to circumvent the enemy's defenses by stopping the bomber out of their range and lobbing the missiles over them.

SRAM has had several predecessors, all expensive, of course; it is not a simple contraption. The predecessors appear in Senator Symington's table. Crossbow, Rascal, and Skybolt were earlier attempts at a stand-off missile; they cost a total of $962.6 million before they were abandoned prior to deployment. Hound Dog A, which cost another $255 million, is another missile in the same family which is no longer deployed. SRAM is very different in capability, range, and complexity. SRAM is intended to do for the bombing plane what penetration aids do for the ICBM. SRAM is supposed to carry all kinds of devices to confuse the radars of the enemy defense.

When Laird appeared before the House Armed Services Committee on March 27 he referred, without further explanation, to "delays experienced in the SRAM development production program." The original Johnson-Clifford budget last January for fiscal 1970 called for the modification of all seventeen B-52 squadrons of series G and H at a total cost of about $340 million to enable them to carry SRAM. The "modification kits," as Laird described them, were to be bought from Boeing "at a total cost of about $220 million," and it was planned to buy kits for twelve squadrons in 1970, leaving the rest to be modified in 1971. Laird proposed to save $30 million in fiscal 1970 by equipping only ten squadrons in 1970 and the remaining seven in 1971. He said "This change will give us a smoother program."

But the White House and the Budget Bureau, desperate for ways to cut, put pressure on the Pentagon and four days later Laird was back before the Armed Services Committee. Now instead of $30 million he proposed a deferral of the SRAM program amounting to $326 million. It now appeared that he had been less than candid with the committee. The cryptic references to "delays" turned out to be quite an understatement. He came forward with new changes in the SRAM program, all of them—he explained—"related to the difficulties encountered in the development of this Short Range Attack Missile." Now it was not "delays," but "difficulties."

Laird went on to quite a revelation. "We have now reached the conclusion," he told the committee, "that procurement of operational missiles should be deferred until the test program conclusively demonstrated that they will work as intended." So "we have deleted most [but not all!] of the missile procurement funds" from fiscal 1969 and 1970, for a total cut in the two years of $153 million.

Then he proposed to defer not only the missiles but the modifications designed to enable the B-52s to carry them. "Inasmuch as we do not know when operational missiles will be available," Laird said, "we have also deferred all special SRAM modification work on the B-52s and FB-111s." The total net deferral—after adding

$17 million to R and D for "a greater portion of the overhead cost" (another consolation fee?)—was to be $326 million.

This shows how much pressure it takes to squeeze the fat out of the military budget, and a little more candor out of the Pentagon. Why didn't Laird tell the committee on March 27 what he revealed on April 1? But for the extra pressure, the Pentagon would have gone on with procurement of the SRAM before knowing whether it would work, and with modification of the strategic bombers to carry the missiles before it was sure that it would have the missiles. What if further testing modifies the missile, and this requires a change also in the kits which modify the planes to carry these missiles? Why risk the waste of millions?

The SRAM story raises similar questions about Laird's rather cryptic references in his budget presentation to a similar deferral of "about $160 million" in the Minuteman ICBM program. The most important part of that "saving" is due, as Laird told House Armed Services on March 27, to "a slowdown in the deployment of Minuteman III." This is the Minuteman which will carry MIRV—"multiple independently targeted re-entry vehicles," i.e., additional warheads independently targeted. It was tested for the first time last August 16 with three warheads.[12] "While we are confident," Laird said, "that the Minuteman III will perform as intended, we believe it would be prudent to reduce somewhat the previously planned deployment rate, at least through the FY 1970 procurement lead-time." Why only somewhat, and what does somewhat mean for the whole program? "This delay," Laird went on, "would serve to reduce the amount of overlapping of R & D and production and provide more time for production." Why risk overlapping altogether until testing has been completed? Laird himself said he was planning to accelerate operational testing "to help ensure that the missile is working well before we return to the originally planned rate in FY 1971." "Mr. Chairman," Laird said, patting himself warmly on the back, "this reflects our determination to minimize cost overruns resulting from R and D modifications after production has commenced." But perhaps more serious cost overruns could be avoided if Minuteman III, like SRAM, were subjected to further deferrals.

A franker if ironic account of the Minuteman III cuts appeared May 5 in *Aviation Week*. It says "The reason for the reduction is fear of reliability problems with the new missile." It said the Air Force had "decided 'to reduce the concurrency of development and production' of the missile in order to insure reliability of all components." Even the Foreign Service could not have hit upon a smoother phrase to equal that "concurrency of development and production." *Aviation Week* added, "The cutback was publicized by some Defense Dept sources as evidence of US willingness to reduce

strategic offensive armaments prior to arms reduction talks with the Soviets, but that was not the reason."

This effort to make the Minuteman cuts look like evidence of Pentagon enthusiasm for arms talks originated in Laird's own presentation on April 1. In a super-slick conclusion he told the Committee, "Our decision to slow the Minuteman III deployment—though necessitated for other reasons—provides a period of time in which arms limitation agreements could become effective at a lower level of armaments. . . . It remains to be seen, of course, whether our potential adversaries will similarly indicate with actions that they, too, are serious about desiring meaningful arms limitation talks." These are the moments when Laird sounds as if he were dreamed up by Molière.

[1] House Document No. 91–100. 91st Congress, 1st Session. *Reductions in 1970 Budget Requests. Communication from the President of the United States*, p. 17.

[2] AP in Omaha *World Herald*, March 7, 1969.

[3] Carl Kaysen, who was Kennedy's Deputy Special Assistant for National Security Affairs, has given us more precise figures than I have ever seen before in the chapter on "Military Strategy, Military Forces and Arms Control" in the Brookings Institution symposium, *Agenda For The Nation* (Doubleday, 1969). He wrote (pp. 562–3) that the decisions of 1961 and 1962 by Kennedy "called for the buildup by 1965 of a US strategic force of nearly 1,800 missiles capable of reaching Soviet targets; somewhat more than a third were to be submarine-launched. In addition, some 600 long range bombers would be maintained. *This was projected against an expected Soviet force of fewer than a third as many missiles and a quarter as many bombers capable of reaching the United States.*" (Our italics.) The "overkill" was worth billions in the aviation and electronics industries.

[4] According to a little-noticed press release by Senator Stephen M. Young (D. Ohio), a member of the Senate Armed Services Committee, which has access to much information otherwise secret, Johnson had originally planned a cutback of troops in Vietnam. Young asked Nixon to recall two divisions before July and more later with an announcement, "We have accomplished our objectives in Vietnam. Our boys are coming home." Young said Johnson had decided on a similar announcement last year but was talked out of it by the Joint Chiefs of Staff.

[5] Since I have been challenged on this "peace dividend" by some colleagues, and others have wondered by what elaborate computation I arrived at it, I give the source, p. 74 of *The Budget of the US Government for Fiscal 1970*. It says, "As shown in the accompanying table outlays in support of Southeast Asia are anticipated to drop for the first time in 1970—declining by $3.5 billion from 1969. This decline reflects changing patterns of combat activity and revised loss projections. *Outlays for the military activities of the Department of Defense, excluding support of Southeast Asia, are expected*

to rise by $4.1 billion in 1970, to provide selected force improvements." (Italics added.)

[6] Even that understates the case. Down near the bottom of the budget outlays table of the Nixon revisions is $2.8 billion more for "civilian *and military* pay increases." (Our italics.) Laird in his April 1 presentation said this would add $2.5 billion but failed to make clear whether this was for the whole government or only for Pentagon civilian and military—almost half the civilian employees of the government work for the Pentagon. Clifford in his 1970 statement gave a figure of $1.8 billion for Pentagon pay increases but did not make clear whether this included the civilian employees. So pay raises will add between $1.8 billion and $2.5 billion to this $3 billion figure.

[7] See page 17 of House Document No. 91–100, 91st Congress, First Session.

[8] House Document No. 91–100. *Reductions in 1970 Appropriation Request. Communication from the President . . . together with details of the changes.* 91st Congress, First Session.

[9] The Johnson budget for 1970 placed the expenditure for strategic forces at $9.6 billion as compared with $9.1 in 1969 and $7.6 in 1968. Much of this is for deployment of new weaponry.

[10] "Such a freeze," Senator Percy declared in a speech April 17, "should be acceptable to the Defense Department. Secretary Laird has testified that our missiles on land and under the seas as well as our long-range bomber force present an overwhelming second-strike array. If a freeze—fully verifiable by both nations through satellite reconnaissance as well as other intelligence sources—is put into effect, the US deterrent will remain credible into the foreseeable future." But if the deterrent remains credible, what will the poor missile salesmen do?

[11] Department of the Army, Senate Hearings, Department of Defense Appropriations for fiscal 1969, 90th Congress, Second Session, Part II, page 868.

[12] "On August 16," said a special survey in *Space/Aeronautics*, page 88, last January, "Poseidon and Minuteman III were launched with ten and three warheads respectively."

Foreign Trade

4. Arms Sales and Foreign Policy

United States Senate Committee on Foreign Relations

I. THE CHANGING PATTERN OF AMERICAN MILITARY ASSISTANCE

Since the Second World War the United States has recognized that it is in the national interest to give military support to friendly countries to enable them to defend themselves against the threat of aggression. The military assistance programs beginning in 1949 with congressional approval of the Mutual Defense Assistance Act have provided various kinds of grant military aid to countries unable to pay for their own defense needs. Over the years the Congress has paid particularly close attention to the military assistance programs with an eye to withdrawing such aid from countries having sufficient resources to maintain their own forces and preventing U.S. military aid from either being misused or overburdening struggling economies.

In recent years both the President and the Congress have become increasingly aware of another responsibility directly related to the use of military assistance. This is the question of conventional arms control in the developing regions of the world. In his message of last January to the Eighteen Nation Disarmament Conference, President Johnson reminded the delegates:

As we focus on nuclear arms, let us not forget that resources are being devoted to nonnuclear arms races all around the world. These resources might be better spent on feeding the hungry, healing the sick and teaching the uneducated. The cost of acquiring and maintaining one squadron of supersonic aircraft diverts resources that would build and maintain a university. We suggest therefore that countries, on a regional basis,

explore ways to limit competition among themselves for costly weapons often sought for reasons of illusory prestige.

Despite President Johnson's concern, the pursuit of "illusory prestige" has recently quickened throughout the developing regions of the world. For example, the United States has agreed to sell to Iran a squadron of F-4 Phantoms, its most sophisticated operational supersonic aircraft. Morocco has purchased 12 F-5's, among the United States most modern fighter-interceptors. The international record of such sales is long: American F-104's interceptors to Jordan, British Hawker Hunter jet fighters to Chile, American A-4B tactical attack aircraft to Argentina, Soviet Mig 21's to Iraq, Czechoslovakian armored cars and bazookas to Cyprus—to cite some recent examples.

What is clearly in process is a competition among the industrial nations to sell arms to the developing nations of the world. In the Indian subcontinent and the Middle East these sales have contributed to an intense arms race; while in North Africa, sub-Saharan Africa and most of Latin America the situation is still, in Lincoln Bloomfield's words, that of an "arms walk." But the arms pace, even where it still remains a "walk," shows every sign of accelerating, unless the major powers take a stronger interest in slowing the pace.

This growing problem of arms competition in the underdeveloped world and the diversion of scarce resources is directly related to a dramatic shift in the composition of U.S. military assistance and sales programs. It seems that at a moment of increasing congressional oversight of the military grant assistance, emphasis has shifted from these programs to a concentration on military sales. In the fiscal years 1952 to 1961 the U.S. military grant aid programs and military sales amounted to a total value of $22 billion—$17 billion in grant aid and $5 billion in sales. According to the Defense Department, the comparative amounts will be radically altered in the 1962–71 period—that is $15 billion in military sales, and $7 billion in grant aid. (In

Staff study prepared for the use of the Committee on Foreign Relations, United States Senate, 90th Congress, 1st Session (January 25, 1967).

fiscal year 1961, for example, sales were 43.4 per cent of grant aid; in fiscal year 1966, sales stood at 235.1 per cent of aid.) Since 1962 the Defense Department has already obtained $11.1 billion in foreign military orders and commitments. The average of all military export sales in the 1952–61 period was around $300 million annually. In fiscal year 1961 military export sales rose to $600 million; they were $1.3 billion in fiscal year 1963; $1.26 billion in fiscal year 1964; $1.97 billion in fiscal year 1965; and were around $1.93 billion in fiscal year 1966. That is a total of some $6 to $7 billion in the past 4 years.

Of the $9 billion in orders and commitments the United States received between 1962 and 1965 almost $5 billion has been received in cash receipts, an amount offsetting almost 40 per cent of the dollar costs of maintaining U.S. forces abroad during that period. Furthermore, these sales offsets have risen from 10 per cent of oversea expenditures in 1961 to 44 per cent in 1965.

Secretary of Defense McNamara made it very clear in 1965 that he considered military grants and the increasing military sales as an important instrument of American foreign policy:

I think it is extremely important to understand that in our military assistance program and in our military sales program we face two extremes.

In the one case we face nations, our allies, who for a variety of reasons may not have developed their defense program to a level commensurate with their economic strength, their obligations to their own people, and their obligations to the alliance of which we are a part. Nations that fall in that category are the developed countries, the countries which have had a remarkable economic growth, in the last decade or two, economic growth in many cases stimulated by Marshall Plan aid.

In these instances it is very much in our interest to work with those nations to expand their defense program, to increase their military personnel strength, to add to their equipment, and where it can be done to our mutual advantage to insure that they buy their equipment from U.S. producers. This we do.

The result has been very substantial increases in the defense budgets of many of the Western nations, Australia, the Federal Republic, to name two. This is ultimately in their interest. It is very much in our interest. In no way does it conflict

with economic development and economic strength which I want to emphasize as Secretary of Defense I consider to be the foundation ultimately of national security. In any case, that is one extreme.

The other extreme is represented by those underdeveloped nations which have not yet met the minimum needs of their people for social and economic progress but who nonetheless are inclined to divert an unreasonable share of their scarce human and materiel resources to defense.

In those cases our first objective is to use the influence that we gain through the military assistance programs and occasionally through the military export sales programs to work with them to reduce the share of their resources devoted to defense and to increase the portion of their human and material capital that is allocated to economic and social programs[*]

It is difficult to fault the objectives and the logic of such an approach to the military assistance and sales programs. But the developing nature of the arms competition seems to defy the best intentions of Mr. McNamara's reasonable explanation of how the United States conducts its arms sales. The question that must be addressed is whether the governmental machinery designed for the management of our military sales program is adequate to the task of bringing the U.S. actions in line with Secretary McNamara's intentions.

There is evidence to suggest that it is not.

II. THE DIMENSIONS OF THE ARMS SALES PROGRAM

Since its establishment in October of 1961 a Defense Department office called International Logistic Negotiations (ILN) has been the center of U.S. military sales. In 1964 the Director of ILN, Henry J. Kuss, was promoted to the rank of Deputy Assistant Secretary of Defense as the result of his success in boosting military sales. ILN's sales force of some 21 professional officers is organized into four teams—red, grey, blue, and white—each charged with particular functional and regional responsibilites. The white team, for example, devotes almost its entire efforts to selling military equipment to West Germany in an effort to offset by military sales the approximately $775 million it costs the United States in

---

[*]News conference, September 16, 1965.

dollars to keep our troops in the Federal Republic (West Germany has bought some $3 billion worth of military equipment in the last 4 years). The measure of ILN's success is the 600-per cent increase in annual military sales over the levels of the 1950's.

The Defense Department's approach to the arms sales field has been dynamic and aggressive. The Department through the Military Export Committee of the Defense Industry Advisory Council has sought the cooperation of industry and the financial community in an effort to further overseas military sales. Defense is also supporting plans to organize symposia throughout the United States aimed at convincing the smaller arms manufacturers, the "non-bigs" as they are called, of the advantages of entering the military export market.

In fostering these commercial ties, the Department of Defense is appreciative of the fact that there are a number of ways by which arms can be sold abroad: private firms selling to a foreign government, private firms selling through an agency of the U.S. Government and government to government sales. There are other possibilities as well, such as a United States manufacturer licensing a foreign firm to produce his products. Because of the variety of ways that arms are sold and distributed it is difficult to know the extent of just how much equipment is being purchased. For example, the F-86's Venezuela recently bought from West Germany were manufactured in Italy under a United States licensing arrangement. The F-86's West Germany "sold" to Iran but which mysteriously seem to actually belong to Pakistan (despite United States efforts to halt the flow of arms into Pakistan) were manufactured in Canada.

In other words, neither the sales figures given by International Logistics Negotiations—which do not include commercial military sales with the exception of those to West Germany—nor even customs statistics would be able to give the full story of the extent of arms traffic for which the United States is responsible.

The Defense Department's interest in the potential of the export market has prompted a number of appeals to the American armament industry to go "international." In a speech before the American Ordinance Association in October of 1966, Mr. Kuss had this comment about the companies who were reluctant to go "international."

This tendency of American companies to refrain from entering into the international arms market is a serious one and affects our entire international posture in a military, economic, and political way.

From the military point of view we stand to lose all of the major international relationships paid for with grant aid money unless we can establish professional military relationships through the sales media. . . .

From the economic point of view the stability of the dollar in the world market is dependent on our ability to resolve balance of payments problems. Failure to resolve these balance of payments problems creates economic pressures in the international and in the domestic spheres. The solution to balance of payments is principally in more trade. All other solutions merely temporize the problem.

From the political point of view international trade is the "staff of life" of a peaceful world. With it comes understanding; the lack of it eliminates communications and creates misunderstandings.[1]

Of particular interest to the Defense Department as a means of furthering its international sales is the eventual creation of a NATO Defense Common Market. Secretary McNamara first proposed the Defense Common Market in May of 1965. Such a common market for defense materials in NATO is also appealing because of the stimulus it would give to the standardization of military weapons and the development of common production facilities. The Department seems most impressed, however with arms sales potential in such a common market area. Mr. Kuss has said that "the highly competitive approach that has been taken here in the United States, particularly as a result of Secretary McNamara's cost reduction programs, places U.S. industries in fit condition for competition throughout the world." ILN estimates that over the next ten years United States allies "may purchase a minimum of $10 to $15 billion of their requirements from the United States by sheer virtue of the fact that most of these items will be a minimum of 30 per cent to 40 per cent cheaper and will be highly competitive from a technical point of view. . . ."[2] An important objective of American military export policies is to break down what ILN has termed "protectionists interests in Europe." For as Mr. Kuss has put it:

We must establish by our actions in Government and industry that there is merit in an orientation toward the United States. We must sell the benefits of collaboration in defense matters with competition. We must demonstrate that the free world has more to gain from the U.S. model of defense competition than it has from the temptation to allocate the market and build little, safe, high-cost arrangements across national borders.

As an example of this temptation, Mr. Kuss cites the recommendations of the Plowden report on the British aircraft industry as ". . . indicative of the frustrations and consequent protectionism that is arising in Europe."[3]

III. THE MILITARY EXPORT MARKETS

For all the excitement generated in the American press over arms sales to Latin America and other developing regions of the world, the fact is that only a small percentage of total United States arms sales is involved. During the period fiscal years 1962–66, $9.85 billion of $11.1 billion in orders and commitments, went to developed countries in Europe and Asia. This is 88 per cent of the total, with $8.7 of the $9.85 billion going to Europe alone. (How much of this equipment is eventually transshipped as surplus to the underdeveloped world is another matter.) By way of contrast, during the same period the United States sold some $45 million to Africa and $162.7 million to Latin America (mainly to Argentina, Brazil, and Venezuela). In the Middle East and south Asia the 1962–66 total was some $972 million or 8 per cent of the grand total (half of this amount went to Iran alone).

Again, these figures do not include grant aid shipments or sales to which the U.S. Government was not a party.

In the case of Latin America, for ex- ample, total sales of U.S. military equipment, including commercial sales, may be 10 or 15 per cent higher than the $162 million. The problem of compilation of total sales is complicated, if not made impossible, by the absence of any public or even Government sources that give totals of all United States military exports to countries or regions.

The fact that sales to underdeveloped countries amount to only 12 per cent of the total military sales handled by the Department of Defense is important for a number of reasons. These figures on sales to underdeveloped countries lead to the conclusion that the U.S. motives in arranging such sales simply cannot be rooted in balance of payments considerations. If the United States were to lose its entire arms market to the underdeveloped world the impact on our overall balance-of-payments accounts would be small. Therefore, our justification for such sales must be based on the other considerations, such as influencing the development of the local military elites or helping a country resist the threat of external aggressions. Preventing the influx of military equipment of other nations, a sort of preemptive selling, has also been a strong United States motive in the underdeveloped areas of the world.

IV. FINANCING MILITARY EXPORTS

Almost two-thirds of all military sales abroad over the past few years have been for cash. The largest cash customer is West Germany, although other industrial nations such as Australia, Canada, and United Kingdom (with the major exception of the billion-dollar F-111 deal) have also normally paid cash. Conversely, sales to the underdeveloped regions of the world have been mainly credit-financed. For example, of the roughly $56 million in arms sold to Latin America through the Department of Defense in fiscal year 1966 only $8 million was for cash. This 7-to-1 ratio of credit to cash probably is common throughout the underdeveloped world.

The International Logistics Negotiations Office, not AID or the Export-Import Bank, has acquired the responsibility of negotiating the terms of the credit extended for military purchases. The sources of this credit are the Eximbank, private banking facilities, and a military assistance account available for the use of the Defense Department under the authority of Section 508 of the Foreign Assistance Act.

Export-import bank

The Eximbank has taken an active interest in the financing of military export sales only since 1963 when the Defense Department was given authority to insure credits.

The Eximbank role is one of providing a service function for the Department of Defense and bringing to military sales on credit the advantages of the Bank's experience in the international credit field. These loans are usually on a medium-term basis, or five to seven years, at an interest rate that now stands around 5½ per cent. Eximbank makes direct loans for military equipment only to industrial nations such as Great Britain, Australia, etc.

In addition, Eximbank makes so-called "country-x loans." Such loans are the result of Eximbank establishing what amounts to an accounts receivable fund for the use of the Department of Defense in arranging loans to underdeveloped countries. The Eximbank does not know or want to know where this money goes. The Department of Defense guarantees these funds through the military assistance account described below. The bank therefore avoids the problem of directly financing military sales to underdeveloped countries.

Private banking facilities

It is not clear how large a role private banking facilities play in the financing of U.S. military exports. According to the Military Export Reporter, a trade journal for United States contractors in the arms business, during the period of fiscal year 1962–65 approximately $2 billion or 40 per cent of total arms sales, were financed by private banks or the Export-Import Bank. Since the Eximbank only entered the field in 1963 and carried only a very small amount of direct credit until fiscal year 1966, it can be roughly estimated that private banks ex-

tended some 90 per cent or $1.8 billion of the funds during that period. But these figures are most tentative. It is safe to say, however, that private banks do not participate in such loans, particularly to underdeveloped countries, without a full guarantee of repayment. In the case of underdeveloped countries, the military assistance credit account serves as the primary source of credit guarantees.

The military assistance credit account

The military assistance credit account is the most useful instrument at the disposal of the International Logistics Negotiations (ILN) office for use in providing credit for arms sales to areas where commercial and direct Eximport credits are unavailable.

The idea that the Department of Defense should have funds available to arrange credit terms for arms sales was initiated with the Mutual Security Act of 1957 when a fund of $15 million was authorized for this purpose. This account officially became a "revolving account" to finance additional sales when the Foreign Assistance Act of 1961 (sec. 508) authorized that repayments from such sales to "be available until expended solely for the purpose of furnishing military assistance on cash or credit terms." Consequently, this fund, through yearly appropriations ranging from $21 to $83 million, has grown to over $300 million. An important amendment to the Foreign Assistance Act came in 1964 when the Defense Department asked for, and received from the Congress, the authority to allow the Department of Defense to guarantee 100 per cent of the credit extended by U.S. banks for arms sales while only obligating 25 per cent of the amount from the military assistance credit account as a reserve to back up the guarantees in the event of a default. In other words, the $300 million in the ever-increasing "revolving account" now allows the Department of Defense to put the full guarantee of the U.S. Government behind over a billion dollars in military credits.

This provision permits ILN to guarantee loans the Export-Import Bank might make available through the "country-x" accounts or to back a loan made by a private bank.

Another option provided for ILN by the Foreign Assistance Act is the use of the military assistance credit account to extend direct credit for foreign purchases. The terms of such credit are at the discretion of the Defense Department and range from commercial rates to as low as a zero interest charge. A low interest charge from the military assistance credit account would normally be used in a package loan, which might include credit funds from a commercial bank and the Export-Import Bank, in order to bring down the overall interest charge to the customer. If the extension of credit were to underdeveloped countries, ILN would probably guarantee the other pieces of the loan package as well.

V. POLICY CONTROL OF ARMS SALES

The magnitude and complexity of the arms sales program would seem to demand a well-developed system of interagency supervision and complete statistics on what is being sold to whom under what terms. In large measure because of the phenomenal growth of the arms sale programs, neither the administrative resources of the executive nor the legislative attention of the Congress have kept pace with the problems these military exports have brought in their wake.

Under the provisions of the post-World War II legislation concerned with the regulation of arms sales (the Export Control Act of 1949, as amended, and the Mutual Security Act of 1954, as amended) the Department of State and the Treasury Department share the responsibility for establishing policy and for enforcing regulations with regard to the sale of arms. As for the obvious connection between arms sales and arms control, the Director of the Arms Control and Disarmament Agency was given the responsibility of Public Law 87–297 in 1961 to:

. . . serve as the principal adviser to the Secretary of State and the President on arms control and disarmament matters. In carrying out his duties under this act the Director shall, under the direction of the Secretary of State, have primary responsibility within the Government for arms control and disarmament matters. . . .

In order to insure that arms exports procedures are consistent with the security of the United States and U.S. foreign policy, the Secretary of State, under the statutory authority of the 1954 Mutual Security Act, established an Office of Munitions Control to control the export licenses of items on the United States munitions list. That is, items the United States considers "arms, ammunition, and implements of war." As a further safeguard the Secretary of State in 1966 established a special interdepartmental committee to make certain that any disclosure of classified military information brought about by military exports would be consistent with national security requirements. This Committee, the successor to the Military Information Committee, is called the National Military Information Disclosure Policy Committee.

In theory, then, the interdepartmental machinery seems adequate to the task of coordinating a national policy of arms sales which would take into full account the military, political, economic, and arms control implications of our expanding sales programs. In practice, the mechanism appears unequal to the task. First of all, the Office of Munitions Control, which should serve as a general clearinghouse for all arms sales, does not have responsibility for handling, or even cataloging, government-to-government military sales—thus it has no influence over the greatest exporter of all, the Department of Defense. Moreover, since 1962 the Office of Munitions Control has not issued a report on just what commercial military items were exported. The problem seems to be a budgetary one of inadequate funding for the necessary staff to compile such a report. As a result, however, there is no way, short of a special request, for Congress or the Secretary of State to know just what is being exported to where by commercial firms. Since the Defense Department submits no composite reports to the Congress on what it sells abroad or even how the military assistance credit account is used, legislative oversight in the arms sales field is haphazard and generally ineffectual.

How and by whom the major decisions on arms sales are made is something of a mystery. There is reported to be a State-Defense Coordinating Committee for arms sales policy consisting of members of Treasury, the State Department, the Defense Department, and presumably the Arms Control Agency and AID. Whether the full Committee actually meets is uncertain. One thing is clear, however, from testimony the Foreign Relations Committee has already heard: the Arms Control and Disarmament Agency, despite its charter, does not sit at the high table when decisions on the sale of arms are made. Another open question is whether the Agency for International Development or the Bureau of the Budget actually participate in the process of making a decision to sell, for example, A-4B's to Argentina or have only the option of attempting to overturn a promise of arms sales already made to another country.

VI. POLICY IMPLICATIONS OF ARMS SALES

The burgeoning arms sales program raises a number of major and intertwined policy concerns: First, what is the effect of U.S. current military export policy on our European alliance relationships; second, what is the effect of these arms exports on the external indebtedness and general financial circumstances of the underdeveloped countries; and third, what are the prospects for arms control in the developing regions of the world given the present pace and pattern of the international traffic in arms?

On the question of the arms sales and United States relations with its European allies, the central fact is that while the financial success of the U.S. military sales is beyond dispute, there is ample reason for concern as to the side effects of the vigorous sales campaigns. American sales efforts have become a source of great irritation in Europe, particularly in West Germany and Great Britain, and may also be a major cause of the increasing interest of Europeans in competing for arms markets in developing regions of the world.

Some of the European resentment over U.S. arms sales efforts has found its way into the European press. In 1965 Britain's Daily Telegraph began a bitter article on American sales by charging:

Growing resentment is being expressed by British defense experts at the effects of ruthless American high pressure salesmanship of arms and aircraft. This has already cost Britain a £ 40 million tank order from Italy.

American efforts to become the monopoly producer of major arms are seen to be producing not only a form of "cold war" within NATO, but an actual weakening of its frontline strength by foisting inferior weapons on it.[4]

Such charges, which have been mirrored less bluntly in the French and Swedish press, are almost certainly overblown; and this particular charge came chiefly as the result of British unhappiness over Italy's decision to buy American M60 tanks instead of the British Chieftain battle tank. Nevertheless, Prime Minister Wilson himself complained to a NATO meeting of the high-pressure salesmanship of the United States in the arms field. In July of 1965 Prime Minister Wilson announced to Parliament that his Government had decided to follow the American lead in arm sales, and would therefore establish its own office of International Logistics Negotiations. Mr. Kuss' counterpart, Mr. Raymond Brown, is called the Head of Defense Sales. In reporting this action, Mr. Wilson explained:

There is a strong desire that we should make more effective arrangements in placing British arms, particularly with our allies, because, as I said in my speech to the NATO conference, one of the things that have unbalanced the situation in the alliance was the high-pressure salesmanship of the Americans — as we found when trying to sell arms to France and Italy.[5]

As for the implications of Britain's new emphasis on arms sales for the worldwide arms control problem, Mr. Denis Healey, the Secretary of State for Defense, told Parliament in January of 1966:

While the Government attach the highest importance to making progress in the field of arms control and disarmament, we must also take what practical steps we can to ensure that this country does not fail to secure its rightful share of this valuable commercial market.[6]

If Mr. Wilson's program of increasing British sales actually resulted in an upturn in sales to the industrial nations, the effect on the arms control problem would be marginal. But the fact is that under present conditions neither Britain, France, nor any other of the industrial nations can compete with the United States in the "Common Defense Market."

Without preferential treatment, Britain cannot even sell enough military equipment to West Germany to offset the small cost of maintaining some 55,000 British troops in the Federal Republic. A combination of technological skills, a high rate of government investment in defense industries, flexible credit arrangements, and the vigorous salesmanship of ILN have virtually put the rest of the Western World out of the sophisticated arms export market. The defense common market is little more than an arena for arms competition between resentful pygmies and an affable giant.

If the increasing arms competition between the United States and the Europeans in the "third" world is an indication of a trend, however, Europeans must feel that in Latin America, the Middle East, and in time, Africa, they can compete on equal terms. At a moment when the United States is attempting to slow the pace of military aircraft sales to Latin America, France has been actively pushing in the area its Dassault Mirage 3, Sweden the Saab J35 Draken, and Britain the Hawker Hunter and the Lightning Mark 3.

Deprived of markets in the industrial countries, the Europeans are anxious to win the next round of jet aircraft competition in Latin America. Most Latin American countries have until recently been content with American surplus F-51 Mustangs and F-80's, the earliest operational U.S. jet, or the equivalent British Meteor or Vampire. Now they want the subsonic jets such as the A-4. Britain has threatened to increase the pace by offering the supersonic Lightning.

In West Germany the situation is somewhat different. The United States has insisted that the West Germans buy approximately $775 million in arms per year in order to offset the cost of maintaining U.S. troops there in the Federal Republic. The problem is that the West Germans, primarily for financial reasons, have become increasingly unhappy and difficult about these purchases; United States pressure on the West German Government to meet this commitment has been intense and re-

portedly injurious to German-American relations.

Chancellor Erhard's failure to gain some relief from the commitment during his last trip to the United States may have contributed to his political downfall.

Over the long run, it is almost certain that this use of arms sales will have to be modified. The cost of maintaining U.S. troops in Germany is rising—it may be as high as $900 million per year by 1970—while West Germany's willingness to purchase the equipment and, equally important, her ability to absorb such equipment is rapidly declining. There are already signs that West Germany is sending surplus military equipment of American origin to areas where the United States would like to prevent the spread of such arms. There are "end use" agreements between the United States and West Germany governing the disposition of surplus equipment. But how long these agreements can be enforced given the present levels of sales is a difficult question.

This problem of the spread of surplus weapons throughout the world is not limited to West Germany and will require increasingly careful consideration by the United States Government. Total U.S. arms sales have now reached something over the $2 billion per year level—not including grant aid. The problem of the disposal of surplus military equipment is certain to grow with this increase in sales. The surplus arms of the industrial nations may provide the ingredients of an arms race in the underdeveloped regions of the world. It should also be noted that some of the arms used by Latin American guerrillas today were exported by the United States—for quite different reasons—yesterday.

The question of what effect American arms sales have on the debt servicing difficulties of underdeveloped nations cannot be answered here. According to the Development Assistance Committee (the DAC) of the OECD, external debts of the most underdeveloped nations "has increased at a considerably higher percentage rate than exports of goods and services, gross national product, or savings."

In Latin America, for example, the Inter-American Committee on the Alliance for Progress (CIAP) estimates suggest that two-thirds of Latin America's foreign exchange deficit is caused by external debt service payments.

Credits for military purchases are usually hard loans with high interest rates and a short repayment period. Development loans are normally just the opposite. Unless all credits to a particular country—both development and military sales—are subject to a comprehensive review how can we know enough about the total economic circumstances of a country to make the right decisions? At the moment there seems to be very little coordination between the right hand of military export credit policy and the left hand of development loans.

Finally, there is the question of the compatibility of our present arms sales policies with the United States' expressed desire to control arms races in the developing regions of the world. The Congress has fully supported the efforts of the executive agencies to administer military assistance and sales with the goal of arms control in mind at all times. The Foreign Assistance Act of 1966, for example, states:

> Programs for the sale or exchange of defense articles shall be administered so as to encourage regional arms control and disarmament agreements and so as to discourage arms races.

In addition, there has been growing concern by individual Senators over the role United States arms are playing in a series of international crises—Kashmir, the Middle East, and in time, perhaps in Latin America. Senator Bourke Hickenlooper expressed such a concern before the American Management Association when he remarked:

> The United States did not cause the Indian-Pakistan war but we did supply most of the rocks and brickbats. I hope we have learned from this experience that foreign military aid must be appraised in the wisest possible context with particular emphasis on what effect this aid will have on regional problems.

What seems to be lacking in the U.S. approach to the arms sales issue is a boldness of policy often demanded of a great power. It is a commonplace to hear discussions on whether the United States should or should not sell military equipment to this or that country end with ". . . but if we don't sell

it to them the Russians (or the British, or the French, etc.) will." Fully aware of this flaw in the U.S. armor, many countries have exploited it in order to acquire equipment we don't really want to sell them. Consequently, the United States often ends up selling, say, the Iranians supersonic F-4 aircraft for defense primarily because the Shah says he will go to the Russians if we don't give him the equipment he wants. When this sort of compelling argument is added to the glint of a balance-of-payments success, a momentum is created which tends to divorce the process from its appropriate overall foreign policy context.

It seems imperative that at some point the United States take the risk that great powers must take and simply say "No—go to the Russians or the British if you must." Furthermore, the risks of such a policy of denial may not be as high as advertised. In considering whether to sell or not we should not ignore the problems of our "competitors." As Prof. John Kenneth Galbraith told the Foreign Relations Committee last year[7]:

> Let me take note in passing of the recurring argument that if we do not provide arms to a country it will get them from the Soviets or possibly China. This is another example of that curious obtuseness which excessive preoccupation with cold war strategy produces in otherwise excellent minds. It was Soviet tanks that surrounded Ben Bella's palace in Algiers when that Soviet-supported leader was thrown out. It was a Soviet and Chinese equipped army which deposed the Indonesian Communists, destroyed the Communist Party in that ruthlessness on which one hesitates to dwell and which left Sukarno's vision of an Asian socialism in shambles. It was Soviet-trained praetorian guard which was expected to supply the ultimate protection to the government of President Nkrumah and which did not. One can only conclude that those who worry about Soviet arms wish to keep the Russians out of trouble. This could be carrying friendship too far.

Surely such a policy of denial will have its dangers; but an effort must be made to slow the seemingly relentless pace of arms competition throughout the underdeveloped world. If Professor Galbraith is correct in suggesting that our competitors may have their own problems with arms assistance and sales, then it may be possible for all the major arms suppliers—including the Soviet Union—to begin to work together to restrict the flow of arms into the underdeveloped regions of the world.

VII. CONCLUDING COMMENT AND RECOMMENDATIONS

Over the past four years there has been a basic change in the composition of American military assistance. The sale of arms has now replaced the giving of arms as the predominant form of U.S. military assistance. While dramatic in character and of major importance in its implications for alliance relationships and for the problem of arms control in the developing regions of the world, the significance of this change has not been fully appreciated by the hierarchy of the American executive branch or the Congress. In Europe, American arms salesmanship has often been zealous to the point of irritation, and overpowering to the point of encouraging Europeans to compete more aggressively for the arms markets in the underdeveloped regions of the world. In some underdeveloped regions of the world—notably Latin America and the Middle East—where there are no significant balance of payment incentives, the United States, when faced with tough decisions as in Iran and Argentina, seems to be drifting into a policy of preemptive selling rather than the more difficult alternative of arms denial.

It is the general conclusion of this study that it is incumbent on the United States to reappraise the adequacy of the present machinery of policy control and legislative oversight governing the sale of arms. On the basis of the available evidence, there is sufficient justification for tentatively concluding that the adjustments in policy and administrative procedure necessitated by the change in the composition of military aid have been marred by a lack of information, by weaknesses in interdepartmental coordination at the highest levels, and, finally, by a lack of serious attention to the problem of reconciling an active arms control policy with an arms sales program.

The specific recommendations of this study are as follows:

1. In order to provide an adequate infor-

mational base upon which to judge the scope of U.S. arms exports, the Munitions Control Office should be directed to compile on a quarterly basis a complete list of all arms exports both commercial and governmental. This report—with a classified annex if required—should be submitted at least to the Secretary of State and the Congress.

2. The Department of Defense should be required to give a full account of the annual use of public funds in the military assistance credit account.

3. The role of the Export-Import Bank in the financing of military exports should be carefully examined by the Congress.

4. Congress should consider making all military export credits and guarantees the subject of a simultaneous review with development loans. Both involve a charge on the resources of the recipient country and both involve the use of U.S. public funds.

5. Congress should examine the decision-making process of the military sales program to determine whether the Arms Control Agency and Agency for International Development are meeting their responsibilities as defined by law.

6. The United States should take the initiative in organizing regional conventional weapons "free zones"; zones that would be free of sophisticated offensive and defensive weapons—missiles, jet aircraft other than subsonic fighters, tanks, etc. Latin America, and perhaps north and sub-Saharan Africa, offer possibilities for such zones. For example, the heads of governments of the Americas meeting now scheduled for the early spring of 1967 could provide the occasion for the United States to take the lead in calling for agreements among the Latin American countries for a Latin American conventional weapons "free zone." Conceivably, the OAS could contribute to the maintenance of such a zone by the creation of an arms inspectorate comparable to the Western European Union's Agency for the Control of Armaments.

---

[1] Speech before the American Ordinance Association on October 20, 1966.

[2] Remarks of Henry J. Kuss before the National Security Industrial Association on October 8, 1965.
[3] Speech before the Los Angeles World Affairs Council on March 24, 1966.
[4] *Daily Telegraph*, April 5, 1965.
[5] *The Times*, July 14, 1965, p. 8.

[6] *Parliamentary Debates* (Hansard), January 25, 1966.
[7] Testimony before the Senate Foreign Relations Committee on the 1966 Foreign Assistance Act, April 25, 1966.

Determinants of Growth

5. The Worried Taxpayer's Guide to the Defense Budget

Richard J. Barnet

One of Robert McNamara's innovations was to provide Congress and the public with a statement each year as to why the Defense Department wants so much money and what it plans to buy with it. Known in the national security world as the Annual Posture Statement, this year's version, prepared by Secretary of Defense Clark Clifford just before leaving office, is designed to convince the reader he is buying $81 billion worth of safety. Here in 165 pages is the most authoritative public account of the American vision of national security. Spread before the reader is a representative sample of the multifarious threats to United States interests as seen through the eyes of the Defense Department and a long list of devices to shoot, burn, blow up, nauseate, disintegrate or otherwise persuade those who might pose such threats. More than any other official statement of national purpose, most of which get the attention they deserve, the Posture Statement must be taken seriously, for it is a credo with a price tag: The concept of national security which emerges from these pages is underwritten by the U.S. taxpayer with more than fifty cents out of every tax dollar.

Writing about the post-Vietnam budget in *Agenda for the Nation*, former Budget Director Charles Schultze points out that we are at a crossroads in military spending. The $30 billion or more spent on Vietnam cannot be automatically rescued for the

Reprinted by permission of the author.

civilian economy. Unless explicit choices are made to reduce defense spending, he argues, the defense budget will almost inevitably grow to absorb "the post-Vietnam fiscal dividend." "If the military budget in the 1970's is not substantially lower than the level implied by current policy, it will quite possibly grow well beyond that level in subsequent years."

Schultze is surely right. The enormous expenditure for the Vietnam war projected in the 1970 budget did not keep the Joint Chiefs of Staff from pressing for about $19.3 billion more for defense "needs" unrelated to that operation. Because Secretary Clifford was able to deny the military some of the hardware on their "wish list," including an expanded missile defense ($8 billion to $14 billion beyond the "thin" system already authorized), and a new missile system ($10 billion to $12 billion), he continually refers to his budget as "austere" and "modest." Melvin Laird's budget, reflecting certain small savings, is about $500 million less, but the rationale for spending the slightly reduced amount remains the same.

Even a cursory reading of the Defense Department's Posture Statement for 1970 should impress would-be budget cutters with the magnitude of the task. For every dollar salvaged from the Vietnam adventure, there are five outstretched military hands, each with a list of "requirements" based on a seemingly inexhaustible supply of "threats." Indeed, the taxpayer learns that he must spend extra billions to protect against "greater than expected" threats. Thus, real dollars must be spent now to counter fantasies. The theory is that for the world's most powerful country "being on the safe side" means that the only limit to our arsenal is the imagination of the military. Thus the Navy justifies keeping bases in Spain by claiming that Algeria might some day attack Spain. Air Force General Powers warns that the Strategic Air Command would still have a job to do even if the communist threat disappeared because of the possible rise of an "African Hitler."

The document describes a list of projects already started. Each incipient military system is a built-in lobby, a concentration of energy, brains and money dedicated to its own self-perpetuation and growth. Steady escalation of military spending in the post-Vietnam world is thus already programmed into the defense system. It cannot be stopped unless the very assumptions which give life and dynamism to the arms race are challenged and rejected. There is no hope of reducing the defense budget significantly and permanently without a radical rethinking of the meaning of national security.

What is the real relationship of defense spending and national security? While "preparedness" has meant good business for some major industrial firms, and challenging work for a growing class of military technicians, (about half of the nation's scientists work directly or indirectly for the Department of Defense), the mammoth investment has not purchased security for the nation as a whole.

Since 1946 the United States has invested more than $1400 billion dollars in military hardware and the men who use it, but by almost any criteria the people of the United States are far less secure than they were when this expensive process started. Twenty-five years ago the territory of the United States was invulnerable. Today, as former Secretary Clark Clifford candidly reminds us, neither the United States nor the Soviet Union "could expect to emerge from an all-out nuclear exchange without very great damage—regardless of which side had the most weapons or which side struck first." With each passing year of the arms race, the Soviets have acquired the capability of killing more Americans. Years ago the military lost the ability to defend American society.

Contrary to the claims of our generals, Sovietologists and other experts on human behavior, challenging the Soviet Union to compete with us in a generation-long military buildup has not taught them the pacific virtues. The present Soviet leadership, encouraged by their technicians and practitioners of violence, are less cautious than Stalin in threatening or using military power beyond their traditional sphere of influence as, for example, Cuba and the Middle East. The Soviet Union is less of an oriental despotism than in Stalin's day but it is more of a great power. It is hardly a national security triumph that they are becoming "more like us" in their dependence upon and use of military power and arms diplomacy.

For most Americans national security means feeling safe. By this criterion the public has not gotten its money's worth either. The level of violence in the United States has kept pace with the rise in arms expenditures. More Americans than ever are worried about their personal safety. As the Defense Department prepares to spend another $80 billion in the national crusade to stamp out violence abroad, an increasing number of citizens are afraid to venture on the streets in their own city.

Robert McNamara introduced the concept of cost effectiveness into Pentagon accounting at the technical level. It is now possible to calculate with some accuracy the cheapest way to kill a man under a variety of conditions. But there is no political definition of "cost" or "effectiveness." A politician or a citizen can read the Posture Statement from cover to cover and have no real sense of what he is buying, why he is buying it, or how much it is costing. Numbers abound. We learn that "an Asian soldier costs about one-fifteenth as much as his American counterpart," that new escort ships are going to cost $5 billion, that testing and developing a new fighter-attack aircraft will cost $414 million, and that we will spend about $6 billion on intelligence and communications and over $8 billion on military research. But the numbers have little meaning. There are no benchmarks for evaluating them other than last year's equally mysterious numbers.

A helpful concept used in economics is to calculate cost in terms of alternatives given up. Thus, to a family, the real cost of a new car may be a foregone vacation.

To a nation the real cost of fifty-eight new submarines might better be expressed in terms of numbers of units of housing not built, numbers of hungry people not fed, or numbers of sick people not cared for. If the Congress and the public are to gain any real understanding of what we spend each year for defense, then they must have a political definition of costs.

A Posture Statement that articulated the real national security needs of the country rather than a shopping list of military hardware would attempt to relate the military "requirements" to the overall requirements of the whole society. It would point out that a wing of F-111's makes an equal demand on resources as, say, 10,000 schools or a rehabilitation program for five cities. Congressmen would then be able to make some rough comparisons of domestic and defense needs and at least be in the position to exercise some choice. They would thus be able to develop some sense of the relative risks to the national security in saying no to the Pentagon's request for additions to the five thousand or more city-destroying nuclear weapons now targeted on the Soviet Union and saying no to Mayor Lindsay's appeal for funds to keep his city from creaking.

No one should be under any illusion that the two investments are equally easy to make. To invest another billion in the defense economy can be accomplished with a few telephone calls, lunches and contract proposals, involving a small number of people with a harmony of interests. To invest a billion dollars to "improve the quality of life" in New York City, requires waging political warfare against a variety of entrenched political and economic interests with strong incentives to preserve the status quo, and reconciling a host of rival claimants on the money.

To invest in the reconstruction of American society means redistributing wealth and power, while the support of our growing war-making class is a welfare system for the rich. The mere comparison of defense and non-defense requirements would not, of course, lead automatically to a transfer from the military economy to the civilian. However, a system that would permit Congress to look at the real costs of defense spending would encourage the legislative branch to assert its constitutional function as guardian of the pocketbook and would help to focus energies on the political obstacles to investment in national reconstruction.

The Posture Statement is as deficient in providing a politically meaningful definition of "effectiveness" as it is in identifying costs. The word is used dozens of times in the document, as are other McNamara favorites such as "options," "capabilities," and "improved performance." The criteria used are invariably narrow and technical. About $10 billion are requested to "improve" the strategic forces so that more nuclear bombs can be delivered with greater accuracy to a greater variety of targets. Despite the frank admission that no additions to the offensive or defensive missile force can protect the United States from a Soviet nuclear attack, again and again the Posture Statement implicitly argues the opposite, giving credence to the myth that more missiles mean more security, that improved performance characteristics can be translated into political advantage.

In the real world of limited resources the accumulation of excessive capacity is called waste, not prudence. Any organization with a real commitment to the concept of effectiveness would determine whether increments in technical capabilities make it possible to accomplish some concrete objective in pursuit of the organization's primary goals that could not be achieved without it. If the Pentagon planners were really interested in defining effectiveness in terms of the national interest rather than the interests of the Air Force, they would ask, "What can we do tomorrow to improve national security after building Minuteman III that we can not do now with Minuteman II, besides kill more people?" "By bringing another major weapons system into the world, are the American people going to face more or less missiles aimed at their cities?" "To what extent will the existence of these new capabilities tempt our leaders to the unwise use of power?"

If these questions were ever raised inside the Pentagon, the debate has left no traces. To read the Posture Statement, the purchase of killing power is an end in itself. Every new weapons system, regardless of cost or redundancy, can be justified as "insurance." Taking out a policy has no effect on the date of my death, but building a new weapons system is a political act which communicates intentions to the adversary that can themselves create the climate of war.

When the Internal Revenue Service finally caught up with Grandpa Vanderhof in George S. Kaufman's play, *You Can't Take it With You* and told the old man who had never paid taxes that the government wanted the money to buy battleships, the agent was at a loss to explain to Grandpa why he needed one. Today an agent can use the Posture Statement.

If, say, a worried taxpayer wanted to know why $9,596 billion more is needed to be spent on the Strategic Forces, i.e. missiles and aircraft capable of dropping nuclear bombs onto Soviet or Chinese cities, he could turn to pages 41–67. The first thing he would learn is that the U.S. lead in nuclear weapons is so great that we have been running much of the arms race with ourselves. Until recently, the Soviets have simply not been pulling their share of the load. Fortunately for those who build their lives around the arms race, the late-starting Soviets have recently tripled their missile force. But according to Secretary Clifford's Posture Statement they do not intend to deploy a new heavy bomber and have curtailed construction of the ABM complex around Moscow. Thus, despite the rapid rise in Soviet missile deployment, the United States retains a lead of almost 4 to 1 in the number of deliverable nuclear warheads. In fact, the disparity is even greater than that because the United States can strike the Soviet Union with short-range missiles and aircraft located in the Mediterranean and other foreign bases. The Soviet Union has no corresponding capability since, except for the abortive attempt to place missiles in Cuba, they have kept their nuclear forces on their own territory.

The continued expenditures for additions to the strategic forces are designed to terrorize Soviet leaders into not doing what they have the physical power to do. No addition to the U.S. arsenal, including the ABM, can keep the Soviets from launching an attack that would destroy at least one-third to one-half of our population if they want to. No one claims that the new weapons are going to cause any more satisfactory damage than the old ones alone could have inflicted. Sensitive to charges of "overkill" and bloodthirstiness, the sophisticated military have for years been telling us that we don't need more weapons for *killing* people, only for making the enemy *think* we're going to kill enough. Thus, the additions to the strategic force designed to buy "Assured Destruction" should properly be thought of as part of the education budget. The per-pupil cost, assuming this expenditure is for the enlightenment of the members of the Soviet praesidium, is about $1 billion.

The Pentagon, emulating Detroit's ideal car purchaser, is very close to embracing the annual trade-in. Minuteman I, which was installed in the 1963–1965 period and beginning in 1967 was replaced by Minuteman II, is now to be replaced by Minuteman III. Minuteman III is no ordinary late model, for it is designed to carry MIRV (Multiple Independently Targeted Reentry Vehicles). This means that the new improved Minuteman can hurl several nuclear weapons at once in several different pre-selected directions. It is a relatively cheap, easy way to spread more destruction. It is also a good way to assure an intensive new round of the arms race, a continuing duel between hydra-headed missiles and anti-missiles.

As Clifford himself puts it, in one of several bursts of candor throughout the document: "We stand on the eve of a new round in the armaments race with the Soviet Union, a race which will contribute nothing to the real security of either side while increasing substantially the already great defense burdens of both."

With this regrettable fact noted, the Secretary goes on to list his strategic requirements. In addition to Minuteman, we need Poseidon, which is an improved version of Polaris, to shoot from submarines, SRAM (Short-Range Attack Missile) to launch from bombers to overcome Soviet air defense and to protect the bomber from any suggestion of obsolescence, SCAD (Subsonic Cruise Armed Decoy), another aspect of the bomber rejuvenation program, ULMS, a new sea-based missile system for use when it is trade-in time for Poseidon, and the marvelously resilient advanced manned bomber, which appears to be impervious to repeated rejection by the civilian leadership of the Pentagon.

The second benefit the American people are getting with the purchase of additions to the strategic force is "damage limitation." In principle, damage limitation is a fine idea, and it is reassuring that men like General LeMay, who have suggested bombing other people into the stone age, are willing to spend a little extra money to see that that sort of thing doesn't happen here. The key to American survival is to be the Sentinel Missile (ABM) now renamed Safeguard.

The ABM is a piece of technology in search of a purpose. During the years of its development it was promoted as a "shield" against Soviet ICBM's. Such a shield, Secretary Clifford admits flatly, is "not attainable." So does Secretary Laird. Even a serious pretense at building a "thick" system would, in the view of long-time Armed Services Committee member Senator Stuart Symington, end up costing about $400 billion. The Johnson Administration was prepared to sell the public a "thin" system good for protection against Chinese missiles for about three years in the mid-Seventies at a cost of $6 billion. The Nixon Administration, reacting to the protests of the very people who were supposedly the beneficiaries of the ABM's, decided to move them away from the cities. The fears of city dwellers nervous about having nuclear warheads in their backyard would be calmed. The technology would be preserved. The option to build a larger system would be kept open. There are only three important disadvantages to the program. The ABM cannot in fact protect a significant number of the one thousand Minuteman missile sites without a "thick" program of astronomical cost. Protection of strategic missiles can be obtained more reliably and at less cost by further "hard-ening" of the sites. A dollar spent on concrete will buy far more protection than a dollar spent on a sophisticated ABM of doubtful effectiveness. Building ABM and MIRV together, as the present budget recommends, is a recipe for a giant escalation of the arms race that will usher in an era of such fear and uncertainty as to make us nostalgic for the "era of confrontation" that is supposed to be behind us.

About $32 billion is allocated to the "General Purpose Forces" which consists "of those land, sea, and air units on which we rely for all military actions short of strategic nuclear war." To understand the true magnitude of the cost of maintaining our forces other than those missiles aimed at the Soviet Union and China one should add another $2 billion for airlift and sea-lift capabilities, another $3 billion for National Guard and Reserve Forces and a major share of the $9 billion budget item (at least two-thirds) for "central supply and maintenance," the $10 billion for "training and medical," and the $1.5 billion for "general administration." In other words, the actual cost of maintaining the present world-wide military for another twelve months exceeds $50 billion. (A glance at Table 1 of Mr. Clifford's statement provides instant understanding of the arcane military term "balanced forces." The money is divided almost equally among the three services.)

The purposes for which this force has been assembled are general indeed. They are to provide the possibility of "forward defense," "collective defense," and to "deter lesser levels of conflict." Whether they in fact do any of these things or how they do it is not demonstrated. In the one case where it is possible for a citizen to evaluate the Department of Defense performance, the Vietnam war, the investment is not promising. We learn from the Posture Statement that we are planning to dump about 90,000 tons of ground ammunition and 110,000 tons of air-delivered munitions each month during FY 1970 on South Vietnam, all at a cost of $5 billion. That comes to two and one-half megatons or 125 times the destructive power of the atomic bomb that levelled Hiroshima. It is perhaps too much to expect the Secretary to offer a moral justification for continuing, in the midst of peace negotiations, to rain death on the inhabitants of a country we are supposed to be defending; but before he drops another $5 billion on the people of South Vietnam, he ought to explain what it is likely to accomplish beyond sheer destruction.

The clearest lesson of the Vietnam War is that the concentration of military power against even one of the world's weakest countries cannot be translated into political power. The United States can destroy Vietnam with our bombs but we cannot create a Vietnamese society to our liking. The unsuccessful attempt to coerce Vietnam into political subservience to American interests has only revealed impotence. The failure to learn this lesson in eight years of war is a classic demonstration of the arrogance of powerlessness. The "capabilities" which we buy to carry on this war are negative assets, for they are the stage props of a gigantic illusion.

Yet the justifications in the Posture Statement for new war-fighting capabilities sound as though either Vietnam did not happen or else was a huge success. There is at least $2 billion in the budget to "improve" airlift and sealift capabilities so that the United States can get into future Vietnams faster. The CA-5 is an airplane capable of transporting a battalion to any "trouble spot" in the world in a matter of hours. The Fast Deployment Ship is designed to make military intervention with even greater forces more rapid and efficient. The FY 1970 Budget is based on the expectation that there will be more Vietnams and that we will fight those wars much as we are fighting the present one, only "with greater effectiveness."

A worried taxpayer or a worried congressman can search Mr. Clifford's statement in vain for an argument as to why speedier military interventions in other countries serve the American national interest. The great debate on America's role in the world that was supposed to emerge from the Vietnam fiasco is being settled in the defense budget. The character of a nation's foreign policy is strongly influenced by its military capabilities. A

country that continues to buy the latest technology of intervention does not forego interventionist policies easily. If the United States decided to adopt a military posture to match the current rhetoric about not being the world's policemen, tens of billions could be saved.

The greatest weapon in the military's arsenal has been mystification. It has been years since a congressman or significant interest group in the United States challenged the basic purposes of massive military spending. Every new weapons system has been presented to the public doubly wrapped, with an inner covering of baffling technical detail and, on the outside, the flag. When the Joint Chiefs of Staff proclaim a new military "requirement" based, as they like to point out, on their 178 years of collective military experience, the poor taxpayer is expected to say thank you for being taken care of so handsomely. The congressman, who by his own admission is likely to have learned about the new plane or bomb from the Reader's Digest or Huntley-Brinkly, dutifully gives his assent in one of our great national rituals, the passing of the Defense Budget in a day and a half in June. The Armed Services Committees, supposedly the watchdogs over the military, play the role of lapdogs, accepting a level of waste, corruption, and inefficiency that can be tolerated only in a system maintained by a subsidized economy and a secular religion.

A recent study by a Budget Bureau staff member of thirteen major aircraft and missile programs costing over $40 billion reveals that only a small minority even approached the technical performance capabilities promised by the contractor. One of the worst offenders, General Dynamics, was rewarded for its poor record with the famous TFX contract, resulting in a plane that has crashed eleven times.

The Posture Statement contributes to the mystification of national security issues by perpetuating the myth that there are clear technical requirements that determine defense spending. But these technical requirements are themselves politically-determined. The assumptions of the DOD are based on a view of the world and what works to change it for the better. It is the classic militarist picture of the planet. Power is the ability to bring order to others by amassing lethal capabilities.

Until the Vietnam war the public embraced the militarist definition of national power and national purpose without question. Despite rumblings over ABM and Vietnam, the public is still sold on the $1400 billion misunderstanding that there is a technical answer to national security — that to be on the frontier of technology in killing power solves national problems instead of complicating them. The defense system cannot be defeated by logic. If reason had been a potent weapon, we would all be richer by a substantial portion of that $1400 billion that has disappeared into the military maw. One can argue about this weapons system or that weapons system while the war machine we have built over thirty years throws up five more to take its place. To make possible the reallocation of national priorities to serve desperate needs of the American people the institutions of militarism themselves must be dismantled.

Market Forecast

6. Cost and Status of Major Weapons Systems

[Note: This tabulation of the costs of weapons systems and budgets is significant as a forecast of what is being programmed by the Department of Defense. The column titled "Estimated Total Cost of Program" shows the size of the commitment in each case. Thus the Administration's budget reductions for fiscal 1972 represent slow-downs in the pace of development or production but not cancellation of the long-range program. The data are published by the Department of Defense; for use here they were selected and adapted from tables that appeared in *National Journal*, Vol. 2, p. 276 and Vol. 3, pp. 170–172, 291. Used with permission. —Ed.]

The table below lists appropriations that the Administration requested from Congress to fund research and development (R & D) and procurement of selected major weapons programs in fiscal 1972. It also lists the increase and decrease of these amounts over the corresponding amounts actually appropriated by Congress for fiscal 1971. The figures are taken from the Pentagon's Selected Acquisition Report, which periodically reports on the costs of weapons programs. The total program costs are estimated by the Pentagon and include funds already spent and yet to be spent. Dollar amounts are in millions and are rounded.

PROGRAM	DESCRIPTION	ADMINISTRATION REQUEST FOR FISCAL 1972		INCREASE OR DECREASE FROM FISCAL 1971 APPROPRIATION		ESTIMATED TOTAL COST OF PROGRAM	STATUS OF PROGRAM
		R & D	PROCUREMENT	R & D	PROCUREMENT		
Air Force							
A-7D	Light attack bomber	1.5	205.2	1.5	−47.7	1,400.0	Production
A-X	Attack plane	47.0	0	19.1	0	1,315.9	Competitive prototype
B-1	Strategic bomber	370.3	0	295.3	0	10,108.0	R & D
C-5A	Transport plane	(Not available)	(Not available)	(Not available)	(Not available)	4,309.0	Production
F-5B	International fighter	48.0	70.4	48.0	52.4		R & D
F-15	Air superiority fighter	414.5	0	44.5	0	7,356.0	Production
F-111A/C/D/E/F	Long-range fighter	0	190.0	−48.2	−324.5	6,381.0	R & D
AWACS	Airborne radar/control system	145.1	0	58.1	0	2,662.0	R & D
Maverick	Air-to-surface missile	7.5	74.0	−17.2	70.9	344.0	R & D
Minuteman II and III	ICBM	186.6	842.0	−37.6	270.4	10,101.0	Production
Sparrow F	Air-to-air missile	0	10.5	0	10.5	66.0	Development (by Navy)
Army							
Cheyenne	Helicopter gunship	0	13.2	−17.6	13.2	202.0[a]	R & D
XM-803	Main battle tank	27.5	59.1	−8.5	18.0	1,826.0	R & D
Chapparal/Vulcan	Air defense missile	3.0	17.0	0.7	−34.9	214.4	Production
HAWK	Air defense missile	5.3	88.5	−1.7	30.3	641.2	Production
SAM-D	Air defense missile	115.5	0	32.4	0	3,414.0	R & D
TOW	Antitank missile	0.7	62.6	−1.3	−48.4	944.8	Production

							Status
Lance	Tactical nuclear missile	29.4	79.1	-22.1	47.2	761.0	Production in fiscal '71
Safeguard	ABM system		(Total of 1,278.0)[b]		(Total of -167.7)	11,900.0[c]	Deployment
Navy							
A-6E	Light attack bomber	0	93.1	0	-34.4	1,457.5	Production
A-7E	Light attack bomber	0	79.0	0	-54.0	1,575.0	Production
EA-6B	Electronic warfare plane	15.0	218.9	5.0	30.9	1,416.3	Production
E-2C	Early warning plane	30.9	241.5	-16.1	198.5	958.5	R & D
F-14A/B/C	Air superiority fighter	228.2	700.6	-90.8	42.6	8,279.0	Production in fiscal '71
P-3C	Antisubmarine plane	0	298.1	0	21.5	2,551.0	Production
S-3A	Antisubmarine plane	207.3	346.6	-58.7	313.9	2,934.0	Production in fiscal '72
ASMS (Aegis)	Ship defense missile	100.2	0	25.2	0		Development
Condor	Air-to-surface missile	19.9	0	-3.4	0	351.0	R & D
Phoenix	Air-to-air missile	3.6	91.1	-13.9	3.5	1,501.0	Production in fiscal '71
Sparrow E/F	Air-to-air missile	0	61.3	-1.4	38.2	1,351.0	E:Production; F:R & D
Standard ER/MR	Surface-to-air missile	6.6	56.3	3.3	-2.3	700.0	Production
Poseidon/Polaris	Strategic missile and submarine conversion	38.9	750.6	-83.7	-71.1	5,115.0	Production
Mark-48	Torpedo	21.1	148.6	-15.2	38.0	3,757.0	R & D
DD-963	Destroyer	0	599.2	0	139.7	4,177.0	Construction
DLGN-38	Nuclear frigate	0	209.2	0	-12.1	5,490.0	Construction
DLG	Frigate conversions	0	90.3	0	-59.7	767.5	Production
SSN-688	Attack Submarine	0	881.0	0	217.0	4,280.0	Construction
ULMS	Submarine/missile system	110.0	0	66.0	0		Advanced design

[a] Cost estimate for R & D only.
[b] The Pentagon did not break down its 1972 Safeguard figure. Of the total 1971 appropriation, $1.016 billion was for procurement and R & D, $429.7 million for construction and other Safeguard costs.
[c] Estimated cost based on "phase I" and "modified phase II" is $5.939 billion; the figure in the table includes costs for "full phase II."

Long-Range Market Forecast

7. Toward a Permanent War Economy?

Walter J. Oakes

[As this article goes to press, the *Wall Street Journal* of Jan. 6 carries a lead story which strikingly confirms one of Mr. Oakes' main points: the scope of the planning now going on for World War III. The *Journal's* Washington correspondent writes:

"The State Department is now considering a big post-armistice stockpile scheme. Under this proposal, which has now reached Secretary Cordell Hull, the Government would accumulate a hoard of strategic materials, mostly from imports, over a period of some five years after the war. Goods like crude rubber and industrial diamonds would be stored above ground in warehouses; commodities such as tin and petroleum would be amassed below ground in vaults, mines and subterranean reservoirs.

"Such a program, say its advocates, would provide a hedge against any future national 'emergency' (presumably, the next war). . . . In addition, it would provide a balance for the large-scale American export program that is in prospect for world reconstruction, offering a way for debtor nations to repay public loans advanced by this country."

The *Journal* also reports that Vice-Chairman Batt of the War Production Board, speaking the same day in Chicago, urged adoption of a similar plan. Indicating the idea has had "more than casual official consideration," Batt suggested it as "a novel means of approaching a balance in our foreign trade picture."

This last argument shows the intimate connection that is coming to exist between war-making and economic stability. The riddle of how the impoverished, relatively backward rest of the world is going to pay for American exports of goods and capital, is neatly solved by importing vast quantities

Reprinted with permission from *Politics* for February 1944.

of raw materials and "sterilizing" them, much as the gold at Fort Knox is sterilized, by burying them in stockpiles withdrawn from the market. War and the prospect of war offer the means for performing this useful economic trick. In war modern capitalism has, as this article shows, an economic stabilizer better than pyramids, cathedrals and PWA rolled into one.— ED., *Politics.*]

As World War II enters its climactic stage, it becomes increasingly clear that this is not the "War to End All Wars." Already there have been many warnings of the "possibility of another war." A growing cynicism is abroad concerning the prospects of durable peace. World War III is not only a distinct possibility, it is inevitable as long as the world's social structure remains one of capitalist imperialism. As Dorothy Thompson puts it in her column of December 6, 1943, "All grand alliances [referring to the Roosevelt-Stalin-Churchill meeting] . . . have existed only as long as it was necessary to win a war, or protect themselves against the aggressions of other powers. Once all enemies are defeated, the only potential enemies left are members of the grand alliance themselves." In more scientific terms—the contradictions which led to this war have not been eliminated; if anything, they have been intensified.

More revealing than any theoretical analysis concerning its inevitability are the obvious preparations that are now being made for World War III. One may dismiss the psychological preparations, designed to condition the population to accept the inevitability of the next war, as too intangible to evaluate. One may shrug aside the political preparations, which are clearly inherent in the power politics now being played by the leaders of the United Nations, on the ground that this is *realpolitik* in a materialistic world. But it is impossible to overlook the unanimity with which the business community approves the maintenance of a large standing army, universal military service and an air force second to none as preconditions of America's "security" in the postwar world. Disarmament, the utopian pipedream of Geneva, is to be abandoned as a slogan after this war—except for the conquered enemy.

Important as are the above more or less obvious types of preparation, currently concealed economic preparations are decisive. In the United States, this question is intimately bound up with the problems of reconversion. Much more is at stake than the question of what to do with the huge government-owned war plants (estimated at $20 billion by the end of the war). A plan for reconversion, no matter how loose and flexible, must be guided by some indication of the type of post-war world that is desired. If war within the life of the next generation is a probability, then it must be planned for on the basis of the lessons learned from this war.

American imperialism, for example, has no intention of entering another war without adequate stockpiles of all critical and strategic military materials. And so we have Senate Bill 1582 (introduced early in December 1943 by Senator Scrugham of Nevada) whose stated purpose is: *"To assure an adequate supply of strategic and critical minerals for any future emergency by holding intact in the post-war period all stock piles surviving the present war owned by Government agencies and by necessary augmentation thereof primarily from domestic sources."* The "future emergency" is subsequently defined as "a total war of three years' duration, or of any equivalent emergency."

In the case of copper, an article in the National Industrial Conference Board's *Economic Record* (November 1943) reveals what would be involved. "As current usage of copper probably is at least 1.5 million tons annually, a supply for a three-year war, as proposed in the Scrugham bill, might require 4.5 million tons. This amount is nearly equal to the entire domestic output of new copper in the Thirties, or four years' output at the peak mining rate of 1.07 million tons in 1942." While the Scrugham bill leaves the question of cost open, it is estimated that the copper program alone would cost well above $1 billion. Clearly, economic preparations for

World War III are beyond the stage of informal discussion.

The big question which all discussions of post-war economy try to answer is, of course: How to achieve full employment? The sad experiences following the last war, culminating in the world-wide depression of the 1930's, give the problem an understandable urgency. Public interest in the question is certainly more widespread than ever before. What better tribute to American advertising genius or what more fitting commentary on the political and economic naivete of the American people, could there be than the $50,000 contest now being held by the Pabst Brewing Company, in commemoration of its 100th birthday, for the best plans to achieve full post-war employment?

There is an urgent political necessity for capitalism to achieve the abolition of unemployment. It is motivated by a much more powerful stimulus than the increasingly-repeated question: "If we can employ everyone in wartime, why can't we do as much in peacetime?" The fact is that the capitalist system cannot stand the strain of another siege of unemployment comparable to 1930–1940. It does not require a far-seeing statesman to picture the revolutionary dynamite inherent in a situation where 10–12 million people are unemployed. And this is a conservative estimate of the size of post-war unemployment, *if the traditional methods, such as those used after the last war, are followed this time.*

The traditional methods (consisting essentially of trying to restore the *status quo ante bellum* as rapidly as possible) will not be followed. Whether Roosevelt presides over the transition period or not, too much water has flowed under the bridge to permit an uncontrolled post-war inflation followed by a resounding and catastrophic depression. This much, at least, the better minds amongst the capitalists see. The Senate will have to intervene. It is a question of how much and in what form.

Here we encounter a problem in semantics. State intervention, as I shall show below, must take the form of maintaining a Permanent War Economy. What is a "war economy"? In an extreme sense, involving the reduction of civilian standards of living to the bedrock minimum in order to permit the maximum expansion of war output, we have not, of course, a war economy today. Russia, since the consolidation of Stalin's dictatorship, and Germany, since the consolidation of Hitler's dictatorship, both in "peace" and in the period of military hostilities, have experienced this type of war economy. They are the only countries in modern times to have experienced a "genuine" war economy, with the possible exception of Japan.

A war economy, as I use the term, is not determined by the expenditure of a given percentage of a nation's resources and productive energies for military purposes. This determines only the *kind* of war economy—good, bad, or indifferent from the point of view of efficiency in warmaking. The question of amount, however, is obviously relevant. At all times, there are *some* expenditures for war or "national defense." How much must the government spend for such purposes before we can say a war economy exists? In general terms, the problem can be answered as follows: *A war economy exists whenever the government's expenditures for war (or "national defense") become a legitimate and significant end-purpose of economic activity.* The degree of war expenditures required before such activities become *significant* obviously varies with the size and composition of the national income and the stock of accumulated capital. Nevertheless, the problem is capable of theoretical analysis and statistical measurement.

Until the present period, in America at least, only one legitimate end-purpose of economic activity has been recognized (in theory); namely, the satisfaction of human wants or, less euphemistically, the production and distribution of consumers' goods and services. In wartime, of course, the legitimacy of war expenditures is never questioned, except by those few who question the progressiveness of the aims of the war. We are now being prepared, however, to recognize as a legitimate economic activity *peacetime* expenditures for war of a sizable nature. Herein lies the real importance of the psychological preparations now under way for World War III.

The state will have to spend for war purposes as much as is required to maintain a "stable and safe" equilibrium. As a result, unemployment will be a thing of the past. Barring the immediate outbreak of World War III—i.e., within five years of the end of World War II—the size of post-war war outlays is not significantly influenced by the potential utility of such expenditures for war-making. *The decisive consideration is the level of employment that it is desired to maintain.* Based on preliminary estimates of national income and capital accumulation in the interim period between World War II and World War III, the United States will achieve a Permanent War Economy through annual war expenditures of from $10 to $20 billion. Thus, the inner functioning of American capitalism will have been significantly altered, with profound consequences for all classes of society.

Why these "balancing" expenditures on the part of government must take the form of war outlays rather than public works requires a brief excursion into the past history of unpaid (surplus) labor.

THE PROBLEM OF LABOR

The root of all economic difficulties in a class society lies in the fact that the ruling class appropriates (in accordance with the particular laws of motion of the given society) a portion of the labor expended by the working class or classes in the form of unpaid labor. The expropriation of this surplus labor presents its own set of problems; generally, however, they do not become crucial for the ruling class until the point is reached where it is necessary to pile up accumulations of unpaid labor. When these accumulations in turn beget new accumulations, then the stage of "primitive accumulation" (designed to build up the physical stock of the country for immediate consumption purposes) ceases and the stability of the society is threatened. The ruling class is impaled on the horns of a most serious dilemma: To allow these growing and mature accumulations to enter into economic circulation means to undermine the very foundations of existing society (in modern terms, depression); to reduce or eliminate these expanding accumulations of unpaid labor requires the ruling class or sections of it to commit *hara-kiri* (in modern terms, the capitalist must cease being a capitalist or enter into bankruptcy). The latter solution is like asking capitalists to accept a 3 per cent rate of profit, because if they make 6 or 10 per cent they upset the applecart and destroy the economic equilibrium. This is too perturbing a prospect; consequently, society as a whole must suffer the fate of economic disequilibrium *unless the ruling class can bring its State to intervene in such a manner as to resolve this basic dilemma.*

Since a class society can support on a relatively stable basis a certain amount of accumulated unpaid labor, the problem becomes one of immobilizing the excess. State intervention is required precisely because no individual member of the ruling class will *voluntarily* give up the opportunity to accumulate further wealth. The State, therefore, acts in the interests of all the members of the ruling class; the disposition of the excess accumulated unpaid labor is socially acceptable, and generally unnoticed by individual members of the ruling class.

Such, for example, was the role performed by pyramid-building in ancient Egypt, the classic example of a stable economy based on the institution of chattel slavery. In feudal society, based on the accumulation of unpaid labor through the institution of serfdom, an analogous role was performed by the building of elaborate monasteries and shrines. These lavish medieval churches were far more than centers of worship and learning, or even than examples of conspicuous expenditure on the part of the ruling classes; they were an outlet for the unpaid labor of feudal society — an outlet which permitted a deadening economic equilibrium for centuries.

Capitalist society, of course, has had its own pyramids. These ostentatious expenditures, however, have failed to keep pace with the accumulation of capital. In recent times, the best examples have been the public works program of the New Deal and the road-building program of Nazi Germany. Both have been accomplished through what is termed "deficit financing." That is, the state borrowed capital (accumulated surplus labor for which there is no opportunity for profitable private investment) and consumed it by employing a portion of the unemployed millions, thus achieving a rough but temporarily workable equilibrium.

While the Roosevelt and Hitler prewar "recovery" programs had much in common, there is an important difference. The latter was clearly a military program; all state expenditures were calculated with a direct military use in view. As such they did not, for the most part, conflict with the direct interests of the capitalist class of Germany who wished to reserve for private capital all opportunities for profitable investment. In the United States, only a minor portion of the W.P.A. and P.W.A. programs possessed potential military usefulness. Consequently, as such expenditures increased, the opposition of the capitalist class rose (this was basically an economic development, although the psychological impetus afforded by recovery from the depths of depression undoubtedly aided the process). The more money the state spent, the more these expenditures circumscribed and limited the opportunity for profitable private investment. The New Deal was dead before the war; the war merely resuscitated its political expression and was, in reality, an historical necessity.

War expenditures accomplish the same purpose as public works, but in a manner that is decidedly more effective and more acceptable (from the capitalist point of view). In this, capitalism is again borrowing from the techniques employed by the more static class societies of slavery and feudalism. War outlays, in fact, have become the modern substitute for pyramids. They do not compete with private industry and they easily permit the employment of all those whom it is considered necessary to employ. True, this type of consumption (waste) of surplus labor brings with it a series of difficult political and economic problems. These, however, appear to be solvable; in any case, they can be *postponed*. The deluge may come but the next generation, not the present one, will have to face it.

A little matter, the tabulation of unemployment, signalizes the profound transformation that our society is undergoing. In prewar days, those employed on public works projects were officially counted among the unemployed. Today, however, not only are those engaged in producing the instruments of war considered to be gainfully employed; even those in the armed forces are classified as part of the employed labor force. It is only necessary to perpetuate into the post-war period this type of bookkeeping which classifies soldiers and munitions workers as "employed," and then war ("national defense") outlays become a legitimate end-purpose of economic activity; a Permanent War Economy is established and socially sanctioned; capitalist society is safely maintained—until the next war.

CAPITAL ACCUMULATION AND STATE INTERVENTION

Perhaps the most distinctive feature of capitalist society—in comparison with earlier class societies, and at the same time that which indicates its superiority over these earlier forms—is the rapidity with which wealth is accumulated. Alternating periods of rising and falling business activity have resulted and have come to be accepted as an inevitable and peculiarly *capitalist* feature of the accumulation of capital. This was, at least, the situation prior to World War II. To understand the basic laws of motion of capitalist society required the application of the fundamental Marxian concepts of the increasingly high organic composition of capital and the falling average rate of profit. With these tools Marx predicted, and one could analyze, the results of capitalist accumulation. The Marxian general law of capitalist accumu-

lation may, for convenience, be expressed as two laws; namely, the inevitable tendencies toward the polarization of classes and the increase in unemployment.

Today, however, this analysis no longer holds good without certain modifications. The new element in the situation is clearly the fact that the entire present period (in the United States, beginning with the advent of the Roosevelt Administration) is one of increasing State intervention. New forces are set in motion and new laws or trends are discernible. The war both obscures and highlights these basic changes in the functioning of capitalism. The role of the State is obviously increased, but the conduct of the war gives rise to the illusion that this is a temporary affair. But the government cannot spend upwards of $300 billion on war expenditures, acquiring ownership of huge quantities of facilities, raw materials and fabricated goods, without having a profound and lasting effect on the body economic. How to dispose of an anticipated $75 billion of government assets at the end of the war is one of the more perplexing questions troubling the best minds among the bourgeoisie today.

If the Republicans are victorious in the 1944 elections, it is conceivable that they might try to restore the *status quo ante bellum*. Reversing an economic trend, however, is far more difficult than reversing a political trend. Destroying or immobilizing $75 billion of government assets is qualitatively a different proposition than the situation which existed at the end of World War I. It would be impossible to do this, and at the same time to maintain employment at a high level and to carry through the international plans of American imperialism. Any such Republican experiment will necessarily be short-lived. As for the Roosevelt Administration—it seems to be "sold" on the Keynesian proposition that public investment must take up the inevitable slack in private investment in order to maintain the savings-investment equilibrium.

Assuming, therefore, that my major thesis is correct and that government balancing operations in the future will consist largely of socially sanctioned war outlays, the question arises: How will the future laws of capitalist accumulation differ from the past?

THE FUTURE LAWS OF
CAPITALIST ACCUMULATION

In the past, the dynamics of capital accumulation have caused a polarization of classes. (On the one hand, concentration of wealth in fewer and fewer monopoly capitalists; on the other, a steady increase in the size of the working class, both factory and non-factory, relative to other classes). The war, far from interrupting, has accentuated both these trends — in general, at the expense of the middle classes.

Although this law will still hold true in the epoch of Permanent War Economy, the increased State military outlays (as compared with prewar State expenditures) will have the effect of slowing up the *rate* of class polarization. This is due not so much to the different economic nature of these expenditures as to their *political* character. Their purpose, it must be remembered, is to stabilize the economy; i.e., by State intervention to freeze class relations *and simultaneously the existing class structure.* That is why the post-war size of the labor force and the national income will be considerably below that achieved during the war. Otherwise, the magnitude of post-war war outlays would be at a level so high as virtually to guarantee widespread political opposition on the part of the capitalist class.

The major revision that will have to be made in the Marxian analysis of capitalist accumulation is in the famous law that an increase in capital means an increase in the industrial reserve army. If the Permanent War Economy succeeds in stabilizing the economy at a high level, unemployment will be eliminated, but only through employment in lines that are economically unproductive. *Thus capitalist accumulation, instead of bringing about an increase in unemployment, will have as its major consequence a decline in the standard of living.*

The decline in the standard of living will be similar in nature to that which is just beginning to take place in wartime. For example, until about the middle of 1942 it was possible for the developing American war economy to support a substantial increase in military production at the same time that a small, but significant, rise occurred in average civilian standards of living. This was due, for the most part, to the fact that in 1939 there was considerable underemployment of both men and resources. Once more or less full employment was attained, however, further increases in military production could only be achieved at the expense of the civilian sector of the economy. Most civilians have not yet felt the full impact of this development because of the accumulation of huge inventories of consumers' goods in the hands of both merchants and consumers. As these inventories are depleted and as consumers' durable goods wear out, the standard of living begins to decline noticeably. If the war continues throughout 1944, with no significant over-all cutbacks in military programs, the decline is apt to become precipitate.

The Permanent War Economy will operate much the same way. At first, of course, there may be a rise in the average standard of living if the levels of national income reached are reasonably close to those now maintained and if, simultaneously, there is a sharp reduction in total military outlays (inclusive of expenditures for "relief and rehabilitation"). Within a relatively short period, however, assuming that the economy is stabilized at the desired level with a minimum of unproductive governmental expenditures, the maintenance of economic equilibrium will require a steadily rising curve of military outlays. The decline in the average standard of living of the workers, at first relative, will then become absolute — particularly on a world scale as all nations adapt their internal economies to conform with the requirements of the new order based on an international Permanent War Economy. Naturally, the decline will not be a descending straight line; it will have its ups and downs, but the long-term trend will definitely be downward.

Three major assumptions are implicit in the above analysis. *First,* any significant increases in real national income or total product beyond the reconversion equilibrium level are excluded, due to the capitalist nature of production. This ties in with the reasons why continued accumulation of capital is necessary and why these additional increments of capitalist accumulation require more or less corresponding (socially acceptable) economically unproductive State expenditures. *Second,* while a portion of the State's consumption of accumulated unpaid labor may take the form of public works, for reasons previously stated only a minor portion of such public works will be capable of raising the standard of living; and these will decline in importance as direct war outlays increase. *Third,* the possible effects of alternative fiscal policies (financing through different methods of taxation and borrowing) to support the Permanent War Economy are excluded as not affecting the basic analysis; although certain methods may markedly accelerate the inflationary process, while others may permit American entry into World War III without having experienced a violent inflation.

Capitalist society is forever seeking a "stable and safe" equilibrium—one which eliminates unemployment or, at least, reduces it to negligible proportions ("stable"); and one which is generally acceptable or, at least, politically workable ("safe").

This is, of course, hardly a new problem. Instability has been a dominant characteristic of capitalism particularly since technological advances in industry have become marked, a matter of some fifty to one hundred years. It is only in recent years, however, especially since the Bolshevik Revolution plainly demonstrated that capitalism is a mortal society and can be succeeded by a different set of socioeconomic institutions, that the problem has taken on a new urgency. Theoretical analysis indicates, and the observations of capitalists confirm, that capitalism would have great difficulty in surviving a depression comparable in severity to the recent one. This must be avoided at all costs, say the more enlightened members of the bourgeoisie, even if far-reaching structural changes are called for. True, this type of motivation has led to fascism and can easily do so again. It is assumed, however, that the ruling class prefers to stave off the advent of fascism as long as possible, and that there is sufficient evidence to indicate that what I have termed "a Permanent War Economy" is coming to be regarded as a feasible, even if temporary, alternative to fascism . . . .

II. THE MILITARY-INDUSTRIAL FIRM

The Economizing Problem

8. A Theory of the Military-Industrial Firm

John Francis Gorgol

The business firm has been analyzed by economists for many years, in an attempt to determine its characteristics, relationships, environment, available strategies, constraints. This is, of course, not all surprising, since a firm is the "key organization in business . . . which produces, exchanges and consumes."[1]

A formal economic theory of the firm has been developed which appears to have the following principal features: The firm has a goal (or goals) toward which it moves in a "rational" manner; its function is to transform economic inputs into outputs in a given operating environment; the theory concentrates primarily on changes in price and quantity of the inputs and outputs.[2]

The goal, in the basic theory, is profit maximization. Rationality means that no decisions will be made which detract from the achievement of this goal. It also implies that all needed information for this type of behavior is available to the decisionmaker, including a complete understanding of the environment in which the firm is functioning. The transformation of inputs into outputs is analyzed quantitatively and qualitatively, with marginal analysis being used to determine both the volume of output and also the "mix" of inputs and outputs which maximize profits. Thus we see that the entrepreneur manager is expected to behave in an "economizing" manner, making a transformation of "inputs to outputs of a higher order of value."[3]

A number of alternate versions of this basic theory have been proposed, based on dissatisfaction with its assumptions and emphasis.

One such set of alternatives stems from the rejection of a single entrepreneurial goal—maximum profit. Thus, one or more additional (dependent) variables will be added to the model of business firm behavior. Some of these are: desire for leisure; maintaining control of the firm, security of profits, maintenance of the firm's share of the market, growth, and liquidity.[4]

Another set is motivated by the separation of ownership and management in modern firms, wherein the managers have an opportunity to set goals which may be directly opposed to profit maximization. One such approach views an *acceptable* level of profits as a constraint on managerial goals of salary, security, dominance, and professional excellence.[5]

This is, obviously, not an exhaustive classification of existing theories of the firm. But whatever organizational goals are selected and whatever personal goals are attributed to the managers, existing economic theories of the firm feature "economizing," that is, the most efficient movement toward these goals. And the point I wish to make is that, whatever form they take, such theories do not adequately apply to one type of firm that has achieved a particular significance in our society. I refer to the military-industrial firm, an enterprise which sells highly technical products to the Department of Defense.

It is my purpose to develop such a theory. I shall begin by demonstrating the ineffectiveness of a conventional "economizing" approach.

Principal managerial (decision-making) activities in the civilian firm

There are a number of managerial decision-making activities which, taken together, give the civilian firm its individual characteristics and provide the impetus for its success in the market place.

Chapter 1 of an unpublished dissertation on the theory of the military-industrial firm. Reprinted by permission from Mrs. J. F. Gorgol.

A. H. Cole identified six areas which, he claimed, "comprehend all the important phases of purpose in the individual business unit, whether it be large or small, or concerned with commercial, industrial, banking or other business activities."[6] These are:

1. The determination of the business objectives of the enterprise, and the change of those objectives as conditions require or make advantageous;
2. The development and maintenance of an organization, including efficient relations with subordinates and all employees;
3. The securing of adequate financial resources, the retention of them, and the nurture of good relations with existing and potential investors;
4. The acquisition of efficient technological equipment, and the revision of it as new machinery appears;
5. The development of a market for products, and the division of new products to meet or anticipate consumer demands; and
6. The maintenance of good relations with public authorities and with society at large.[7]

An important premise here is that there are meaningful choices available to the decision-maker. While the freedom of choice may not be unbounded in all of the areas listed, there are usually many alternatives available in each of them. The "economizing" suggested in a theory of the firm is the result of an optimal selection from among these alternatives. The sum of the individual area choices should move the firm closer to its goal (or goals) than any other possible combination.

From within these rather broad channels of activity, the following more specific decision-making requirements of an industrial firm have been selected for this evaluation of the military-industrial firm (MIF):

1. What shall be produced? What shall the specifications for the product/service be?
2. What quality attributes shall be selected for the various products/services? How shall these be tested?
3. What quantities shall be produced?
4. How shall the product be distributed?

5. How shall the product be made?
6. What shall the price be?
7. What will the working capital requirements be, and how shall they be met?
8. What investments shall be made in plant, equipment, research, etc.?

This list certainly does not exhaust the previous one, but I believe that it contains enough of the critical managerial activities found in the civilian firm to support the following claim: If an enterprise does not have freedom of choice in most of these areas, and/or if the majority of these decisions are made for it by agencies outside the enterprise, then the classic, free-enterprise theories of the firm will not apply to it in a meaningful way, and it should be considered as some different kind of entity.

The MIF's customer

Our intention is to show that the MIF either does not have decision-making autonomy in the areas listed above or else that it is not really necessary for it to be concerned about them. In so doing, we show that the MIF does not belong in the category of free-enterprise firms and we demonstrate the need for a special theory to describe its functioning.

For this purpose, we shall define the MIF as any organization which acts as a supplier for the military establishment and restrict our evaluation to this view of its total activity. A more precise definition is introduced later on for the development of our theory.

When we talk about the military, we are including its three procurement agencies: Defense Supply Agency, Defense Communications Agency, and Defense Atomic Support Agency. Each of these is responsible directly to the Secretary of Defense. In addition, we are concerned with the buying done by the three operational units: the Army, the Navy, and the Air Force. In each of these departments, there is an assistant Secretary in charge of military procurement — the Assistant Secretary of the Army (Installations and Logistics), the Assistant Secretary of the Navy (Installations and Logistics), and the Assistant Secretary of the Air Force (Installations and Logistics). Each department also has an Assistant Secretary for Research and Development.

At the next lower echelon, a military official in each department coordinates and directs the overall procurement operation.[8]

The basic law which governs defense procurement is Title 10, Chapter 137 of the United States Code (referred to as the Procurement Act). A number of supplementary publications have been issued by the Department of Defense (DOD) or its divisions to serve as instructions and guides for this activity. Thus, we have the *Armed Services Procurement Regulation* (ASPR), jointly issued by the military departments, which is supposed to provide uniform policies for carrying out provisions of the Procurement Act and to establish policies in areas not covered by it. There are also departmental regulations, which implement ASPR. The Navy issues the *Navy Procurement Directions.* The Army has its *Army Procurement Procedures.* The Air Force uses the *Air Force Procurement Instructions.* The Defense Supply Agency provides the *Defense Supply Procurement Regulations.* Finally, there are numbers of special instructions, directives, circulars, notices, issued both by the DOD and the military departments to deal with special situations.

This brief description of the procurement organization and regulations is presented primarily to give notice that a highly developed and systematized buying function exists in the DOD and to suggest that neither its power nor the extent of its influence should be considered accidental or fleeting.

We now return to our task, which is to demonstrate that the critical decision-making areas of the civilian firm (as listed in the previous section) do not apply to the MIF.

What shall be produced by the MIF?

The military customer will specify (usually in great detail) the nature of the product he wishes to buy. If a firm wishes to become a supplier, it must produce according to these specifications. The importance of properly describing the supplies or services being procured and the possible implications of not doing so are spelled out in the following advice to DOD procurement officials:

The description of the required supplies or services is a critically important element of the procurement request. From the statement of what is required, the other elements of the procurement proceed: The method of procurement is determined, the source list is compiled, the contract terms and conditions are selected, the work is performed, and the results are evaluated. If the description is defective or inconsistent, prospective contractors may take exception to it and include contingency factors in their bids or proposals. After contract placement, a poor description may create costly difficulties in performing the required work.[9]

The DOD has prepared the *Index of Specifications and Standards,* which includes all military specifications and all governmental specifications used by the Defense Department.

But even where the nature of the work is not readily amenable to standardization and specification, the DOD attempts to approach the task in a way which makes at least some circumscription possible. For example, certain projects funded as Research, Development, Test and Evaluation (RDTE) activities may be required to engage in a "Project Definition Phase" (PDP), which

. . . is a period of time set aside for precise planning of engineering, management, schedule, and cost factors. During PDP, the proposed project is analyzed in detail to derive more realistic estimates of what will be developed — how it will be developed — how much it will cost — and how long it will take to complete.

The PDP is generally conducted as a DOD-financed effort by two or more contractors working in close collaboration with the (military) Department having development responsibility. Competition is maintained until negotiations for a satisfactory contract for the Phase II effort have progressed, in the judgment of the project manager, to the point where competition is no longer required.[10]

The influence of the DOD in determining the specifications for future (Phase II) work is clearly apparent.

What quality attributes shall be selected and how shall these be tested by the MIF?

The decisions on quality are made by the DOD customers, who have drawn up some detailed procedures and standards:

In addition to describing the required supplies or services, the solicitation must also describe the methods that will be used to control their quality. The control methods will vary with the nature of the end item: Some will outline what the contractor must do; others will define the Government's task. But most of the time they will be determined by whether the item is simple or complex, and the stage of its development. The term "quality assurance" includes all the methods used to control quality.

Simple off-the-shelf items—such as shoes, clothing, and standard capacitors—usually require relatively simple quality program provisions. In some cases, the standard ASPR inspection clauses may be sufficient. In others the end-item specification or the procurement request may state that a Qualified Products List item is desired. Or they may specify other quality assurance requirements. In first-production procurements, the contractor may be required to submit preproduction models for approval before he can go on to full production. More complex items may require inclusion of a quality program system specification such as MIL-Q-9858. Even more complex items—missiles, for example—may require provisions calling for special reliability programs.[11]

There is even a DOD decision regarding where the inspection is to take place. In this connection, we have the following instructions:

The solicitation should also indicate the point of inspection for the procurement. Supplies are often inspected at source—that is, where they are produced. For example, source inspection is performed when inspection at any other place would require uneconomical disassembly or destructive testing of the end item. It may be desirable when large lossed would result from shipment of unacceptable supplies or delay in correcting them. It may also be necessary when special test instruments, gauges, or facilities required for inspection are available only at source or when inspection at any other point would destroy (or require replacement of) costly special packing and packaging.[12]

What quantities shall be produced by the MIF?

The importance of properly determining the quantities which the MIF shall produce and the assumption of this responsibility by the DOD are underscored in the following instructions:

Determination of the quantity of an item to be procured is the responsibility of the requesting activity. The activity makes this determination on the basis of approved program directives, regular supply-demand reviews, and other known requirements for the item. When the contracting officer receives the request, he analyses the stated quantity for its contractual implication. He considers how quantities will affect price, competition, authority to negotiate, and so forth. He also determines whether the stated quantity makes it possible to implement certain Government policies—small business and labor surplus area participation in the procurement, for example; and maintaining or broadening the industrial base. In all these areas he coordinates, as necessary, with other specialists—technical, engineering, small business—before he proceeds with the procurement.[13]

The above paragraph also suggests the assumption of responsibilities on the part of the procurement official which deal with regulating or influencing the general economy and which seem quite a departure from the mere acquisition of military supplies.

We also find evidence of a policy which seeks to expand the military-industrial base in the following advice:

Dividing the procurement among several suppliers is also a useful way of developing new sources. A new source can be tested without risking the whole procurement. This holds true even when delivery of a portion of the item is urgent. Dividing the procurement thus allows the Government to tool up the new sources while the urgent delivery requirements are met by an experienced supplier.[14]

How shall the product be distributed by the MIF?

The DOD customer decides on the delivery point of the order. He is given specific instructions concerning this decision:

To determine whether use of a Government bill of lading is more economical, solicitations should generally request prices for both origin and destination delivery. Data on the cubage, weight, and dimensions of the supplies may also be needed. When bids or proposals are received, the contracting officer determines the cost of shipping the described items on a Government bill of lading. This information may be obtained from his transportation officer or from the cognizant office of the Defense Traffic Management Service. He compares this with the transportation costs quoted by the offerors. Origin delivery is then specified if Government transportation is cheaper. Otherwise, destination delivery is normally required.

There are three circumstances that usually necessitate delivery at origin, regardless of the quantity involved. One is when the ultimate destination is not known. The second is when the destination is likely to be changed before the supplies are delivered. However, if the precise destination is uncertain but it is known that the supplies will be required in a general location—such as the east or west coast—an appropriate destination should be chosen simply to evaluate transportation costs of bids and proposals.

The third circumstance permitting delivery at origin is when domestic purchases are destined for ultimate delivery outside the country. The Government obtains rate benefits for those shipments; it is also able to select the port of export and the most economical mode of ocean transportation.[15]

Further concern with the methods of transportation manifests itself in the following requirement:

Special rate adjustments for volume movements of Government traffic are provided for under the Interstate Commerce Act. Production schedules and planned destinations will be established after contract award. As soon as this has been done, ASPR requires procurement personnel to refer a copy of all contracts involving volume movements to the transportation office that services their area. The transportation office will report back on planned volume movements. On this basis, a review is made of current rates and the necessary adjustments are sought.[16]

How shall the product be made by MIF?

The control which is exercised by the DOD customer over the actual production process takes a variety of forms. We shall describe some of the more prominent ones:

1. Approval of the process before the contract is awarded. In the award of contracts for research and development work, the DOD procurement office is told to ask for "technical proposals" in addition to the price quotations. These proposals should contain sufficient information to make possible an evaluation of:

(i) a prospective contractor's understanding of the Government's requirement;
(ii) his proposed method of approach in conducting the work;
(iii) the major problem areas he expects to encounter and his plans for solving them:
(iv) the types of scientific, technical, or engineering talent and the levels of effort that he proposes to devote to the work;
(v) the nature and scope of any consulting or subcontracting services he plans to employ;
(vi) his past experience in similar technical

areas or with comparable development projects;
(vii) his other qualifications for performing the work.[17]

The evaluation, which really means approval or disapproval, obviously implies the authority to require changes if certain aspects of the proposal do not satisfy the DOD decision-maker (DM).

2. Formal reporting systems to give the DOD control over progress. An obvious difficulty in maintaining control over progress and decision-making on highly technical projects is their complexity, which may require a multitude of simultaneous activities, often occurring at widely separated points. In an effort to minimize the inherent confusion of these projects, the DOD has required its contractors to institute formalized planning and control systems, the best known of which is probably the Program Evaluation and Review Technique (PERT). Its value is described as follows:

PERT provides, first, a detailed, integrated view of all segments of a research and development program. Second, it provides periodic review of the total program. This review is based on a comparison of results actually achieved with the scheduled objectives in the original plan. The technique is used by the contractor and the Government to monitor complex system, subsystem, and component development programs. It is usually updated on a biweekly basis. Specifically, PERT provides:

(i) A systematic approach to the detailed planning and scheduling of the program.
(ii) Frequent, accurate communications relating actual and planned achievement.
(iii) Continuous, timely progress reports that identify potential problem areas where action can be taken at once to avoid more serious problems later.
(iv) A basis for simulating the effects of alternative decisions under consideration and an opportunity to study their impact on the program deadlines before implementation.[18]

And, lest there be any doubt about the DOD's intent regarding the uses of PERT and similar systems, we find the following statement:

When the PERT process is complete, the Government has information to make any trade-off decisions that are necessary. A trade-off is a transfer of resources or altering of objectives to optimize the program goals. The PERT system thus permits the Government to maintain close and continuous control over the program schedule.[19]

3. Make-or-buy decisions. The civilian firm very often must decide whether a component shall be manufactured or purchased. But the firm which acts as a supplier to the DOD must realize that the customer has the power to make this decision and will very often exercise this power. Consider the following comment:

It may be possible to remove from the procurement in question the fabrication or purchase of certain equipments, components, parts, and the like. These items might then be procured directly by the Government and provided as Government-furnished property to the sole-source prime contractor. Again, this is a technical decision. It must be considered and planned for long before it is presented.[20]

What is particularly interesting about the above statement is that it comes from a section dealing with contract negotiations. It is offered as a strategy for keeping the MIF in line while a price is being negotiated.

4. Premium-pay work. The use of overtime and multishift work as a form of increased resource allocation to projects or products which require accelerated processing is a clearly recognized option of the civilian firm's management. But the MIF must deal with the following policy:

Tight delivery schedules and performance problems often raise the question of premium-pay work on defense procurements. Premium-pay work includes overtime, extra-shift, and multishift effort. The question may arise either before or after award. Before award, the contracting officer may have to decide whether to accept the costs of such work in the proposed price. . . . After award, he will have to authorize previously unanticipated premium-pay work at Government expense where specified cost-reimbursement type contracts are used. But—regardless of when the question arises—it is DOD policy to hold overtime, extra-shift, and multishift work at Government expense to a minimum. ASPR Section XII, Part 1, requires sound justification and written Government approval for premium pay effort.[21]

5. Quality programs. Although the DOD customer's control over quality specifica-

tions has been described earlier, the extent of this control may be great enough to influence the process itself.

Thus, on very complex projects, the contractor may be required to conduct a reliability program such as the one specified by MIL-R-27542 (USAF), "Reliability Program Requirement for Aerospace Systems, Subsystems, and Equipment":

It outlines the steps required of the equipment developer in consulting a reliability program. It specifies reliability criteria for such matters as design, program planning, program review, statistical methods, demonstration testing, manufacturing, failure analysis, and other elements of the work. The contractor applies the criteria to the specific development task. He then recommends a reliability program that will suit the objectives of the procurement.[22]

6. Conditions of employment. While we are not assigning the same value to the restrictions imposed on the MIF in determining the conditions of employment as we would to some of the other aspects of the DOD-MIF relationship, the fact remains that these restrictions do exist and they do add support for the argument that control over how a product is to be made belongs to the DOD more than it does to the MIF. We shall not include the laws which are applicable to all employment in interstate commerce (nondiscrimination, Fair Labor Standards, etc.) but only those which apply specifically to performance on government contracts. We also shall not list, but merely acknowledge the existence of a multititude of laws, regulations and procedures which deal with security clearance and, thus, the choice of employees.

a. *Walsh-Healey Public Contracts Act.* Sets standards for wage rates, hours of work, minimum age, health and safety.

b. *Contract Work Hours Standards Act.* Requires overtime pay for laborers and mechanics working on certain government contracts.

c. *Davis-Bacon Act.* Requires payment of certain minimum wages for laborers and mechanics on construction contracts over $2,000 taking place in the United States.

d. *Copeland ("Anti-Kickback") Act.* Its

purpose is to prevent extortion of money from workers employed on construction work.[23]

The principal conclusion to be drawn from the six discussions which related to the question, "How shall the product be made by the MIF?" are:

1. The DOD has the right to approve or reject (and, thus, influence, if not determine) the production system to be used in manufacturing its products.
2. The DOD, through its monitoring activity, is at least theoretically able to control the progress of production and has the authority to make significant decisions concerning future operations.
3. Certain important managerial decisions, such as make-or-buy and the design of reliability programs, may be made by the DOD customer.
4. The MIF must follow DOD-set regulations in the matter of hours and conditions of work.

What should the price be for the MIF's products?

In the classic civilian firm, management has the responsibility to determine the relationships between the prices of its products and the demand for them. It then is expected to exploit these relationships to the firm's advantage.

But in the MIF we have an entirely different situation. Pricing is still a critical matter, but the approach to it is not the same. This subject is the basis of one aspect of our MIF theory and is given extended treatment in chapter 3. We shall simply demonstrate the fact that the MIF does not have the same kind of autonomy in this area which one usually assigns to a civilian firm.

In the first place, more than 80 per cent of all procurement by the DOD is done through negotiation.[24] This automatically brings the DOD customer into price-setting activities, which in itself might not be too radical if the military negotiator had the same goals as the firm. But, in reality, his objective is quite different:

The negotiator's pricing objective is to achieve a price that is fair and reasonable to both the contractor and the Government (ASPR 3-801.1

and 3-806). This may be defined as a price that provides the contractor with an incentive to do a good job and does not impair his ability to perform. This does not mean, of course, that a fair and reasonable price is always determined solely by the contractor's costs to perform. Other factors may affect the price. Nonmonetary advantages may accrue to the contractor. Or perhaps the contractor needs business during a slack period. Thus, a contract price may be reasonable even if less, at times, than the contractor's normal "costs plus a fair profit."[25]

Now, consider the less than 20 per cent of procurement done through the solicitation of bids and the award of contracts on the basis of some fixed price. If we could assume that the contract was always awarded to the firm which submits the lowest bid, then we could recognize this as a situation in which the MIF sets its own price in accordance with conventional economic practices. But this is not the case.

The award procedure has the following qualification:

To receive (the) award, the lowest bidder must be responsible.[26]

This "responsibility" is given further meaning in the following instructions:

Although procurement at the lowest cost may be highly advantageous [an] award solely on a price basis to a marginal low bidder is not justified. Prospective contractors must demonstrate their capability to perform successfully. If the contracting officer is unable to obtain enough information to permit an affirmative finding, he must make a determination that the contractor is not responsible. Doubt as to the contractor's capabilities that cannot be resolved dictates a determination of nonresponsibility.[27]

It is clear that the DOD is buying more than a product. The same kind of extension of DOD managerial control over areas of internal MIF operation is demonstrated here that was evident in previously described activities. To facilitate this control, we find the military customer requesting that certain information be provided by the firm:

Of course, prospective contractors may also be required to submit detailed cost breakdowns to support their offers. Other pertinent business or management information may be requested, too. This will help in evaluating the contractors' qualifications to perform the proposed work successfully.[28]

What will the working capital requirements be, and how shall they be met by the MIF?

The civilian firm's cash flow is a priority concern of management. Inability to finance work-in-process until it is converted into finished, delivered goods and payments are received has been a principal cause of business failures. Management must anticipate its financing requirements and develop effective sources of money supply under conditions of substantial risk.

The DOD customer does not insist that its contractor face these uncertainties and problems. We find the possible alternatives described as follows:

To promote private financing, for example, the Government permits the contractor to assign his claim for payment. It may also guarantee his private loans in suitable cases. To reduce the need for such financing, the Government makes intermediate payments of two kinds: partial payments on fixed-price contracts and interim payments on cost-reimbursement procurements. These increase the contractor's cash inflow from the contract; thus, they reduce the amount of working capital he must obtain from other sources.

The Government may also provide direct contract financing in appropriate instances. Customary progress payments are used most often. Unusual progress payments and advance payments are also available. All three may be used in any combination that is needed and justified by the financing regulations, ASPR Appendix E. Contract financing, too, may materially increase the contractor's cash inflow. Thus, the Government and the contractor have considerable flexibility in ensuring adequate working capital for the procurement. [29]

What investments shall be made in plant, equipment, research, etc. by the MIF?

Management in the civilian firm must decide how to allocate its earnings in an effort toward the attainment of multiple and conflicting goals. In military procurement we often find that the customer will provide the MIF with the equivalent of capital investments in an effort to strengthen the supply base. This subject is discussed at

length in chapter 4,[30] in connection with another hypothesis of MIF operation.

At this point, we shall merely give evidence of the formal acceptance of this practice by the government and also one example of how this practice ties in with the apparent takeover of MIF management by the DOD.

To show that the provision of government property for use in connection with the performance on contracts for supplies or services is an accepted DOD procedure, we need only to cite the following excerpt from the *Armed Services Procurement Regulations:*

The Government shall deliver to the contractor for use in connection with and under the terms of this contract, the property which the schedule or the specifications state the Government will furnish (hereinafter referred to as Government Furnished Property). The delivery or performance dates for the supplies or services to be furnished by this contractor under this contract are based upon the expectation that Government Furnished Property of a type suitable for use will be delivered to the contractor at the time stated in the schedule or if not so stated in sufficient time to enable the contractor to meet such delivery or performance dates. In the event that Government Furnished Property is not delivered to the contractor by such time or times, the Contracting Officer shall if requested by the contractor, make a determination of the delay occasioned the contractor thereby, and shall grant to the contractor a reasonable extension of time in respect of such delivery or performance dates. [31]

That the military customer is aware of the power which accrues to him as a result of this practice, and that he may be expected to use this to his advantage, may be easily seen from the following strategy suggestion offered to DOD contract negotiators:

A major defense contractor will often have in his possession a large number of Government-owned facilities not essential to the sole-source contract being negotiated. If these facilities are being used solely for commercial work, they can be taken away. If they are idle, they can be removed if their possession would improve the contractor's competitive position in future Government work. The mere threat of such action, if credible, may soften the contractor's attitude toward current negotiations. [32]

CONCLUSION: THEORIES OF THE CIVILIAN FIRM DO NOT APPLY TO THE MIF

In the eight areas discussed above, the MIF was shown to be highly dependent on its customer (the DOD) for decisions relative to product, process and resources. These decisions in the civilian firm will, for the most part, be made by the company's management and their effectiveness will be established in the market place. There is no claim of complete autonomy for the civilian firm. Certainly, some examples may be found (especially in the case of industrial goods producers) where there are similar interactions between the' supplier and the buyer, but any situation in which the firm has abdicated so much of its conventionally defined autonomy must be recognized as one in which the classic theories of the firm would not be *appropriate*. Since the firm does not make decisions in these areas, it cannot be expected to "economize" in the classic sense. This is not to say that the MIF does not try to use its resources in the best possible way. But we claim that the choices open to it (whatever they may be), are not the same as those available to the civilian firm. The MIF obviously does care whether or not it makes a profit, and it must be concerned with certain aspects of its performance in a sense which, although not identical with, say, the price-elasticity notions of the conventional analysis, will, nevertheless, be determinants of its success. It may be that it is under less severe pressures to economize, but one cannot entirely discard, for example, the substitutability of similar products as a major consideration in its operations. The point is that its concern with such economization lies in areas quite alien to those associated with the civilian firm.

The MIF is a new entity, created by its unique environment

A new sort of entity has come into being with the MIF. It is not like the classic free-enterprise firm, because it has lost much, if not most, of the autonomy which is associated with the principal decision-making in the firm.

It is possible to see the relationship of the MIF and the government as having an un-usual duality. There is, first, the role of the Department of Defense as customer for the MIF's products. But the total dependence of the MIF on the DOD for most of the decisions regarding product, process, distribution, etc. defines yet another relationship. Figuratively, it may be said that the Secretary of Defense functions as the chief executive of the MIF, with the President of the United States as chairman of the board. . . .

It is necessary only that we emphasize an almost complete dependence of the firm on the DOD for decisions which are equivalent to basic policy formulation in the free enterprise system.

The singularity of the MIF has an additional dimension. This is the relationship of the employee to management. A superficial examination of the MIF would disclose no apparent discrepancy between the way it applies the conventional management principles such as scalar authority, delegation, unity of command, etc., and their normal use in the civilian firm. But the workers, as citizens and members of the electorate, vote for the "figurative" company president. Through their senators and representatives they determine the amount of money which will be available for the company's operation. These same elected representatives may often be called upon to exert some influence in attempts to favor a particular plant, i.e., to see that it does not lose out in getting orders from the DOD. The successful continuation of a political career may depend on such effort. It is easy to see the strong similarity between these relationships and those which exist in a socialist economy, such as, say, the Soviet Union. . . . The principal reason for introducing it now is to propose that a set of circumstances surrounding the MIF's functioning have produced a mutation in the model of a free-enterprise firm.

ASSERTION: THE MIF NEEDS A THEORY OF ITS OWN

The net effect of the above situation is the MIF's need for a set of decision rules which are unique and differ from those commonly associated with the civilian firm in a free-enterprise system. It is my purpose to develop a set of such rules after first identifying the principal decision-making situation. The result will be a theory of the MIF, whose nature and value will be discussed in the sections which follow.

Comments on theories of the firm

I believe that the theory of the MIF should satisfy the following requirements:

a. It should be derived from observations which lead to a set of hypotheses dealing with the principal characteristics of the phenomenon it is intended to explain. The theory may be considered as the totality of these hypotheses.

b. It should possess both internal and external logical consistency: internally, from its assumptions; externally, it should be consistent with other laws, theories and facts.

c. It should be as simple as possible.[33]

The substantial amount of literature dealing with the theory of the firm contains a variety of approaches and is based on a variety of assumptions. The objectives of all these efforts have been similar in that they are concerned with describing or recommending rules of conduct for some organizational sector (ranging from an individual decision-maker charged with limited responsibility to the direction of the total organization). Furthermore, the individual approaches usually reflect the academic background (economics, psychology, sociology, etc.) of the analyst.

Dean Joseph W. McGuire has summarized and classified the bases of existing theories as follows:

a. Holistic concepts, based on the following assumptions: collective rather than individual action, predetermined rational behavior patterns, clearcut goals for firms, an external environment which creates the need for action.
   (1) The economic concept, in which the firm is considered in terms of entrepreneurial behavior which manipulates quantities of product and selects factors of production in accordance with variation in process and costs.
   (2) The theory of games concept, in which the firm is considered to be a "rationally choosing player confronted by opponents or cooperators in a game defined by predetermined rules."
   (3) The cybernetics concept, in which the firm is considered to be a closed system constantly seeking an equilibrium position.

b. Behavioral concepts, based on the following assumptions: (1) that it is actors within the firm, rather than the firm itself, that act; (2) that behavior is conditioned by personality as well as environmental factors; (3) that, as a minimum, the behavioral processes examined must take into account the cognition, perception, beliefs, and knowledge of the actor(s); and (4) that rewards, or goals, are oftentimes complex.
   (1) The firm as a bureaucratic organization, based on the notion "that firms are adaptive, or functional organizations," although some of the theorists "postulate dysfunctional elements that retard the tendency of firms to adapt themselves to their environment." Included in this category are such contributors as Max Weber, Robert K. Merton and Philip Selznick.
   (2) Organizational concepts of the firm, the majority of which "appear to possess at least three features in common: (1) the concept of the firm as a complex pattern of personal relationships rather than a framework in which actors perform; (2) the omission of the traditional assumption of strict rationality, and its replacement with any one of several types of qualified assumptions of rationality; (3) the assumption, often only implicit, that the firm is a homeostatic socioeconomic organization with the underlying goal of survival." The works of Chester Barnard, Burleigh Gardner, and Herbert Simon are placed here.
   (3) The firm as a collection of small groups possessing three major attributes: "Activity which is what the members of the firm do as members; interaction, the relationships between members of the firm; and sentiment, which is the additive total of the individual group member's feelings toward the group's activities." This is the contribution of George C. Homans.[34]

The above is not offered as an exhaustive list of alternative ways in which the firm may be studied, but merely to give evidence of the existence of such alternatives.

A definition of the MIF

In order to qualify as a model MIF for which a theory will be developed here, a firm's activities must satisfy the following conditions:

a. The problems and projects worked on are complex in nature and require considerable innovation in their completion.
b. The effort expended upon them requires the coordinated effort of scientists and engineers, whose contribution constitutes a significant part of the total venture.
c. The company functions in a monopsonistic situation, i.e., that there is only one customer—specifically, the Department of Defense. Even though a number of DOD agencies may be involved as actual purchasers, the firm would still qualify.

Note that this definition is based on characteristics of product and customer. Thus, the MIF would cease to exist if all contracts with the DOD were terminated and the company started mass producing a consumer item. Also it is possible, with this definition, to include a division, plant, or some other portion of a company which is engaged in both military and civilian effort, since only contributors to the DOD product become members of the MIF. Such activities as university research or research done by non-profit organizations may be included. And, finally, it is not difficult to see that the theory of the MIF might be applied to the increasing number of companies doing work for other government agencies, notably NASA.

A large portion of this activity is financed by DOD contracts classified as EDT&R (Experimental, Developmental, Test and Research), which have been described qualitatively and quantitatively as follows:

(a) Research: increased knowledge of natural phenomena (4%).
(b) Exploratory Development: effort directed toward the solution of specific military problems short of major development projects (15%).
(c) Advanced Development: all projects which have moved into the development of hardware for experimental or engineering test (14%).
(d) Engineering Development: development programs being engineered for service use but not yet approved for procurement or operation (21%).
(e) Operational Systems Development: research and development effort directed toward development, engineering and test of systems which have been approved for production and service employment, but otherwise have the same characteristics as engineering development programs (29%).
(f) Management and Support: effort in support of installations or operations required for general research and development use, such as test ranges and maintenance support of laboratories (17%).[35]

The percentage figures are based on the budget programs for Fiscal Year 1963.

We are not concerned here with such suppliers to the military as dairies selling ice cream and milk to military installations, clothing manufacturers making uniforms, construction contractors building troop barracks, or truck manufacturers supplying relatively standard diesel engines. The reasons for excluding these companies are:
a. Their DOD activities are often mere extensions of their functioning in the civilian economy. While their military business operates under a different set of rules, these do not exert a significant influence on their principal management activities. The mutation of these firms is not as complete as it is for those included by our definition. Their activities are totally bounded by DOD regulations.
b. The value of our theory for future applications is increased by applying the restrictions in the definition. . . .

Set of hypotheses for a theory of the MIF

From a study of the MIF's operations, it was possible to infer a set of five hypotheses dealing with its principal decision-making activities. These have been developed against a background of civilian activities which are replaced by these unique activities. . . .
a. The MIF's basic product is "competence" to invent and discover.
b. The MIF's "selling" activity is really an attempt to influence the customer's selection of a technical goal. . . .
c. The MIF's pricing activity consists of mustering resources which are superior to those of the MIF during the process of negotiating contract prices. . . .
d. A prime MIF managerial effort is concerned with the acquisition of govern-

ment-owned resources in support of a contract.

e. Top management in the MIF functions as representatives of the political force inherent in the enterprise and attempts to increase its likelihood of winning contracts by effective wielding of this force. . . .

[1] Joseph W. McGuire, *Theories of Business Behavior*, Englewood Cliffs, New Jersey: Prentice Hall, Inc., 1964, p. 47.

[2] *Ibid.*

[3] *Ibid.*, p. 57.

[4] *Ibid.*, chap. 5.

[5] Oliver E. Williamson, *The Economics of Discretionary Behavior: Managerial Objectives in a Theory of the Firm*, Englewood Cliffs, New Jersey: Prentice-Hall, Inc., 1964, chap. 3.

[6] Arthur H. Cole, "An Approach to the Study of Entrepreneurship" in *Enterprise and Secular Change*, (Ed. F. C. Lane and J. C. Riemersma), Homewood, Illinois: Richard D. Irwin, Inc., 1953, pp. 185–186.

[7] *Ibid.*, p. 186.

[8] This description of the defense procurement organization and its activities is largely based on material found in the Department of Defense, *Defense Procurement Handbook*, Washington, D.C.: U.S. Government Printing Office, 1965.

[9] *Ibid.*, p. II-3.

[10] *Ibid.*, p. II-13.

[11] *Ibid.*, p. II-21.

[12] *Ibid.*, p. II-25.

[13] *Ibid.*, p. II-29.

[14] *Ibid.*, p. IID2.

[15] *Ibid.*, p. IIF2b.

[16] *Ibid.*, p. IIF2b.

[17] *Ibid.*, p. II-45.

[18] *Ibid.*, p. XIIc6a.

[19] *Ibid.*, p. XII-11.

[20] *Ibid.*, p. IXE4a.

[21] *Ibid.*, p. XII-19.

[22] *Ibid.*, p. II-27.

[23] *Ibid.*, chap. 2, section L.

[24] *Background Material on Economic Impact of Federal Procurement-1966*. Materials prepared for the Subcommittee on Federal Procurement and Regulation of the Joint Economic Committee, Congress of the United States, March, 1966, Washington, D.C.: U.S. Government Printing Office, p. 32.

[25] *Defense Procurement Handbook*, p. IX-29.

[26] *Ibid.*, p. IDI.

[27] *Ibid.*, p. III-41.

[28] *Ibid.*, p. II-45.

[29] *Ibid.*, p. IV-39.

[30] *Infra* p. 95.

[31] Department of Defense, *Armed Services Procurement Regulations*, 1963 edition. Washington, D. C.: U.S. Government Printing Office, 1963.

[32] *Defense Procurement Handbook*, p. IX-47.

[33] Based primarily on insights gained from the following sources: C. West Churchman, *Prediction and Optimal Decision*, Englewood Cliffs, New Jersey: Prentice-Hall, Inc., 1961, Richard M. Cyert & James G. March, *A Behavioral Theory of the Firm*, Englewood Cliffs, New Jersey: Prentice-Hall, Inc., 1963, and Joseph W. McGuire, *Theories of Business Behavior*, Englewood Cliffs, New Jersey: Prentice-Hall, Inc., 1964.

[34] McGuire, *Theories of Business Behavior*, chapter 2.

[35] "Five-Year Trends in Defense Procurement, 1958–62," Department of Defense, *Convertibility of Space and Defense Resources to Civilian Needs*, Volume 2, 1964, p. 612.

Monopoly, Monopsony

9. Firms Without Enterprise

Seymour Melman

The National Aeronautics and Space Administration gave one of America's leading military electronics firms a contract to devise an advanced piece of electrocardiograph for use by Colonel Glenn on his space flight. The machine was constructed. It was attached to the Colonel while he orbited the earth, and it performed admirably. The marketing department of this company decided that its new electrocardiograph, which gives more information about heart function than ordinary machines, might be sold to the medical profession. So the firm prepared a machine for demonstration for a heart specialist.

The equipment was boxed in an available container, a military type (sturdy olive drab), and carried off to the doctor's office. There a demonstration of the machine's capabilities was given, and the physician was genuinely impressed. He turned to the marketing men and asked, "Has the AMA approved this machine?" The marketing men were a bit nonplused, thinking to themselves: What does the American Management Association have to do with all this? The doctor soon made it clear to them that it was approval by the American Medical Association that was of interest to him.

From *Our Depleted Society*, Chapter 5, by Seymour Melman. Copyright © 1965 by Seymour Melman. Reprinted by permission of Holt, Rinehart & Winston, Inc., New York.

No, the machine had not been shown to any formal body of the Medical Association. The physician then asked: "Is the firm prepared to take out a $1 million liability insurance policy on the use of this machine so that if a doctor's patient should suffer some mishap while he was attached to this machine, the doctor would be covered for medical liability?" The company men, as they reported it, were rather upset: "Do you mean," they said to the doctor, "that you want us to pay for a $1 million liability policy while we are selling you this advanced machine for a mere $6,500?" The heart specialist clarified the point for the military technicians, explaining that such insurance coverage was conventional for medical machines.

Then there is the matter of the $6,500 price which made this machine exactly ten times as expensive as the ordinary, first-rate electrocardiograph machine already being used by physicians. The high price of the machine made it unattractive to the doctor. When the marketing man in charge of this venture told me his story, I asked, "Before you saw the physician and set this price, did you find out how many pieces of equipment in a modern hospital might cost $6,500 or more?" "No," he said, "no attempt was made to get such information."

The end of the tale is that the marketing department of the military-electronics firm gave up on the whole affair, and decided to try to turn their new machine over to a company already established in the medical-instrument field.

This incident is characteristic of the behavior of many military-industrial firms during the last few years. From time to time, engineers and others on their staffs decided that some particular product might be commercially marketable. Whereupon, efforts were made in that direction and, with rare exception, they failed. A regular pattern was to be discerned: These companies, and their employees, no longer had the capability to design, manufacture, and sell to the civilian markets. Long experience in servicing the defense agencies of the Government, under conditions where cost had been a secondary matter, resulted in a trained incapacity, among many military-industrial firms, and their staffs, to operate in a civilian market.

Management of the ordinary sort of industrial firm, in the civilian field, involves deciding on what shall be produced, how it will be produced, in what quantity, and how to dispose of the product. Before all this, the management must also gather the capital and organize the human and technical resources required for production. The ability to do all these things is the essential nature of "entrepreneurship," or, in more recent usage, enterprise. The inability of military-industrial managements to do work within this range has caused them to become the chiefs of firms without enterprise.

The private firm raises capital from its own surpluses, the result of previous activity, or by means of loans from banks, or by inviting the general public to invest in securitites. One of the principal differences between the procedures of the private firm and the military-industrial firm is that the larger military-industrial firm has drawn heavily upon Government as a source of capital. Thus, Federal defense agencies have become the principal owners of metal-working machinery in the United States. The Department of Defense itself owns 341,000 buildings within the United States (some proportion of these are factory buildings). These buildings encompass almost 2 billion square feet of floor space, and their value, taken together with the attached land, and facilities, amounts to almost $37 billion.

What should be produced? In a civilian firm, this decision is based on an estimate of the market, the functional requirements to be met by the product, an estimate of its ability to attract purchases at an acceptable price. In a military-industrial firm, of course, the Department of Defense makes the principal decision about the nature of the product to be produced. Very often, the Department of Defense invites advice from the research and allied departments of principal military contractors. Study contracts are issued for research to be done on possible new weapons systems. The research reports are submitted to the Department of Defense and provide a basis for decisions about what should be produced.

Research and development is one of the key activities in an industrial firm, since it affects and shapes the technical position of the firm among its competitors. In a civilian-oriented enterprise, decisions about industrial research are based upon the characteristics of civilian products and their sales potential. Those performing such research for the civilian firm have access to the general body of literature in the areas of science and technology. Further, the amount of money spent on research by the firm must be controlled by the amount the sale of the product brings. In the case of the military-industrial firm, new technology is freed from cost restraint, for new military technology is justified as an end in itself, and so cost considerations take a back seat. In addition, there is no built-in restraint in military industry to determine what is a reasonable level of expenditure for research affecting new military technology. Since refined methods in the military art are regarded as important for attaining and holding military advantage, great pressure has built up behind research into new military techniques.

In the aerospace industries, for example, the level of spending per research engineer and scientist in the larger companies reached the level of $55,700 per man, while in all American industries combined, the equivalent figure was $34,700 per research engineer. Finally, military-industrial research is segregated from civilian research because of access to a "classified" body of literature unavailable to civilian researchers. This, of course, involves the operation of libraries of classified information under special security controls.

The structure of management in the military firm, and its cost, are significantly different from structure and cost in a civilian firm. While there has been a tendency toward growth in the relative cost of management in all industry during the last half century, restraints on administrative costs of the sort operative in civilian firms do not appear to be dominant in the military-industrial enterprise. A good illustration of an aspect of this condition is found in an electronics firm I visited in 1963. This firm was in the unique position of producing an instrument whose working parts were assembled on a chassis in two different departments. One department packaged the equipment in a case for civilian use; the second department packaged it in containers for military use. The main production operation therefore included both civilian and military shipments. However, in this plant (all under one roof) two separate management offices were maintained. The military administrative office included functionaries not found on the civilian side. In order to meet the requirements of the Department of Defense the defense section included a property officer, security officers and guards, a contract administrator, contract lawyers, contract auditors, contract negotiators, contract re-negotiators, and contract-termination specialists. Also, the firm employed a larger number of technicians in the military administrative section than in the civilian counterpart. The result was that the overhead rate on direct costs on the civilian side was 80%, while the overhead charge on the military side was 135%. In military-industrial firms administrative costs have reached hitherto unknown heights.

How should a product be produced? In a civilian enterprise the production methods chosen are usually those that minimize costs while turning out a functionally satisfactory and salable item. In a defense-oriented enterprise, the operating characteristics of the product take first importance. Indeed, there is sustained pressure for "improving" the product in detail, while cost considerations take a definitely secondary role.

In order to meet the requirements of firms that are asked to undertake the production of new products, the Department of Defense has long practiced the pattern of writing contracts which pay the contracting firm for all the costs incurred, and in addition, pay the firm a profit over and above the cost. This sort of contract inevitably involves an incentive to maximize and not minimize costs. In an effort to hold down costs of military materiel, the Defense Department has tried to shift to contracts based on a fixed price, or contracts that include an incentive toward lower costs. In each case, however, the prior cost experience in these fields was the available basis, or standard, for setting the fixed price, or for setting the level of costs to serve as the target for an incentive system. Where the experience of cost-plus-profit is the basis for setting fixed price, the experience biases the decision in favor of high costs as a basis for setting a fixed price. In the case of incentive-type contracts, the target cost has again been the subject of bargaining. In this case the military-industrial firm is given an incentive to set the target cost as high as possible so that an incentive could be readily earned by operating under the target cost. (At this point, I think many people who know something about methods of industrial management in the USSR will feel they are on partly familiar ground. Their intuition is probably correct, and can be checked out by an examination of two books that treat this style of Soviet industrial management. I recommend Joseph S. Berliner, *Factory and Manager in the USSR,* Harvard University Press, 1957; and David Granick, *The Red Executive,* Doubleday, 1960.)

Industrial relations are a most important function of the civilian industrial manager, since the level of wages has an important effect on the competitive position of the firm. Therefore, industrial relations are treated as a major part of management's concern, in the effort to protect the firm's competitive position. Among military-industrial firms, however, the situation is rather different. There, the customer (the Department of Defense), is the one who pays. Accordingly, in many military-industrial firms, the custom has developed of consulting with the Department of Defense before new contract arrangements are concluded. Through such arrangements the management of the military-industrial enterprise becomes merely the nominal contracting party with the labor union, because the crucial decisions on these matters are made by the Government-customer.

Decisions on how much to produce are made in the civilian firm on the basis of estimates of markets and the relation of costs and price. The Department of Defense, however, decides for the military-industrial management.

Marketing strategy is a primary function for the civilian manager, as disposition of the product is his responsibility. For the military-industrial firm, all of this is subordinate to the customer's decision, and the Department of Defense decides on shipments, their timing and quantity, to suit its convenience.

Customer relations in the civilian enterprise have an essentially commercial basis, notwithstanding a degree of applied personal leavening. In the military-industrial enterprise, however, the critical considerations in customer relations are a combination of technical and political considerations. On the technical side, there is the requirement of demonstrated competence to produce particular goods, with cost again of secondary importance. The political aspect of military customer relations involves not only the personnel of the Department of Defense, but also members of Congress and other public officials. Recently the custom has developed of permitting Members of Congress to make the first public announcements of the award of new contracts in their respective districts or states. Some Members of Congress devote a considerable part of their working time to helping military-industrial enterprises in their districts secure particular contracts. This involvement in contract competition culminated in the remarkable spectacle of the long-drawn-out 1964 hearings on the so-called TFX aircraft in which the principal issue was never, "Should this plane be produced?" but only, "Who should have gotten the contract?"

In a civilian firm, the most efficient utilization of the equipment and labor force is characteristically obtained under conditions of stable operation—where the rate of output is not permitted to vary widely.

By contrast, the military-industrial enterprise is best enabled to enlarge, adding to research staff and production facilities, under conditions of instability, of major changes in the work done and the products produced. These changes became the opportunity for increasing research and production staffs and for drawing on fresh Government capital for these purposes.

In the private, civilian firm, the main criterion for the investment of productive capital is an estimate of the future activity and earnings of the particular enterprise. Forecasting the future condition of the market involved is thereby a primary requirement of its management. On the military side, however, judgments about investments must necessarily be based almost exclusively on current earnings. Estimates of future conditions must be based primarily on contracts already in hand. Beyond the terms of the contract, the future of the enterprise is not in the hands of its management but lies rather with the officers of the Federal Government's defense agencies.

The ways of birth and death of enterprise differentiate the civilian from the military firm. In the case of the private firm, both starting and terminating an enterprise are based primarily on private decision. In the military sphere, however, the birth of enterprise may be a private decision or a government agency's decision, or a mixture of the two. The Air Force, for example, initiated the formation of special firms based in California to supervise the detailed management of many missile contracts. A privately-owned firm, though heavily engaged in contract work for a government agency, can be legally terminated by decision of its management. But managements are not oriented toward terminating their enterprises. Rather, there is a strong drive in every industrial management to continue and to expand the operation of the firm. The more critical test of the unique characteristic of the military-industrial enterprise is the reaction of such a firm to the sort of grave financial difficulty that could ordinarily result in the termination of a private enterprise. By decision

of the Department of Defense, for example, particular firms can be made unsinkable, financially speaking. A case in point is the General Dynamics Corporation, which has for many years been the number one military-industrial contractor in terms of the volume of work done. One of the divisions of this firm is the Convair aircraft group with principal factories in San Diego and Fort Worth. The Convair Division undertook the design and manufacture of the Convair 880 airplane. This enterprise, in competition with the 4-engine jets of Boeing and Douglas, produced long-delayed aircraft at costs that netted General Dynamics a loss of about $440 million. The same division of the same firm was subsequently awarded the multi-billion-dollar Air Force contract for the manufacture of the highly controversial TFX airplane. The effect of this contract award was certainly to sustain the firm as an available military contractor.

Both the location and primary function of top management differ sharply in the civilian as against the military-industrial enterprises. In the private firm, the final veto in decision-making is usually found in the most senior officers of the firm itself. This final veto power pertains to virtually the whole range of operations of the firm. Not so in the military-oriented enterprise; there, final veto power is located in the Department of Defense or in the other governmental agencies to which the firm is beholden, and the principal duties of top management in this case are to maintain satisfactory relations with the government agencies.

In some military-industrial enterprises, the managers resemble the men in charge of a subdivision of a major central-office firm, rather than the operators of autonomous enterprises. These managers operate nominally independent firms; they do not, however, perform those functions classically understood as entrepreneurship, management, or enterprise.

Another aspect of operating that differentiates the military-industrial firm from the civilian one is the role of the union. Classically, the trade union, in the realm of private industrial enterprise, has functioned as an autonomous organization of workers, housing among them an evolving process of mutual decision-making. This is expressed in the contract relations between union and management which have developed, in ever greater detail, the terms of worker employment. Because of the important decision-making role of the Federal Government agencies, the trade union, in military-industrial enterprises, has entered into unique relationships with both local management and the decision-making group in the Federal Government.

Union officers, in these firms, have often become important participants in the marketing function. Union leaders have learned to use political contacts and political methods to help get preference in the allocation of contracts to their enterprise. This has involved delegations to the Department of Defense, and the establishment of Washington offices, an important part of whose business is to lobby at the Department of Defense and in the Congress in favor of procurement programs for their industries and to see that contracts are allocated to their firms.

Government Controls and Regulations

10. Free Enterprise and National Defense

Jack Raymond

In the new warfare, the engineering factory is a unit of the Army, and the worker may be in uniform without being aware of it.

— HAROLD LASKI

How free is free enterprise?

About 25,000 privately-owned industrial facilities across the nation operate under security regulations devised by the Pentagon and carefully checked by visiting military teams.[1] More than four million industrial employees have been required to obtain security clearances over a ten-year period.[2] In 1963 the Pentagon issued a manual "for the purpose of establishing uniform security practices within industrial plants or educational institutes and all organizations and facilities used by prime and subcontractors having classified information of the military departments or certain foreign governments in their custody." The manual has seventy-seven pages of

detailed regulations on how to handle classified materials, check employees, supervise visitors and other admonitions normally associated with military installations. Big corporations have found the "industrial security officer," who previously worried mainly about pilferage, vandalism, embezzlement, sabotage and fire, an increasingly important member of management. As in wartime employees wear lapel badges, sign in and out of certain areas of their plants and perform their tasks under constant surveillance. The situation recalls the prediction by Harold Laski that "In the new warfare, the engineering factory is a unit of the Army, and the worker may be in uniform without being aware of it."[3]

The problem of security has become so vast that in the fall of 1962 the American Society for Industrial Security had 2,490 members with chapters in forty-eight states.[4] What troubles many of these security men, it appears, is that they now have multiple responsibilities—to their superiors in management, to their fellow employees and to the government. "The security officer has to exercise company loyalty and still think like a government security officer," one of them commented. "If you don't think like a government supervisor, you jeopardize your company's defense contracts." A spokesman for one firm said that his company could lose 60 per cent of its business overnight if a military agency should become dissatisfied with its security program and withdraw clearance of its facilities. In the summer of 1962 all pending new military contracts for Westinghouse Electric Company's Baltimore plant were held up when "discrepancies" were uncovered in a routine Navy inspection of the plant.[5] According to an article in *Business Week*, management is not happy when a key employee is required to act on so marked an outside loyalty. "But this is part of the price of doing business with the government," sighed one business executive. As a consequence, security officers, operating under guidance from military authorities and often to the displeasure of company officers, have taken over substantial portions of the functions of personnel divisions. In theory, they are not supposed to hire and fire. In practice, their word often is law. "If security frowns at a prospective employee, we won't touch him even if he is a Nobel Prize winner," said one company executive.

Fear of being chided or even punished for failing to meet the Pentagon's security requirements has compelled some firms to enforce military-type security regulations throughout the entire company, instead of limiting these only to the defense areas. As a consequence, production, marketing and promotion chiefs bristle when they find good men for important jobs being kept in "deep freeze" for weeks and even months while references are being cleared in the same way that clearance is required for government work itself, that is, with elaborate checks into the backgrounds of the prospective employees.

The resultant picture of a large portion of American industry being policed by the government conflicts with the image of independence nurtured in the folklore of American free enterprise. If the need to protect national security is unanswerable, however, defense industrialists have found other irritations that put them at the mercy of Washington defense policies and changing military technologies. The arms industry of America has become permanent, but permanent only, it appears, in over-all spending. Each individual military manufacturer may find himself blessed with

sudden riches or on the brink of disaster as weapons objectives shift. The impact on the community where the manufacturer's plant is located is almost immediate and dramatic. At Denver, Colorado, onetime Rocky Mountain trading post and cattle town, the annual stock show still opens with a cowboy parade. But the barren-looking plain east of the city is the site of a Titan missile complex of underground silos, and the Martin Company's production line has brought more jobs and money than Denver ever contemplated. A television program produced these interviews:

Representative Peter Dominick, a Republican: "Well, the whole Denver area has an enormous amount of defense installations which have come in—I think—within the last fifteen years. The added salaries and income which they bring in have, of course, contributed to the general welfare of that community, and I think it's had some impact in avoiding some of the rather bad effects of recessions which have gone on over the past six years."

A real estate entrepreneur: "We're building houses in Cherry Wood Village, some 750, and they're a semi-custom-type home ranging in price from $17,000 to $25,000. In our first filing we sold to approximately 50 per cent Martin personnel, so, as you can see, they've had a very decisive effect upon our company."

A banker: "We've run several estimates of numbers of depositors that are direct Martin employees and feel that from our information probably 25 to 30 per cent of our total deposit numbers are Martin employees."

An economist: "I think the Martin Company installation here in Denver has had several effects. First of all, of course, the direct impact total is something in excess of twelve thousand employees. In the manufacturing industry in Denver that is considerable. It's now by far the largest single manufacturing enterprise in the metropolitan area. Secondly, there have been other effects from the standpoint of requirements the Martin Company has had in supporting industry, such as job shop welders, heat-treating, machine shops. These have introduced new technology on the part of the service industries in metropolitan Denver—both manufacturing and warehousing—which gives Denver a base from which it can supply other nondefense, as well as other defense industries, which five years ago it did not have."

A subcontractor: "We are subcontractor to the Martin K. Eby Company here and the Martin K. Eby Company is a subcontractor to the Martin Company. The Martin Company is considered prime contractor to the Air Force—so you have a long chain of command."

Martin Miller, County District Attorney: "Before the Martin Company came into the Denver area we were a two-or-three-industry establishment town. Wages were not low, but they weren't high either. The Martin Company brings in a great demand for specialists, plumbers, mechanics and electric people—not just simply college-trained, but the production people. This has had a tremendous impact on the community. The Martin Company has created new shops, a demand for new stores, new housing; new schools are going up and the entire feeling is that the Martin Company is—well, it's just like having a direct Federal subsidy, that's what it is."[6]

But at another Martin Company plant, in Baltimore, the reverse impact was evident. There the TV interviewers found unhappy men and women at a plant that was built to produce aircraft, but now the Martin Company, after fifty years of pioneering with planes, has given up producing aircraft to devote itself entirely to missiles. The facility in Baltimore was not designed for missiles. The total work force was reduced by seven thousand within a period of four years. In a single month, fifteen hundred workers were laid off. The TV interviews were as follows:

A worker, seated with his wife: "I've been working at Martin's for ten years and then two years before that. And all at once, the thing drops out. Nothing."

The wife: "I don't know. I just know that the bottom can fall out of government work and that's it. I mean, one day it's here and next day it's gone. We came here in 1948. Why, everything was going! And we've seen this place build up. One time here

there was one schoolhouse; now there's three elementaries and three junior high. We've seen it come up like that, and then one time this Middle River Church was in another building—they have a big church now. And then all at once it's all gone, and we don't know where the people are going to."

Not only big businesses but small businesses throughout the country rise and fall in accordance with the garrison economy. For example, a modest-sized machinery fabricator in Birmingham, Alabama, won a $335,000 contract in mid-1961 to build steel containers for the Army's Little John missile. The order, along with other military business, more than doubled the total production volume of the firm. The owners, believing their break into the big time had occurred, erected a $77,000 plant addition to their factory. They soon regretted that they had ever won the first contract. A year afterward, when they sought to continue their container work, they found themselves underbid by 30 per cent by a Virginia firm which got the contract. In thirty subsequent bids, the Birmingham firm was unsuccessful. In April, 1963, their plant addition was silent and the owners of the firm were saddled with $690 monthly payments on a loan they took out to finance the initial construction.[7]

Nevertheless, like moths around a flame the small businesses continue to seek the brilliance of defense industry stoking furnaces, fed annually by more than $25 million in procurement contracts. The Pentagon in the Sixties buys more than two million items a year, ranging from shoelaces to submarines. The Defense Department's seven million separate contractual transactions a year are multiplied several times in subcontracts that spread the military business throughout the country. Under a special plan, dubbed "Operation Booster," Army, Navy and Air Force officials are admonished to disperse small business awards wherever possible. The law specifically forbids "the payment of a price differential on contracts . . . for the purpose of relieving economic dislocations." Thus the government has found it hard to control the clustering of defense business with certain big firms and in certain geographical areas.

But it is possible under the law to create some spread in these contracts through the so-called "set-asides" for small business, by definition a business with five hundred or fewer employees. By 1965, it is expected that the spread of defense business, as a result of special provisions, will provide small businesses with $10 billion out of the total defense procurement.

Small American businessmen, no less than their big counterparts, complain about the difficulty of doing business with Uncle Sam—the red tape, the costly delays, changing designs and complicated specifications that are difficult to interpret and difficult to satisfy. "Military subcontracting is a wild brutal battle," said the president of a firm in Orlando, Florida, near the huge Martin-Marietta plant. "Bidding is so close, work becomes a matter of survival instead of profit." Yet there is no lack of defense contractors. The successful counterpart to the unsuccessful Birmingham defense contractor was a onetime awning manufacturer in Miami. He made silicon-coated Dacron radome covers and halved his overhead from 35 per cent of sales volume to 13 per cent. "This helps us get more business," the company head enthusiastically told a *Wall Street Journal* reporter. "Where we once needed a 40 per cent markup to make a profit, we now get the same profit with a 25 per cent markup and can quote lower prices."[8]

A few outstanding examples of contemporaries who have waxed big and powerful in defense business have provided sufficient incentive for small businesses despite the teeter-totter fortunes of many of them. The Winfield, Alabama, Manufacturing Company, producers of cotton trousers and jackets, started out as a new business in 1960 and by 1963 had three hundred employees; Brown Engineering Company, in Huntsville, Alabama, jumped from three employees in 1954 to 2,700 in 1963; Northwestern Motors Company, Eau Claire, Wisconsin, doubled its dollar volume of business from $1.5 million to $3 million in eighteen months.[9]

Virtually every community in America is supported in part by the economic radiation of the defense program. In words that were reminiscent of, but not intended to reinforce, General Eisenhower's observations about the "military-industrial complex," Secretary of Defense McNamara told Congress: "We are aware that the award of new defense contracts and the establishment of new defense facilities in a particular area can make the difference between prosperity and depression."[10] The Secretary did not at that time mention the unashamed struggle for defense contracts, particularly in the aerospace industry, that was exemplified in the titanic competition for a potential $7 billion contract for a new Air Force-Navy biservice jet fighter plane, the F-111. This was the controversial TFX (tactical fighter, experimental) airplane contract which precipitated a lengthy Congressional hearing. Along with the TFX hearings (which will be discussed later), another airplane contract came under fire and was subjected to a Congressional investigation. This was for the V/STOL (vertical or short take-off and landing) aircraft, known as the X-22. The discussion of the merits of the awards was drowned in partisan debate. But the cases forced attention to the procedures of defense contracting and what is known as "source selection." These have developed against a background of conflicting impulses. One factor has been the nation's historic concern over "war profiteering." The other has been its readiness, proved repeatedly, to throw out the rule book in the interests of national defense.

The simplest form of contract calls for a fixed price for a specific quantity of specifically described goods. But when the government operates in an atmosphere of emergency, it may choose to attract producers with CPFF (cost plus fixed fee) contracts, guaranteeing the bidder a profit above costs. In wartime, the device was used to finance the construction of new plants and to cover expensive shifts in requirements. In peacetime, however, the public has resented the fixed fee guarantee, regarding it as a built-in profit. And the Kennedy Administration particularly sought to replace the CPFF with incentive contracts. The form of any contract inevitably is complicated and many of the details must be negotiated. In fact, officials have learned from experience that due to changes imposed by technology as well as exaggerations by eager designers even the costs that are estimated in tough negotiations must be modified in the light of experience. Thus when the competitors for the V/STOL development contract estimated their initial costs for two models around $14 million, the Navy immediately estimated it would come to more than $20 million. And the first contract was concluded at $22 million.

Related to the type of contract to be let is the degree of competition considered feasible in selecting a contractor. Sometimes there is only a single logical source for a weapon. In such a case it is considered cheaper and more efficient to negotiate a contract than to open it to competitive bidding. But even in negotiated contracts there are many competitive elements. The terms "competitive" and "negotiated" are defined in regulations. Thus firms may compete bitterly for the opportunity to be considered for a contract, but the contract itself is technically regarded as negotiated if the detailed terms are negotiated following the initial competition. A Defense official explained the procurement process in this way: "If a new gun is desired, the Pentagon calls a meeting of potential bidders, explains its ideas and invites proposals. Responses. let us say, come from eleven bidders. The Pentagon then selects three of them and asks them to produce a weapons prototype. The samples then are tested and the final choice made. If the actual price is negotiated after the selection, the contract is considered to be negotiated."[11]

In huge or complex weapons systems such as a bomber, missile, submarine or even the controversial TFX airplane, the possible number of original bidders is obviously small. A decision must be made fairly early in the contracting process whether the manufacturers are expected to produce and compete with an actual plane—as was the case with the highly successful Navy F-4B jet plane—or produce only a set of estimates—as in the competition to get missiles contracts. The presentation of estimates, sometimes assailed as "brochuremanship," has been relied upon increasingly as military costs have risen. In the TFX case, the Defense officials were so concerned with the possibilities of unanticipated costs they introduced a new form of competion which they labeled "program definition." In this competition, after all but two firms were scratched, officials and experts of the Pentagon were assigned as teams to work with the two selected competitors and to cooperate with each of them as if they had already been assigned the contract. Thus the competition was carried out on paper in an effort to avoid the cost of producing two planes for competition in the air. The rival firms were each paid a fee during the paper competition, but this was much smaller than the fees that would have been paid each rival to produce competing flight models.

Aside from the political charges that developed in the TFX case, it illustrated the intimacy between the military services and the defense contractors. The Pentagon's Director of Research and Engineering once pointed out: "In the civilian economy the product is produced first and the customer decides to buy the product or not. . . . Survival of the United States depends upon the high quality of the military weapons which are produced and in what numbers. This is not the case for vacuum cleaners or washing machines. It is thus clear that a much closer partnership between the government, particularly the defense contractors—almost a symbiotic relationship—is needed, a relationship very different from that which can prevail between the producers and consumers of automobiles.[12]

Claude Witze, an authoritative writer on Air Force affairs, expressed pride that weapons systems defending the free world were based on concepts that originated on the drawing boards of private corporations. Not suprisingly, the writer said, General Eisenhower had described military-industrial relations as a "complex." To some it was a wonder that the military-industrial relationship was not even closer. "There have been serious discussions," he went on, some of them on paper, of the plausibility of having the contractor go a step beyond the design, development and production of weapons systems. His support already is essential to maintenance—he has technical representatives at every major air base and missile launching site, including those under the sea—and the only phase of the life of a system where he has no mission is the actual destructive use of the weapons.[13]

Witze added that the "extreme" would be to have a contract between the government and a private consortium providing for expert operation of the weapon system under the direction of a military command. This, he said, "is so remote as to be ridiculous." Yet, he added, in a tenor that suggested he did not consider it so ridiculous after all, the defense contractor is knowledgeable "across the whole spectrum of military operations." He added: "The designer and builder of a modern system must be familiar with enemy capabilities, he must know what future wars wars will be like, and how to fight them."[14]

The foregoing is a perfect example of how the proper boundary between public and private spheres of interest and responsibility has become blurred in the permanent mobilization of the post-World War II era. The Bell report to the President on government contracting for Research and Development, previously cited, observed: ". . . the developments of recent years have inevitably blurred the traditional dividing lines between the public and private sectors of our nation. A number of profound questions affecting the structure of our society are raised by our inability to apply the classical distinctions between what is public and what is private."

Defense contractors themselves are aware of and concerned over this phenomenon. The most conspicuous group of contractors, the Aerospace Industries Association of America, Inc., asked the Stanford Research Institute, Menlo Park, California, to study the industry-government relationship in the aerospace field. One of its reports observed that the line between "public" and "private" was being breached from both sides, due largely to three interrelated but separate patterns of action. First: the "growth in power and influence of many private organizations that is occurring as a natural outgrowth of our maturing technical-economic system. As a result these organizations achieve a greater capacity to affect the public welfare." Private firms become "vested with public interest," become subject to increasing regulation and control, but also are assisted by the government in their capacity to grow. Second: "the delegation of public authority to private agencies," particularly when a single firm or group of firms is made responsible for an entire weapons system. Third: "the efforts of private organizations to identify themselves with the public good and demonstrate their public responsibility." This "reflects their search for a new legitimacy for their endeavors to replace the one that was once provided by the 'rights' of ownership."

"The elaborate arguments advanced to 'prove' that private corporations are truly responsible to the public are so familiar that they hardly need repetition," the Stanford report commented with remarkable candor for a study prepared for such corporations.

Through skillful public relations programs, the corporation is cast in an image of public concern and its actions justified in terms of some view of the "public interest." Stockholders are described as "public" owners; boards of directors as "public" representatives; corporate charters as acknowledgments of the "public" nature of the organization's purposes. The "public good" is advanced as the legitimate corporate aim.[15]

The mantle of public service may be assumed in order to forestall government intervention. But it often has the opposite effect. When private corporations are identified as operating in the public good, it is logical to demand special demonstrations of public responsibility. The consequence is often regulation.

In reaction, the private corporations supporting defense production have sought to evidence their good faith through "more frequent and vigorous efforts to influence government decisions," the report continued.

This has run the gamut from old-fashioned legislative lobbying to more sophisticated attempts to guide the bureaucracy, often from the inside. It has included attempts to effect the selection of key officials and the announcement of corporate stands on controversial public issues. The corporation has brought itself into politics in insignificant and often dramatic ways. The unfortunate thing is that whether public-spirited or self-serving, open or covert, such actions tend to obscure further the distinction between public and private institutions and to provide additional justification for the regulation of private corporate power.[16]

With all the antiprofiteering and security controls, both workers and managers in the defense industries must find it little different from working directly in the government. Yet the old-fashioned arsenal system has been considered inadequate in the post-World War II period; private companies are said to be more efficient than government arsenals, due to competition and the profit incentive. This is the "American way." Some have argued that the United States has avoided large-scale peacetime armaments in the past so there really is no precedent. But the trend away from the arsenal system continues. Early in the Kennedy Administration, Dr. Harold Brown, the Defense Research and Engineering Chief, said the free enterprise system would be used "maximally" to permit the government's exercise of the best possible options. Yet private financing of weapons system development is considered impossible. Development costs can run into billions of dollars. A low rate of profit for speculative investment, risks of obsolescence and changes in government policy discourage private investment in defense.

Discussing this point, Witze, one of the most competent writers in his field, observed: "What they [the Administration] should say, and what Congress should acknowledge—possibly by revising the procurement legislation—is that characteristics of the customer and the product and the requirement for infallible technical capability narrows the source selection to a point where open competitive bidding is neither realistic nor practical."[17] Thus competition is found by its chief exponents to be an anachronism. The renegotiation law—which permits the government to reclaim any excessive profits accruing to the defense contractors—also disturbs the defense business community because, as Witze pointed out, it is really an out-of-date precaution against venality. The statu-

tory profit limits and renegotiation laws grew out of abuses that existed when defense merchandise was primarily munitions and long before the auditing forces of the military had moved into the production plants.

But if profits have been low, where is the harm in renegotiation? And why the apparent fierce striving for defense dollars? At the time of the TFX airplane contract controversy General Dynamics had a backlog of government contracts of $2,065 million; Grumman, its partner in the contract, $315 million and contracts in process which would bring the total to more than $700 million; and Boeing, the loser in the competition, had a total backlog of $1,620 million of which $744 million was from nongovernment sources. "I feel that these companies have had tremendous government business and none has any special claim for any special favor from the government," observed Congressman Mahon, the chairman of the Defense Appropriations Subcommittee, during a budget hearing. "Amen," echoed Representative Daniel Flood of Pennsylvania.[18] A hybrid arms industry, financed by the government, controlled by the government, but labeled free enterprise, is one of the characteristics of the military-industrial complex.

If the premises for a private military aerospace industry have seemed troublesome if not confusing, the naval industry is a perhaps more complicated problem. In 1962 Congress passed a law requiring that at least 35 per cent of naval ship overhaul, repair and conversion work go into the private shipbuilding yards. The reasons given were that private builders were more efficient and, second, they needed the work. The Congressional action caused a furious debate on the merits of private versus government shipyards. Depending upon the advocate, including many members of Congress who came before the House Appropriations Subcommittee to argue in behalf of the yards in their districts, government ownership of shipyards was "socialistic" or private ownership was greedy. Said Edwin M. Hood, vice president of the shipbuilders council: "Oddly enough, this complex exists half free and half nationalized, in contradiction to the free, competitive, economic system we cherish and strive to nourish. Oddly enough, we have the anomaly of nationalized industrial activity competing with private industry. If seminationalization is good for naval purposes, why, then, aren't all other industries furnishing weapons, aircraft, and other military matériel similarly nationalized?"

To which Representative Robert A. Leggett, of California, whose district included the Mare Island Naval Shipyard in Vallejo, retorted: "It sticks a little bit in the craw of myself and many of my fellow Vallejoans to now hear a few Johnny-come-lately alleged private shipbuilding companies claiming that the socialistic Democratic Administration should get out of the shipbuilding business and leave this area to good old private enterprise. The government's getting out of the shipbuilding business is like effecting postal service by competitive contracts, or farming out our Army and Navy on a soldier-of-fortune basis. . . .It just did not happen that our naval shipyard complex has thrived for better than a hundred years. Private enterprise has fouled the ball for decades."

When President Johnson took office, the naval shipyards found themselves again in the path of an economy drive. Repeated studies had shown that private yards can build and repair ships for less money than it costs to maintain naval yards. The private yards need no special facilities for Navy personnel and are not bound by Civil Service regulations regarding layoffs in slack times. In the past the naval yards have been maintained with arguments that they constitute a mobilization base for national emergency. John F. Griner, president of the American Federation of Government Employees, used it when he said: "The naval shipyards are too important an arm of our national defense to be judged wholly on standards which properly apply only to a profit-making enterprise."[19] That argument, reinforced by local political and economic influences, has been demolished by "cost-efficiency" standards. On the other hand ship-building costs in the private yards

are so high in comparison with foreign countries that the government must subsidize merchant ship construction. Will it be found that when the government inevitably closes the naval yards such subsidies will have to be increased to permit the maintenance of the fleet? Once again, to what extent is a private enterprise a free enterprise when its existence depends on military contracting?

Both the relatively new aerospace industry and the shipbuilding industry that originated in colonial days exemplify the complicated, deep-rooted grip of the defense economy. From the time of Eli Whitney down to the end of the First World War, as Walter Millis has pointed out, the armaments industries in the United States were never more than an auxiliary to industry's main business of supplying civilian markets. Steel, shipbuilding and other industries might seek government contracts in slack time; holders of armaments patents might compete for contracts; but mostly the government rather than the industries pressed for military production. Out of the Second World War emerged a new phenomenon, multibillion-dollar private armaments industries, almost wholly dependent on government orders.[20]

As the Kennedy Administration military budgets rose spectacularly to $52.4 billion in the fiscal year ending June 30, 1964, the claim by a Columbia professor, Seymour Melman, that it could be cut to $34 billion received some notice, although few endorsements. One aspect of Melman's study seems to deserve more serious attention than it has received. This deals with certain consequences of the military preoccupation of large sectors of the economy. The following points were made: that the American shipbuilding industry is becoming increasingly less competitive in the world market; that Belgian and French sources are increasingly supplying iron and steel for Midwestern industries; that the American heavy electrical machinery manufacturers are competing with Europeans only through drastic price-cutting; that the American machine tool industry, once a world leader, has dropped to fourth or fifth place in the volume of its output; that the United States typewriter industry, which in 1948 supplied virtually all United States requirements, now supplies only 60 per cent, while the remainder are imported from Europe; that with the notable exception of earthmoving equipment, the machinery-producing industries of America are growing obsolescent; that the American machine tool industry, in particular, is obsolescent.

The differences in industrial growth between countries of the European Common Market and the United States were indicated in part by these estimates: that in 1960 United States military expenditures amounted to 9.2 per cent of the Gross National Product, while the average among Common Market members was 4.2 per cent; that the expenditures in the United States on machinery and equipment was 5.4 per cent of the Gross National Product, while the expenditures for this purpose among members of the Common Market totaled 10.2 per cent.[21]

An impressive observation in the foregoing analysis of the consequences of military orientation of a large part of American industry is this: One of the characteristics of military products is that they are end products. Once they are made, there is little use for them except in war. The fact that more than half of all research and development is paid for by the United States Government has caused considerable concern among educational and scientific leaders. Its consequences for American business also has drawn attention. In a report to the Senate Small Business Committee, in August 1962, Assistant Democratic Majority Leader Hubert Humphrey said:

In Germany, 85 per cent—85 cents out of every research dollar—is private, and less than five cents of that goes into the civilian economy, so that today the German plant competition for world markets of civilian goods is being automated, modernized, equipped in the latest and best fashion, and new products are developing, while we are developing new wrappings. . . . What is happening to our civilian economy as we plow more and more of our scientific personnel, our brains, into atomic energy for military purposes? Where are we going to end up in this trade competition with these Belgians and these Dutch, who are clever, who are spending more money for civilian aspects and will develop products cheaper, better and more serviceable?

Senator Humphrey's question seems to be answered by Professor Melman's study.

---

[1] Department of Defense estimate in response to author's inquiry, December 23, 1963.

[2] *Business Week*, November 10, 1962.

[3] Cf. Footnote 17, chapter 1, *Power at the Pentagon*.

[4] *Business Week*, November 10, 1962.

[5] *Ibid.*

[6] NBC White Paper, "Arms and the State," March 25, 1963. Author served as adviser for this TV program.

[7] *Wall Street Journal*, April 3, 1963.

[8] *Ibid.*

[9] Examples provided author by Department of Defense, June 18, 1963.

[10] Testimony, House Armed Services Committee, January 30, 1963.

[11] Author's interview with Thomas D. Morris, Assistant Secretary of Defense for Logistics and Installations, March 5, 1963.

[12] Speech by Dr. Harold R. Brown, Director of Defense Research and Engineering, before Convention of Armed Forces Communications and Electronics Association, June 12, 1962.

[13] Claude Witze, senior editor, *Air Force and Space Digest Magazine*, September 1962 issue.

[14] *Ibid.*

[15] Stanford Research Institute Report, Menlo Park, California, May 1963.

[16] *Ibid.*

[17] Claude Witze, cited earlier.

[18] House Defense Appropriations Subcommittee Hearings, May 6, 1963.

[19] Testimony, House Defense Appropriations Subcommittee, May 17, 1963.

[20] Walter Millis, *Arms and Men*, New American Library, a Mentor Book reprint, p. 274. Original edition published by G. P. Putnam's Sons, 1956, New York.

[21] As cited by Seymour Melman in *A Strategy for American Security*, including statistical material from *U.S. Statistical Extract*, 1962: *American Machinist Magazine*, November 26, 1962.

11. The Economics of Military Procurement

Congress of the United States, Joint Economic Committee

INTRODUCTION

Last year, fiscal year 1968, $44 billion was spent on defense procurement, equivalent to about 25 per cent of the Federal budget. Total defense spending reached $80 billion. In recent years numerous instances of inefficiency, excessive profits, and mismanagement in defense contracting have been revealed by this subcommittee, other committees of Congress, and the General Accounting Office. Increasing concern over the enormous amounts spent on military procurement prompted the Subcommittee on Economy in Government of the Joint Economic Committee to hold hearings on profits and cost control in defense procurement. Testimony was received on November 11, 12, 13, and 14, 1968, and January 16, 1969.[1][2][3]

The subject matter of the hearings, economic aspects of military procurement, may be perceived as a relatively narrow set of issues. In the subcommittee's view, however, the enormous commitment of national resources to military systems makes the details and facts of procurement practices a central public policy issue. The wasteful, inefficient practices uncovered in the course of the hearings raise basic questions concerning the Defense Department's management of its own affairs. It also makes us skeptical concerning the effectiveness and care with which the Defense budget is scrutinized by pertinent agencies outside of the Pentagon. If this government is to serve the public interest, close scrutiny of these billions of dollars of expenditures must be given high priority.

Report of the Subcommittee on Economy in Government of the Joint Economic Committee, Congress of the United States (May 1969).

In the judgment of the subcommittee, there is a pressing need to reexamine our national priorities by taking a hard look at the allocation of Federal revenues between the military and civilian budgets. Indeed, the inefficiencies described in this report, in addition to being difficult to contend with, raise questions about the very nature and size of the Department of Defense, its place within the framework of the executive branch of Government, and its relationship and responsiveness to Congress. The real needs of the Nation, military and civilian, are too important to endanger through bureaucratic arrangements in an agency which in too many instances has been unable to control costs or program results.

I. MILITARY PROCUREMENT POLICY: A PROBLEM OF UNCONTROLLED COSTS

A. There exists in the Department of Defense a set of practices and circumstances which lead to:

1. Economic inefficiency and waste

The extensive and pervasive economic inefficiency and waste that occurs in the military procurement program has been well documented by the investigations of this subcommittee, by other committees of the House and Senate, and by the General Accounting Office. The absence of effective inventory controls and effective management practices over Government-owned property is well known. In the past, literally billions of dollars have been wasted on weapons systems that have had to be canceled because they did not work. Other systems have performed far below contract specifications. For example, one study[4] referred to in the hearings shows that of a sample of 13 major Air Force and Navy aircraft and missile programs initiated since 1955 at a total cost of $40 billion, less than 40 per cent produced systems with acceptable electronic performance. Two of the programs were canceled after total program costs of $2 billion were paid. Two programs costing $10 billion were phased out after 3 years for low reliability. Five programs costing $13 billion give poor performance; that is, their electronics reliability is less than 75 per cent of initial specifications.

Actual costs of expensive programs frequently overrun estimated costs by several hundred per cent. Assistant Secretary of the Air Force Robert H. Charles testified that "The procurement of our major weapons systems has in the past been characterized by enormous cost overruns — several hundred per cent — and by technical performance that did not come up to promise." The greatest amount of cost overruns occur in negotiated, as opposed to competitive, contracts. Even where overruns do not occur, there is evidence that prices are being negotiated at too high a level from the beginning. Most procurement dollars are spent in the environment of negotiation. It is precisely in this area that the DOD has the heaviest responsibility for obtaining the best military equipment and supplies at the least possible price. In the judgment of the subcommittee, the DOD has not adequately fulfilled this responsibility.

2. A subsidy to contractors

The major portion of procurement costs are in the costs of research and development, material, labor, and overhead for which contractors are reimbursed. In theory, competition requires contractors to be efficient in order to minimize costs and maximize profits, and inefficient contractors should not be able to underbid their more efficient competitors. Competition is a method of cost control. However, as we have said, most defense contracts are awarded through negotiation, not competition. A number of mechanisms, such as the cost and other price data submissions required by the Truth-in-Negotiations Act, and incentive contracting, have been designed to act as cost controls for negotiated contracts, in lieu of competition. In the judgment of the subcommittee, these mechanisms have not constituted an effective system of controls over the costs of procurement.

The result of the absence of effective cost controls, coupled with a number of policies and practices discussed in this report, has resulted in a vast subsidy for the defense industry, particularly the larger contractors. These practices include loose handling of Government-owned property, interest-free financing of contractors, absence of comprehensive profits reports and studies, lack of uniform accounting standards, reverse incentives, and a special patent policy lucrative to the contractor. All of these things tend to benefit the contractor at the public's expense.

3. An inflated defense budget

The total effect of unnecessary cost overruns, of hidden profits in "fat" contracts, of inefficiency and waste, and of the absence of cost controls is to create a bloated defense budget. Admiral Rickover testified that $2 billion of excessive costs results from the absence of uniform accounting standards alone. There is evidence that literally billions of dollars are being wasted in defense spending each year.

It is the judgment of the subcommittee that the defense budget has been bloated and inflated far beyond what an economy-minded and efficient Department of Defense could and should attain.

B. These practices include:

1. Low competition and high concentration

Defense buying practices are reducing competition for Government contracts and increasing economic concentration within the defense industry. Formally advertised competitive military contract dollar awards dropped from 13.4 per cent in fiscal year 1967 to 11.5 per cent in fiscal year 1968. Single source procurement increased to 57.9 per cent. These figures constitute a record low for competition and a record high for single source procurement over the past 5 years. Negotiated procurement in which more than one source was solicited comprised 30.6 percent of total contract awards, also a record low over the past 5 years.

The DOD maintains that there is a substantial degree of competition in negotiated procurement where more than one source of supply was solicited. However, too often in these cases technical performance rather than price has been the basis for contract awards. Competition must involve dollar cost as well as nonprice elements such as technical performance and date of delivery. Activity involving only one nonprice element usually cannot be considered competition, nor does it contribute beneficially to the public interest in defense procurement.

It is widely acknowledged that *true* competition significantly reduces the costs of procurement. Some experts believe that in the absence of effective competition, procurement costs are 25 per cent to 50 per cent higher than what they would be under competitive conditions. However, instead of competition, it is becoming increasingly clear that the "buy-in, get well later" method is commonly employed by contract rivals. Under this approach, a contractor may bid a lower price, higher performance, and earlier delivery than his rivals, knowing Pentagon officials will accept increased costs, less than promised performance, and late delivery. Inadequate management controls at the highest levels of Government have contributed to the development of these practices. The prevalence of these practices goes far in explaining why the estimated costs of individual contracts almost always increased and the performance of the weapon procured was often less than promised. Weapons procured in this manner, in the absence of true competition, have been characterized by high costs, poor performance, and late delivery of the end product.

DOD procurement is highly concentrated. A relatively small number of contractors receive most of the dollar value of defense contract awards. In fiscal year 1968, the 100 largest defense contractors were awarded 67.4 per cent of total defense contracts, the highest percentage since 1965. To get on the list of the top 100 in fiscal year 1968 required $50 million in awards, up from $46 million in fiscal year

1967. These large contractors generally have assets of $250 million or more. Small firms (as defined by the Small Business Administration) received only 18.4 per cent of defense prime contracts in fiscal year 1968, down from 20.3 per cent in fiscal year 1967 and 21.4 per cent in fiscal year 1966.

The larger, dominant defense firms tend to hold entrenched positions. Eighty-four of the top 100 firms appeared on both the fiscal year 1968 and fiscal year 1967 lists. Eighteen of the top 25 in 1967 were in the top 25 in 1968. The same five companies received prime contract awards of more than $1 billion each in fiscal year 1968 as in fiscal year 1967. There is other evidence of entrenchment and concentration in the defense industry, such as the tendency of divisions of certain large contractors to obtain major contracts from one service, for example, the Air Force, while divisions of the same or other large contractors consistently obtain major awards from the other services. In some specific areas of military procurement the Government does business not only with sole-source suppliers, but with absolute monopolies. The nature of the purchases and the limited quantities may not be adequate to justify more than one producer. For this reason, the Federal Government must improve its capability to control procurement costs in the absence of competition.

2. Government-owned property

In addition to the lack of competition for defense contracts, the Defense Department's policy of providing Government-owned property and working capital to defense contractors constitutes a government subsidy and contributes to concentration within this industry. The cost of Government-owned equipment supplied to contractors sometimes exceeds the value of property owned by the company. While the total value of Government-owned property in the hands of contractors declined from $14.6 billion in fiscal year 1967 to $13.3 billion in fiscal year 1968, reflecting primarily a drop in the amount of materials, in the important category of industrial plant equipment costing over $1,000, there was an increase from $2.6 to $2.7 billion. A disproportionate amount of this equipment was held by the larger contractors. Defense Department assurances that it is aware of the problems surrounding the use and control of the enormous amount of Government-owned property have so far yielded little tangible results in the form of improved performance in this area.

Last year this subcommittee found loose and flagrantly negligent management practices in defense procurement largely on the basis of facts surrounding Government-owned property furnished to contractors.[5] The subcommittee has no reason to alter this judgment.

3. Progress payments

The Pentagon makes so-called progress payments to reimburse contractors for up to 90 per cent of incurred cost, on a pay-as-you-go basis. These payments are not necessarily related to progress in the sense of work completed. Costs are often incurred greatly in excess of original estimates. It is possible, for example, for a contractor to incur costs equal to 75 per cent of the original contract price while completing only 50 per cent, or less, of the job. A more accurate term would be "incurred-cost reimbursement payments."

The important point is that the payments are made interest-free, prior to completion or delivery of the end-product. The contractor could operate largely without his own working capital, on capital supplied by the Federal Government, particularly in expensive, long leadtime procurement. For example, in the C-5A case, Lockheed received "progress" payments of $1.207 billion on reported incurred costs of $1.278 billion, as of December 27, 1968. In addition, the contract is being performed in a Government-owned plant. The plant and the Government-owned facilities employed at the plant have an original acquisition cost of $113.8 million.

In effect, considering the extensive use of Government-owned property and Government-supplied working capital—"progress payments"—the Defense Department provides negative incentives for the use of private capital, and tends to develop a financial stake in its contractors, especially those larger contractors which it favors with great amounts of Government-owned property and interest-free working capital. Contractors so favored have a sizable competitive advantage over others in the defense and civilian industries, and are actually highly subsidized.

Money advanced to contractors in the form of progress payments are really no-interest Government loans which inflate contractors' profits. Armed with free working capital a contractor may be able to bid low for more Government work, "finance" commercial work, or otherwise compete unfairly in the commercial market.

4. Patent policy

The Government's patent policy similarly tends to reduce competition and increase the concentration of economic power. Briefly, the Government permits contractors to obtain exclusive patent rights, free of charge, on inventions produced in the performance of Government contracts. The Defense Department normally retains only a nonexclusive royalty-free license for itself. The contractor, in other words, obtains a monopoly which he can exploit for his own private gain in the commercial market for inventions paid for by public moneys. This "fringe benefit" of doing business under Government contracts does not get reported as part of the contractor's profits. In effect, the public pays twice. Once through the Government contract; again in the marketing of the private monopoly.

It should be noted that the contractor's own patent policy differs from that of the Department of Defense. When contractors award contracts to independent research institutes, the contractors, not the research institutes, retain the patent rights. Further, the employees of contractors generally must agree that the contractor gets the patent rights to any inventions developed during their employment.

Admiral Rickover and Professor Weidenbaum agreed that permitting contractors to obtain patent rights from Government contracts reduces competition in defense industries because the "ins" get a competitive advantage over the "outs." Rickover stated that one-half of the patents acquired by contractors as a result of Government-financed research and development work are owned by 20 large corporations, " . . . the very same companies that receive the lion's share of contracts."

In contrast to general Government policy, the Atomic Energy Commission and the National Aeronautics and Space Administration are required by law to take Government title to inventions developed under Government contracts, subject to waiver of rights by the Government. The Government's policy amounts to a special privilege to contractors at the expense of taxpayers.

5. Subcontracting and profit pyramiding

The study of subcontracting in defense procurement is important for at least two reasons. First, subcontracting can provide an opportunity for small business to participate in Government work. Most small businesses cannot obtain prime contract awards. But they can supply prime contractors with a variety of goods and services. Second, profits in subcontracts turn up as part of the costs of the prime contract. Information about the amount and type of subcontracting and of subcontract profitability could be a valuable guide to current procurement costs and future policy. Unfortunately, the Defense Department has not been able to supply good information on these subjects.

DOD's collection of subcontracting data is inadequate. The only data which has been collected is the percentage of subcontracts that go to small business, on the basis of sampling. In fiscal year 1968, 886 large prime contractors awarded subcontracts worth $15.2 billion. Of this sum, $6.5 billion went to small businesses, according to DOD. DOD also *estimates* that approximately 50 per cent of the total amount of prime contract awards is subcontracted. This estimate seems to be based on data gathered by DOD during 1957–63 when prime contractors were required to report such information. Data on the total amount of subcontracting has not been collected since 1963. DOD

cannot state with certainty whether subcontracting has increased or diminished since 1963, or whether prime contractors are tending to keep more or less of their work in-house.

Because DOD no longer collects complete data on subcontracting, we cannot know whether subcontracting is being awarded competitively or through sole sources, what kinds of work are being subcontracted, or whether subcontractors are required to submit cost data in compliance with the Truth-in-Negotiations Act. Admiral Rickover testified that there is a lack of effective price competition both at the prime contract and subcontract levels in shipbuilding procurement and that some major subcontractors have never provided the cost data required by the Truth-in-Negotiations Act.

Another serious omission has been the failure to collect information on subcontractor profits. The DOD profit review system compiles profit data for a sample of prime contract awards. These figures do not reflect profits taken by subcontractors which could involve several tiers. For example, a prime contractor might purchase a piece of machinery from a subcontractor. The subcontractor might purchase a component for the machinery from another subcontractor, and so on. Each of the subcontractors will earn a profit on the item supplied. The same final item, therefore, is likely to include a profit as part of its cost for each time it changed hands. In this manner, subcontractor profits are pyramided, layer upon layer, into the final cost.

When the prime contractor obtains the item, he, too, will add his profit to its cost. The Government pays for it on the basis of the prime contractor's cost plus the prime contractor's profit. Included in the prime contractor's cost are the pyramided profits of several subcontractors. However, profits are often considered to be only the amount realized by the prime contractor. Profit studies normally do not consider the hidden, pyramided layers of subcontractors' profits buried in the prime contractor's costs. Whether subcontractor profits are reasonable is entirely unknown to DOD or any other Government group. For this reason alone, defense profits may be seriously underestimated because the studies include only prime contractors' profits. The present policy of not gathering adequate information on subcontracting could be calculated to minimize the total amount of defense profits that are reported and to frustrate the thorough study of this important subject.

It is well recognized that subcontractors doing Government or non-Government business should be allowed to earn reasonable profits for their work. The issue here is that the DOD does not collect sufficient information to know whether subcontractors' profits on defense contracts are reasonable or excessive. The available data is also inadequate to reveal the level of competition among subcontractors, and the precise interrelationships between the prime contractors and the subcontractors. Further, it is presently not possible to determine whether prime contractors are charging the Government unreasonably for work done by subcontractors. In the subcommittee's judgment, the thorough study and full disclosure of all the facts with respect to subcontractors' costs and profits, and their effects on the final costs to the Government, is frustrated by the DOD's present policy and practice.

6. Noncompliance and waiver of the truth-in-negotiations act

The Truth-in-Negotiations Act was passed in 1962. Its purpose was to give the Government better access to contractors' cost data so as to place Government on a more equal footing with industry in negotiating the prices of contracts. The Act is supposed to protect the taxpayer against overpricing where there is not true competition.

Investigations by this subcommittee and others over the past 2 years have demonstrated widespread noncompliance and other shortcomings with truth in negotiations. The Government's failure to fully implement it seems to be one of the major reasons. Lack of implementation occurs in two ways. First, the Government contracting officer can make a determination

that competition is adequate, or that the price is based on a standard catalog price, and therefore that the Act should not apply. Such determination can be made with respect to a negotiated procurement even though there is, in fact, little or no actual competition for the contract. Once there is a determination that adequate competition exists, the Government does not obtain or evaluate cost and pricing data, or require the contractor to reveal the basis for his cost estimates, or to certify the completeness or accuracy of his cost information. Nor does the Government subsequently review the contractor's books or records. In effect, the price is set on the basis of uncertified, unevaluated data supplied by the contractor.

Second, the Government can waive the requirements under the Act for cost data. There is evidence that waivers are granted to many large contractors. In one recent case, the Navy waived the requirement for cost data in a $10 million procurement of propulsion turbines. According to Admiral Rickover, the price of the equipment was substantially higher than for similar equipment on a prior order. In addition, the price included a profit of 25 per cent of costs. The contractor was one of the only two available sources capable of building the machinery. In response to requests for cost data, the contractor declined on the grounds that the proposed price was established "in competitive market conditions" and that "to supply any cost estimating data could only lead to misunderstanding." The waiver was granted over Admiral Rickover's objections.

The subcommittee also received evidence that the manufacturers of large computers are simply refusing to supply information specified in the Truth-in-Negotiations Act on orders for new design computers. In the face of contractor refusals to supply cost or pricing data for computers costing millions of dollars each, the Government has waived the provisions of the Act. According to the testimony of the General Services Administration, the Government is faced with a take-it-or-leave-it situation. The contractor will simply refuse to sell if the Government insists on the cost data. Moreover, there is evidence that few basic material suppliers such as steel mills, nickel producers, and forging suppliers comply with the cost data provisions of the Act. Again, the tactic is (1) to persuade the Government contracting officer that competition is adequate, or that the price is based on a standard catalog price, and that the Act should not apply; or (2) to obtain a waiver of the cost data provisions.

The Truth-in-Negotiations Act permits the Government to make preaward audits of contractors' books to determine the adequacy of cost data in cases where the Act is applied. Investigations by GAO have revealed substantial overcharges to the Government as a result of the failure of the Department of Defense to obtain adequate cost and pricing data. Because preaward audits were not always effective in disclosing inadequate cost estimates, Congress amended the act to give the Government postaward audit rights, Public Law 90–512. The effectiveness of the postaward audit provision has not yet been determined. However, it should be kept in mind that the postaward audit provision cannot solve the problem of the failure to apply the Act, or the granting of waivers. Furthermore, the Comptroller General testified to this subcommittee in 1967 that a GAO review showed there had been full compliance with the Act in only about 10 per cent of the transactions tested. We are not aware that the record of compliance has improved.

7. Absence of uniform accounting standards

In addition, the Truth-in-Negotiations Act often cannot place the Government on a more equal footing with industry in negotiating the prices of contracts, even when there is compliance, because of the inherent difficulties of determining costs and profits under present accounting practices.

For example, it may not be possible for the Government to determine whether direct and indirect costs on Government and commerical work have been properly allocated by the contractor. In one case,

reported by Admiral Rickover, the Navy allowed a shipbuilder to charge salaries and other pay directly on Government contracts, while similar costs on commercial contracts were charged as overhead and allocated to both Government and commercial work. The Government was thus paying directly for work done on Government contracts and indirectly for work done on commercial contracts. The Navy had accepted these costing methods because the contractor's system conformed to "generally accepted accounting principles." In this particular case the GAO eventually found that the Government had been overcharged by over $5 million.

The fact is that there is wide disagreement on how particular costs should be handled and profits calculated under "generally accepted accounting principles." For this reason, experts may come to completely different conclusions about costs or profits in an individual case. In a case still pending, where the Government entered into several multimillion dollar contracts with the Westinghouse Co. for nuclear propulsion components, the contractor indicated his price included a 10 per cent profit based on costs. GAO found that the contractor made actual profits of 45 to 65 percent of costs, and that he knew or should have known at the time he submitted cost breakdowns that the higher profits would be realized. Later the Defense Contract Audit Agency decided the contractor should have expected to realize 20- to 27-per cent profits. Thus, two different Government auditing agencies are in sharp disagreement over the amount of profits in these contracts. The vagueness of "generally accepted accounting principles" is generally acknowledged. In a recent case, the Armed Services Board of Contract Appeals stated in its opinion:

"Except insofar as the ASPR (Armed Services Procurement Regulation) cost principles themselves reflect generally accepted accounting principles, it is difficult for the Board or the parties to cost contracts to govern their determinations by such an elusive and vague body of principles."

Under the Armed Services Procurement Regulations, cost principles are set forth for cost-reimbursement-type contracts for the purpose of denying certain costs, such as bad debts. These principles are not mandatory in fixed-price contracting. Yet fixed-price contracts constitute more than 75 per cent of defense procurement. Thus there are no mandatory cost principles in the regulations for 75 per cent of defense procurement. The cost principles that do exist have the effect of only disallowing certain items. They do not constitute uniform standards.

Finally, contractors are not required to maintain books and records on firm-fixed-price contracts, constituting 53 per cent of defense procurement. Where contractors are required to maintain records, they must conform only to "generally accepted accounting principles," and may not show the cost of Government work. Admiral Rickover testified that a sole-source supplier of nuclear propulsion units refuses to keep accounting records showing the cost of manufacturing the components. Thus, although he complies with the Truth-in-Negotiations Act, the absence of accounting records prevents a determination of whether his prices are reasonable. For example, a contractor may submit cost data at the time the price of the contract is being negotiated, but afterwards, during performance of the contract, not keep adequate books and records. Colonel Buesking testified, "I have yet to see a contractor's accounting system in major programs that can adequately determine the unit cost of hardware."

Uniform accounting standards for all defense contracts have been advocated to facilitate the measurement of costs and profits. The GAO is now undertaking a feasibility study of such standards at the direction of Congress. Regardless of the outcome of the study, it is clear that the Government often cannot determine the reasonableness of costs or profits on defense contracts under present cost accounting methods.

8. Voluminous change orders and contracters' claims

It is often necessary to make changes in the design or production of an item after the contract is awarded. This is especially true for the more complex weapons and equipment such as missiles, fighter planes, bombers, and their electronic components. There may be thousands of changes on such procurements. The production of the B-47 bomber in the 1950's involved about 8,000 changes. The Minuteman program has involved at least that number. Change orders generally increase the cost of a contract.

The Government pays the price if it originated the change or was in any way responsible for it. Because of the great number of changes, and the fact that the total cost of the changes may exceed the original price of a given contract, it would be reasonable to assume that records are maintained of the cost of each individual change and of their origin as to the Government's liability. Again, DOD has failed to keep adequate records or to even require that contractors keep adequate records.

Contractors are not required to account for change notices separately. As a result, it is usually not possible to determine the cost of individual changes. Typically, the Government is forced to negotiate a lump-sum settlement to pay for numerous changes since most changes are not priced in advance of the work, and the Government has not checked to see what the cost of the change should have been. Admiral Rickover testified.

Thus, contractors can use change orders as a basis for repricing these contracts. They have almost unlimited freedom in pricing change orders because their accounting system will never show the cost of the work. The Government can never really evaluate the amounts claimed or check up to see if it paid too much.

Under the present system of nonaccountability, it is possible for contractors to inflate costs by pricing changes, and to attribute cost overruns to contract changes. In the vernacular of the world of defense contracts, change notices are sometimes referred to as contract nourishment.

Many claims against the Government result from formal contract changes. Others are produced by constructive change notices which may occur in a telephone conversation between a DOD official and an officer of the contracting company. The contractor might obtain relief orally from meeting a contract specification, or claim that an act of God or a strike prevented him from meeting the contract schedule.

Regardless of the origin of a claim, the Government is often at a disadvantage in meeting it. A contractor may have a large staff begin preparing and documenting a claim the day work begins on the contract. Although fully documented, however, accounting records seldom support the costs claimed. Nevertheless, the claim may be pursued over a period of years until it is finally disposed of. DOD does not keep records of unfounded or exorbitant claims, nor does it consider such information in awarding subsequent contracts.

9. The failure of incentive contracting

Another attempt to find a substitute for competition has been the use of incentive contracts. The Defense Department began using incentive contracts extensively in 1962. The shift in emphasis reflected the widely held belief within the Defense Department that the cost-plus-fixed-fee (CPFF) contracts commonly used up to that time for major weapons systems procurement did not result in adequate control over costs. Since 1962 the decline of CPFF contracts and the increase of incentive contracts has been substantial.

The goal of the incentive contract is to motivate the contractor to be efficient and control his costs. The mechanism is a provision in the contract entitling the contractor to retain a portion of any cost underrun as additional profits. That is, the Government and the contractor agree on a target cost as part of the contract price. They also agree on a profit as part of the price. If the actual costs turn out to be less than the target cost, the contractor retains part of the underrun as an increased profit. If the actual cost exceeds the target costs, the contractor must bear a portion of the overrun and his profit is reduced. The profit-sharing provision is the hoped-for incentive which will cause

the contractor to increase the underrun so as to increase his profit.

The Defense Department has maintained that incentive contracting is an improvement over cost-plus-fixed-fee contracts. Beyond question, the problem of cost control during the period when CPFF contracts predominated was very great. Assistant Secretary of the Air Force Robert H. Charles referred in his testimony to the "enormous cost overruns of several hundred per cent" for major weapons systems procurement in the past. He attributed a substantial portion of the cost overruns to the use of cost reimbursement type contracts and the absence of price competition.

The question, however, is, first of all, whether incentive contracting is, in principle, an effective means of controlling the costs of procurement, and secondly, whether it has succeeded in practice. The Defense Department claims success on both counts, although conceding the difficulty of demonstrating the effectiveness of incentive contracts as opposed to CPFF contracts, since they cannot both be utilized on the same project at the same time. On the other hand, much evidence was received which casts doubt on the proposition that incentive contracts result in cost savings, at least in practice.

Indeed, the experience of incentive contracting shows that it can increase both profits *and costs*. For while a contractor may increase his profit by performing efficiently to produce an underrun, another way of producing an underrun is to inflate the original target cost as much as possible. As Irving Fisher of the RAND Corp. pointed out in the hearings November 13, 1968, the problem of overstated target costs is significant because most weapon system procurement is negotiated without price competition, and many of the development contracts awarded competitively are awarded on the basis of technical or nonprice rivalry. In situations where target costs are negotiated, the opportunity for contractors to increase them is great.

The evidence suggests that incentive contracts have not accomplished their intended goal of increased efficiency or reduced costs, and that they may actually be contributing to a general upward shift in target costs. Whether this is inherent in the incentive contracting approach, or the result of poorly applied but valid concepts, we are not prepared to say. However, we feel that burden of proof that the concept is indeed valid rests squarely on the Department of Defense. We are so far unconvinced that this approach is the best that can be designed to effectively control procurement contract costs.

10. The conceptual problems in using historical cost analysis and the failure to use "should costing"

The analysis of cost and pricing data is a crucial factor in determining the amount the Government spends on weapons programs. Without good cost analysis and cost estimation, the Government is unable to control the costs of procurement, much of which is based on original estimates. That is, the price of a contract is negotiated on the basis of cost estimates submitted by the contractor. An inflated estimate can result in an inflated price unless DOD can properly evaluate estimated cost data. Yet, as indicated above, the Defense Department's ability to adequately analyze cost data is severely limited by the lack of information on profitability, the absence of data on subcontracting, the shortcomings of the Truth-in-Negotiations Act, and the nonexistence of uniform accounting standards.

Another obstacle to adequate analysis is the fact that cost estimation presently relies extensively on past experience; that is, historical costs are used to provide estimates of the future costs of proposed weapons systems. Historical costs refer to the actual costs of performing earlier contracts. They are often insufficient and misleading guides to estimating the costs of new contracts for several reasons. For example, it is possible for the cost of performing a contract to be inflated intentionally or through contractor inefficiency, and for the costs of that contract to influence the estimation of costs on subsequent contracts.

As the testimony showed, historical costs are no better than the underlying data on which they are based. If the costs of previous procurements were obtained without competition, estimates based on them probably would not be comparable to costs determined competitively. As we know, most procurements in the DOD data bank were not awarded competitively. In fact, many of the earlier contracts were the CPFF type in which some of the most extreme cases of cost overruns occurred.

The use of historical costs may give the contractor a premium to inflate his cost base. The inflated costs of previous contracts may then become the new cost base figure for subsequent production runs and subsequent contracts. If profit is calculated by DOD as a percentage of costs, the contractor may be given a profit motive to increase costs. The only party hurt in this scheme is the American taxpayer.

Implicit in the criticism of historical cost is the point that the cost of a particular contract may have been excessive because of contractor inefficiency. The possibility that contractor inefficiency may be a significant problem was brought out in the testimony of Colonel Buesking (U.S. Air Force, retired) and A. E. Fitzgerald, Deputy for Management Systems, Office of the Assistant Secretary of the Air Force. Both witnesses compared the probable cost approach, which employs historical costs, and the should-cost approach to Government estimates.

The should-cost approach attempts to determine the amount that weapons systems or products *ought* to cost given attainable efficiency and economy of operation. The method of determining the should-cost figure is based on a combination of industrial engineering and financial management principles. Briefly, a study is made at a contractor's plant of each of the cost elements of the contractor's operation to ascertain what the product should cost the Government, assuming reasonable efficiency and economy on the part of the contractor. Obviously, this approach differs sharply from the traditional one in which costs are estimated in advance on the basis of earlier costs, and in which the

Government thereafter reimburses the contractor for incurred and allocable costs without finding out whether the costs were reasonable.

According to the testimony, when the should-cost approach was employed by the Navy in connection with the TF-30 engine contract for the F-111 program, substantial inefficiencies were detected in the contractor's plant. As a result of the study, the contract price was later reduced by more than $100 million.

It is difficult to see how the Government can be assured that incurred costs will be reasonable on negotiated contracts without the benefit of a should-cost type in-depth study and evaluation. Col. A. W. Buesking (U.S. Air Force, retired) testified that selected evaluations of resource planning and control systems conducted to assess contractor's capability to meet standards of efficiency revealed that control systems essential to prevent excessive costs were absent. He estimated that costs in such plants are 30 to 50 per cent in excess of what they might be under competitive conditions. When Admiral Rickover was asked to comment on Colonel Buesking's statement, he said, "His estimate is a conservative one." Establishing objective cost performance standards would be an important step toward cost control.

11. Absence of ongoing cost reports to congress

Equally important is the need for devising a method to periodically report actual costs to Congress as they are incurred on large negotiated contracts. Presently, it is difficult for the Members of Congress and the public to know whether a program is staying within or exceeding original cost estimates and the negotiated price, during the period of contract performance. Reports of actual costs should be correlated with planned cost of work segments satisfactorily completed. In this way, cost estimates could be compared with incurred costs.

It may also be desirable to relate progress payments to real progress, in the sense of work segments satisfactorily completed, rather than simply incurred costs, and to

report the volume and cost of contract change notices. Finally, a full cost report system would include the profit rate negotiated and realized, and estimated and realized profits as a return on investment. If this were done, Congress would at least have available to it indicators of contract objectives and contract costs which would make it possible to detect serious overruns and delays, and to determine on an ongoing basis the cost status of the contract.

C. The manifestations of these practices are:

1. High defense profits

Perhaps the most glaring fact about defense profits is that not enough is known about them. The DOD cannot accurately state what profits are in defense procurement. First, it defines profits as a percentage of costs, and does not report profits as a return on investment. Second, DOD does not obtain complete information about profits on firm fixed-price contracts. During fiscal year 1968, firm fixed-price contracts made up about 53 per cent of total expenditures for defense procurement. Third, without uniform accounting standards, it is difficult, if not impossible, to discover the costs and profits in defense production unless months are spent to reconstruct contractors' books. The reason for this is that contractors are not required to maintain books and records on most defense contracts. Thus, while the profit *rate* is designated at the time a contract is negotiated, the profit actually realized in the performance of the contract cannot be known and verified without an expensive, time-consuming audit.

The DOD collects data on less than half of annual contract awards, and the data it collects is inadequate. Studies conducted independently of the Pentagon are admittedly sketchy. Among other problems, (1) the trend toward conglomerate mergers among large defense suppliers obscures the opportunity for determining defense profits as their data is published in the aggregate without separating sales and profits by division, and (2) neither the DOD nor their contractors will readily furnish profit data to congressional or academic investigators.

No complete and comprehensive study of this subject has ever been made by any agency of the executive branch or by the GAO. Contractors are not required to report their profits on most Government contracts. The DOD does not keep adequate records of contractors' profits. In view of the tens of billions of dollars of taxpayers' money spent on defense contracts each year, the Government's lack of knowledge about defense profits is inexcusable.

One difficulty is in defining what is meant by profits. GAO and DOD surveys deal with profits as a percentage of costs. On this basis a 10-per cent profit rate on a contract for a weapon that cost $1 million to produce would result in a profit of $100,000. But profits as a percentage of costs or sales is often an inaccurate indicator of true profits. For example, if a contractor is able to use Government-owned equipment or operate in a Government-owned plant, he may have a relatively small investment in a given contract. In such a case, his profit may be more accurately measured as a percentage or return on investment. Thus, on a $1 million contract, performed in a given year, where the contractor had an investment of $500,000 worth of plant and equipment, a $100,000 profit would be equal to a 20-per cent return on investment.

An example of how a low profit as a percentage of costs can be misleading is found in a case decided by the Tax Court involving Air Force contracts (*North American Aviation Inc.* v. *Renegotiation Board, 1962*). In that case, while the contract provided for 8 per cent profits as a percentage of costs, the Tax Court found the contracts returned 612 per cent and 802 per cent profit on the contractor's investment in 2 succeeding years, according to Admiral Rickover. In that case 99 per cent of the contractor's sales was to the Government. Indeed, profits as a return on investment is the preferred method of measuring profitability. Stockholders are concerned with the return on their investment, not with profits as a percentage of costs or sales. Return on investment is also a better indicator of the profit relation to the contractor's input.

It is interesting to note that defense companies operate on smaller profit margins, based on percentage of costs, than do typical industrial corporations. Basically, this is because they often operate with large amounts of Government-supplied capital. Professor Murray Weidenbaum studied a sample of large defense contractors doing three-fourths or more of their business with the Government compared with similar sized industrial companies doing most of their business in the commercial market. Net profits as a percentage of stockholders' investment was 17.5 per cent for the defense contractors and 10.6 per cent for the industrial firms, for the period 1962–65.

The first question asked in this investigation was whether defense contractors' profits are too high. Much criticism of defense profits has been made in recent years. Critics maintain there is a serious problem of excessive profits. Others assert the opposite, that defense profits may be too low.

Although our present knowledge is incomplete, there is evidence that profits on defense contracts are higher than in related nondefense activities, and higher for the defense industry than for the manufacturing industry as a whole. There is also evidence that this differential has been increasing. The arguments of the Department of Defense to the contrary are unconvincing. The Pentagon's own figures show a 22-per cent increase in profit rates on negotiated contracts under the weighted guidelines method of profit computation. GAO found a 26-per cent increase in a study comparing the 5-year period from 1959 through 1963 with the average profit rate negotiated during the last 6 months of 1966. DOD claims the increases relate only to "going in" profits negotiated, and that actual "coming out" or realized profits are less. But the DOD in-house profit review survey shows that contractors are coming out with profits that are substantially the same as the going in rates. In addition, when Admiral Rickover made a comparison of profits reported and actual profits as determined by Government audit for five contractors, actual profits were found to be much higher than profits reported. Admiral Rickover also testified that suppliers of propulsion turbines are insisting on 20- to 25-per cent profit on costs as compared with 10 per cent a few years ago, that several nuclear equipment suppliers are requesting 15- to 20-per cent profit, that profit percentages on shipbuilding contracts doubled in the past 2 years, and that a large company recently priced equipment to a Navy shipbuilder at a 33-per cent profit.

Col. A. W. Buesking testified that profits based on return on investment in the Minuteman program, from 1958 to 1966, were 43 per cent. Profits for the large companies seem to be relatively higher than the smaller and medium-sized ones, according to the studies already completed.

Officials of the Department of Defense have attempted to answer the criticism of high profits in defense contracting by citing Renegotiation Board figures. Yet, in the annual reports, the Renegotiation Board warns against using its figures for generalizing about defense profits. One of the reasons for not using these figures is the fact that a large amount of contract awards are exempt from renegotiation and therefore do not show up in the totals for renegotiable sales. In addition, the Board does not publish figures for profits as a return on investment, nor does it disclose the names of contractors who have been ordered to return excessive profits to the Government and the amounts involved. Unless such disclosures are made so that profits on renegotiable sales can be fully analyzed, we agree that Renegotiation Board figures should not be used to generalize about profitability in defense contracting.

Officials of the Department of Defense have also attempted to answer its critics with the results of a study performed by the Logistics Management Institute (LMI). LMI was created by the DOD and in the past has worked almost exclusively for DOD. The LMI profits study was financed by DOD.

The LMI study used unverified, unaudited data which was obtained through the voluntary cooperation of a sample of defense contractors. Those who did not wish to do so did not participate in the study. Forty-two per cent of those contacted provided no data. As Admiral Rickover pointed out, one of the faults with such a study is that the contractors making high profits would naturally be reluctant to supply information and could simply choose not to participate. In addition, the study fails to distinguish between profits of the larger contractors and the medium sized and smaller ones.

These facts are cited to underline the continued need by Congress for an objective, independent, and comprehensive study of defense profits. This need cannot be satisfied by a DOD in-house study, or by an organization dependent upon the DOD for its funds.

2. Cost overruns: The C-5A cargo plane

The Air Force selected the Lockheed Aircraft Corp. as the airframe prime contractor for the C-5A, a large long-range, heavy logistic aircraft, on September 30, 1965, after proposals had been received in response to Requests for Proposals (RFP) from 5 firms, and preliminary contracts had been entered into with 3 of them in 1964. It is not clear, from the evidence, how much *price* competition had to do with the selection. Secretary Charles testified that there was competition among the firms. But when asked how low Lockheed's bid was compared to the others, he refused to disclose the figures on the grounds that "this is company proprietary information." A similar procedure resulted in the selection of General Electric as the engine manufacturer.

The contract with Lockheed is a negotiated, fixed-price incentive-fee contract. It is also the first contract utilizing the total package procurement concept (TPPC). Two major objectives of the concept, according to the Defense Department, are to discourage contractors from buying in on a design-and-development contract with the intention of recovering on a subsequent production contract, and to motivate contractors to design for economical production and support of operational hardware. Thus, TPPC is supposed to act as a deterrent against cost overruns and less-than-promised performance. To accomplish this, all development, production, and as much support as is feasible of a system throughout its anticipated life, is to be procured in a single contract, as one total package. The contract includes price and performance commitments to motivate the contractor to control costs, perform to specifications, and produce on time. As the C-5A is an incentive contract (TPPC does not necessarily result in incentive contracting) it contains the usual financial rewards and penalties associated with incentive contracting.

The C-5A contract for the airframe provides for 5 research, development, test and evaluation (R.D.T.&E.) aircraft plus an initial production run of 53 airplanes (the total of 58 planes is called run A), and a Government option for additional airplanes. The present approved program for the C-5A is 120 airplanes comprised of run A (58 airplanes) plus run B (57 airplanes) plus 5 airplanes from run C.

The testimony received during the November 1968 hearings indicated a cost overrun in the C-5A program totaling as much as $2 billion. A "cost overrun" is the amount in excess of the original target cost. According to the testimony, the program originally called for 120 C-5A airplanes to cost the Government $3.4 billion, but because of cost overruns mainly being experienced in the performance of the Lockheed contract actual costs would total $5.3 billion.

Following the November hearings, Senator Proxmire asked GAO to investigate into the causes and amount of the C-5A overruns and other matters relating to the contract.

On November 19, 1968, the Air Force announced, in a press release, that the original estimate for 120 C-5A aircraft was $3.1 billion, compared to the current estimate of $4.3 billion. Subsequently, in response to a request by the subcommittee, Mr. Fitzgerald, who was responsible for the development of the management controls used on the C-5A and who was on a steering committee directing a financial review of the C-5A, supplied a breakdown of the estimates of C-5A program cost to completion. This data showed Air Force esti-

mates for 120 airplanes was $3.4 billion in 1965, and $5.3 billion in 1968, indicating an overrun of about $2 billion. The difference between the Air Force press release and the data supplied by Mr. Fitzgerald seems to be accounted for in the figures for spare parts. The data supplied by Mr. Fitzgerald shows $0.3 billion for spares estimated in 1965, and $0.9 billion in 1968. If the figures for spares are added to the estimates in the Air Force press release, the two sets of figures are close to one another.

In the January 16 followup hearing, GAO reported on its investigation. . . . Briefly, GAO transmitted to the subcommittee figures supplied by the Air Force 2 days prior to the hearing. These figures indicated a substantial overrun but a smaller total cost for the overall C-5A program than the $5.3 billion figure shown in the November hearings. The reason for the lower total was the omission by the Air Force of the costs of the spares.

Nevertheless, testimony and other evidence received in the course of the hearings confirmed the existence of the approximately $2 billion overrun in the C-5A program, the reverse incentives contained in the repricing formula, and large overruns in other Air Force programs. The latest estimate of the total cost of 120 C-5A's, including spares, provided by Secretary Charles, is $5.1 billion. This is close to the estimate previously supplied by Mr. Fitzgerald, and about $2 billion more than was estimated in 1965. The table below shows the estimates supplied by Mr. Fitzgerald, the Air Force press release of November 19, 1968, and Assistant Secretary Charles.

The cost growth in the C-5A program can be seen in the table. The figures supplied by Fitzgerald show an increase from $3.4 billion in 1965 to $5.3 billion in 1968. The Air Force press release can be reconciled with the Fitzgerald figures if the AFLC investment (spares) is added to each of the estimates. Thus, the $3.1 billion estimate for 1965 would total $3.4 billion, and the $4.3 billion estimate for 1968 would total $5.2 billion. Secretary Charles' own figures for 1968 total $5.1 billion. The subcommit-

Comparison of estimates of C-5A program

[in billions of dollars]

	FITZGERALD		AIR FORCE PRESS RELEASE[1]		CHARLES	
	1965	1968	1965	1968	1965	1968
120 aircraft:						
R.D.T. & E. plus production . . .	$3.1	$4.4	$3.1	$4.3		$4.3
AFLC[2] investment	.3	.9				.8
Total	3.4	5.3	3.1	4.3		5.1

[1] The Air Force press release of Nov. 19, 1968, did not provide cost breakdowns between R.D.T. & E. (research development, testing, and engineering), production runs, and AFLC investment. The figures given seem to omit AFLC investment.

[2] AFLC (Air Force Logistics Command) investment submitted by Fitzgerald includes spare parts; that submitted by Charles includes initial spares, replenishment spares, and support. Table submitted by Secretary Charles (Hearings, Pt. 1, p. 311) does not include estimates for 1965.

tee rejects the attempts of Air Force spokesmen to minimize the size of the program or the size of the overrun by removing spares as an item of cost. Spares are an integral part of the C-5A program and should be included in any consideration of costs.

According to the Air Force, the cost growth in the C-5A program has resulted from normal development problems associated with complex weapons and inflation. However, the subcommittee notes that the C-5A was chosen for the first application of the total package procurement concept partly for the reason that it was not considered a highly complex weapons system requiring technological advances beyond the state of the art. The inflation argument, which is supposed to account for $500 million of the cost growth, appears questionable. The contract contains an inflation provision to protect the contractor from unforeseeable price changes in the economy, to go into effect 3 years after the issuance of the initial contract, that is, October 1, 1968. The initial 3-year period was supposed to be considered a normal business risk. The Air Force official explanation of this provision states: "The contract thus included in the price an amount which reflected a projection of the mounting cost trend in the economy of labor, materials, equipment, and subcontract prices." If future inflation for at least 3 years was included *in the price*, it is hard to see why inflation should be a major factor in later

increasing the price. Without a more thorough investigation of the C-5A program, the technical problems encountered, the failure to anticipate them at the time of the negotiations, and operations of the inflation provision, the subcommittee cannot form any firm conclusions about the reasons for the enormous overrun.

A repricing formula built into the contract was also revealed in the November testimony. The repricing formula is one of the most blatant reverse incentives ever encountered by this subcommittee. It should be recalled that the C-5A contract is supposed to represent an important step toward cost control. An Air Force manual on the total package procurement concept dated May 10, 1966, states that "It should produce not only lower costs on the first production units, but, in turn, a lower take-off point on the production learning curve, thus benefiting every unit in the production run." The facts about the C-5A are just the reverse. Costs for the first production units are greatly exceeding original estimates, resulting in a higher take-off point on the production learning curve, thus inflating every unit in the production run. In addition, the contract is supposed to provide the Government with binding commitments on price and performance. Obviously, there is in fact no binding commitment on price if the price can be modified upwards, as is being done in the C-5A, because actual costs are exceeding estimates. Whether the actual performance of the C-5A lives up to its promise remains to be seen. On the matter of delivery, it is interesting to note that the Air Force announced on February 25, 1969, a 6-month delay in the first operational C-5A aircraft, from June 1969 to December 1969.

Not only were the price increases made possible by the repricing formula, but the cost overruns which are resulting in the higher prices may very well have been encouraged by the existence of the formula and by the nature of the formula. For the mere fact that a repricing provision existed in the contract constituted a built-in get-well remedy for almost any kind of cost growth. According to this provision, the price of the second increment (run B) could be increased on the basis of excessive actual costs on the first increment (run A). The motivation, if any, of the incentive feature of the contract is thereby largely nullified, provided the contractor is confident that the Government will exercise the option. Why bother to keep costs down if their increase forms the basis for a higher price? Additionally, because of the nature of the formula, the higher the percentage of overrun over the original contract ceiling price on the first increment, the higher the percentage by which the second increment is repriced.

The subcommittee learned, on the morning of the January 16, 1969, hearing, that the Air Force had exercised the run B option for 57 additional C-5A aircraft, apparently committing the Government to spend at least $5.1 billion on aircraft originally estimated to cost $3.3 billion. The subcommittee was dismayed to learn that this decision was made before the completion of the GAO investigation and without a full disclosure of the reasons for the cost overruns. The public interest in economy in Government was not served by this precipitous decision, announced a few hours before the start of a congressional hearing and a few days before the inauguration of the new President.

3. Cost control as an antisocial activity

Considerable testimony was received on the need to protect and encourage Government personnel attempting to keep the costs of procurement down. But cost control has been interpreted by many within and outside of Government as antisocial activity. The phenomenon of officials in the bureaucracy pushing for ever-enlarged programs is widely known. To such bureaucrats, any employee who wants to cut costs, and possibly reduce the size of the program, is stepping out of line.

The problems encountered by Fitzgerald in connection with the C-5A were underlined by Admiral Rickover. According to the admiral, subordinates in DOD are supposed to "hew to the party line." Personnel who speak out against excessive costs may be subjected to disciplinary action. Rickover testified: "We have all heard of cases where Government personnel were apparently 'punished' for speaking out against the policies of their superiors. I do not mean the spectacular punishments that might be meted out to a dissenter in other countries; but there are subtle methods of reprisal that have been brought to bear against subordinates who publicly refuse to toe the agency line."

Colonel Buesking similarly observed that the sanctions have been imposed on those who have attempted to bring about major improvements in reducing costs. He testified: "It has been my personal observation that a number of competent people who did attempt to stimulate major change in the cost environment are no longer involved in working that particular environment."

In a written statement submitted for the record by Fitzgerald, a civilian employee of the Navy, Mr. Gordon Rule, cautioned his fellow employees engaged in controlling costs to expect resistance not only from the contractor but from people in the Government as well. Mr. Rule stated: "This 'homefront' resistance can be much more brutal than that from a contractor."

The subcommittee is deeply disturbed over the evidence of the lack of support for those conscientious individuals in DOD who want to reduce procurement costs. The negative attitude toward cost control and the apparent hostility against those who try to perform this function, is another example of "reverse incentives" in military procurement.

Complicating the job of cost control for

cost-conscious personnel is the relationship of DOD with the defense industry as seen in the interchange of personnel. A preliminary survey has revealed over 2,000 retired, high-ranking regular military officers now employed by the 100 largest contractors. Only officers of the rank of Army, Air Force, and Marine Corps colonel, or Navy captain and above were included in the survey. The total represents almost three times the number of retired military employed per company that existed 10 years ago. The survey did not include former DOD civilian employees now working for contractors, nor did it include the number of former contractor officials now employed by DOD. Admiral Rickover and many other persons believe that the heavy interchange of personnel is at least partly responsible for the absence of adequate cost controls in military procurement.

[1]Due to the pressure of other responsibilities, Senator Symington was unable to fully participate in the hearings and other committee deliberations pertaining to this report and makes no judgment on the specific recommendations made therein.

[2]Congressman Donald Rumsfeld, Senator Len B. Jordan, and Senator Charles H. Percy, while in general agreement with this report, call attention to the fact that all the information and testimony cited in this report relate to procurement contracts in effect prior to the end of 1968. It is their belief

that the irregularities and deficiencies in the procurement process reported here will encourage the new administration, which took office January 20, 1969, after the conclusion of this subcommittee's hearings, to press forward with the reforms necessary to save the American taxpayers millions of dollars while providing the defense capability necessary for peace and security.

They are encouraged that on April 30, 1969, Defense Secretary Melvin R. Laird expressed his concern over the costly C-5A transport plane and ordered the Air Force to make a thorough review of the multibillion-dollar contract. Secretary Laird said:

I am determined to insure that full and accurate information on C-5A procurement, and all other procurement matters, is given to the Congress and to the public promptly. I also am determined to insure that past mistakes in the procurement of this transport aircraft will not be repeated.

They believe that the healthy, constructive pressures of a free enterprise system must be allowed to operate to provide a rebirth of competition in many of the sectors of the economy which provide the material needed for our national security. The leadership and stimulation needed in these areas must come from the new civilian leadership in the Department of Defense and the White House. It is their hope and belief that the new Administration will provide this leadership.

[3]Representative Barber B. Conable, Jr., states: "The hearings on this matter were held last year prior to my appointment to the Joint Economic Committee. Since I did not have an opportunity to hear the testimony, I neither endorse nor dissent from the conclusions herein."

[4]"Improving the Acquisition Process For High Risk Military Electronics Systems" Richard A. Stubbing, *Congressional Record*, Feb. 7, 1969, p. 1450.

[5]Economy in Government Procurement and Property Management, Report of the Subcommittee on Economy in Government, Joint Economic Committee, April 1968.

Productivity

12. Defense Waste and the Industrial Engineer
A. E. Fitzgerald

Since last November I have been privileged to testify several times before the Senate Subcommittee on Economy in Government. In these appearance I and others have discussed problems and opportunities in controlling major weapon acquisition costs. The reactions to this testimony have been remarkable.

Following my first appearance, in which

I confirmed the information that the Government estimates for the cost of the C-5A aircraft had increased dramatically, I found myself in very serious difficulty with the management of the Department of Defense. Despite attempts on my part to settle the inadvertently generated conflict, my personal difficulties persisted. When these difficulties were publicized by the press and the Congress, I began to hear from large numbers of people throughout the country, practically all of whom agreed with my views on costs of big defense systems.

I have maintained that we commonly have excessive costs in the operations of the giant contractors who develop and manufacture our major weapons systems. By major weapons systems I mean such things as the F-111, Minuteman, and the C-5A. I have presented evidence to demonstrate that a major reason these problems exist and are not corrected is that the intent and determination to require efficiency in the operations of the larger contractors are insufficient on the part of the Government management. I emphasize the term "larger contractors" since it is my conviction that the Government is much more solicitous of the contractors' welfare in dealing with giant systems contractors than with smaller suppliers.

In various appearances before the Joint Economic Committee I have attempted, in addition to citing the intent problem, to popularize some of the more technical aspects of controlling costs on these complex programs. One of these aspects which I have discussed in some depth is the type of cost estimating employed in setting the prices of large weapons systems.

Basically, I have discussed the two approaches to estimating now recognized in defense acquisition. The two different approaches produce either the so-called probable-cost estimates or should-cost estimates. Probable-cost estimates are by far the most widely used. These estimates project program or contract costs based on experience on the same or similar programs without considering the possibility that the bases for projection may be inflated by ineffective performance. Should-cost estimates attempt to project costs attainable by reducing inefficiency and waste.

The should-cost estimates have been vigorously opposed by both the Government and contractor segments of the acquisition community. On the other hand, the acquisition community has adopted the probable-cost estimating techniques with enthusiasm for negotiating costs of new contracts and changes. It is indeed a more comfortable mode of operation. It allows negotiations to be conducted in a gentlemanly manner, which helps Government-industry relations no end. The only people who suffer are the taxpayers, who are generally ignorant of the process and consequently do not complain.

I have heard responsible Government managers oppose should-cost pricing by rationalizing contractor inefficiency as a good thing — creating more employment, keeping the large contractors financially healthy, and the like. This group, which I call the "social goals" faction, has exerted a powerful influence on defense acquisition in recent years. The argument that we must allow excessive costs in order to "maintain capability" (keep contractors in business) is also heard often.

Associations' influence

The political potency of the large contractors and their supporters in all branches of the Government is often cited as an obstacle to improvement. I have personally observed the effectiveness of the large industry associations such as AIA (Aerospace Industry Associations) and CODSIA (Council of Defense and Space Industry Associations) in opposing measures beneficial to the taxpayers. Most major changes in the acquisition process are cleared in advance with these contractor associations.

The Industry Advisory Council (IAC), a joint Department of Defense/contractor group, is also a strong force in opposing changes not beneficial to the acquisition community. Conversely, changes beneficial to major contractors, such as the increases in progress payment or reimbursement percentages, breeze through the IAC.

Given the overall climate and the level of opposition to cost reducing measures (reinforced by occasional examples of personal disaster visited on economy proponents), it is not surprising that most working-level Government acquisition managers shy away from tough cost control actions. The most successful Government project managers take a detached view of all financial matters once they make sure they have enough money to cover their contractors' requirements.

The environment I have described is hardly conducive to motivating major contractors to do the things necessary to run efficient operations. Given an environment without effective penalties for poor performance, I can honestly think of no valid business reasons why the major contractor community should extend itself to improve its cost performance on Government contracts, so long as it is assured of our continued patronage.

Despite evidence of vast increases in discretionary expenses, shocking inefficiencies, and unnecessary activities, I do not know of a single effective program under way to capture the cost improvement potential in these areas today. Broad but nonspecific commitments to improved efficiency are often heard, but the hard means of attainment are resisted.

I do not intend to suggest that the subject of why we have excessive acquisition costs is a simple one or that there is a single easy remedy. However, I do believe the permissive or, at best, indifferent environment of past years has been the prime factor in erosion of the buying power of the defense dollar.

Loose acquisition practices

Taken together, I believe the broader effects of loose aquisition practices on major programs make up one of our most severe national problems. Some of these effects are 1) Inflation and higher taxes. The contribution of waste in major acquisitions to inflation and higher taxes is probably the most obvious of its adverse effects. Not only are the expenditures themselves mostly nonproductive in a purely economic sense, but higher contractor prices also condition buyers to view continuing upward trends as inevitable.

For example, the runaway contractor overhead rates, plummeting labor efficiency, and sharply increasing average pay of the ballistic missile contractors during the early 1960's — a period of relative price stability — were the precursors of our present inflation.

The higher prices caused by degraded performance spread throughout the major acquisition community, encouraged by the permissive climate for cost growth. Smaller suppliers were forced to follow suit to remain competitive for employees, services, and material. This situation compounded the effect of increases in volume of procurements after 1965. General inflation followed, and higher taxes, including the surtax, were imposed to pay the bills.

2) Limitations on military hardware and services. During periods of stringent budget limitations, high and ever-increasing costs limit available and planned military hardware and services.

It is puzzling that the strongest opposition to improved cost control measures comes from some of the most verbally hawkish elements of the acquisition community. It is also strange to find that these same verbally hawkish elements are strong supporters of the theory that defense inefficiency is necessary to the attainment of "social goals," and that they often rationalize excessive costs on the grounds of "maintaining capability."

As something of a hawk myself, albeit a parsimonious one, I find these arguments fascinatingly illogical. Even if the Government desired to spend a given amount of defense money to "maintain capability," to employ the disadvantaged, or whatever, I see no reason why we should not try to get full value in return. This is particularly true in periods when it is argued that we need more or newer defense hardware.

3) Poor product quality. Product quality is inevitably affected adversely by the poor management and worker discipline encouraged by loose acquisition policies. In some contractor operations, workloads are so low that workers do not maintain concentration on their widely spaced essential activities. Workmanship suffers greatly under these conditions.

In all the major weapons systems I am familiar with, those which experienced severe technical and quality problems were affected to some degree by this underlying cause.

4) Impact on international trade. General domestic inflation is often cited as a growing problem in maintaining a favorable trade balance. A more persistent and possibly irreversible problem, which may be obvious at present only to industrial specialists, is the effect of undemanding acquisition cost management practices on our nation's management and work habits.

The poor management and work habits typical of the larger defense plants rapidly infect entire communities. There is a growing body of opinion which asserts that this situation is one of the root causes of a national productivity problem which threatens our competitive position in world markets and, hence, our balance of trade.

Until recently, American management and labor were so efficient compared to foreign competitors that they could be paid considerably more than their foreign counterparts and still compete successfully in world markets. There are increasingly fewer market areas where our margin of effectiveness is sufficient to offset differentials in rates of pay.

Achieve social goals?

5) Failure to achieve "social goals." It is ironic that even with the strong position enjoyed by the "social goals" faction in the defense acquisition community, avowed "social goals" are not being achieved. The reason for this is quite simple. Most defense acquisition activities are very poor vehicles for employing those who could not otherwise be employed in a healthy economy.

Some time ago, this fact was recognized, and an effort was made by the Department of Defense to encourage defense contractors to hire low-skilled and poorly motivated employees from among the hard core unemployed. Authority was granted to pay up to a 33 per cent price premium for materials and services supplied by the disadvantaged. Armed Services Procurement Regulations requirements and restrictions in the Defense Appropriations Act were bypassed by transferring defense funds to the Small Business Administration for their subsequent contracting. The SBA is not bound by Armed Services Procurement Regulations or restrictions in the Defense Appropriations Act.

Even with all this activity, the hard core unemployed remain largely unemployed. Furthermore, those few who have been employed have, for the most part, been introduced to an undemanding, subsidized type of industrial activity which will equip them very poorly for the competitive world. I believe we should do much more to help the disadvantaged become more productive citizens and thereby have a better life. We should make sure they have a fair chance to fill legitimate, necessary jobs in the defense industry.

However, it is quite clear that extra-cost employment of the disadvantaged could be brought about much more efficiently outside the defense establishment. The specialized nature of the defense business, coupled with the inefficient management now prevalent in the industry, results in huge Government administrative and contractor overhead costs which must be paid in order to employ the disadvantaged. These expenses could be much less if extra-cost programs to employ the disadvantaged were assigned to agencies other than the Defense Department.

I believe employment of the disadvantaged in economically productive activities would be more beneficial to both the national economy and the disadvantaged. Finally, a significant excuse for inefficiency would be removed.

6) Failure to "maintain capability." At many contractor facilities where the Government has spent vast sums of money to "maintain capability," it appears that the opposite result has been achieved. Often these organizations have been sustained in near idleness long enough to impair seriously their ability to become effective producers. The effect on these companies is as tragically demoralizing and debilitating as the effect of prolonged welfare payments on a healthy family.

Worst of all, from the standpoint of organizational potential, most of the best producers among the staffs of the "maintained" companies have long since departed. Top people, particularly creative ones, simply will not tolerate the deadly, stagnant atmosphere of near idleness and make-work if opportunities for challenge and growth exist elsewhere. The atrophy of major industrial suppliers could have diastrous consequences should the time come when national survival depends upon our ability to outproduce any other nation.

7) Breakdown of trust in Government. By far the most disturbing implication of continued drift in defense cost control policy is the danger of losing the trust and faith placed in the Government by the American people. Until quite recently, defense waste and its causes were seldom discussed publically. However, as the procurement community has grown larger and

less efficient, it has also become more visible to the grassroots taxpayer.

Since my difficulties in the Pentagon were publicized, I have heard from literally hundreds of private citizens who expressed their own conviction, usually based on personal experience, that there is enormous waste in defense acquisition. These citizens generally have difficulty putting a dollar price on their own particular horror stories and often have difficulty detecting and explaining the causes. However, they are convinced of the avoidability of waste and object to the increased tax burden to pay for it.

Public being milked

There is another group of people who feel even more strongly than the average taxpayer group that the American public is being milked. These are the professional management people who have attempted to correct defense cost abuses and have suffered personal reverses as a result. All these people deeply resent being told in official pronouncements that all is well and that the ever-increasing defense money requirements are solely the result of the necessity to counter "threats" or of inexorable economic processes. They know better.

An increasing number of people believe that a prime purpose of defense expenditures is to enrich the so-called military-industrial complex. This belief is fed by obvious waste, frank admissions of protecting supplier interests at the taxpayers' expense, and delays in corrective actions by the Government. In these circumstances, we might reasonably ask how long we can expect the annual recurrence of the miracle of April 15 in which millions of our citizens give up sizable portions of their bank accounts with minimum protest.

I am told by friends from abroad that this phenomenon is almost unique in the free world and that foreign governments view it with awe and envy.

It is by no means certain that our heavily burdened taxpayers will continue to provide the still enormous sums for the necessary portions of the defense budget if the taint of waste is not removed. Moreover, oratory and superficial, isolated demonstrations of toughness will not suffice. Hard-nosed corrective action on a broad scale is needed. More than any other area of government, stewardship of the defense appropriation should be above reproach. At present, it is not.

Although I have painted a gloomy picture and a somewhat frightening one, I believe our present difficulties offer opportunities for improvement in the future. The possibility of capturing the cost reduction potential represented by excessive costs in our major weapons systems presents a genuine opportunity to find money for other national requirements at minimum risks to our security. We might even consider cutting taxes.

Training influences views

I recognize that my views on this subject are heavily influenced by my training and experience as an industrial engineer. Unquestionably, this background causes me to view industrial and business operations much more critically than most other managers in the weapons acquisition business. However, there are thousands of other experienced industrial engineers who have had the same exposure to defense inefficiencies as I, though rarely on so broad a scale.

As a long-time worker in industrial engineering professional association activities, I have met and talked with hundreds of these people over the years. Many are long-time friends. I know of none who have shared my experiences who will disagree with my appraisal of the problems and the opportunities in the acquisition of major defense systems. Because of our special skills, I believe that we professional industrial engineers have a particular responsibility to speak out on these subjects. Yet how many have? Unfortunately, not many.

The reason for my professional colleagues' silence is crystal clear to me. Those who have the best opportunity to view at close hand the situations I have described are engineers in the employ of large defense contractors. Clearly, these people could not make public disclosures of their convictions without jeopardizing the interests of their employers, at least in the short run. Also, they probably would be fired. Unquestionably, an industrial engineer who offended his employer in this way would have great difficulty obtaining responsible employment.

Despite my sympathy and understanding of these individuals' situations, I cannot avoid the question of whether industrial engineers can truly be called professional under these circumstances. By a loose definition, all employed industrial engineers are professional in that they get paid for their activities and have thereby lost their amateur standing. However, I believe the hallmark of true professionalism is an overriding dedication to the public good.

No one would argue the fact that a professional civil engineer should not approve a faulty design for a bridge or public building simply because his employer wished him to do so. I recognize that the issues in such decisions are not always clear-cut or precisely stated, and I am not so naive as to believe that the judgments are completely unaffected by employer interest. However, open advocacy of jeopardizing

the safety of people using the structures would never be tolerated. Should such a practice become commonplace and known to the public, the approval of the civil engineer would become meaningless and his professionalism would be destroyed.

Attain true professionalism

Given this unfavorable comparison with other professional disciplines, accentuated by the dilemma faced by industrial engineers in the defense industry, I have concluded that we as a group cannot truly lay claim to professional objectivity at present. At the same time, I am convinced that I and others of my craft can somehow overcome the obstacles to attainment of true professionalism.

I would be most interested in the views of my colleagues on the subject. We have a golden opportunity to make a major contribution to the national well-being, and the mood of the country demands that we try.

Product Quality

13. Weapons Systems: A Story of Failure
Bernard D. Nossiter

The complex electronic gadgetry at the heart of new warplanes and missiles generally works only a fraction of the time that its builders had promised.

The performance of the multi-billion-dollar weapons systems started in the 1950s was bad; those of the 1960s are worse.

The Pentagon appears to be giving the highest profits to the poorer performers in the aerospace industry.

These are the conclusions of an abstruse 41-page paper now circulating in Government and academic circles. The document,

Reprinted from *The Washington Post*, January 26, 1969; © *The Washington Post.* Reprinted by permission.

a copy of which has been made available to *The Washington Post,* is believed to be the first systematic effort to measure how well or ill the Pentagon's expensive weapons perform.

Its author is a key Government official with access to secret data and responsibility for examining the costs of the Pentagon's complex ventures. He and his agency cannot be identified here.

His paper, entitled "Improving the Acquisition Process for High Risk Military Electronics Systems," aims at bringing down the costs and bettering the dismal performance of weapons. It does not discuss a question that might occur to others: if these weapons behave so badly, why is the money being spent at all?

For security reasons, many of the planes and missiles examined are not identified by name.

The paper first examined 13 major aircraft and missile programs, all with "sophisticated" electronic systems, built for the Air Force and the Navy beginning in 1955 at a cost of $40 billion. Of the 13, only 4, costing $5 billion, could be relied upon to perform at more than 75 per cent of their specifications. Five others, costing $13 billion, were rated as "poor" performers, breaking down 25 per cent more often than promised or worse. Two more systems, costing $10 billion, were dropped within 3 years because of "low reliability." The last two, the B-70 bomber and the Skybolt missile, worked so badly they were canceled outright after an outlay of $2 billion.

Loses further luster

The paper sums up: "Less than 40 per cent of the effort produced systems with acceptable electronic performance—an uninspiring record that loses further luster when cost overruns and schedule delays are also evaluated."

The paper measure "reliability" in this context: The electronic core of a modern plane or missile consists essentially of three devices. One is a computer that is supposed to improve the navigation and automatically control the fire of the vehicle's weapons and explosives. Another is radar that spots enemy planes and targets. The third is a gyroscope that keeps the plane or missile on a steady course.

When the Pentagon buys a new gadget, its contract with the aerospace company calls for a specified "mean time between failure of the electronic system." In lay language, this is the average number of continuous hours that the systems will work.

In a hypothetical contract for a new jet bomber, Universal Avionics will sell the Air Force on its new devices by promising that the three crucial electronic elements will operate continuously for at least 50 hours without a breakdown. In the reliability measures used in the paper described here, the plane is said to meet 100 per cent of the performance standards, if, in fact, its gadgetry did run 50 consecutive hours. However, if a key element breaks down every 12.5 hours, it gets a rating of 25 per cent; every 25 hours,

50 per cent and so on. Should a system operate with a breakdown interval of 62.5 hours—a phenomenon that happens rarely —its reliability is rated at 125 per cent.

Test for the pilot

Quite obviously, the more frequent the breakdown, the more the pilot of a plane has to rely on his wit and imagination to navigate, find targets and fly a steady course. Over-frequent breakdowns in a missile can render it worthless as an instrument of destruction. . . .

The document first looks at the performance record of the electronic systems in 12 important programs begun in the 1950s. As the accompanying chart shows, all but four missiles can be identified by name without breaching security.

Of the 12, only five perform up to standard or better; one breaks down 25 per cent more frequently than promised; four fail twice as often and two break down four times as frequently as the specifications allow.

The document discusses some of the good and bad performers in this group. It observes that the F-102, the Delta wing interceptor for the Air Defense Command, was bedevilled by an unsatisfactory fire control system. Its first had to be replaced; the next was also unsatisfactory, and an extensive, two-year program to modify the device was then undertaken.

Sidewinder did well

In contrast, the Sidewinder, a heat sensing missile, performed very well. The study attributes this to the fact that the missile was developed in a leisurely fashion, without a "crash" schedule, and that several contractors were brought in to compete for key components.

The paper next examines eleven principal systems of the 1960s. These cannot be identified beyond a letter designation.

Thus, in the chart, A1 is the first version of a plane or missile; A2 is the second version, possibly one for a sister service; A3 is the third version and so on. B1 is the first version of an entirely different system; so are C1, D1, and E1.

To make the best possible case for the

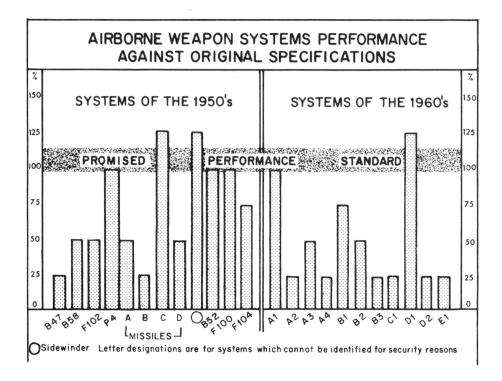

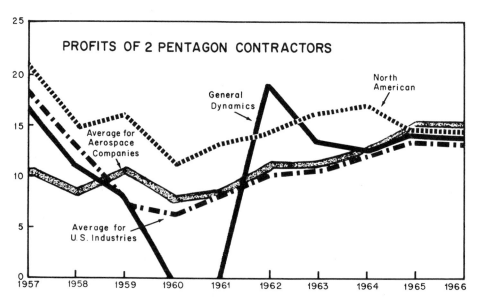

During this ten-year period, General Dynamics built seven weapons systems and none measured up to expectations. North American was responsible for six and one met specifications, one was canceled and four broke down four times as rapidly as contracts provided.

Pentagon and its contractors, this survey does not include two systems costing $2 billion that performed so badly they were killed off. The eleven systems of the 1960s evaluated here account for more than half of those begun in the most recent decade and their electronic hearts cost well in excess of $100 million each.

Of the eleven systems, only two perform to standard. One breaks down 25 per cent more rapidly than promised; two break down twice as fast and six, four times as fast.

As a group, the eleven average a breakdown more than twice as fast as the specifications demand. Oddly enough, the first version of the system designated as "A" met the standard. But the same unidentified contractor produced three succeeding versions that fail on the average more than three times as often as they should. All these successors, the paper observes, were ordered on a "pressure cooker" basis, on crash schedules.

Highest rewards

The paper also examines the relationship between contractors' profits and performance, and suggests that, contrary to what might be expected, some of the most inefficient firms doing business with the Pentagon earn the highest rewards.

The second chart looks at profits, after-tax returns as a percentage of investment, the only valid basis for determining profitability, for the ten years from 1957 to 1966. During the decade, the aerospace firms managed to earn consistently more than American industry as a whole, piling up nine dollars (or billions of dollars) in profits for every eight garnered by companies not doing business with the Pentagon.

Even more peculiar is the brilliant earnings record of two of the biggest contractors, North American and General Dynamics. Both, except for a brief period when General Dynamics tried its hand at some civilian business, made profits far above the industrial average and generally in excess of their colleagues in aerospace.

During the ten years, North American did all but 2 per cent of its business with the Government. The study reports that it produced one highly successful plane in the mid-50s, another system that met performance specifications, one that was canceled, and four that broke down four times as frequently as promised. Nevertheless, the company's profits were 40 per cent above those of the aerospace industry and 50 per cent above the average for all industries.

None measures up

General Dynamics had, as the chart shows, a much more uneven profits record. But its years of disaster and even losses were those when it ventured into the economically colder climate of the civilian world to produce a commercial jet airliner. Having learned its lesson, it retreated to the warmer regions of defense procurement and, in recent years, has netted more than the industry average. It has compiled this happy earnings score, the study observes, despite the fact that none of the seven weapons systems it built for the Pentagon "measured up to expectations." Its most notorious failure is the F-111 swing-wing fighter-bomber.

As a final touch, the study notes that complex electronic systems typically cost 200 to 300 per cent more than the Pentagon expects and generally are turned out two years later than promised. But both of these phenomena have been examined so frequently by specialists in the field that the paper does not dwell on them.

How much protection?

These findings raise some serious questions. Perhaps the most important is how much protection the United States is getting for the tens of billions of dollars invested is expensive weaponry. Another is whether the whole process should be turned off and improvements made in the existing devices. Secretaries of Defense have repeatedly assured the nation that present weaponry guarantees the destruction of any nation that attacks the United States.

The document under study here, however, takes a different line, one aimed at getting less costly weapons that measure up to the promised performance.

It blames the dismal record on several factors. One is the relentless search for newer and more complicated electronic "systems." The aerospace contractor has an obvious vested interest in promoting "breakthrough" gadgetry. This is the way he gets new, and clearly profitable business.

Close correlation shown

But the study asks, do the services need it? Since the Air Force and the Navy almost always accept a plane or a missile that performs at a fraction of its promised standard, it would appear from an exclusively military standpoint that a device of a much lower order of performance fits the nation's defense needs.

The document also shows a close correlation between "crash" programs and poor performance. Thus, it proposes more realistic schedules. If a weapon is wanted in short order, five years or less, the study recommends that its electronic gadgetry be limited to familiar items.

If the Pentagon wants something that makes a "technical breakthrough," it should allow a minimum development period of five to seven years, it is pointed out.

Another factor in poor performance, the study says, is the absence of competition for new systems after the initial designs are accepted. Typically, the Pentagon requires five or so aerospace firms to bid on its original proposal. But typically, it selects one winner on the basis of blueprint papers. The study says that the military could save more money and get a better product if it finances two competitors to build prototypes after the design stage. Such a technique was followed, it recalls, with the F-4, a supersonic Navy interceptor. Even though the F-4 employed both a new radar and a new computer, it performed up to the promised standard.

At first glance, such a technique might seem like throwing good money after dubious dollars. But the study contends that if two aerospace competitors are forced to build and fly prototypes before they win the big prize — the contract to produce a series of planes or missiles — they will be under a genuine incentive to be efficient, hold costs down, and make things that work.

III. ECONOMIC CONSEQUENCES OF MILITARY INDUSTRY FOR THE ECONOMY AS A WHOLE

The Mixed Economy

14. The Defense Sector: An Evaluation of Its Economic and Social Impact

Arthur F. Burns

In his famous farewell address, President Eisenhower warned the nation to remain vigilant of what he called "the military-industrial complex." This warning needs to be remembered and pondered by thoughtful citizens. An age of nuclear weapons leaves no time for assembling the military and industrial forces needed to repel an aggressor. Once a nation is attacked, it can be practically destroyed in a matter of minutes. For this reason as well as because of the unhappy state of our relations with the Communist bloc, "normalcy" for us has come to include since 1950 a formidable military establishment in a state of constant readiness, if need be, for war. But "the conjunction of an immense military establishment and a large arms industry," as President Eisenhower has observed, "is new in the American experience. The total influence—economic, political, even spiritual—is felt in every city, every statehouse, every office of the Federal government." My purpose today is to consider with you some of the ways in which the emergence of a massive and permanent defense sector has already changed and is continuing to change our economic and social life.

From *The Defense Sector and the American Economy*, The Moskowitz Lectures, Number VIII. Copyright © 1968 by New York University Press. Reprinted by permission.

I

To begin with, the defense sector has revolutionized governmental finances in our generation. In fiscal year 1948, Federal expenditures came to $36 billion. In fiscal 1964, well before Vietnam became a significant financial burden, spending on national defense alone amounted to $54 billion, or half as much again as the total budget in 1948. In the current fiscal year, the defense budget may amount to about $80 billion, but this huge sum still does not indicate the full financial cost of defense activities. The Federal government expects to spend another $5 billion on international programs and also $5.25 billion on space research and technology. These activities, of course, are mainly pursued in the interests of our national security. Moreover, the Federal budget allows $10.5 billion for interest on the public debt and over $6.5 billion for veterans' benefits, the former being preponderantly and the latter entirely a legacy of past wars. Thus, defense-related expenditures will probably come this year to over $100 billion—a sum that represents more than $500 for every man, woman, and child of our population.

The large and rising cost of defense activities would have caused financial problems even if other costs of government had not changed. In fact, as we all know, the range of governmental activities has greatly increased. Since the end of World War II, the American people have come to expect their government to maintain economic conditions that are generally conducive to full employment. The Federal government has been also under increasing pressure to enlarge social services—that is to say, improve the nation's schools, help support universities, improve hospitals and medical facilities, facilitate home ownership, reduce urban slums, promote safer and faster air travel, raise social security and related welfare benefits, train manpower for the needs of industry, seek ways of reducing air and water pollution, and even concern itself with problems of traffic congestion and police protection. These expanding interests of the Federal government are a political response to the increasing urbanization of modern life, the new opportunities opened up by advances in technology, and the growing impatience for better living on the part of many citizens who have been left behind by the march of progress. Thus, at the very stage of history when demographic, technological, and political trends have been releasing powerful forces to raise the costs of government, the defense sector likewise became an increasing burden on the Treasury. The inevitable result has been a vast growth of Federal spending—from $36 billion in fiscal 1948 to $120 billion in 1964, and probably $175 billion, if not more, this fiscal year.

The upsurge of Federal spending on defense and on civilian activities has naturally resulted in much higher taxes. To be sure, we have recently become accustomed to deficits when the economy is booming as well as when the economy is depressed. The role of deficits in governmental finance, however, is commonly exaggerated. From mid-1946 to June, 1967, the cumulative revenue of the Federal government covered all but 2 per cent of its expenditures, so that Federal taxes have in fact grown just about as rapidly as expenditures. Our economy has also grown substantially during this period, but not enough to prevent taxes from siphoning off an increasing portion of the national income. In fiscal 1940, Federal revenues came to about 7 per cent of the gross national product, in 1950 to 15.5 per cent, in 1960 to 19 per cent, last year to 20 per cent. Meanwhile, state and local taxes have also moved up—indeed, they have grown even more rapidly during the past ten or twenty years than Federal taxes. According to the national income accounts, the combined revenue of all governmental units amounted in the past fiscal year to about 29 per cent of the gross national product and 32 per cent of the net national product; and even the higher figure may understate the tax burden, since it makes inadequate allowance for the capital used up in the process of producing goods and services.

This year, with the war in Vietnam escalating and social expenditures also rising, the Federal budget deficit may well exceed $20 billion unless steps are taken to raise taxes and curb expenditures. To reduce the enormous deficit now in sight, President Johnson has proposed a 10 per cent surcharge on income taxes, but the Congress has thus far failed to adopt the proposal. Some members of Congress feel that the tax burden is already so heavy that it would be wiser to cut governmental expenditures than to raise taxes. Others would be willing to accept higher taxes provided substantial reductions in expenditures were simultaneously made. With financial markets disturbed and interest rates rising above last year's abnormally high level, a great debate is now raging both within and outside governmental circles about the relation of the Federal budget to economic activity, interest rates, and inflation. What is critically at issue in this debate is not whether Federal spending should be permitted to rise, but the size of the reduction—if any—in the projected scale of spending on nondefense programs. No matter how this issue is resolved, spending in the aggregate will still go up, and—if history is any guide—taxes will follow; so that we now face the prospect of higher income taxes besides higher social security taxes and assorted increases of state and local taxes.

We also face the prospect of paying more for foodstuffs, clothing, automobiles, and whatever else we buy. The causes of inflation are complex, and it is never strictly true that an increase in spending on defense or on business equipment or on any other category is the sole cause of inflation. In principle, the government can always adjust its monetary and fiscal policies to economic conditions so as to keep the price level reasonably stable. If the government had foreseen how rapidly the cost of the Vietnam war would mount and if it had taken promptly the restraining measures needed to keep the aggregate demand for goods and services from outrunning the nation's capacity to produce, the new round of inflation that we have experienced since 1964 could have been prevented. But if we blame the government for its lack of foresight or courage in this instance, we should also bear in mind that the theoretical ideal of price stability has rarely, if ever, been closely approximated under wartime conditions.

When demand presses hard on a nation's resources, as it generally does at a time of war, it becomes very difficult to adjust tax, credit, and expenditure policies on the scale needed to prevent advances in the price level. The doubling of wholesale prices between 1940 and 1950 was obviously linked to the enormous expansion of military spending during World War II. Since then, the trend of prices has continued upward at a much slower pace, and no single factor stands out so prominently among the causes of inflation. Indeed, prices have risen less in our country since 1950 than in most others, despite our exceptionally large military burden. It is nevertheless true that the greater part of the recent advance in both wholesale and consumer prices came in three spurts — between 1950 and 1952 when the Korean War was raging, between 1955 and 1957 when a fairly rapid increase of military contracts for newly developed weapon systems paralleled a booming trend of business investment in new plant and equipment, and since mid-1965 when our ground forces shifted to an active role in Vietnam. It appears, therefore, that the sudden surges within the defense sector have contributed to the inflationary trend which has been gradually eroding all savings accumulated in the form of bank deposits, life insurance, savings bonds, and other fixed-income assets, besides complicating life for everyone whose money income fails to respond to the rising cost of living.

The defense sector has also contributed to the deficit in our balance of payments. Since 1950 the receipts from our sale of goods, services, and securities to foreign countries have run considerably below the sums that we need to pay foreign countries. One reason for this persistent deficit is the large expenditure that is required, year in and year out, to maintain our military forces abroad. Foreign assistance programs have also been adding to the deficit, although their foreign exchange cost is now much smaller. Since the revenue derived from our foreign transactions has been insufficient to cover the required payments, our stocks of gold have shrunk from $24.5 billion at the beginning of 1950 to about $13 billion at present. Meanwhile, the dollar balances that are held here by foreigners have also grown, so that the United States finds itself in the position of a banker whose short-term liabilities are steadily rising while his reserves keep dwindling. In order to check the deterioration in our international financial position, the Department of Defense has lately been favoring domestic over foreign suppliers even at cost differentials of 50 per cent. More disturbing still, the government has found it necessary to impose restrictions on the outflow of capital — an interference with private investment that is contrary to our national traditions. Even so, the deficit in the balance of payments has persisted, and — at least partly as a result of the war in Vietnam — it is larger this year than last. International confidence in the dollar, which is of such immense importance to America's political leadership as well as to our economy and that of the rest of the world, is still strong, but we can no longer count on it as we did ten or twenty years ago.

II

I have been concerned thus far with the financial aspects of national defense — its impact on governmental expenditures, taxes, the price level, and the balance of payments. Financial transactions and the price system, however, are merely mechanisms for putting a nation's resources to work and for distributing what is produced among people and their government. The resources that we devote to national defense are not available for making consumer goods or for adding to the stock of industrial equipment or for public uses in the sphere of education, health, or urban redevelopment. To the extent that we allocate labor, materials, and capital to national defense, we cannot satisfy our desires for other things. The civilian goods and services that are currently foregone on account of expenditures on national defense are, therefore, the current real cost of the defense establishment.

This cost has become very large, as my observations on governmental finance have already suggested. Its magnitude can perhaps be grasped best by considering the amount of labor devoted to national defense. In fiscal 1965, the armed forces numbered close to 2.75 million. They were supported by over 900,000 civilian workers attached to the Department of Defense and by another 2.1 million civilians employed in private industry who worked, directly or indirectly, on military supplies. Thus the total employment on defense goods and services amounted to 5.75 million, or to 86 out of every 1,000 employed workers in the country. Two years later — that is, during the fiscal year which ended June, 1967 — the number was nearly 7.5 million, or 103 out of every 1,000 employed workers. The employment currently attributable to national security expenditures is still larger; for the figures that I have cited, besides not being fully up to date, take no account of the activities of the Atomic Energy Commission, the National Aeronautics and Space Administration, or other defense-related efforts.

A mere count of numbers, moreover, does not convey adequately the drain of the defense establishment on the nation's work force. Men differ in quality, and we need to take account of the fact that those involved in the defense effort are, on the average, superior from an economic viewpoint to workers engaged in civilian production. Military technology and operations have become very sophisticated in our times. The armed forces now have a highly skilled core and are very selective in accepting men for service. Indeed, the proportion of personnel who completed high school is much larger in the armed forces than in the comparable age group of the civilian population, while the proportion of college graduates is not materially lower. Training and skill count even more heavily among the civilians involved in defense activities. Last year professional workers accounted for nearly 16 per cent and skilled blue-collar workers for 21 per cent of the civilians employed on defense work, in contrast to about 13 per cent for each of these groups in the total working population. One out of every five of the nation's electrical and mechanical engineers in civilian jobs, two out of every five airplane mechanics, two out of every five physicists outside of teaching, and three out of every five aeronautical engineers were employed on defense goods during the past year. And even these figures understate the skill dimension of defense employment, for they again leave out of account the highly technical activities originating in the Atomic Energy Commission and the Space Administration.

The heavy emphasis on skill and brainpower in defense employment reflects, of course, the explosion of military technology to which modern science has been contributing so much of its finest energy. Since the Korean War, defense contractors have been devoting themselves not only to the production of extremely complex weapons but also to developing entirely new weapon systems that no one as yet knew how to produce. Much of the defense sector of our economy has come to consist, therefore, of research and development work. The President's budget for this fiscal year, for example, allots about $16 billion to research and development, of which $9 billion is to be devoted to defense and another $5 billion to space activities. Since 1960 defense and space programs have consistently accounted for over 80 per cent of the rapidly increasing Federal funds devoted to research and development. More important still, they have amounted to about 54 per cent of the expenditure on research and development carried out in the entire nation — that is, by the Federal government, industry, universities and colleges, research centers affiliated with universities, and other nonprofit institutions. During the 1950's the proportion of the nation's research and development effort devoted to defense-related activities was only a little lower.

By diverting to its interest so much manpower, especially scientific and engineering skills, the defense establishment has left its mark on both the structure and the functioning of our economy. The effects are all around us. Some defense-oriented industries—notably, the aerospace group, electronics, and communications—have become a major factor in the economy, and their development has favored many communities—for example, Los Angeles, San Diego, Seattle, Baltimore. Some large firms have aquired marvelous technological competence from their work on defense or space contracts and this rather than any immediate profit has commonly been their chief reason for wanting the contracts in the first place. Not a few of the scientists and engineers who received their training in the more sophisticated enterprises have moved into traditional lines of activity, bringing something of the spirit of research and innovation with them. Many of the men released by the armed forces have been able to put the technical skills acquired during their military service to effective use in civilian jobs. Nondefense activities have shared in the increased supply of engineers, scientists, and technicians that has been stimulated by the defense-related demand. And not a few of the processes or products developed for the military have found application in civilian life—for example, jet transports, advanced computers, radar, miniaturized components, and nuclear power plants.

But if the defense sector has stimulated economic development in some directions, it has retarded growth in others. Many civilian-oriented laboratories of business firms have found it difficult to match the salaries or the equipment that subsidized defense firms offer to scientists and engineers. Research and development work in behalf of new products and processes for the civilian economy has therefore been handicapped. Small firms have derived little benefit from military or space contracts. The draft has added to the labor turnover of all businesses, large and small.

The lack of opportunity in the defense sector for poorly educated and unskilled workers has not helped the rural Negroes who have flocked into the cities in recent years in search for jobs and a better life. Moreover, a new class of business executives has arisen, consisting of men whose understanding of marketing and cost controls is often deficient, but who know how to negotiate effectively with government officials handling military or scientific problems. While knowing the right people or having friends in the right places can sometimes advance the interests of an enterprise better than plain business ability, the nation's economic efficiency is not likely to reap a corresponding advantage.

In any event, the economic growth of a nation is a blind concept unless we consider what is produced as well as the rate of growth of what happens to be produced. During the decade from 1957 to 1966, our nation spent approximately $520 billions on defense and space programs. This sum is almost two-and-one-half times as large as the entire amount spent on elementary and secondary education, both public and private. It is two-and-three-quarter times as large as the amount spent on the construction of new housing units. It exceeds by over a fourth the expenditure on new plant and equipment by the entire business community—manufacturing firms, mining concerns, transportation enterprises, public utilities, and all other businesses. To be sure, an extra billion dollars' worth of bombs or missiles will increase current production just as much as an extra billion of new equipment for making civilian goods. Bombs or missiles, however, add nothing to the nation's capacity to produce, while new equipment serves to augment production in the future. The real cost of the defense sector consists, therefore, not only of the civilian goods and services that are currently foregone on its account; it includes also an element of growth that could have been achieved through larger investment in human or business capital. But even if we assumed that the conflicting influences of the defense sector on economic growth canceled out, its real cost is still enormous.

Unhappily, we live in dangerous times which make large national security expenditures practically unavoidable. Nevertheless, there are always some options in a nation's foreign and military policy, and we therefore must be alert to the opportunities that our military establishment forces us to forego. For example, if the resources devoted to military and space activities during the past decade had been put instead to civilian uses, we could surely have eliminated urban slums, besides adding liberally to private investment in new plant and equipment as well as to both public and private investment in human capital.

III

It follows from our analysis that the military-industrial complex, of which President Eisenhower spoke so perceptively in his farewell address, has not only been enlarging the scale of governmental operations and thereby complicating financial problems. By changing the thrust of economic activity and by making the economy more dependent on government, it has also been affecting profoundly the character of of our society. Nor have the social effects been confined to the kinds of goods that we produce. Hopefulness about the future, optimism about success of new undertakings, impatience to complete satisfactorily whatever is begun—these psychological qualities have been peculiarly American characteristics, and they account in far greater degree than we may realize for the remarkable achievements of our economic system and the vigor of our political democracy. These qualities are deep-rooted in American experience and they continue to sustain us. Nevertheless, the development and spread of thermonuclear weapons, the frustrations of the cold war, and now the brutal struggle in Vietnam have left us, despite our awesome military power, more anxious about our national security than our fathers or grandfathers ever were.

Adults whose habits were formed in an earlier generation may put the dangers of nuclear catastrophe out of mind by losing themselves in their work or by seeking solace in religion. That is more difficult for our children who increasingly wonder what kind of world they have inherited by our doings. There can be little doubt that the lively competition among the great powers in devising instruments of terror is one of the underlying causes of the restlessness of modern youth.

Moreover, young men of military age are bearing a disproportionately large part of the defense burden. That is unavoidable at a time of war, but our generation has institutionalized compulsory military service even when the nation is at peace. It is undoubtedly true that many young men derive deep satisfaction from helping to protect their country by serving as soldiers, sailors, or aviators. Not only that, many have also found useful careers in the armed forces, or have benefited in their civilian jobs from the skills and discipline acquired during military service, or have gained a larger understanding of life by associating with men of widely different backgrounds or by being stationed abroad for a time. But just as these benefits deserve recognition, so too does the fact that the draft has by and large proved to be a seriously upsetting factor in the lives of young people. Not knowing when they would be called up for military service or whether they would be accepted, many have found themselves marking time. Those who are accepted have often had to interrupt their schooling or careers, perhaps alter plans with regard to marriage, and in any event be content with substantially lower pay than they could earn as a rule in civilian work. Moreover, the administration of the draft over the years, particularly the handling of student deferments, has raised troublesome moral questions in the minds of young people—and, for that matter, in the minds of older citizens as well.

The emergence of our country as a great military power, having world-wide political responsibilities, has also affected our educational system. Greater emphasis on science, mathematics, and modern languages in secondary schools and colleges, new area institutes, and schools of international affairs in the universities, advanced courses in the esoteric languages and customs of the Far East and Africa—

these educational developments not only reflect the widening scientific and geographic interests of modern business; they are also a response to urgent requirements of national security. But it is in the area of research, rather than teaching, where the impact of the defense establishment on our universities has been particularly felt. Colleges, universities, and research centers associated with universities spent in the aggregate $460 million on the performance of research and development in 1953, with something over half of this sum financed by the Federal government. Last year, the sum so spent was six-and-one-half times as large, and the federally-financed portion rose to 70 per cent. Clearly, Federal funds are mainly responsible for the extraordinary growth of research activities in universities, and the chief—although by no means the sole—reason for this governmental involvement is the intensive search for new knowledge on the part of defense-related agencies. During 1963–1966, the Department of Defense, the Atomic Energy Commission, and the Space Administration together accounted for five-eighths of the dollar value of Federal grants for research and development to institutions of higher learning, and their proportion in immediately preceding years was even larger.

The huge influx of governmental research funds has served to enrich the intellectual life of numerous colleges and universities, especially in the larger institutions where the grants have been mainly concentrated. By virtue of research grants, professors have better equipment to work with and more technical assistance than they had in former times. They also travel more, keep in closer contact with their counterparts in other universities, and mingle more freely with government officials, business executives, and scientists working for private industry. The gulf that previously separated a university from the larger interests of the community and the nation has therefore narrowed very significantly.

However, governmental research grants have created problems for universities as well as new opportunities for useful service.

The greater interest of a faculty in research is not infrequently accompanied by lesser devotion to teaching. No little part of the time set aside for research may in practice be consumed by travel and conferences of slight scientific value. However welcome grants from military and space agencies may be, their concentration on the physical and engineering sciences makes it more difficult for a university to maintain the balance among various branches of learning that is so essential to the intellectual and moral improvement of man. Some military contracts involve classified research, and the secrecy which attends such work introduces an entirely foreign note in institutions that have traditionally taken a strong pride in completely free and uninhibited communication among scholars. Not less serious is the tendency, which appears to be growing among university scholars, to forsake the research to which they are drawn by intellectual curiosity in favor of projects that have been designed by, or contrived to suit the tastes of, government officials or others who take care of the financing. All universities and many of our colleges are struggling with this and other problems that the defense sector has created or accentuated.

The danger of diminished independence is not confined to research activities. If college or university presidents no longer speak out as vigorously on national issues as they did a generation or two ago, one major reason is that the institutions over whose destiny they preside have become heavily dependent on Federal contracts and subsidies. Even professors who are benefiting from Federal research grants or consulting relationships, or who expect to be able to do so in the future, have been learning the occasional value of studied reticence. And if discretion is tempering the spirit of forthright questioning and criticism in our universities, its power is all the stronger in the business world. It is hardly in the interest of businessmen to criticize their customers publicly, and by far the largest customer of the business world is clearly the Federal government itself. Some firms sell all and many sell a good part of what they produce to the Federal government, and there are always others that hope to be in a position to do likewise in the future.

To be sure, the great majority of business executives, even those who manage very large enterprises, prefer commercial markets to governmental business; but they have become so sensitive nowadays to the regulatory powers of government that they rarely articulate their thoughts on national issues in public. Trade union leaders are typically more candid and outspoken on governmental issues than business executives; but they too have become dependent in varying degrees on the goodwill of government officials and therefore often deem tact or reticence the better part of wisdom. Not only that, but it is no longer unusual for the government in power, whether the administration be in Democratic or Republican hands, to suggest to prominent businessmen, trade union leaders, attorneys, journalists, or university professors that they support publicly this or that administration proposal. And men of public distinction at times comply regardless of their beliefs, perhaps because they are flattered by the attention accorded them, or because they vaguely expect some advantage from going along, or simply because they feel that they dare not do otherwise. Thus the gigantic size to which the Federal government has grown, for which the defense sector bears a heavy but by no means exclusive responsibility, has been tending to erode perceptibly, although not yet alarmingly as the open discussion of the war in Vietnam indicates, the spirit of rational and constructive dissent without which a democracy cannot flourish.

The huge size of military budgets and incomplete disclosure concerning their management carry with them also the danger of political abuse. Since money spent in the interest of national security necessarily has economic effects, the government in power may sometimes be tempted to ease domestic problems by adjusting the scale or direction of military spending. For example, raw materials may be stockpiled beyond the minimum military target, or the target itself may be revised upward, in order to grant some relief to a depressed industry. Or at a time of general economic slack, the government may begin to look upon military spending as if it were a public works program. Worse still, considerations of political advantage may play a role in deciding whether contracts are placed in one area rather than another, or with this firm instead of that. Such practices confuse military officers, lead to waste, and might even exacerbate international relations. Nevertheless, they are not entirely unknown to history, including our own. Fortunately, our government officials have generally been reluctant to tamper with something so fundamental to the nation as its defense establishment; and even on the rare occasions when they have strayed from virtue, the sluggishness of a governmental bureaucracy in carrying out any plan has kept down the scale of mischief. But if politics is ever effectively computerized, as some students believe it will be, we may have less protection against political abuse within the defense sector in the future.

Any enlargement of the economic power of government, whether brought about by military expenditures or through other causes, can eventually result in some infringement of liberty. However, because of the sense of urgency in troubled times, the requirements of national security may lead more directly to restriction of freedom. Necessary though the draft may be, it still constitutes compulsion of the individual by the state. Necessary though security clearances may be, they still constitute an invasion of privacy. Necessary though passport regulations may be, they still restrict the freedom of individuals to travel where they choose. Fortunately, the vitality of our democracy has thus far proved sufficient to limit restrictions of freedoms such as these. Not only that, it has enabled us to put an end to the nightmare of McCarthyism, to suppress the interest of the Central Intelligence Agency in our colleges and universities, and even to fight the war in Vietnam without imposing price and wage controls. We cannot take it for granted, however, that our formidable defense establishment will not give rise to more serious dangers to our liberties and the democratic process in the future.

IV

Throughout the ages, philosophers and religious teachers have lamented the horrors of war and searched for the keys to peace. Yet their noblest thought has been frustrated by the course of human events. Our country has been more fortunate than most, but we have had our share of the destruction of life and property that is the universal coin of warfare. Every American of age fifty or over has lived through two world wars, the Korean War, and now the smaller but still very costly and protracted struggle in Vietnam. When this war ends, military expenditures will probably decline for a while, as they have in fact after every war in our history. We cannot look forward, however, to demobilization on anything like the scale experienced after World War I or World War II, when the military budget was reduced by about 90 per cent within three years.

The reason for the difference, of course, is that the cold war is still with us, just as it was when the Korean hostilities ended. After the cessation of that conflict, the defense budget was reduced merely by a fifth. If the cost of the Vietnam War remains at approximately the current rate, it is doubtful whether a ceasefire will be followed by a reduction of even the Korean magnitude. A return to the defense budget of fiscal 1964 or 1965 would indeed involve a cut of roughly 35 per cent from this year's expenditure; but in the absence of a dramatic change in our international relations, this is quite unlikely. In the first place, prices are higher at present than they were in 1964 or 1965, and they will probably be higher still when the war phases out. In the second place, it may well be necessary for us to keep many more troops in Vietnam after a ceasefire than was the case in Korea and also to become more heavily involved in the task of reconstruction. In the third place, while stocks of military equipment were built up during the Korean War, they have been seriously depleted—particularly for the Reserve and National Guard units—by Vietnam. They will need to be rebuilt when hostilities come to an end, and this demand will be reinforced by the deferred procurement of newer models to replace equipment now in inventory.

Nevertheless, a sizeable reduction of military spending will take place in the year or two after the ceasefire, and we will have the opportunity to concentrate more of our resources on the arts of peace. In the past, the American economy has demonstrated a remarkable ability to adjust speedily to cutbacks in military spending, and we can be confident of doing so again. After World War I the conversion from war to peace was carried out with only a mild and brief setback in total economic activity. The like happened after World War II, despite the fact that more than two-fifths of our nation's resources were devoted to military uses at the peak of the war. Between 1945 and 1946, spending on the manufacture of defense goods dropped drastically and the number of men in the armed forces declined from 11.5 million to 3.5 million. Nevertheless, the unemployment rate remained below 4 per cent. The termination of the Korean War was followed by a recession but the return of peace was not its sole cause. In any event, unemployment during this recession was less serious at its worst than during the recession which came just before or just after it. With the experience that our country has gained during the past two decades in coping with economic fluctuations, with both the Executive and the Congress obviously eager to prevent unemployment, and with plans for dealing with post-Vietnam problems already beginning to take shape, there should not be much difficulty in adjusting Federal tax, expenditure, and credit policies so as to maintain aggregate monetary demand at the level needed to assure reasonably full employment when hostilities cease. Some sizeable adjustments will still need to be made by numerous communities and industries; but even they should prove manageable since the military cutbacks are likely to be largely concentrated on items produced by business firms that are closely oriented to our diversified and resilient civilian markets.

The highly specialized aerospace, electronics, and communications industries will probably not bear much of the burden of post-Vietnam cutbacks. Indeed, once the curve of military spending turns upward again, as it well may two or three years after the ceasefire, these are the very industries that are likely to benefit most from the dynamism of modern technology. To maintain a sufficient strategic superiority to deter any aggressor, we have been devoting vast sums to research and development, as I have already noted. The fantastic new weapons and weapon systems devised by our scientists and engineers soon render obsolete some of the existing devices, which themselves were new and revolutionary only a short time ago. But until the new devices are ready. those that were only recently new cannot be abandoned and may even need to be augmented. Meanwhile, strategic concepts may shift, as they did during the sixties from reliance on massive nuclear deterrents to developing a capability for limited warfare and counterinsurgency operations. One way or another, therefore, costs tend to multiply all around. The Soviet Union, of course, will not stand still while our military prowess increases. On the contrary, it is striving through a remarkably enterprising and inventive military-industrial complex of its own to establish military parity, if not actual supremacy. For example, we have recently learned of the deployment of an anti-ballistic missile system around Moscow and Leningrad, of a novel ship-to-ship missile of Russian origin fired in the Mediterranean, and of the apparent development of an orbital bomb capability by the Soviet Union. Communist China has also been developing, and with greater speed than was generally anticipated, the ability to make and deliver sophisticated weapons. In turn, our military establishment, besides innovating vigorously on its own, keeps devising countermeasures to what the Russians or Chinese have or may have in hand. Both its reaction and its fresh challenge to potential aggressors can be expected to become stronger once Vietnam no longer requires top priority.

As we look beyond the cessation of hostilities in Vietnam, we therefore need to recognize that the scale of defense expenditures has, to a significant degree, become a self-reinforcing process. Its momentum derives not only from the energy of military planners, contractors, scientists, and engineers. To some degree it is abetted also by the practical interests and anxieties of ordinary citizens. Any announcement that a particular defense installation will be shut down, or that a particular defense contract will be phased out, naturally causes concern among men and women who, however much they abhor war and its trappings, have become dependent for their livelihood on the activity whose continuance is threatened. With a large part of our economy devoted to defense activities, the military-industrial complex has thus acquired a constituency including factory workers, clerks, secretaries, even grocers and barbers. Local politicians and community leaders may not find it easy to plead for the extension of activities that no longer serve a military purpose. Many, nevertheless, manage to overcome such scruples. Indeed, candidates for the Congress have been known to claim that they are uniquely qualified to ward off military closings or even to bring new contracts to their districts, and their oratory has not gone unrewarded by the electorate. The vested interest that numerous communities have acquired in defense activities may therefore continue to run up costs on top of the rising budgets generated by the momentum of competing military technologies.

If this analysis is at all realistic, the military-industrial complex will remain a formidable factor in our economic and social life in the calculable future. It will continue to command a large, possibly even an increasing, part of our resources. It will continue to strain Federal finances. It will continue to test the vigor of our economy and the vitality of our democratic institutions. It will continue to confuse understanding by suggesting to many foreign citizens, as it sometimes does even to our own, that our national prosperity is based on huge military spending, when in fact we could be much more prosperous without it.

For all these reasons, while we need to recognize the high and honorable national purpose of our military-industrial complex, we also need to remain continually vigilant of its activities and seek to protect ourselves against its possible abuses, just as we long ago learned to guard the public interest against business monopolies and as we are beginning to protect ourselves against labor monopolies.

V

The scale and activities of our defense sector are now being subjected to a searching public discussion. Two major schools of political thought have become locked in a contest for the mind and soul of America. One school draws much of its strength from the revolution of military technology, the other from the revolution of rising expectations. One school tends to regard communism as a centrally directed conspiracy that threatens our survival as a free people. The other school believes that communism is breaking up into independent national movements, and sees the main threat to free institutions in the deterioration of our cities and the sickness of our society. One school seeks overwhelming military power to deter fresh Communist adventures, and is willing to risk war in order to prevent the geographic expansion of communism. The other school seeks wider social justice and better economic conditions for Negroes and others who have not participated fully in the advance of prosperity, and holds that the force of moral example can contribute more to our national security than additional bombs or missiles.

Both schools have focused attention on the Federal budget and neither has been satisfied by the treatment accorded its claims. From 1955 to 1965, Federal spending on nondefense activities increased faster than spending on defense. Since then, defense expenditures have gone up more rapidly, though not much more rapidly. Looking to the future, professional economists never tire of pointing out that our growing economy will make it possible to have more butter and, if they are needed, also more guns, even as we have been managing to do while the war in Vietnam is being waged. Their reassurance, however, does not satisfy those who feel that our national security requires not just more guns, but many more guns, and that we therefore need to give up some of our butter. Nor does it satisfy those who feel that we need not just more butter, but much more butter, and that our statistics of the gross national product are misleading us by their failure to allow for the pollution of our water, the poisons in our air, the noise of our streets, the rats in our slums, the rioting in our cities, and the destruction of life on our highways. Debate along these lines has reached a high pitch of intensity and even bitterness as the war in Vietnam has dragged out. It has become a divisive force, and it has brought anguish to our people. Its effect on the conduct of the war, however, is likely to count for less than its effect on the general direction of our foreign and military policy in the future.

For the debate is demonstrating to thoughtful citizens that our national security depends not only on awesome military forces. It depends also on the strength of our economic system, on the wholesomeness of our social and political life, and particularly on how well governmental objectives express the national will and purpose. As this lesson sinks in, we will want to try far harder than we ever have, both in our personal capacity and through our government, to bring the armaments race under decent control. And if the cracks of freedom within the Communist system of tyranny widen, as they well may in coming decades, we can count on being joined in this quest by the people of the Soviet Union and eventually by the people of mainland China as well. That, at any rate, is the only real basis for hope of saving ourselves and the entire human family from catastrophe.

15. Profits Without Productivity

Seymour Melman

In 1959, "A group of foreign businessmen was touring the Underwood typewriter plant in Hartford, Conn. A workman turned from the assembly line and asked, 'You guys Italians?' One of the visitors nodded. 'You here to learn how to make typewriters?' The reply was soft but firm: 'No. We are here to teach you.'" The visitors were in fact members of the new top management team which Olivetti of Italy sent over to refurbish the Underwood firm.

The United States typewriter industry is an example of what can happen when the depletion of metal-working production equipment and technique continues over a long period of time. There are a number of important typewriter factories in the New England area, which once supplied virtually all the typewriter requirements of the United States. However, by 1963, about 60% of the typewriters sold in America were being imported.

One of the major typewriter-producing factories in the United States is housed in a graceful, old, multistory factory that is a fine specimen of late nineteenth-century New England textile-mill architecture. While a beginning was recently made toward modernizing this plant, the manufacturing continued with machinery that will soon qualify for museum status; while painting was done with ultramodern automatic equipment, the factory continued making small parts on lathes turned by overhead belts just like those in illustrations of the early Industrial Revolution. The management of this firm, over a long period, withdrew profits and did not reinvest in new production equipment. Research and development were substantially

From *Our Depleted Society*, Chapter 3, by Seymour Melman. Copyright © 1965 by Seymour Melman. Reprinted by permission of Holt, Rinehart & Winston, Inc., New York.

neglected and newer developments in production were not introduced. The firm relied on the stockpile of "Yankee know-how" and mechanical ingenuity that was available among its foremen and skilled workers. That class of production technique is not adequate for producing efficiently enough to absorb modern wage rates, while manufacturing a quality product at a price low enough to sell. I think it noteworthy that the Olivetti company of Italy purchased one of the major American typewriter firms, Underwood, and immediately began modernization of its factories and methods; but certainly the interests of Olivetti, with its Italian-based operation, will also be served by supplying its American sales organization with products from its home-based factories. Profits will probably be sustained from sales in the United States, but an important part of the production base of Olivetti-Underwood is not in this country.

Among the depleted industries the pattern varies: profits from U.S. sales while production is done abroad by foreign firms buying into American companies; American firms maintaining a production base in the United States, but putting fresh capital abroad; profitability maintained for a few firms that service a government market—as in shipbuilding—while the whole level of activity of the industry declines; general decline in an industry owing to long-standing management failure to invest enough in new technology—as in fishery industries, railroads. The common feature of all the depleted industries is less work in the United States.

The one industry which may be said to be most basic to a society utilizing metal and machines is the machine-tool industry. Machine tools are usually understood to include all those machines that remove metal in the form of chips, or that shape metal by pressing it between dies. The products of this industry, the lathes, milling machines, drills, and the like, are machines which are used to manufacture all other machines.

In 1963, the United States reached the position of operating the oldest stock of metal-working machinery of any industrial country in the world. In that year 64% of American machine tools were ten years old, or older. The figure for West Germany was 55%, for the Soviet Union about 50% (a declining percentage), while the American stock continues to age.

Here is a portrait of antiquity in American production. The percentage of machines in use that was twenty years old or older in 1963:

	%
Machine Tools	20
Ships and Railroad Equipment	41
Construction, Mining, Materials Handling	25
Precision Instruments and Mechanisms	15
Electrical Equipment	16
Automobiles	23
Office Machines	14
Special Industry Machinery	28

Since 1925 the McGraw-Hill organization has been conducting national "inventories" of the machine tools and other equipment in American industry. The following data show the proportion of metal-cutting machines in American industry found to be ten years old or older at the indicated times:

1925 44	1945 38
1930 52	1949 43
1935 67	1953 55
1940 72	1958 60
	1963 64

The growing age of the machine tools in use in American factories means that 2.2 million basic manufacturing machines are not being replaced by newer equipment that could incorporate many technical improvements. The replacement is not made because the firms using the existing machine tools are unable to justify investment in new machines except when the savings from their introduction will pay off the initial cost of the machine within a period of perhaps four to five years, or even sooner.

This means that it is not enough for new machines to have a higher output per hour of use, that is, greater productivity. It means that it is also necessary for the new machine's price to be low enough to permit higher physical productivity to be registered in the form of a lower production cost—almost immediately. Owing to relatively high production costs, the prices of machine tools during the last decade have been too high to be attractive to machine-tool users on a large scale. The result is that the demand for American-built machine tools has been so low that the metal-working machinery stock of the United States industry has been aging. The net effect of this stagnation, relatively speaking, is that the metal-working industries of the United States have a less efficient set of basic production machines available to them than would be the case if machine tools produced here were lower in price.

The high cost of producing machine tools in the United States can be traced to the market for machine tools which has been classically unstable. This instability has made it difficult for the machine-tool makers to introduce high-efficiency operations into their factories. Therefore, the instruments of mass production are being fabricated in factories that do not themselves use mass-production techniques. In order to preserve the position of single firms, managements attempt to diversify the products produced, and to differentiate their own product design from those of other firms. As a result the firms of this industry become involved in producing small quantities of many products. This raises the cost of manufacturing and becomes the basis for a high selling price. At the same time, standardization is not pursued by the managements of the machine-tool industry because that would open up the possibility of customers securing attachments or parts from other firms. Indeed, to my knowledge, there has been no extensive study of the cost-saving that might be obtained in the machine-tool industry if standardization were to be widely practiced.

In October, 1959, I produced a report for the European Productivity Agency on

"The Productivity of Operations in the Machine-Tool Industry in Western Europe." The recommendations for defining major new avenues for improving productivity in the European machine-tool industry, given in that report, apply equally well to the United States. At that time they included projected studies for discovering what proportion of machine tools could be constructed from standardized components; the possibility of building machine tools on the basis of standardized modules; devising methods for formulating and adapting design standards; defining the cost and productivity of alternative production systems for the manufacture of machine tools; problems of controlling quality on precision components in small and large quantity production; and finally, possible methods for offsetting market fluctuations in order to insure stable production conditions in this industry. The crucial fact is that no studies along these lines have been carried out, either in Western Europe, or in the machine-tool industry in the United States, where this report was widely circulated. This means that there has not even been a serious attempt to discover the possibilities for productivity improvement and cost reduction along the recommended lines.

In the last decade the American machine-tool industry has been very active in developing its overseas operation. The principal firms of the industry are involved in investment in Western Europe and elsewhere, and in licensing arrangements with foreign firms, which often enable American firms to import machine tools manufactured in Western European plants for sale through the American firms' sales organization. An examination of any current issue of the machine-tool industry's principal trade journal *American Machinist* discloses that advertising by foreign machine-tool firms has increased in importance during this period.

While the American machine-tool industry has invested in manufacturing facilities overseas, the American market for machine tools has come to include the Government as a principal customer. By 1957, it was estimated that the Federal Government owned about 15% of all the machine tools in the country and thereby became the largest single owner of such equipment, valued at about $3 billion.

The headquarters of the National Machine-Tool Builders' Association was once in Cleveland, a long-standing center of the metal-working industries; but the headquarters have been moved to Washington, D.C., which, although not a metal-working center, is now the location of the industry's principal customer. Major sales to the Department of Defense and the Atomic Energy Commission have the effect of discouraging emphasis on cost reduction in the manufacture of machine tools. For the armed services, desirous of buying machines with particular capability, have tended to give cost consideration secondary importance. Since the Department of Defense has become the single largest customer for the machine-tool industry, the industry is thereby made less sensitive to pressures from other customers for reducing the prices of its products.

At the same time the machine-tool industry of the United States has had and continues to have a world-wide reputation; the quality of its product is widely respected. Nevertheless, failure to produce quality products at low prices, because modern production techniques are not used in its operation, has the effect of leaving U.S. metal-working industries without the flow of higher-efficiency machines at modest prices which U.S. industry must have to maintain a major productivity advantage over foreign competitors—and thereby offset higher wages to American workers. If, in a given industry, U.S. wages per hour are twice those of European workers, then, in order for the American factory to be competitive, its man-hours must be twice as productive as those of the Europeans. This is only possible if the productivity margin is maintained by constant replacement with more productive equipment. That is why the slowdown in machinery replacement and an aging stock of metal-working machinery is a danger signal for the economic viability of a whole sector of American industry.

On Sunday, January 5, 1964, the New

York *Times* ran a full-page ad boldly titled "Trains vs. Planes." The text of the ad, under a page-wide photograph of a fast-moving streamliner train read:

You might think planes have the edge. Not entirely true. The new Hitachi Superexpress streaks down the tracks at a phenomenal 155 miles per hour.

When the Superexpress goes into operation in late 1964 it will equal total airline time on Tokyo-Osaka run, 320 miles in only three hours! A new era in railroading is about to begin.

Add to the speed the convenience of one carrier, no to and from airport travel, no waiting. You go downtown to downtown in one comfortable seat. The Superexpress achieves what many experts believed impossible—trains that effectively complete with aircraft.

The Superexpress is guided by electronic control in the train, a motorman, and a supervisory control room in Tokyo. The train automatically increases speed when the line is clear, slows down or stops when the line is not clear. The human error factor is eliminated.

This is only one example of Hitachi versatility in industry, any industry. Hitachi manufacturers more than 10,000 basic products from turbines and generators to transformers and trains. Anything powered by electricity and a few things that are not.

Hitachi brings you the finest first. Look for the name and buy with confidence.

There are 215,000 miles of principal railroad trackage in the United States. But the sort of capability implied in the Hitachi ad is not part of recent American experience. Both the volume and the quality of railroad service on the whole, have been deteriorating, not improving.

An examination of journals that report on railroad developments around the world shows that in Western Europe, the Soviet Union, and in the Far East, the railroads, far from being abandoned, are being intensively developed with respect to the speed and quality of both freight and passenger service. The Italian State Railway expects to raise the maximum of its top electric train to 112 miles per hour in the near future. In West Germany 1,988 miles of main rail line are being converted to standards necessary for high-speed operations, 124 miles per hour, for passenger travel. The investment for rebuilding the lines is estimated at about $416,000 per mile. In 1965 British Rail-

ways is going to institute 75-mile-per-hour fast freight flyers between the principal cities of the British Isles. British Railways is stimulating vacation and tourist travel by "car-sleeper" trains. You drive your automobile onto a flat car, and then you ride in the sleeper. In Australia, the rail system is being unified and rebuilt and the two principal cities, Melbourne and Sidney, are linked by highspeed train systems. In France, railroad timetables show 38 point-to-point runs timed at better than 75 miles per hour. The total mileage of these fast rail runs adds up to 5,597 — more than double the United States total.

The decay of the railroad system in the United States has imposed high costs for freight and passenger travel because people and freight can be carried much more cheaply by rail than by private motor vehicle.

There is no development in the United States that parallels the new Japanese express. It is perfectly obvious that this would be a superior transportation service between major American cities. But American railroads, and their equipment suppliers, Westinghouse, General Electric, General Motors, *et al.*, have become technologically inert. Innovations have been few and far between. And so deterioration of the railroads has continued; the public is serviced with more expensive transportation, while the number of railroad employees has dropped from 1,200,000 in 1950, to 700,000 in 1962.

What is the cause of this inertia? After all, alternative technical ideas are readily available. Why are they not applied?

From the standpoint of investing fresh industrial capital, the easiest way is to purchase a going, successful enterprise. Thereby, managerial, marketing, and production competence is bought in one package. Next in line of difficulty is the investment of new funds in new manufacturing facilities, in new "growth" industries. Under these conditions the investing management takes responsibility for the detailed equipment of plant, the organization of management, of staff, the training of a work force, and the development of markets.

The most difficult management situation is the technical renewal and reorganization of existing industrial operations. When the designs of products are changed, and new manufacturing methods are introduced, this immediately implies a requirement for learning new occupational skills by managers, engineers, foremen, and workers. Re-equipping factories, learning new skills, and regrouping job responsibilities on a large scale are the most difficult sorts of tasks for an industrial management. But this is precisely the requirement in the whole range of basic American industries which have operated for a long time and whose competent functioning is essential for a productive society.

In the absence of strong encouragement and assistance for industrial updating by industry associations, by government, and by journals of opinion, it is no wonder that the managers of many industrial firms have sought easier ways of handling the investment of their funds, thereby making it possible to earn profits on investment while not advancing the productivity of many of America's basic industries. After all, advancing productivity is not a conventional yardstick of business success. If a firm shows "growth" and profits, its management is usually regarded as competent.

The firms in these industries have lacked the industrial engineering staffs and allied specialists needed for continuous technical and managerial review and renewal. The firms in civilian machinery industries that are economically and technically healthy have generally had this self-renewal tradition.

The sewing-machine industry offers a good example of how money-making and basic economic deterioration can go hand in hand. The Singer Company operates a factory in Elizabethport, New Jersey, that has a special claim for distinction. It is the last place in the United States where household sewing machines are manufactured. About 10,000 people worked there in 1947. By 1964 about 3,000 workers were left to man a factory composed of primarily antiquated manufacturing equipment.

Aged equipment, together with rather old-fashioned engineering and operating methods, have been used to produce fine sewing machines, but at high cost and high price.

Yet, at the same time, *Fortune* magazine wrote about the "Spryer Singer" in December, 1963, acclaimed recent sales of $631 millions and profits of $29.2 millions, and declared the Singer of today a company ". . . aggressively looking to the future instead of resting on its past."

Where did all this money come from? Classically, we understand that new wealth must be created by someone's productive work. The financial vigor of the Singer firm contrasts with the declining quantity and relatively low efficiency of its American production operations in the sewing-machine field.

All the sewing machines needed in the United States used to be manufactured by American factories. By 1964 about 1½ million sewing machines were sold for American home use, but some 66% of them were imported, mainly from Japan and Western Europe. How did this happen? Let us understand that no great technological breakthroughs have been scored in sewing-machine design for many years. Is it possible that the level of wages paid to American workers makes the economic production of sewing machines impossible in the United States? That cannot be the case since sewing machines enjoy a market of about 1,500,000 units per year in this country, and that surely is a market for mass-production manufacturing. In the case of the automobile industry, the record is that with the highest wages in the world to automobile workers, the major U.S. firms are still able to produce cars at the lowest price per pound of fabricated vehicle in the world. What makes this possible is high productivity of labor by means of mechanization and systematic organization of the work. What happened to the United States sewing-machine industry?

The essential weakness of the Singer operation in Elizabethport is this: In order to produce sewing machines that are competitive with the output of Japanese workers, paid one sixth of United States wages, it is essential that productivity in the U.S. plants exceed the productivity of operations in Japan by a factor as much as five times as large. But such productivity has been made impossible by the failure of the Singer management to install modern high-productivity equipment which could indeed produce up to the desired level. The production workers in Elizabethport operate a stock of largely aged equipment. For example, 40% of their foundry equipment was twenty years old or more by 1963. Nationally, only 5% of foundry equipment was that old. Of the metal-cutting machine tools in the factory 80% were over twenty years old, as contrasted with 37% of that vintage in U.S. manufacturing as a whole.

Furthermore, redesigning of the product (to simplify its manufacture) has been neglected. For example, the Singer Company has had no standardization system for components that makes use of conventional screw threads. The firm manufactures its own screws, and the tools for making them to special dimensions. This is costly and technically wasteful. In another era this may have seemed a shrewd way to generate a captive spare-parts business, but by the middle of this century it became clear that the manufacture of parts in relatively small quantities made production costs too high. Singer has 91 colors for their machines, and over 80,000 different parts in inventory. There are about 100 sorts of flat, metallic washers with less than 1″ outside diameter. The Singer Company, and its former U.S. competitors, have not bothered to do the job of standardization now being done so competently by the Japanese sewing-machine industry.

How did the Singer Company develop its strong financial position under such conditions of depleted technical efficiency?

The Singer Company and its reputable sewing machines have been household words in the United States and other countries for over a century; Singer employs 81,000 people in 95 countries. Since the Second World War the Singer Company has expanded in the following ways: New sewing-machine factories have been erected abroad; production of new products has been undertaken abroad, either directly, or by other firms, to Singer's order; sewing machines and other products produced abroad have been sold there and also imported into the United States for sale through Singer's far-flung retailing organization. Finally, within the United States, Singer has bought up several going concerns, including several in the "space age" industries.

By 1953 Singer factories for sewing machines were located in 6 countries. Thereafter, an expansion program was set in motion to manufacture in 16 countries, with 12 additional assembly plants and parts factories in various lands. In Western Europe, and in the Far East, Singer undertook the sales of various household appliances manufactured there to its requirements. These included vacuum cleaners, washing machines, refrigerators, hi-fi equipment, typewriters, and TV sets.

Sewing machines made in Singer's plant in Scotland are imported for sale in the United States; so are portable typewriters made in Europe. In 1963, on the West Coast, Singer began to market Japanese-made TV sets carrying the Singer name. No sophistication in production methods is required to use low-wage labor for making products to sell competitively in the United States.

At the same time, the Singer management has bought up companies in the United States in various fields: military cameras, textile machinery, electrical and electronic instruments, and data processing machines. All the firms involved, of which the Friden business-machines firm is most important, were successful operations when Singer bought them. *Fortune* in December, 1963, reported that these non-sewing-machine firms made up about 20% of Singer's sales in 1962, and contributed 25% of the firm's total profits.

The formula for financial success adds up to this: expansion of production and sales abroad; expansion of ownership in the United States; expansion of sales in the United States, based upon overseas production with low-wage labor; *contraction* of sewing-machine production within the

United States, owing to failure to offset U.S. costs by improved productivity.

By the conventional tests of financial success the Singer record is entirely commendable. By the test of participation in a viable American production system, the Singer record is calamitous.

If this sort of pattern were the performance of a few firms, a rarity, a set of exotic contrasts, then there would be little point in pursuing this analysis. But the combination of financial success and decaying productive capability has become a far-ranging pattern that threatens the viability of the American industrial system at its base.

The shipbuilding and ship-operating industries are good illustrations of managements that are financially successful while contributing to industrial depletion.

The United States still possesses one of the largest merchant fleets in the world, but between 1955 and 1963, it was the only major merchant fleet in the world that declined in size while all others registered considerable growth. The principal maritime countries of the West increased the tonnage of their merchant fleets from 72 to 96 million gross tons between 1955 and 1963, while American tonnage declined from 25 to 22 million gross tons. Exactly what is the nature of the incapacity that seems to have seized the American merchant marine?

Recently constructed Swedish shipyards, equipped to build vessels of the largest size, are highly mechanized; closed-circuit television is used for central control of internal movement of steel plates, and the like. In one of the yards a vessel is assembled inside a building. As each section of the ship is built, mainly from prefabricated assemblies, it is pushed out of the building into a dock area by hydraulic jack. Then work begins on the next section, and then the next, in a continuous pattern, until, like toothpaste squeezed out of a tube, the whole vessel is in the outdoor dry dock from which it is finally floated. By such methods it has been possible to produce a ship of the largest merchant class (a 36,000-ton ore carrier) in 27 weeks, working only one shift. Compare this with the customary 40 weeks spent doing the same job by conventional methods.

Unfortunately, the point of all this is that the semiautomated shipyard is located in Sweden, not the United States, and further, that the plausible methods of modern production engineering that have been applied in the Swedish yard do not exhaust the possibilities of further technological refinements in the art of shipbuilding. And virtually none of this is going on in American shipyards.

In 1964 the United States attained the distinction of operating the world's oldest oil-tanker fleet. The tanker fleets of other countries, notably that of the Soviet Union, with an annual increase of 29% since 1953, have been growing while the American fleet has been diminishing. In 1962 only 9% of the ocean-borne cargo of the United States was carried by vessels of American registry, as against 43% in 1954. The U.S. performance in 1962 was the lowest per cent among the principal maritime countries of the West; the merchant marine of France carried 59% of its cargo; Denmark, 23%; Sweden, 33%; and the United Kingdom, 52%.

Why is the merchant marine of the United States declining? Basically, because the cost of building merchant ships in the United States has been about twice the cost of building similar ships elsewhere in the world. Three important factors contribute to the incompetence of U.S. commercial shipbuilding: the system of subsidies to shipbuilders and ship operators; the dominance of naval shipbuilding in the United States; and, finally, the failure of the shipbuilding industry to make use of modern design and production-engineering techniques.

The subsidy system for shipbuilders and ship operators follows a remarkable pattern. Under the Merchant Marine Act of 1936, provision was made for a differential construction subsidy for vessels of American registry to be used in the foreign commerce of the United States. This subsidy may not exceed 55% of the cost of the vessel, which means that if you are the prospective buyer of a commercial vessel, you go to a naval architect in the United

States and commission a set of drawings for a vessel to your specifications. You then proceed to get a quotation on the price of building such a vessel from an American, and a foreign, shipbuilder. If you want the vessel built in the United States, you can get the difference between the American quoted price and the foreign quoted price from the Federal Government. This will amount to about 50% of the U.S. quoted price, because shipbuilding costs are twice as high in the United States as elsewhere. Obviously, this style of operating cannot offer much incentive to the American shipbuilding industry to improve the efficiency of its operation and make the changes necessary to improve productivity and thereby equal overseas ship costs and prices.

Then there are the operating subsidies. An operating differential subsidy is given to American ship operators to place American vessels on a parity with those of foreign competitors. This is based on the difference between "the fair and reasonable cost of insurance, maintenance, repairs, and wage and subsistence of officers and crews, and the estimated costs of the same items if the vessels were operating under foreign revenue." Such payments are authorized by the Merchant Marine Act of 1936. At the same time, the Act provides that any profits made by the ship operator in excess of 10% of the capital employed are to be shared 50-50 between the ship operator and the Federal Government. This subsidy system does not apply to domestic trade.

In 1963, the construction subsidy cost the Federal Government $91,996,000. The operating subsidy cost the Federal Government $220,677,000 in 1963.

In 1963, in the various navy yards of the United States, 90,000 men were employed; 118,000 men worked in the private shipbuilding industries. However, about 60% of the tonnage under construction in the private shipyards has recently consisted of naval vessels. Accordingly, we may estimate that about 47,000 men were employed in commercial shipbuilding in 1963, while 161,000 men were employed in military shipbuilding. The number of men working in commercial and naval work

is important because of the sharp difference in the costs of ship construction in each case.

The Polaris-type submarine has become an important class of naval shipbuilding. These vessels, excluding major weapons, are built at the cost of about $12 per pound. On the other hand, large oil tankers constructed in the United States cost about 20¢ per pound. This dramatic difference in cost between naval and commercial vessels also defines the gap in the style of design and methods of construction.

The essential point is that in naval construction, cost considerations take a definite second place, while for commercial vessels, cost considerations must be paramount as the criterion requisite to their construction. A production manager in one of the major shipbuilding firms once put the contrast between the two types of shipbuilding to me as follows: "If I were asked to construct naval vessels in the same shipyard with commercial vessels, the first thing I would do is erect a very large fence between the naval and commercial sections of the yard. I would regard this as essential to prevent contamination of the standard of work in each case by the other."

The methods of designing and building commercial vessels in the United States are so anachronistic that a cautious estimate points to the possibility of reducing the manufacturing costs of commercial vessels by 30%. A more adventurous exploration of technological possibilities, already encompassed by other industries, leads to a possible 50% reduction of shipbuilding costs. The latter case would make the elaborate Federal subsidy system unnecessary, and American shipbuilders would once more be competitive in the world shipbuilding market. At the same time, this cost reduction would be an incentive for American shipping firms to purchase and use American-built ships. Both developments would cause expanded employment in the shipbuilding industry, and in ship operations, even though more sophisticated productivity techniques would be used both in the construction and operation of commercial vessels.

However, the possibility for substantially

improved productivity in shipbuilding awaits reorganization of methods within the industry. The principal commercial shipbuilding firms still do virtually no research on ship design. Neither do they operate substantial design organization. The naval architects who design ocean-going vessels operate as a separate profession, removed from the shipbuilding industry itself. This is like having a chemical industry with no chemists on the staff, or an electric-power industry without electrical engineers.

Further, the technique of standardizing ship components is virtually unknown. There is no active shipbuilding standardization movement in the United States. A contrast may be seen in Japan where the shipbuilding industry has a vigorous program of standards development. The Japanese industry has published a major volume depicting its standards for ship structure as an instrument for industry-wide advertising throughout the world.

Since research and development in shipbuilding in the United States is concentrated in the naval field, one might expect the state of the art to develop rapidly in the naval-vessel direction, while the technology of commercial shipbuilding, design, and construction remained stagnant; and that is exactly what has been happening. The result is that even construction subsidies of as much as 50% have not been sufficient to turn the American shipbuilding industry into a vigorous builder of commercial vessels.

As a result of these several factors—depending upon Government subsidies, more money and imagination invested in naval construction, and a technology of design and production unsuited to cost conditions—the American shipbuilding and ship-operating industries are reaching a terminal condition of depletion. Mr. Ralph E. Casey, President of the American Merchant Marine Institute, warned in March, 1964, that unless major policy decisions were made soon, the United States must prepare to lose more than half of its merchant fleet in a very few years. He pointed out that in 1945, with 5,000 ships, the United States operated

the largest merchant fleet in the world. By 1953 the number had dropped to 1,258, and ten years later to 983. Mr Casey's warning was directed to the Congress, pressing the Federal Government for even greater subsidies and more Federal funds to sustain the merchant marine in its present style of operation.

But the point is rather that the technological and economic renewal of the merchant marine, and the shipbuilding industry, requires a fundamental change away from a style of operation that has up until now generated economic and technical depletion. This change is required *before* the introduction of new technology and fresh productive capital. Such an orientation has yet to be considered seriously by the shipbuilding industry or the merchant-marine operators.

The United States fishing industry, with 3,000 aging and relatively inefficient fishing vessels, is closely linked to the depletion process in the shipbuilding industry. Modern, large capacity trawlers operating in fleets around ocean-going fish-processing vessels are unknown to America. Elsewhere in the world, trawler fleets of modern design operate with high efficiency to produce an increasing stock of fish food from the world's oceans. In the past ten years the United States has dropped behind Peru, Communist China, and Soviet Russia and now ranks fifth among the fishing nations. The tendency is for the American fishing fleet to decrease in size while the total market for fish grows. As a result, the value of U.S. fishery imports during the period 1953–63 has exceeded exports by more than $3 billion.

A hopelessly inefficient fishing fleet cannot hold the world market, or even serve the domestic American market. But there is no American center, or institute, or set of firms now practicing design for, or construction of, modern fishing vessels. The technological talent that might be applied to this function has been substantially pre-empted by naval design and naval ship construction. Therefore, American fisheries which provided employment for 263,000 men in 1950 could employ only 217,000 by 1962. Like the merchant marine and major shipbuilding industries, the fishery and fishing-craft-construction industry could provide an increasing volume of employment because of the predictable expansion of the market for fish products. But the men and the capital required for this industry have instead been given strong incentive either to move abroad and operate with low-cost labor in foreign countries, or to abandon the industry altogether. The fishing industry is therefore in decline at the very same time that the market for its product in the United States is rapidly expanding and being supplied, increasingly, by imports. . . .

Do high wages necessarily mean high costs and high prices?

In response to economic incentives, American agriculture has drawn upon varied technological capability to make possible production of foodstuffs in prodigious volume at low cost. Research support from the agricultural experiment stations, new developments by farm-machinery firms and the chemical industries — all of these made possible the growth of U.S. agricultural productivity to the point where U.S. farm products are the single largest class of U.S. exports able to hold their own and then some in many world markets.

Again, the point is not that the United States can or should function as an autarchic economy. Rather, I regard these data as evidence against the proposition that a high wage automatically means high product cost and price. What counts is the wage and other cost per unit of product. Essentially, the choices in methods available in modern technology make it feasible to offset high labor and capital costs by efficient methods in production and organization. High wages can be combined with low prices.

But making this happen takes some doing; capital, management talent, and technical skills must be systematically applied in a self-renewal process. During the 1950's and 1960's, capital has been available in large amounts in the United States. On the other hand, important kinds of managerial talent and technical skills have been in short supply.

During the last decade, there has been a growing alarm over reduction in employment owing to mechanization and automation in industrial and other kinds of work. The depleted industries manifest decline in employment not because of change in the way the work is done, but *because of the decline in the total amount of work performed by these industries in the United States.* The growing reliance on imports, in industries integral to an industrial system, has resulted in a decline in employment in the United States. This decline is unrelated to whether or not the factories supplying the United States from abroad were owned by American firms.

Our economists have tended to view the decline of a firm or an industry as part of an ordinary and recurring process of the decay and growth of the enterprise. The assumption has been that if a given management is not competent to meet the market demand for a product, another management will in due course recognize opportunity, move into the field, and serve the market anew. This natural process of economic correction has been substantially checkmated by the development of government-controlled industries and markets dominated by the military sphere of society. By offering superior salaries that could be absorbed by selling to Federal defense agencies, the military contractors, and their nonprofit adjuncts, have absorbed a massive proportion of the available technological talent. At the same time, capital has been attracted to the new rapid growth of defense and space industries. The result is that the normal process of correction of economic depletion has been rendered inoperative.

Another aspect of the depletion process is the growth of dependence on foreign sources of supply. Here again, economists have tended to view this as an essentially desirable pattern when it occurs for particular firms and industries. The reasoning has been: If foreign sources of supply are more economic, then those suppliers should be drawn upon. Let each country produce and sell what it is naturally competent to do. In that way, there will be an international division of labor and everyone will be served from sources of supply that are most efficient. Thereby every country will stand to benefit. The awkwardness of the present problem, however, arises from the fact that the depletion of American industries has not been a spotty, random affair, relegated to a few firms. In-

	UNITED STATES	COMMON MARKET
Military Spending as % of GNP	9.2	4.2
Machinery and Equipment as % of GNP	5.4	10.2

stead, the process of depletion has been concentrated in the class of machinery-producing industries which lie at the base of any modern industrial system. The conventional economist's view does not take into account our present condition, under which industrial depletion has become epidemic, and the "natural" economic correction process frustrated by the unavailability of fresh capital and technological talent. While depletion in industry has been spreading, the public is reassured

by reports of general economic growth. At the same time talent, capital, and society-wide attention have been lavished on the defense and space industries.

The American way of using up productive capital and talent has not been followed in the countries of the Common Market. Here is the contrast with the United States in 1960:

The Common Market countries have enjoyed healthy economic growth and full employment.

Many people, including some engineers, have concluded that the depleted industries are those concerned with "unsophisticated" products and technologies, and might just as well be located abroad. These industries, badly needed for a healthy economy, have not been given technological updating in product design or production methods.

Research, Development and Growth

16. Federal Science, an Economic Drag, Not Propellent

Amitai Etzioni

The United States is presently the most affluent country in the world. However, there is wide concern about our rate of economic growth, which is surpassed by the Western European countries (which give us increasing competition) and even many of the new, underdeveloped countries, from Brazil to Formosa. In its campaign to get America moving again, the New

Frontier administration placed high on its list of priorities an increase in our rate of economic growth. But by the end of 1963 our growth rate was still only half of the rate of many other countries. The race to the moon was supposed to invigorate our science and technology and thus act as a propeller on our economy; instead there is enough evidence to convince a jury that it served as a drag.

Until recently we thought that, as the London *Economist* of October 5, 1963, put it, "prosperity depends on investment, investment on technology and technology on science. Ergo, prosperity depends on science." J. A. Schumpeter, a most distinguished economist, pointed out that the economy will not run out of new things to produce, as long as science keeps feeding it with new ideas of new things it can manufacture. According to Leonard Silk, Senior and Economics Editor of *Business Week*, "there can be little doubt that the most important element in economic growth is in expansion of scientific and technological knowledge. . . . In our own time some economists have reached the conclusion that technological advance has accounted for about 90 per cent of the rise in productivity—output per man-hour—in the United States since the latter part of the 19th Century." The amount a country invests in research and development was, and still is in many places, viewed as a measure of its scientific and hence economic vitality.

Britian was one of the first countries to note that this is not necessarily the case. Its expenditure on R&D increased by almost 60 per cent in the five years between 1958 and 1963, but its economy in the same period grew much less than that of most Western European countries and many underdeveloped ones. Similarly, the American government's expenditure on R&D soared almost 450 per cent over the last ten years; and the total expenditure on R&D in the United States grew from $5.1 billion in 1954 to $16.9 billion in 1963; yet the rate of economic growth remained small, smaller than in the earlier period, when R&D expenditures were low, below $5 billion a year.

Economist Robert A. Solo put the science-equals-growth formula to a statistical test and found that "after 1953, while expenditures for R&D skyrocket, the rate of increase in output per man-hour slumps." At the same time Solo found no positive association between levels of national expenditure on R&D and the rate of economic growth, or other economic indicators, including the rate of increase in the gross national product (GNP). I might add that while 25 per cent of the R&D expenditure goes into aero-space and electronics, these industries account for only 3.5 per cent of the GNP.

Seeking to explain this unexpected lack of propelling power of the American R&D,

Solo, writing in the *Harvard Business Review* (November-December 1962), separates R&D into two kinds: the first goes into civilian industry, seeking better production techniques or new products; this is "growth-oriented R&D." The other part, which goes into defense and space, need not raise productivity and accelerate economic growth, since orbiting objects or miniaturizing atomic war-heads does not have an automatic stimulant effect on the production of consumer goods. Solo incidentally includes medical research in the non-growth-oriented R&D. But it seems to me that, by increasing the number of productive years and working hours, medical research leads to better utilization of the existing manpower. Hence I would not lump it with space and defense R&D, but view it as growth-oriented R&D.

Barriers have sprung up between the defense and space R&D and the civilian economy, and as these are not surmounted, there is but little spillover and an actual *drag on the economy* as space-defense R&D drains creative manpower from civilian use. Five out of every eight American R&D scientists and engineers work for space or defense enterprises; and out of every ten now being graduated, as many as eight end up working in these non-growth sectors.

By Solo's calculations, the growth-oriented R&D has been, since 1955, below the 1953 level. During the same time, the non-growth R&D increased by 233 per cent! The civilian economy gained little from this monumental growth, but it may have lost a lot. The Western European societies, with small defense and next to no space R&D, have invested their R&D funds and manpower mainly on civilian development. This is widely viewed as one of the major secrets of their continued and high economic boom, which has now lasted more than fifteen years.

NASA advertises an "astronautical fallout" of findings from space research which, it claims, will spur the economy to ever higher levels of activity and technological refinement. As I read the extravagant statements about the benefits the space R&D presumably rains on the economy, I often feel Congress should ask NASA to finance even a small part of its budget from those "gigantic" gains, by selling to civilian industry that endless flood of new techniques, materials, and fuels that presumably pours forth from its research centers. We had better realize, however, that the operation of bringing back one astronaut from his postorbital swim could not be financed by this income.

Like a celestial Santa Claus, the space program will, according to its promoters, provide the earth with an amazing bag of goodies:

Exotic new fuels, such as liquid hydrogen, based on new chemical knowledge, especially high-temperature and high-pressure fuels.

New "wonder" materials, including metals and alloys, that are lighter and stronger than any known to man, such as tantalum and bergelium.

Improved building and bonding techniques to join materials, new and old.

Increased reliability and miniaturization. Since everything that goes into orbit has to be A-OK, and space repairs are prohibitive and accident a constant possibility, a great increase in reliability of instruments is expected. Small transistors and diodes will allow the production of desk (maybe pocket?) computers which, according to Dr. G. T. Seaborg, will eventually be in general use—to figure out family budgets and income tax, and to translate foreign languages.

Packaged power in silicon solar cells, small atomic power packs, and thermoelectric converters will be produced, to turn chemical reactions into electricity.

Improved vacuum techniques will have a wide use in electronics, and will foster industries on the moon which work in that vacuum better than on earth.

Psychological testing will benefit from new insights gained in the screening of space pilots, and social workers—from studies of the relationships among astronauts, crammed together into a small space for long interplanetary voyages. One authority envisions the possible evolution of new patterns of sexual behavior following such trips.

Unknown advances. Following the principle that science is unpredictable it is assumed that *some* advances will be made above and beyond those actually predicted.

"In astronautics," we are warned by two leading space experts, Wernher Von Braun and Frederick I. Ordway, III, "we tend to underestimate what we shall accomplish twenty-five years from now, yet overestimate what we can accomplish tomorrow." But Congress—notoriously impatient —might not be willing to wait a quarter of a century for results. Hence NASA is engaged in a campaign to sell taxpayers and industrial leaders on the here-and-now benefits of pouring billions into space. To this end Norman O. Miller, Jr., reports in the September 12, 1962, issue of the *Wall Street Journal,* NASA has used a New York public relations agency report on the immediate "civilian dividends from space research."

Here is some of the lunar manna NASA already "found":

•In working on "softening" the moon landing of the Apollo spacecraft, NASA's Langley Research Center came up with a new aluminum alloy that is relatively shockproof. It is now used in the bottom of elevator shafts and is being tried on helicopters and airplanes.

•NASA's Marshall Space Flight Center discovered an improved welding head, now in the process of being adapted for use by a farm machinery manufacturer.

•A manufacturer of furnaces and air conditioners is using a "pressure-sensitive" fiber-glass adhesive tape, which NASA researchers discovered.

•Von Braun and Ordway report in the November 1962 issue of the *Bulletin of Atomic Scientists:* "A ceramic material developed to protect nose cones of atmospheric re-entry vehicles is now being used to make cooking utensils that can be taken directly from the freezer and placed on open flame."

Nor are the social problems neglected. Space research, according to the same source, has already provided a bonus for both mental health and juvenile delinquency. "A derivative of hydrazine, a liquid propellant for spacecraft, is now being used experimentally to treat certain mental disorders . . . [and] the system of rewards and punishments used to train Enos [a chimpanzee] for his duties in the Mercury capsule might be adapted to rehabilitating juvenile delinquents when social and clinical procedures prove unsuccessful." Neal Stanford reports in the *Christian Science Monitor* of September 15, 1963, from a NASA source, that "the work NASA is doing to provide pure water and air for astronauts making long voyages to distant planets is being closely watched by big cities which have major water and air-pollution problems."

NASA, according to the same source, tells the following heart-warming story of a small hat manufacturer in Oklahoma who was having trouble because the resin he used to stiffen hats often stuck to the heating block. "From NASA he learned of a non-stick coating that had been developed in connection with space research on solid rocket fuels. Felt no longer sticks to the hatmaker's molds."

In the medical field there are hints of cancer cures in the future, but meanwhile the instruments used for measuring the heartbeat, pulse rate, and brain waves of the astronauts are adapted to enable one nurse seated at a central station to monitor the reactions of many patients.

Many of these declared space bonuses are sale claims; undeniably there are some technological benefits from the space race. Weather prediction *will* improve. Management methods *will* benefit. But most of the promised payoffs rest safely in the unknown future. The same holds true for most of the claims about new material, fuels, and production techniques derived from space research. In order not to confuse hopeful expectation with realization, let us take a little closer look at word and deed, or, as it might well be put, at fact and fantasy.

Although NASA says that manufacturers are "now adapting" materials found by space research, it is not certain that they will actually use them. When a drug is "experimentally used," this means that its value has not been established. One would hope that big-city management has better things to do than "closely watch" NASA men sifting air and water for three people, under the special circumstances of a closed capsule traveling in a high vacuum at fantastic speed, in the hope of learning how to purify the air and water for, let us say, eight million New Yorkers.

"Heat-resistant metals developed for rocket nozzles and winged space vehicles also should find their way into future plane engines and nuclear reactors," NASA says. They "should," but so far even NASA does not claim that they have. Slight exaggerations and exercises in semantics are perhaps forgivable, but what about statements by federal officials that simply do not check with the facts?

According to NASA, it provided new ceramics for kitchenware. But the *Wall Street Journal* of September 12, 1963, reports: "Corning Glass Works says its glass-ceramics material 'was not developed specifically for [missile] use, although the first practical application was indeed for nose cones.' It was happenstance that the new materials developed for pots and pans first found use in the space program." . . .

A House subcommittee report maintains that *of nearly 1200 prime research contracts and many thousands of subcontractors, NASA received only 159 invention disclosures from commercial contractors and authorized patent application on only 23 developments.* The promise is, of course, that this ratio will improve greatly as years go by. This must be viewed with considerable skepticism, however, as the spillover from defense research, which is much older, is still meager. Close to two thirds of the total American expenditure on R&D, private and public, goes into space and defense. Since the promise of research dividends for the economy as a whole is a major justification for this expenditure, the question of the flow of new knowledge from these sectors to others is of major importance for national policy.

The fallout from space research cannot be sufficiently increased to compensate for the drain it imposes on creative man-power. Hence space (and defense) R&D should be cut sharply as soon as possible. A civilian space program of a half to one billion dollars a year, growing as the economy does, might be quite adequate for real American needs. But since some time will pass before such a cut is implemented, since some space R&D ought to be re-tained, and because some of the same problems are faced in defense and poten-tially in other programs, we must look for *ways to increase the economic fallout of federal research,* putting aside the question of the appropriate size of the federal space (and defense) drag on the economy. . . .

Only a small part of the scientific in-formation currently generated by federal R&D is available *at all.* Although the Department of Defense has approximately 10,000 prime and associate contractors, and more than 300,000 subcontractors and sub-subcontractors, technical docu-ments are received from a mere 1900 companies. To be sure, a proposed change in Department of Defense regulation is expected to raise the annual receipt of technical documents from 30,000 to 300,-000. Yet the division that deals with these documents (Armed Services Technical Information Agency) now has the resources to process only *half* of the technical doc-uments it is *currently* receiving.

The reasons for collecting are as varied as the collectors. For private industry, there is often more money to be made in collecting than in analyzing; for govern-ment agencies, more headlines in orbiting the heavens than in armchair work on earth. The skills required for analysis are harder to come by than those needed for collecting. Foundations are generous in financing the "field" stages of studies, but skimpy when the researcher seeks a year to pore over his data. There is thus a great tendency to publish material raw or half digested, and a general lack of in-terest in codification and theorizing, which is often the best and only way to bring out the import of different bits of information.

What is needed is a change of heart,

a maturity of scholarship, a reflective spirit showing as great an interest in the pro-cessing and utilizing of findings as in the more active field work. Studies must be designed to include a full period of gesta-tion, and no research team should be viewed as having discharged its duties until it has digested its findings and made them available to others in a coherent form. A *new authority within the federal network of R&D should be set up,* entrusted with the responsibility of countering this ten-dency to collect but not analyze, of sal-vaging the mountains of unanalyzed data already in existence, of developing better techniques for analysis, and of training scholars in the requisite special skills. . . .

Least amenable to direct treatment is the growing gap between the kinds of knowledge produced by the arms-and-space race and that which is consumable by civilian industry. Federal R&D deals mainly with a special set of circumstances such as a presumed human enemy, while industry faces a cooperative, if not down-right submissive, consumer; space efforts face an extremely hostile environment, from super speed to super vacuums and the extremes of heat or cold, while most consumer industry aims at an environment no more challenging than the living room or the side of the pool. Reliability for most lunar hardware has to be extremely high; most washers and driers, their reliability improved ten times, are still "imprecise" instruments by comparison. Commercial use of atomic energy, mail by missiles, and tourism on the moon are still years away. In brief, both new space products and information are difficult to translate *directly* into new civilian terms, a task NASA became engaged in, the Atomic Energy Commission is pursuing, and the Defense Department is touching upon. . . .

NASA cannot pay for the breakfasts of its astronauts with the money it has made from its research fallout — not only because much of it lies in the future, or on public relations drawing boards instead of R&D's, but because most of the civilian patents that grew directly out of research NASA paid for do not bring in any royalties. The issue finally came before Congress in 1963 but meanwhile *most of the by-products of federal research have been a giveaway to private industry.* Most of the federal R&D goes to five industries, and a full 30 per cent to four giant corporations— Lockheed, General Dynamics, Boeing, and North American Aviation. Federal agencies, however, usually get a royalty-free license so that they will not have to pay royalties if they use the civilian patents that grew out of the research they paid for in the first place.

Regional Input-Output

17. The Balance of Military Payments Among States and Regions

James R. Anderson

The direct military budget of the United States has grown over the last decade to approximately $75 billion per year. The magnitude of such a sum makes it difficult for citizens and public officials alike to visualize its impact on the well-being of individuals and their communities. In this essay I will compare the flow of military expenditures into specific states and regions with the flow of federal taxes out of states and regions. The data will show 1) which states and regions are suffering the most severe drain upon their resources; 2) which states and regions most benefit from military expenditures, and 3) the extent and intensity, on a per capita basis, of these gains and losses.

Previous studies of the distribution of federal revenues and expenditures (civilian and military) have indicated that their primary effect is toward redistribution of income from high-income states and regions to lower-income states and regions. A 1965 study by Weidenbaum confirms this general conclusion, with the specific qualification that military expenditures tend on the whole to favor the high-income states and regions, such as New England, the Mideast, and the Pacific coast.[1]

The Weidenbaum study, while accurate in terms of the gross aggregates and areas considered, is limited in several respects. Its data are drawn from the period prior to the Vietnam war buildup in the military budget, when military expenditures rose nearly 60 per cent, from $50 billion to nearly $80 billion. Second, the study is limited by its lack of data with respect to the revenue and expenditure flows of specific states. This can distort the distribution perspective, in that one state may dominate or determine the picture of an entire region: Texas dominates the West South Central region. Third, the study does not make sufficient allowance for the per capita levels of revenue and expenditure in specific states, which leads to a degree of miscalculation of the actual impact of gross outlays in certain areas. For example, Pennsylvania, with a 1965–67 average military expenditure of $1.3 billion, is significantly less affected on a per capita basis than is Kansas, with half that in gross military outlay, and Pennsylvania's overall revenue loss is not compensated by military expenditures to nearly the extent that Kansas is benefitted by such expenditures. Fourth, and this point may be open to some debate, it seems to this writer that Weidenbaum's study, and others similar to it, are much clearer and more forceful with respect to the beneficiaries of military expenditure policies than with respect to the serious imbalance that exists among the separate states regarding the financing, through tax levies, of these expenditures. Finally, the Weidenbaum study gives insufficient attention to the political and strategic factors which can influence, and in certain cases govern, the allocation of federal tax resources. Certain patterns of allocation, inexplicable by any strictly economic factors, are readily understood in terms of certain concentrations of political power.

The principal facts and comparisons of this study are presented in four tables of data. They are derived from a report on federal revenues and expenditures for states and regions for the fiscal years 1965–67 compiled by a committee of the U.S. House of Representatives.[2] All of the data drawn upon for the present paper comprise averages for the fiscal years 1965–67. The timing and focus of this congressional study are particularly fortunate in that this period matches the time of the major expansion of the military budget for the Vietnam war.

Certain factors should be stressed at the outset. First, this essay will be exclusively concerned with the quantitative aspects of the flow of revenues and military expenditures among states. No effort will be made to assess the character or the economic and political quality of these outlays. Our efforts will be confined to an exploration of the imbalances generated or influenced by heavy outlays for military purposes. Second, it should be emphasized that the data used represent approximations of federal revenues and expenditures. Thus, because of subcontracting, the state in which a prime contract is received is not necessarily the location of all the subcontracted work. Third, certain classes of federal expenditure, for the Atomic Energy Commission and the Veteran's Administration, are military either in origin or character, but are included in the civilian categories of expenditure in the congressional study. Therefore, we are justified in stating that what follows represents a series of understatements as to the impact of federal military expenditure within the United States. This conclusion is supported by the fact that only prime military contracts of $10,000 or more are included in the congressional study (which partly accounts for the fact that the military outlays reported are somewhat below the actual outlays for fiscal years 1965-67).

Table 1 shows, on a per capita basis, the tax revenues originating in each state and region, as well as the federal expenditures in each state and region. The difference between the per capita revenues and expenditures, multiplied by the population of each state and region, represents the total gain or loss for the specific entity as a consequence of federal tax policy. The ratio of federal payments to each state and region as against federal tax revenues originating in the particular state or region, along with the corresponding ranking in terms of this ratio, gives us a quick indication of the degree of gain or loss to each unit from the standpoint of federal levies and outlays. Several aspects of this table are notable.

First, a total of twenty-one states, comprising nearly 110 million persons, suffered net drains ranging from $20 million (Vermont) to $7.5 billion (New York) in their transactions with the Federal Government and its agencies. Although many of these twenty-one states are above average in terms of per capita income, it is significant that some of the poorest states in the United States experience net drains in their balance of payments with the Federal Government. West Virginia and Tennessee, of the Appalachian region, are injured rather than benefitted by federal taxation. West Virginia lost an average of $110 million each year during the three years covered by our data. Despite many words to the contrary by federal officials over the last decade, it appears that West Virginia has been severely drained, rather than benefitted, by federal taxation.

Another particularly striking feature of the data in Table 1 is the magnitude of the tax drain out of the Middle Atlantic and East North Central regions. The Middle Atlantic region, comprising New York, New Jersey, and Pennsylvania, experiences a net loss approaching $13 billion per year. The East North Central region, comprising the Great Lakes states of Ohio, Indiana, Illinois, Michigan, and Wisconsin, experiences a net drain of more than $12.7 billion per year.

It is doubtful that any sovereign government in similar circumstances could be regarded as either economically healthy or, from a political standpoint, as master of its own destiny. The mounting symptoms of social and economic dislocation in these regions, such as the "brain drain" out of the Great Lakes region, may be due in no small measure to the acute strain imposed on these areas by federal taxation and military priorities.

The federal military allocations to these regions, as indicated in Table 2, compensate for only a small portion of the net loss suffered. Military (Department of Defense) spending includes industrial as well as base operations (including payments to civilian employees and local purchases of goods and services). The latter Department of Defense payments are large in certain states (Alaska, Hawaii, South Carolina, Virginia, Georgia, etc.) and dominate the per capita military payments in such states.

The Middle Atlantic region, as a whole, receives only about $5.5 billion in military outlays. This is a large sum in the aggregate, but in per capita terms it leaves the Middle Atlantic region near the bottom in rank among the nine regions of the United States. The East North Central region, with a net per capita drain of $331, receives only about $116 per capita in military outlays.

The South Atlantic region, well below average in total personal income per capita, derives very substantial benefit from military outlays. A total net gain, for the region, of $3.2 billion is due to a total military outlay within this region of $9.3 billion. Of this total, Maryland, Virginia, North Carolina, Georgia, and Florida all receive outlays of $1 billion or more, which is high both in absolute and per capita terms.

Being the nerve center of American military power and bureaucracy, as well as the location of a number of exceptionally powerful senators and congressmen, is much more significant as a determinant of military allocations to this region than is the advanced technology and industry of the Great Lakes, Middle Atlantic, and New England regions. The extremely high total and per capita military outlays for the Pacific coast likewise seem to be accounted for only partly by advanced industry and technology. Strategic and political factors contribute to explain the scene in this region, as much or more than economic considerations.

Tables 3 and 4 display military expenditures in the states and regions in close detail. What emerges here is that there is no particular correlation between the income level of a state and the military allocation to that state. Many states with above-average per capita income are below average, sometimes substantially so, with respect to per capita military outlays. Conversely, many states with below-average per capita income receive per capita military outlays well above the national average. (The Pacific coast, which is highest in per capita income, is also highest in per capita military outlays, while the Middle Atlantic region, which ranks second in per capita income, ranks eighth among nine regions in per capita military outlays.) The highest per capita military expenditure is to be found in Alaska, a fact that is unrelated to its level of industry and income, but rather to its strategic importance.

The payments imbalance condition of Michigan and other states is disclosed in the data of Tables 1 and 4, which enable us to compare both aggregate and proportional data regarding the flow and balance of revenues and expenditures in the various states and regions. Michigan, although ranking eleventh in the United States in per capita personal income, and eleventh in taxes paid to the Federal Government, ranks fiftieth, almost last in the nation, in federal expenditures per person. During the years 1965–67, Michigan paid more than twice as much in federal taxes as it received in federal expenditures. Revenues totalling $6.4 billion per year were taken from Michigan, while only $3.2 billion per year was returned to Michigan in the form of various federal programs. This means that Michigan suffered a drain of more than $3 billion per year.

It appears that the states in which the military-industrial system is most strongly centered, and in which its bases and personnel are located, benefit most from this maldistribution. California and Texas, for example, together receive over $3 billion

TABLE 1. Estimates of Per Capita Federal Revenues and Expenditures by State and Region; Fiscal Years 1965-1967, Average for Period.

Region / State	Per Capita Personal Income	Rank	Federal Per Capita Revenues Originating in State	Rank	Per Capita Federal Expenditures in State	Rank	Total Gain or Loss (Millions of Dollars)	Rank	Per Capita Gain or Loss	Rank	Ratio of Total Federal Payments in State to Tax Revenues from State	Rank
New England	$3,133	3*	$800	2*	$654	4*	–$1,636.0	7*	–$146	7*	.82	7*
Maine	2,388	37	577	32	579	29	+1.9	29	+2	30	1.00	30
New Hampshire	2,703	27	703	13	511	36	–129.6	36	–192	39	.73	41
Vermont	2,469	32	631	25	581	28	–20.2	31	–50	35	.92	34
Massachusetts	3,181	10	783	8	611	26	–923.1	43	–172	38	.78	39
Rhode Island	2,935	17	713	12	721	13	+7.3	28	+8	28	1.01	29
Connecticut	3,558	2	983	3	783	9	–572.3	42	–200	41	.80	37'
Middle Atlantic	3,227	2*	820	1*	471	8*	–12,761.0	9*	–349	9*	.57	8*
New York	3,408	6	893	4	481	40	–7,458.1	51	–412	49	.54	48
New Jersey	3,355	8	826	7	509	37	–2,173.1	46	–317	47	.62	44'
Pennsylvania	2,868	18	703	14	433	46	–3,129.8	48	–270	44	.62	44
East North Central	3,109	4*	743	4*	412	9*	–12,726.6	8*	–331	8*	.55	9*
Ohio	2,945	16	702	15	426	48	–2,845.1	47	–276	46	.61	46
Indiana	2,956	15	659	21	429	47	–1,132.2	45	–230	42	.65	43
Illinois	3,412	5	845	6	433	45	–4,417.4	50	–412	49	.51	49
Michigan	3,139	11	761	11	378	50	–3,206.8	49	–383	48	.50	50
Wisconsin	2,855	19	644	23	373	51	–1,125.7	44	–271	45	.58	47
West North Central	2,724	5*	615	5*	610	5*	–70.5	6*	–5	6*	.99	6*
Minnesota	2,777	23	625	26	503	38	–435.9	41	–122	37	.80	37
Iowa	2,822	21	594	30	514	35	–220.0	38	–80	36	.87	35
Missouri	2,736	25	688	16	649	23	–176.1	37	–39	33	.94	33
North Dakota	2,308	39	464	44	836	8	+240.4	13	+372	4	1.80	4
South Dakota	2,288	42	463	45	665	19	+138.2	19	+202	7	1.44	7
Nebraska	2,720	26	605	28	654	21	+70.8	26	+49	24	1.08	25
Kansas	2,757	24	572	33	710	15	+312.2	12	+138	13	1.24	14
South Atlantic	2,473	7*	601	6*	711	2*	+3,174.6	1*	+110	2*	1.18	1*
Delaware	3,439	3	1,301	1	602	27	–355.7	39	–699	51	.46	51
Maryland	3,125	12	783	9	908	4	+446.5	8	+125	15	1.16	17
D.C.	3,839	1	1,068	2	1,975	2	+728.2	4	+907	2	1.85	3
Virginia	2,521	30	594	29	888	5	+1,307.5	2	+294	5	1.49	6
West Virginia	2,107	47	480	42	420	49	–109.7	35	–60	34	.87	35
North Carolina	2,161	44	476	43	498	39	+107.6	23	+20	27	1.04	28
South Carolina	1,947	49	402	49	552	30	+374.1	10	+150	11	1.37	9
Georgia	2,270	41	507	39	668	17	+706.9	5	+161	10	1.32	10
Florida	2,532	29	672	17	665	18	–40.8	32	–7	32	.99	31
East South Central	2,019	9*	433	9*	505	7*	+926.9	3*	+72	5*	1.17	2*
Kentucky	2,144	45	460	46	523	32	+201.1	17	+73	21	1.14	18'
Tennessee	2,135	46	487	41	470	42	–62.9	33	–17	31	.97	32

	Value	Rank	Value	Rank	Value	Rank	Value	Rank	Value	Rank	Value	Rank
Alabama	1,992	48	420	48	548	31	450.1	7	+128	14	1.31	12
Mississippi	1,696	51	328	51	473	41	338.6	11	+145	12	1.44	7
West South Central	2,337	8*	520	8*	605	6*	1,573.1	4*	+85	4*	1.16	4*
Arkansas	1,927	50	394	50	443	44	94.8	24	+49	25	1.12	24
Louisiana	2,187	43	457	47	522	33	233.9	15	+65	23	1.14	18
Oklahoma	2,377	38	531	37	628	24	239.8	14	+97	17	1.18	15
Texas	2,453	34	562	35	657	20	1,004.6	3	+95	18	1.17	16
Mountain	2,593	6*	597	7*	690	3*	715.9	5*	+93	3*	1.16	3*
Montana	2,517	31	570	34	753	10	128.8	22	+183	8	1.32	10
Idaho	2,416	36	515	38	518	34	1.7	30	+3	29	1.00	27
Wyoming	2,664	28	664	19	842	7	57.9	27	+178	9	1.27	13
Colorado	2,818	22	505	22	743	11	183.0	18	+94	19	1.14	18
New Mexico	2,308	40	586	40	735	12	231.6	16	+230	6	1.46	5
Arizona	2,469	33	541	31	671	16	134.5	20	+85	20	1.14	18
Utah	2,436	35		36	614	25	72.4	25	+73	21	1.13	23
Nevada	3,422	4	868	5	650	22	-94.0	34	-218	43	.75	40
Pacific	3,279	1*	751	3*	864	1*	2,770.4	2*	+113	1*	1.15	5*
Washington	3,061	13	667	18	711	14	132.0	21	+44	26	1.07	26
Oregon	2,837	20	661	20	463	43	-386.1	40	-198	40	.70	42
California	3,372	7	781	10	894	5	2,098.5	1	+113	16	1.14	18
Alaska	3,336	9	637	24	2,569	1	512.1	6	+1,932	1	4.03	1
Hawaii	2,961	14	615	27	1,188	3	413.9	9	+573	3	1.93	2

SOURCE (FOR COLUMNS 2, 3, & 4): U.S. Congress, House of Representatives, 90th Congress, second session, 1968, Committee on Government Operations, *Federal Revenue and Expenditure Estimates for States and Regions, Fiscal Years 1965–67.* pp. 25–26, 32.

[1]Duplicate numbers in rank column indicate tie.
*Denotes regional ranking.

Table 2. Military (Department of Defense) Outlays by State and Region; Estimates for Fiscal Years 1965–67

	AVERAGE ANNUAL PAYROLL MILITARY PERSONNEL (IN $ MILLIONS)	AVERAGE ANNUAL PAYROLL: D.O.D. CIVILIAN PERSONNEL (IN $ MILLIONS)	AVERAGE TOTAL DOD PAYROLL ($ MILLIONS)	MILITARY OUTLAYS LESS PERSONNEL ($ MILLIONS)	TOTAL MILITARY OUTLAYS ($ MILLIONS)	RANK	PER CAPITA MILITARY OUTLAYS	RANK
50 States & D.C.	8,521	7,343	15,864	30,044.6	45,908.6	—*	$ 236	—*
New England	313	397	660	2,675.6	3,335.6	6*(R)	298	3*(R)
Maine	63	11	74	141.1	215.1	39	219	29
New Hampshire	35	62	97	57.9	154.9	43	230	27
Vermont	2	1	3	66.6	69.6	51	171	34
Massachusetts	151	183	334	949.6	1,283.6	12	240	25
Rhode Island	42	63	105	168.8	273.8	35	307	14
Connecticut	20	27	47	1,291.6	1,338.6	9	469	5
Middle Atlantic	455	928	1,383	3,997.6	5,480.6	3*(R)	150	8*(R)
New York	175	312	487	2,216.5	2,703.5	3	149	38
New Jersey	203	198	401	1,088.4	1,489.4	7	218	30
Pennsylvania	77	518	595	692.7	1,287.7	11	111	45
East North Central	553	751	1,304	3,150.2	4,453.5	5*(R)	116	9*(R)
Ohio	126	336	462	927.9	1,389.9	8	135	41
Indiana	47	98	145	537.4	682.4	19	137	40
Illinois	256	208	464	797.7	1,261.0	13	118	42
Michigan	104	92	196	648.3	844.3	17	101	46
Wisconsin	20	17	37	238.9	275.9	34	66	49
West North Central	544	237	781	2,211.7	2,992.7	7*(R)	188	6*(R)
Minnesota	25	15	40	363.6	403.6	31	114	44
Iowa	8	5	13	235.7	248.7	38	90	48
Missouri	148	141	289	832.1	1,121.1	15	225	28
North Dakota	68	8	76	123.3	199.3	40	309	13
South Dakota	36	9	45	59.1	104.1	47	152	37
Nebraska	91	27	118	153.1	271.1	37	187	32
Kansas	168	32	200	444.8	644.8	21	241	24

South Atlantic	2,441	1,785	4,226	5,140.8	9,330.8	2*(R)	308	2*(R)
Delaware	44	9	53	91.7	144.7	44	284	17
Maryland	279	345	624	709.9	1,333.9	10	375	8
D.C.	173	210	383	116.7	499.7	28	622	3
Virginia	503	578	1,081	875.4	1,956.4	4	440	6
West Virginia	3	8	11	74.2	85.2	49	47	51
North Carolina	385	75	460	776.8	1,236.8	14	250	22
South Carolina	230	115	345	423.1	768.1	18	299	16
Georgia	455	256	711	989.4	1,700.4	5	385	7
Florida	369	189	558	1,047.6	1,605.6	6	275	18
East South Central	592	417	1,009	1,135.2	2,144.2	9*(R)	167	7*(R)
Kentucky	220	94	314	312.3	626.3	22	197	31
Tennessee	90	46	136	433.9	569.9	26	148	39
Alabama	156	231	387	163.2	550.2	27	158	36
Mississippi	126	46	172	225.8	397.8	32	171	33
West South Central	1,338	730	2,068	3,006.2	5,074.2	4*(R)	272	5*(R)
Arkansas	55	30	85	110.4	195.4	41	100	46
Louisiana	166	49	215	362.3	577.3	24	161	35
Oklahoma	182	197	379	197.5	576.5	25	233	26
Texas	935	454	1,389	2,336.0	3,725.0	2	350	9
Mountain	576	446	1,022	1,178.5	2,171.5	8*(R)	286	4*(R)
Montana	53	8	61	110.5	171.5	42	244	23
Idaho	26	3	29	51.5	80.5	50	116	43
Wyoming	25	4	29	57.4	86.4	48	265	21
Colorado	191	107	298	370.4	668.4	20	342	10
New Mexico	100	81	181	139.0	320.0	33	318	11
Arizona	118	53	171	314.4	485.4	29	305	15
Utah	26	171	197	75.2	272.2	36	272	19
Nevada	37	19	56	60.1	116.1	46	269	20
Pacific	1,654	1,592	3,246	7,581.7	10,828.7	1*(R)	440	1*(R)
Washington	221	176	397	554.9	951.9	16	315	12
Oregon	23	24	47	75.2	122.2	45	63	50
California	1,077	1,188	2,265	6,481.0	8,746.0	1	470	4
Alaska	153	55	208	223.0	431.0	30	1,626	1
Hawaii	180	149	330	247.6	577.6	23	800	2

SOURCES (COLUMNS 2, 3, & 4): U.S. Department of Commerce, *Statistical Abstract*, 1968, p. 250. (FOR COL. 5) U.S. Congress, House of Representatives, 90th Congress, second session, 1968, Committee on Government Operations, *Federal Revenue and Expenditure Estimates for States and Regions, Fiscal Years 1965–67*. pp. 30–31.

°Note.—"°R" at the right of a number in the ranking columns denotes a regional ranking.

Table 3. Per Capita Military (Department of Defense) Expenditures by State & Region, Relative to Non-military Expenditures; Averages for Fiscal Years 1965–67.

	PER CAPITA MILITARY EXPENDITURE	RANK	PER CAPITA MILITARY EXPENDITURE, RELATIVE TO U.S. AVERAGE	PER CAPITA MILITARY EXPENDITURE AS PROPORTION OF TOTAL PER CAPITA INCOME	RANK
50 States & D.C.	$ 236	—	—	8.2%	—
New England	298	3*	+$ 62	9.5	5*
Maine	219	29	− 17	9.2	25
New Hampshire	230	27	−6	8.5	27
Vermont	171	34	−65	6.9	36
Massachusetts	240	25	+4	7.5	32
Rhode Island	307	14	+ 71	10.5	18
Connecticut	469	5	+233	13.2	11
Middle Atlantic	150	8*	−86	4.6	8*
New York	149	38	−87	4.4	44
New Jersey	218	30	− 18	6.5	38
Pennsylvania	111	45	−125	3.9	46
East North Central	116	9*	−120	3.7	9*
Ohio	135	41	−101	4.6	43
Indiana	137	40	− 99	4.6	42
Illinois	118	42	− 118	3.4	47
Michigan	101	46	− 135	3.2	49
Wisconsin	66	49	− 170	2.3	50
West North Central	188	6*	−48	6.9	7*
Minnesota	114	44	−122	4.1	45
Iowa	90	48	−146	3.2	48
Missouri	225	28	−11	8.2	29
North Dakota	309	13	+73	13.4	10
South Dakota	152	37	−84	6.7	37
Nebraska	187	32	− 39	6.9	35
Kansas	241	24	+5	9.0	26
South Atlantic	308	2*	+72	11.2	3*
Delaware	284	17	+48	8.3	28
Maryland	375	8	+139	12.0	14
D.C.	622	3	+386	16.2	5
Virginia	440	6	+204	17.5	3
West Virginia	47	51	−189	2.2	41
North Carolina	250	22	+14	11.6	15
South Carolina	299	16	+63	15.4	6
Georgia	385	7	+149	17.0	4
Florida	275	18	+ 39	10.9	17
East South Central	167	7*	−69	8.3	6*
Kentucky	197	31	− 39	9.4	24
Tennessee	148	39	−88	6.9	34
Alabama	158	36	− 78	7.9	31
Mississippi	171	33	−65	10.1	20
West South Central	272	5*	+36	11.6	2*
Arkansas	100	46	−136	5.2	39
Louisiana	161	35	−75	7.4	33
Oklahoma	233	26	− 3	9.8	22
Texas	350	9	+114	14.3	7

Table 3. Per Capita Military (Department of Defense) Expenditures by State & Region, Relative to Non-military Expenditures; Averages for Fiscal Years 1965–67. *(Continued)*

	PER CAPITA MILITARY EXPENDITURE	RANK	PER CAPITA MILITARY EXPENDITURE, RELATIVE TO U.S. AVERAGE	PER CAPITA MILITARY EXPENDITURE AS PROPORTION OF TOTAL PER CAPITA INCOME	RANK
Mountain	286	4*	+50	11.0	4*
Montana	244	23	+8	9.7	23
Idaho	116	43	−120	4.8	40
Wyoming	265	21	+29	9.9	21
Colorado	342	10	+106	12.1	13
New Mexico	318	11	+82	13.8	9
Arizona	305	15	+69	12.4	12
Utah	272	19	+36	11.2	16
Nevada	269	20	+33	7.9	30
Pacific	440	1*	+204	13.4	1*
Washington	315	12	+79	10.3	19
Oregon	63	50	−173	2.2	51
California	470	4	+234	13.9	8
Alaska	1,626	1	+1,390	48.7	1
Hawaii	800	2	+564	27.0	2

SOURCE: Data derived from Table 1.
* Denotes regional ranking.

Table 4. Relationship of Department of Defense to Other Federal Expenditure, by State & Region, Averages for Fiscal Years 1965–67.

	TOTAL FEDERAL REVENUES	TOTAL MILITARY (DOD) EXPENDITURE ($ MILLIONS)	TOTAL CIVILIAN EXPENDITURE ($ MILLIONS)	RATIO OF TOTAL MILITARY (DOD) TO CIVILIAN EXPENDITURE	RANK
50 States & D.C.	139,949.3	45,908.6	87,040.7	.53	—
New England	8,945.1	3,335.6	3,973.5	.84	2*
Maine	565.4	215.1	352.2	.61	25
New Hampshire	423.8	154.9	189.3	.82	13
Vermont	257.1	69.6	167.3	.41	37
Massachusetts	4,203.4	1,283.6	1,996.7	.64	23
Rhode Island	637.0	273.8	370.5	.74	18
Connecticut	2,808.4	1,338.6	897.5	1.49	3
Middle Atlantic	29,983.6	5,480.6	11,742.0	.47	7*
New York	16,188.2	2,703.5	6,026.6	.45	35'
New Jersey	5,655.2	1,489.4	1,992.7	.75	17
Pennsylvania	8,140.2	1,287.7	3,722.7	.35	42
East North Central	28,585.6	4,453.5	11,405.5	.39	9*
Ohio	7,235.5	1,389.9	3,000.5	.46	32
Indiana	3,242.5	682.4	1,427.9	.48	30'
Illinois	9,057.3	1,261.0	3,378.9	.37	40
Michigan	6,376.3	844.3	2,325.2	.36	41
Wisconsin	2,674.0	275.9	1,272.4	.22	48

	TOTAL FEDERAL REVENUES	TOTAL MILITARY (DOD) EXPENDITURES ($ MILLIONS)	TOTAL CIVILIAN EXPENDITURE ($ MILLIONS)	RATIO OF TOTAL MILITARY (DOD) TO CIVILIAN EXPENDITURE	RANK
West North Central	9,771.0	2,992.7	6,707.8	.45	8*
Minnesota	2,225.6	403.6	1,386.1	.29	44
Iowa	1,638.1	248.7	1,169.4	.21	49
Missouri	3,120.0	1,121.1	1,822.8	.62	24
North Dakota	299.7	199.3	340.8	.58	28
South Dakota	317.2	104.1	351.3	.30	43
Nebraska	878.3	271.1	678.0	.40	38
Kansas	1,292.1	644.8	959.4	.67	22
South Atlantic	17,373.8	9,330.8	11,217.6	.83	3*
Delaware	662.1	144.7	161.7	.89	10
Maryland	2,792.1	1,333.9	1,904.7	.70	20
D. of C.	857.5	499.7	1,086.0	.46	32
Virginia	2,642.5	1,956.4	1,993.6	.98	9
West Virginia	870.1	85.2	675.2	.13	51
North Carolina	2,357.0	1,236.8	1,227.8	1.01	8
South Carolina	1,033.5	768.1	649.5	1.18	5
Georgia	2,239.5	1,700.4	1,246.0	1.36	4
Florida	3,919.5	1,605.6	2,273.1	.71	19
East South Central	5,563.4	2,144.2	4,346.1	.49	6*
Kentucky	1,461.2	626.3	1,036.0	.60	26
Tennessee	1,874.2	569.9	1,241.4	.46	32
Alabama	1,465.6	550.2	1,365.5	.40	38
Mississippi	762.4	397.8	703.3	.57	29
West South Central	9,701.6	5,074.2	6,200.5	.82	4*
Arkansas	769.3	195.4	668.7	.29	44
Louisiana	1,635.6	577.3	1,292.2	.45	35
Oklahoma	1,313.6	576.5	976.9	.59	27
Texas	5,983.1	3,725.0	3,262.7	1.14	6
Mountain	4,599.1	2,171.5	3,143.5	.69	5*
Montana	400.1	171.5	357.4	.48	30
Idaho	357.7	80.5	278.9	.29	44
Wyoming	216.5	57.4	217.0	.26	47
Colorado	1,268.6	668.4	783.2	.85	11
New Mexico	508.5	320.0	420.1	.76	16
Arizona	932.5	485.4	581.6	.83	12
Utah	540.8	272.2	341.0	.80	14'
Nevada	374.4	116.1	164.3	.70	20
Pacific	18,425.9	10,828.7	10,367.6	1.04	1*
Washington	2,013.2	951.9	1,193.3	.80	14'
Oregon	1,287.5	122.2	779.2	.16	50
California	14,512.5	8,746.0	7,865.0	1.11	7
Alaska	168.8	431.0	249.9	1.72	2
Hawaii	443.9	577.6	280.2	2.06	1

SOURCE (COLUMN 3): U.S. Congress, House of Representatives, 90th Congress, second session, 1968, Committee on Government Operations, *Federal Revenue and Expenditure Estimates for States and Regions, Fiscal Years 1965–67.*
' Duplicate numbers in rank column indicates tie.
* Denotes regional ranking.

more in federal expenditures than they contribute in revenues, primarily because both are among the top six states in military contracts. California was third in 1967, while Texas was sixth.

The data examined here lead to a series of observations regarding the performance of the Federal Government as an instrument of equitable income distribution, particularly as effected by military spending priority in its budgets. 1) Some poor states, it appears, are either clearly harmed or benefitted very little by federal taxation. 2) Some large, urban states appear to be so severely drained that one must raise the question of equity, even while granting that the prosperous states should provide some measure of assistance for the poorer ones. 3) A number of states with favorable ratios of federal expenditures to tax revenues, particularly those of the Appalachian and Rocky Mountain regions, appear to be having difficulties maintaining their populations and prosperity in spite of this advantage. This raises questions as to the particular persons who benefit from expenditures in the states of these regions. 4) The large imbalances in military expenditure, along with the corresponding revenue drain from more than half the population of the country, are economically ominous. It appears that the economic

equivalent of bloodletting is being imposed on substantial portions of the United States, while the federal doctor, like his medieval counterpart, assures his patient that such a treatment is making him stronger and more secure. 5) The flow of military expenditure, with accompanying research and industrial activity, and the corresponding drain from some regions of the country, go far toward explaining the gradual shift of population and political power to the South and West.

The data of this brief study probably underestimate the situation and the actual imbalance generated by the flows of federal taxes and expenditures. With fully 70 per cent of federal employment committed to military purposes, we are very likely justified in concluding that until such priorities undergo fundamental examination and reversal, the inequities will not be corrected.

---

[1] Weidenbaum, Murray L., "Shifting the Composition of Government Spending: Implications for the Regional Distribution of Income," Peace Research Society (International), Papers, Volume V, 1966, pp. 15–41.

[1] U.S. House of Representatives, Committee on Government Operations, 90th Congress, 2nd Session. *Federal Revenue and Expenditure, Estimates for States and Regions, Fiscal Years 1965–67.* U.S. Government Printing Office, Washington, D.C., 1968.

Technology

18. Who Decides Technology?

Seymour Melman

Contrary to current fears, there is little evidence, I believe, to support the notion that man is simply the passive creature of technology. Moreover, there is considerable unclarity as to how technology gets to be the way it is in the first place.

While the outer limits of feasibility in technologies are set by knowledge of na-

ture, the selection (design) of preferred technology, in industrial society, is controlled by social, largely economic, criteria. Men select from an array of available or conceivable technological options to suit specific social requirements. Change the criteria for design and the resultant technology is altered. Thus appliances, machines, and vehicles would be rather different if designed with safety and durability as prime design criteria. Neither is the nature of preferred technology determined in any traceable way by factors that inhere in technology itself.

A most important demonstration of the socially determined nature of technology was the decision by the U.S. in 1961 to build an overkill force of over 1,000 intercontinental ballistic missiles. This was not determined by what was technically essential for actually defending the U.S. from external attack. Rather, the controlling considerations were the political aims of the Kennedy-Johnson administration.

At the opening of the Kennedy-Johnson administration the White House was engaged in a political struggle with the Air Force. The Air Force was denied a new big bomber program and it had to be given something. Second, the administration was looking for ways of stimulating general economic activity by quick injection of large capital funds by government. The Kennedy administration soon discovered that of all major federal agencies the Department of Defense was obviously best equipped to put money into circulation rapidly, with blueprints in hand and industrial contacts arranged. Also, newly created theories about politically rational management of nuclear and conventional forces were deployed to explain how having 1,000 intercontinental missiles would help to ensure the "stability of the deterrent." Plainly, the massive program for the construction of an overkill missile force was not determined by technology having an initiative of its own, by what was technically possible. Rather, this arms race escalation was determined by social—in this case largely political—considerations.

So if we want to know why our current technology is what it is, we should look to who decides what that technology shall be.

A management is identified functionally as a group that gathers capital and decides what shall be produced; that determines how production shall be carried out and what quality standards are to be satisfied; that decides about cost keeping, price, and the shipment of goods. In the Department of Defense such decisions are made over an industrial network comprising the largest firm in the nation.

Studies of the operation of military industry disclose that Robert McNamara's most important contribution has been the creation in the Department of Defense of a central administrative office over military industry. This central management group controls industrial production valued at about $40 billion a year and carried out by diverse units throughout the country.

The new management group is housed in a new organization, the Defense Supply Agency. Subsections of this agency perform functions relating to the so-called contractor firms similar to those performed by the top management of Ford, General Motors, or General Electric with respect to the divisions of those firms. As in every large industrial corporation, the new management does not own—it merely controls. With respect to the military "contractors" the control relationship is the sort that renders the "contractors" a functional part of one management organization.

It is therefore invalid to hold that the men in the several contracting firms and the men in the Defense Department management are all part of an essentially homogeneous group (Galbraith's "technostructure"), more or less similar in their capabilities and work performances. With respect to decision power some are more equal than others. That inequality in decision power is defined by the place where final decisions are made: final means the person whose decision cannot be vetoed by anyone else. By that test it is the management of the Department of Defense and its senior personnel—finally, the Secretary of Defense and the President of the United States—who are the top decision makers in this firm.

The consequences from this development for the American economy and society are extensive. Studies in process on the operating characteristics of this organization suggest that a true transformation of the essential character of American society has been fashioned within the government of the United States. The location of peak economic and political decision power in the same hands is one of the essential and characteristic features of a Soviet-type society. This feature is precisely what has been wrought in the U.S. through the new industrial management in the Department of Defense.

The following is a list, with brief comments, of statements of ideology that are specific to and contribute to the maintenance and extension of the decision power of America's new military industry management:

1. *Growth is a hallmark of economic health.* This statement does not differentiate growth—it implies that any kind of growth is healthy. From the standpoint of economic function, it is possible to differentiate clearly between growth that is parasitic and growth that is productive. Productive growth is activity whose products, goods and services, are parts of the level of living or contribute to further production. Growth in outputs of civilian goods and services of all sorts is readily recognized as contributing to productive growth. The contrast is parasitic growth—output of goods and services that are not part of the level of living and cannot be used for further production—characteristics of military goods and services. The common use of the money unit to measure all economic activity masks the functional difference between parasitic and productive growth.

2. *As long as the Gross National Product rises, income and resources are available for new programs.* This is not necessarily true. Insofar as GNP increases occur in sectors of parasitic growth, then the increased quantity of money-valued goods and services is not necessarily available for productive uses.

3. *The productive resources of this nation are so great that an indefinite number of public programs, foreign and domestic, can be pursued simultaneously.* Not necessarily. The U.S., with a GNP per person of over $4,000 per year, is nevertheless constrained in its work capabilities by a finite stock of manpower, especially skilled manpower. When this manpower has been allocated, then further economic growth, of whatever sort, that requires skilled manpower cannot be performed.

Under such conditions, the creation of more money or the appropriation of money for additional work will not make it happen. Thus, with the lion's share of the nation's research and development talent pre-empted by the armed forces and organizations that serve them, it is unfeasible for American railroads to operate other than Toonerville Trolleys on passenger services. The same military priority system does make it possible to have commercial airplanes that are adaptations of military airplanes. Similarly, it is now impossible for the U.S. to do what is needed to maintain health services: for example, we need 3 new medical schools *per state* while present programs are for the construction, by 1975, of 13 new medical schools for all 50 states. There will be a decline in health services for the American people.

Despite such demonstrations, the assumption that the productive resources of the nation are indefinitely large remains a piece of conventional wisdom that is widely trusted by senior officers of the U.S. government and by their ideologists.

At this writing parasitic military spending by the U.S. amounts to over $80 billion per year, two-thirds of the federal budget. If one adds the capital investment required for an anti-ballistics missile system, the civil defense program that must accompany it, multiple independent re-entry vehicles (new nuclear warheads), the C5 aircraft program (700 soldiers per intercontinental jet), and the counterinsurgency forces, one discovers an additional capital outlay for parasitic growth of not less than $500 billion. If the work were to be done over a five-year period this would require more than doubling the military budget. To the extent that such plans are given first priority, an inevitable consequence will be to make unavailable all manner of crucial resources for other work in this society.

4. *Military industry and research help civilian industry via "spillover" in knowledge and design factors.* True, the development of computers for civilian use got something from the investment made in computers for military use. True, the commercial jetliner came, in part, from the Air Force's jet refueling tanker. True, we have nuclear energy capability that may be increasingly useful for civilian purposes. Do these economically meaningful "spillovers" justify the use of over three-fourths of the government's research and develop-

ment budget for military and allied purposes?

None of these "spillover" effects justify the gross depletion and deterioration in many of our civilian industries. I recorded the first draft of this paper on a tape recorder that was made in Japan, not Schenectady. Americans did major theoretical work in the physics of the solid state, and enormous work on the application of the solid state for technological purposes. But those technological applications have been, mainly, military applications. That is why for the first time, a new, mass-produced, durable-goods product was designed, produced, and marketed outside the United States. The inexpensive transistor radio, TV set, and tape recorder are products of the electronics industry of Japan, whose young electronics engineers have no place to go except to civilian industry employers.

5. *Military priority produces domestic stability because of high-level economic activity.* On the contrary, sustained military priority and the unavailability of resources for much civilian investment is producing insurrection at home. Military priority over a long period makes impossible the reconstruction of the cities and the investment in human capital and in new work places that is essential if 30 million Americans are to be economically developed. About 7.5 million American families live in poverty. One estimate of the capital outlay required for their economic development is $30,000 per family. Thus, a capital fund of $225 million is required to raise the impoverished of our own country to productive status. That capital fund, and the manpower it must represent, are both unavailable and inaccessible today and in the foreseeable future, so long as the present military priority is sustained.

6. *Military organizations yield stability abroad.* The most recent data assembled by the U.S. Arms Control and Disarmament Agency show that the less developed nations of the earth have been spending more on arms than for education and public health. This sort of priority curtails economic development and breeds movements of rebellion against the regimes that are responsible for human neglect.

7. *Individual, corporate, and govern-* *ment money-making is a competent test* *of economic productivity.* We may ask: productive in what sense? Is the outcome productive growth or is it parasitic growth? And productive in what moral sense? After all, values do count for something. If the money-making activity is done in the furtherance of illegality, if it is done in complicity with violation of the laws of war (i.e. war crimes), then is that to be regarded as acceptable economic performance? Constraints are indispensable. Money-making *per se* cannot be regarded by society as a sufficient end in itself.

8. *Military-industrial firms are new industries with a high level of technical competence and represent a general enrichment of the technical and managerial resources of the nation.* Close scrutiny suggests that managements of these subsidiaries of the national military-industrial firm are infused with a trained incapacity for operating civilian enterprises functioning in the civilian market place. Attempts by these managements to enter civilian markets have mainly failed. The failures did not result from personal incompetence. Rather they stemmed from the fact that the management methods, costs, and technological requirements for the military market are inappropriate in the civilian sphere. Thus, the management style, technology, equipment, and practices required for producing certain nuclear submarines at $12 per pound are hopelessly inappropriate for producing commercial oil tankers at less than $1 per pound.

9. *Military-industrial firms can readily convert to civilian work if that is required.* The evidence of the 1963–64 period when there were minor curtailments in military contracts instructs us to the contrary. It will be necessary to motivate these organizations strongly to attempt possible conversion planning. Beyond that it will be necessary to salvage the bulk of the individuals involved in the military-industrial sector with appropriate retraining and relocation programs for transferring them to civilian work.

10. *We might just as well maintain military priorities, for even if we tried to realign priorities, Congress would not allocate the funds needed.* In 1939–40, the Congress

of the United States appropriated 42 per cent of the federal budget for social welfare, community development, health, education, housing, and allied purposes. The same set of purposes recently received about 10 per cent of Congressional appropriations. There is no science from which to forecast that if Congress could do it in 1940, it could not do it again, today. There is nothing in the nature of Congress as an institution that precludes changing an order of priorities.

11. *Concentration of decision power in the federal government is inevitable and, in any case, desirable, as in the Department of Defense, in the name of economic-industrial efficiency.* Efficiency indeed. Under the guidance of the Secretary of Defense, the F-111 airplane program was supposed to cost $3.4 billion. The latest estimate is $12 billion. This ratio between expected and actual costs is fairly typical of industrial performance for the Department of Defense. Wherever the customer or competitor constraints of a commercial market are operative, this sort of cost performance would compel either a change of management or bankruptcy, or both. In the land of military industry gross inefficiency has become normal. And so the polite thing is to be learned about the programs for "cost effectiveness" and the miracles generated by "cost-benefit analysis," thereby detracting attention from staggering cost-excesses that would be self-penalizing elsewhere. There is little evidence to be found in these spheres of ordinary work-a-day economy and efficiency.

12. *The diminishing level of U.S. Treasury gold reserves is an economic-technical detail and the present condition is simply a stepping stone to a new and better monetary order.* On the contrary, the decline of the gold reserve is a very real threat to the value of the dollar. The decline is the consequence of a chronic imbalance of payments that has been generated by parasitic military spending abroad. If the trend is not arrested and reversed, the consequences for the world position of the United States will necessarily be the same as those Great Britain has suffered.

13. *The management of the Department*

of Defense uses modern techniques to make rational decisions and employs resources to yield high returns to the taxpayer. The total cost of military operations in Vietnam approaches $100 billion, or about half the capital fund required for a major economic development program in the U.S. for 30 million Americans who are visibly underdeveloped. Moreover, military operations in Vietnam would not score well under any serious evaluation in terms of cost-effectiveness or cost-benefit analyses. The major field operation under McNamara, with Joint Chiefs given unprecedented resources, has been a military and political failure.

In the strategic sphere, the Department of Defense has built a nuclear arsenal with a delivery capability of more than six tons of TNT per person on the planet. However, since it is not reasonable to assume that competence for killing people more than once exists in the Department of Defense — or anywhere else — we must conclude that the squandering of the resources of this society on overkill capacity is a piece of monumental irrationality. Nevertheless, the overkill program does make professional good sense for the new military industry managers. For these military expenditures tend to maintain and extend the decision power of this new managerial unit at the peak of the federal government.

14. *If university professors and students would work on research problems of interest to the Department of Defense, then all will be well for the national defense, for the universities and for the nation as well.* This is not necessarily true. There are strong grounds for supposing that long concentration on military priorities, with the proliferation of military research activity, threatens the integrity of the university and undermines the traditional function of the university: generating new knowledge and teaching people.

Military technology, like other technology, and its consequences are plainly cast in the image of man's social condition. Political purpose has been imprinted on the design of our military establishment and on the very design of its weapons. The root is not in technology, but in man.

Opportunity Cost

19. The Price of War

Who pays for defense? A cost/benefit analysis of the American empire.

Bruce M. Russett

"Peace" stocks are up; "war" stocks are down; congressmen scrutinize Pentagon expenditures with newly-jaundiced eyes. Any (New Left) schoolboy can rattle off a list of the top ten defense contractors: General Electric, Boeing, General Dynamics, North American Aviation. . . . Scholars and journalists have worked hard lately, and now almost everyone knows who *profits* from defense spending. But who knows who *pays* for it?

Nothing comes free, and national defense is no exception. Yet curiously little attention has been paid to the question of which segments of American society and its economy are disproportionately sacrificed when defense spending rises. Despite some popular opinion to the contrary, our economy is a good deal less than infinitely expansible. Something has to give when military expenditures take larger bites out of the pie. But when this happens, what kinds of public and private expenditures are curtailed or fail to grow at previously established rates? What particular interests or pressure groups show up as relatively strong or relatively weak in maintaining their accustomed standards of living? And which of them are better able to seize the opportunities offered when international conflict cools off for awhile?

The questions, of course, are implicitly political, and they are important. But the answers have to be sought within economic data. What we want, in a sense, is a "cost-benefit" analysis of war or the preparations for war, an analysis that will tell us not only who most profits from war, but who most bears its burden. Apart from the direct costs in taxation and changes in wages and prices, which I will not go into

Reprinted from *Trans*-action, October 1969. Copyright © October 1969 by *Trans*-action, Inc., New Brunswick, New Jersey.

here, there are the equally significant costs in social benefits, in opportunities foregone or opportunities postponed.

What I want to do here is to examine *expenditures*—by categories of the Gross National Product, by their function and by governmental unit—to see what kinds of alternative spending suffer under the impact of heavy military spending. The necessary data are available for the period 1939–68, and they allow us to see the effects of two earlier wars (World War II and the Korean War) as well as the burdens of the current Vietnam venture.

First, however, an overview of the changing level of defense expenditures may be helpful. For 1939, in what was in many ways the last peacetime year this nation experienced, defense expenditures were under $1.3 billion. With the coming of war they rose rapidly to a still unsurpassed peak of $87.4 billion in 1944. The 1968 figure was by contrast around $78.4 billion, reflecting a build-up, for the Vietnam war, from levels of about $50 billion in the first half of this decade. The raw dollar figures, however, are deceptive because they reflect neither inflation nor the steady growth in the economy's productive capacity that makes a constant defense budget, even in price-adjusted dollars, a diminishing burden.

The graph shows the trend of military expenditures as a percentage of Gross National Product over the past thirty years. We immediately see the great burdens of World War II, followed by a drop to a floor considerably above that of the 1930's. The Cold War and particularly the Korean action produced another upsurge in the early 1950's to a level that, while substantial, was by no means the equal of that in the Second World War. This too trailed downward after the immediate emergency was past, though again it did not retreat to the previous floor. In fact, not since the beginning of the Cold War has the military accounted for noticeably less than 5 percent of this country's G.N.P.; not since Korea has it had as little as 7 percent.

This repeated failure to shrink the mili-

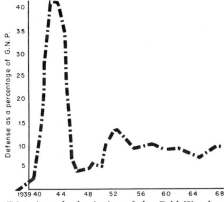

"Not since the beginning of the Cold War has the military accounted for noticeably less than 5 percent of this country's G.N.P.; not since Korea has it had as little as 7 percent."

tary establishment back to its prewar level is a phenomenon of some interest to students of the dynamics of international arms races and/or Parkinson's Law. It shows up even more clearly in the data on military personnel, and goes back almost a century to demonstrate the virtual doubling of the armed forces after every war. From 1871 to 1898 the American armed forces numbered fewer than 50,000; after the Spanish-American War they never again dropped below 100,000. The aftermath of World War I saw a leveling off to about 250,000, but the World War II mobilization left 1,400,000 as the apparent permanent floor. Since the Korean War the United States military establishment has never numbered fewer than about 2,500,000 men. Should the post-Vietnam armed forces and/or defense portion of the G.N.P. prove to be higher than in the early and mid-1960's, that will represent another diversion from private or civil public resources and a major indirect but perhaps very real "cost" of the war.

Returning to the graph, we see the effect of the Vietnam build-up, moving from a recent low of 7.3 percent in 1965 to 9.2 percent in 1968. This last looks modest enough, and is, when compared to the effects of the nation's two previous major wars. At the same time, it also represents a real sacrifice by other portions of the economy. The 1968 G.N.P. of the United States was well in excess of $800 billion;

if we were to assume that the current war effort accounts for about 2 percent of that (roughly the difference between the 7.3 percent of 1965 and the 9.2 percent of 1968) the dollar amount is approximately $16 billion. That is in fact too low a figure, since some billions were already being devoted to the war in 1965, and direct estimates of the war's cost are typically about $25 to $30 billion per year. The amounts in question, representing scarce resources which might be put to alternative uses, are not trivial.

I assume that defense spending has to come *at the expense* of something else. In the formal sense of G.N.P. proportions that is surely true, but it is usually true in a more interesting sense as well. Economics is said to be the study of the allocation of scarce resources; and, despite some periods of slack at the beginning of war-time periods (1940–41 and 1950), resources have generally been truly scarce during America's wars. Major civilian expenditures have not only lost ground proportionately (as would nevertheless happen from a military spending program financed entirely out of slack) but they have also failed to grow at their accustomed rates, they have lost ground in constant dollars as a result of inflation, or they have even declined absolutely in current dollars. During World War II, for example, such major categories as personal consumption of durable goods, all fixed investment, federal purchases of non-military goods and services, and state and local expenditures all declined sharply in absolute dollar amounts despite an inflation of nearly 8 percent a year.

Some observers argue that high levels of military spending are introduced to take up the slack and maintain demand in an otherwise depression-prone economy. If this were the case, opportunity costs would be minimal. But there is little evidence for that proposition in the American experience of recent decades. Certainly the Vietnam experience does not support it. I assume, *pace* "Iron Mountain," that with the demonstrable public and private needs of this society, and with modern tools of economic analysis and manipulation, full or near-full employment of resources would be maintained even in the face of major cuts in military spending. Because of the skill with which economic systems are now managed in modern economies, defense expenditures are much more likely to force tradeoffs than they were some thirty years ago. Hence the point of my original question, "Who pays for defense?"

I do not argue that defense expenditures are necessarily without broader social utility. Spending for military research and development produces important (if sometimes overrated). technological spillovers into the civilian sector. The education, skills and physical conditioning that young men obtain during service in the armed forces are likely to benefit them and their society when they return to civilian life. Nevertheless the achievement of such benefits through spill-overs is rarely the most efficient way to obtain them. While scientific research may be serendipitous, the odds are far better that a new treatment for cancer will come from medical research than from work on missile systems. Therefore we must still consider as real costs the trade-offs that appear when defense cuts deep into the G.N.P., though they are not quite so heavy as a literal interpretation of the dollar amounts would imply.

One must also recognize that some civilian expenditures—for health, for education and for research—have been stimulated by Cold War and ultimately military requirements. Such were various programs of the 1950's, when a greater need was felt for a long-run girding of the loins than for more immediate military capabilities. Still, to concede this is far from undercutting the relevance of the kind of question we shall be asking. If civilian and military expenditures consistently compete for scarce resources, then the one will have a negative effect on the other; if both are driven by the same demands, they will be positively correlated. If they generally compete but are sometimes viewed as complementary, the negative correlation will be fairly low.

An evaluation of the relationship of defense and alternative kinds of spending in this country requires some explicit criteria. There is room for serious argument about what those criteria should be, but I will suggest the following:

1. It is bad to sacrifice future productivity and resources for current preparation for war or war itself; insofar as possible such activities should be financed out of current consumption. Such an assumption might be easily challenged if it were offered as a universal, but for the developed countries of North America and Western Europe in recent years it seems defensible. All of them are now, relative to their own past and to other nations' present, extremely affluent, with a high proportion of their resources flowing into consumption in the private sector. Furthermore, for most of the years 1938–68, the demands of defense have not been terribly great. Since the end of World War II, none of these countries has had to devote more than about 10 percent of its G.N.P. to military needs, save for the United States during the Korean War when the figure rose to just over 13 percent. It is surely arguable that such needs rarely require substantial mortgaging of a nation's future.

a. By this criterion one would hope to see periodic upswings in defense requirements financed largely out of personal consumption, with capital formation and such social investment in the public sector as health and education being insensitive to military demands.

b. Another aspect of this criterion, however, is that one would also anticipate that in periods of *declining* military needs the released resources would largely be *kept* for investment and education rather than returned to private consumption. In a strong form the criterion calls for a long-term increase in the proportion of G.N.P. devoted to various forms of investment, an increase that would show up on a graph as a fluctuating line made up of a series of upward slopes followed by plateaus, insensitive to rising defense needs but responsive to the opportunities provided by relaxations in the armament pace.

2. Another point of view, partially in conflict with the last comment, would stress the need for a high degree of *insulation from political shocks.* A constant and enlarging commitment to the system's

social resources is necessary for the most orderly and efficient growth of the system, avoiding the digestive problems produced by alternate feast and famine. Some spending, on capital expenditures for buildings for instance, may be only temporarily postponed in periods of fiscal stringency, and may bounce back to a higher level when the pressure of defense needs is eased. To that degree the damage would be reduced, but not eliminated. In the first place, school construction that is "merely" postponed four years will come in time to help some students, but for four years a great many students simply lose out. Secondly, boom and bust fluctuations, even if they do average out to the socially-desired dollar level, are likely to be inefficient and produce less real output than would a steadier effort.

GUNS, BUTTER AND STRUCTURES

Calculation of a nation's G.N.P. is an exercise in accounting; economists define the Gross National Product as the sum of expenditures for personal consumption, investment or capital formation, government purchases of goods and services and net foreign trade (exports minus imports). Each of these categories can be broken down. Private consumption is the sum of expenditures on durable goods (e.g., automobiles, furniture, appliances), nondurables (e.g., food, clothing, fuel) and services (airline tickets, haircuts, entertainment); investment includes fixed investment in non-residential structures, producers' durable equipment (e.g., machinery), residential structures and the accumulation or drawing down of stocks (inventories); government purchases include both civil and military expenditures of the federal government and spending by state and local units of government. Except for inventories (which fluctuate widely in response to current conditions and are of little interest for this study) we shall

The Effect of Defense Spending on Civilian Activities in the United States, 1939–68

	% OF VARIATION	REGRESSION COEFFICIENT	INDEX OF PROPORTIONATE REDUCTION
Personal Consumption Total	84	—.420	—.041
Durable Goods	78	—.163	—.123
Nondurable Goods	04	—.071	—.014
Services	54	—.187	—.050
Fixed Investment Total	72	—.292	—.144
Nonresidential Structures	62	—.068	—.140
Producers' Durable Equipment	71	—.110	—.123
Residential Structures	60	—.114	—.176
Exports	67	—.097	—.115
Imports	19	—.025	—.037
Federal Civil Purchases	38	—.048	—.159
State & Local Gov't Consumption	38	—.128	—.105

look at all these, and later at a further breakdown of public expenditures by level and function.

In the table, the first column of figures — the percentage of variance explained — tells *how closely* defense spending and the alternate spending category vary together — how much of the changes in the latter can be "accounted for" by defense changes. The regression coefficient tells *the amount in dollars* by which the alternate spending category changes in response to a one dollar increase in defense. The proportionate reduction index shows the damage suffered by each category relative to its "normal" base. It assumes for illustration a total G.N.P. of $400 billion, an increase of $25 billion in defense-spending from the previous period, and that the alternative expenditure category had previously been at that level represented by its mean percentage of G.N.P. over the 1946–67 period.

This last measure is important for policy purposes, since the *impact* of the same dollar reduction will be far greater to a $100 billion investment program than to a $500 billion total for consumer-spending.

Looking at the table, one can see that, in general, the American experience has been that the consumer pays most. Guns do come at the expense of butter. Changes in defense expenditure account for 84 percent of the ups and downs in total personal *consumption*, and the regression coefficient is a relatively high –.420. That is, a one dollar rise in defense expenditures will, all else being equal, result in a decline of $.42 in private consumption.

Of the subcategories, sales of consumer durables are most vulnerable, with 78 percent of their variations accounted for by defense. Spending on services is also fairly vulnerable to defense expenditures, with the latter accounting for 54 percent of the variance. But the negative effect of defense spending on nondurables is not nearly so high, with only 4 percent of the variance accounted for. This is not surprising, however, as needs for nondurables are almost by definition the least easily postponed. Moreover, during the World War II years new consumer durables such as automobiles and appliances were virtually unavailable, since the factories that normally produced them were then turning out war material. Similarly, due to manpower shortages almost all services were expensive and in short supply, and long-distance travel was particularly discouraged ("Is this trip necessary?"). Hence, to the degree that the consumers' spending power was not mopped up by taxes or saved, an unusually high proportion was likely to go into nondurables.

Investment (fixed capital formation) also is typically hard-hit by American war efforts and, because it means a smaller productive capacity in later years, diminished investment is a particularly costly loss. Defense accounted for 72 percent of the variations in investment, which is only a little less than that for defense on consumption, and the reduction of $.292 in investment for every $1.00 rise in defense is substantial. The coefficient is of course much lower than that for defense and consumption (with a coefficient of –.420) but that is very deceptive considering the "normal" base from which each starts. Over the thirty years for which we have the figures, consumption took a mean percentage of G.N.P. that was typically about five times as great as investment. Thus in our hypothetical illustration a $25 billion increase in defense costs in a G.N.P. of $400 billion would, *ceteris paribus,* result in a drop in consumption from approximately $256 billion to roughly $245 billion or only a little over 4 percent of total consumption. Investment, on the other hand, would typically fall from $51 billion to about $44 billion, or more than 14 percent. *Proportionately,* therefore, investment is much *harder* hit by an expansion of the armed services than is consumption. Since future production is dependent upon current investment, the economy's *future* resources and power base are thus much more severely damaged by the decision to build or employ current military power than is current indulgence. According to some rough estimates, the marginal productivity of capital in the United States is between 20 and 25 percent; that is, an additional dollar of investment in any single year will produce 20–25 cents of annual additional production in perpetuity. Hence if an extra billion dollars of defense in one year reduced investment by $292 million, thenceforth the level of output in the economy would be *permanently* diminished by a figure on the order of $65 million per year.

This position is modified slightly by the detailed breakdown of investment categories. Residential structures (housing) vary less closely with defense spending than do non-housing structures or durable goods for producers, but its regression coefficient is the strongest and shows that it takes the greatest proportionate damage. Within the general category of investment, therefore, nonresidential structures and equipment usually hold up somewhat better proportionately than does housing. Doubtless this is the result of deliberate public policy, which raises home interest rates and limits the availability of mortgages while trying at the same time to maintain an adequate flow of capital to those firms needing to convert or expand into military production.

The nation's international *balance of payments* is often a major casualty of sharp increases in military expenditures; the present situation is not unusual. Some potential exports are diverted to satisfy internal demand, others are lost because domestic inflation raises costs to a point where the goods are priced out of the world market. Imports may rise directly to meet the armed forces' procurement needs—goods purchased abroad to fill local American military requirements show up as imports to the national economy—and other imports rise indirectly because of domestic demand. Some goods normally purchased from domestic suppliers are not available in sufficient quantities; others, because of inflation, become priced above imported goods. If the present situation is "typical," the Vietnam war's cost to the civilian economy would be responsible for a loss of more than $1.5 billion dollars in exports.

The import picture is more complicated. According to the sketch above, imports should *rise* with defense spending, but in the table the percentage of variance explained is very low and the regression coefficient is actually *negative*. This, however, is deceptive. The four years of World War II show unusually low importation due to a combination of enemy occupation of normal sources of goods for the United States, surface and submarine combat in the sea lanes and the diversion of our allies' normal export industries to serve *their* war needs. To assess the impact of defense expenditures on imports in a less than global war one must omit the World War II data from the analysis. Doing so produces the expected rise in imports with higher defense spending, on the order of +.060. This suggests that the current effect of Vietnam may be to add, directly and indirectly, over $1 billion to the nation's annual import bill. Coupled with the loss of exports, the total damage to the balance of payments on current account (excluding capital transfers) is in the range $2.5–$3.0 billion. That still does not account for the entire balance of payments deficit that

the United States is experiencing (recently as high as $3.4 billion annually) but it goes a long way to explain it.

THE PUBLIC SECTOR

In the aggregate there is no very strong impact of defense on *civil public expenditures*. The amount of variation accounted for by defense is a comparatively low 38 percent; the regression coefficients are only –.048 for federal civil purchases and –.013 for state and local governments. During the four peak years of World War II changes in federal civil expenditures were essentially unrelated to changes in defense spending. Samuel P. Huntington, however, notes, "Many programs in agriculture, natural resources, labor and welfare dated back to the 1930's or middle 1940's. By the mid-1950's they had become accepted responsibilities of the government," and hence politically resistant to the arms squeeze. If so, the overall inverse relationship we do find may be masking sharper changes in some of the less well-entrenched subcategories of central government budgeting. Further masking of the impact on actual programs may stem from the inability of government agencies to reduce costs for building-maintenance and tenured employees, thus forcing them in dry times to cut other expenses disproportionately.

When relating state and local government expenditures to defense some restraint is required. There really is no relationship except *between* the points above and below the 15 percent mark for defense. During World War II state and local government units did have their spending activities curtailed, but overall they have not been noticeably affected by defense purchases. Quite to the contrary, spending by state and local political units has risen steadily, in an almost unbroken line, since 1944. The rise, from 3.6 percent of the G.N.P. to 11.2 percent in 1968, has continued essentially heedless of increases or diminution in the military's demands on the economy.

When we look at the breakdowns by function, however, it becomes clear that the effect of defense fluctuations is more serious, if less distinct than for G.N.P. categories. I have chosen three major items—education, health and welfare—for further analysis, on the grounds that one might reasonably hypothesize for each that expenditure levels would be sensitive to military needs, and, for the first two, that a neglect of them would do serious long-term damage to the economy and social system of the nation.

All three are sensitive to defense spending, with *welfare* somewhat more so than the others, which is not surprising. In most of this analysis reductions in expenditure levels that are forced by expanded defense activities represent a *cost* to the economic and social system, but welfare is different. Insofar as the *needs* for welfare, rather than simply the resources allocated to it, are reduced, one cannot properly speak of a cost to the economy. Rather, if one's social preferences are for work rather than welfare, the shift represents a *gain* to the system. Heavy increases in military pay and procurement do mean a reduction in unemployment, and military cutbacks are often associated with at least temporary or local unemployment. The effect seems strongest on state and local governments'

welfare spending. In fact, the inverse relationship between defense and welfare at most spending levels is *understated* at 54 percent on the chart. At all but the highest levels of defense spending achieved in World War II, the inverse relationship is very steep, with small increases in military needs having a very marked dampening effect on welfare costs. But manpower was quite fully employed during *all* the years of major effort in World War II, so ups and downs in defense needs during 1942–45 had little effect.

Both for education and for health and hospitals, the relationship to the immediate requirements of national defense is less powerful (less variance is explained), but nonetheless important. Furthermore, the regression coefficient is quite high for education, and since the mean share of G.N.P. going to education is only 3.5 percent for the period under consideration, the proportionate impact of reductions is severe.

A widespread assumption holds that public expenditures on *education* have experienced a long-term secular growth in the United States. That assumption is correct only with modifications. The proportion of G.N.P. devoted to public edu-

---

The Effect of Defense Spending on Public Civil Activities in the U.S., Fiscal Years 1938–67

	% OF VARIATION	REGRESSION COEFFICIENT	INDEX OF PROPORTIONATE REDUCTION
Education—Total	**35**	**—.077**	**—.139**
Institutions of Higher Ed.	12	—.013	—.146
Local Schools	34	—.053	—.125
Other Ed.	19	—.014	—.265
Federal Direct to Ed.	16	—.013	—.309
Federal Aid to State & Local Gov'ts for Ed.	08	—.004	—.140
State & Local Gov't for Ed.	24	—.060	—.124
Health & Hospitals—Total	**32**	**—.017**	**—.113**
Total Hospitals	30	—.014	—.123
Fed. for Hospitals	25	—.004	—.130
State & Local for Hospitals	29	—.011	—.120
Other Health—Total	**22**	**—.003**	**—.087**
Fed. for Health	06	—.001	—.101
State & Local for Health	45	—.002	—.078
Welfare—Total	**54**	**.019**	**—.128**
Fed. Direct for Welfare	13	.003	—.493
Fed. Aid to State & Local Gov'ts for Welfare	17	—.005	—.087
State & Local for Welfare	30	—.011	—.134

cation has increased by three quarters over the period, from 3.0 percent in 1938 to 5.3 percent in 1967. But it has by no means been a smooth and steady upward climb. World War II cut deeply into educational resources, dropping the educational percentage of G.N.P. to 1.4 in 1944; only in 1950 did it recover to a level (3.6 percent) notably above that of the 1930's. Just at that point the Korean War intervened, and education once more suffered, not again surpassing the 3.6 percent level before 1959. Since then, however, it has grown fairly steadily without being adversely affected by the relatively modest rises in defense spending. Actually, educational needs may have benefitted somewhat from the overall decline in the military proportion of the economy that took place between the late 1950's and mid-1960's. The sensitivity of educational expenditures to military needs is nevertheless much more marked on the latter's upswings than on its declines. Education usually suffers very immediately when the military needs to expand sharply; it recovers its share only slowly after defense spending has peaked. Surprisingly, *federal* educational expenditures are less related (less variance explained) than is spending by state and local units of government; also, local schools at the primary and secondary levels are more sensitive than are public institutions of higher education, whose share has grown in every year since 1953.

Public expenditures for *health* and hospitals are only a little less sensitive to the pressures of defense than are dollars for education. Here again the image of a long-term growth deceptively hides an equally significant pattern of swings. Health and hospitals accounted for a total of .77 percent of G.N.P. in 1938; as with education this was sharply cut by World War II and was not substantially surpassed (at 1 percent) until 1950. Once more they lost out to the exigencies of defense in the early 1950's, and bounced back slowly, at the same rate as did education, to recover the 1950 level in 1958. Since then they have continued growing slowly, with a peak of 1.23 in 1967. Thus, the pattern of health and hospitals is almost identical to that for education — some long-term growth, but

great cutbacks in periods of heavy military need and only slow recovery thereafter. In detail by political unit the picture is also much the same — despite reasonable a priori expectation, federal spending for this item is less closely tied to the defense budget than is that by state and local governments. It should also be noted that the *impact* of defense on health and hospitals is slightly less severe than on education.

It seems fair to conclude from these data that America's most expensive wars have severely hampered the nation in its attempt to build a healthier and better-educated citizenry. (One analyst estimates that what *was* done to strengthen education accounted for nearly half of the United States per capita income growth between 1929 and 1957.) A long-term effort has been made, and with notable results, but typically it has been badly cut back whenever military needs pressed unusually hard.

It is too soon to know how damaging the Vietnam war will be, but in view of past patterns one would anticipate significant costs. The inability to make "investments" would leave Americans poorer, more ignorant and less healthy than would otherwise be the case. We have already seen the effect of the war on fixed capital formation. Consumption absorbed a larger *absolute* decline in its share of G.N.P. between 1965 and 1968 than did fiscal investment — from 63.3 to 62.1 percent in the first instance, from 14.3 to 13.8 percent in the second; but given the much smaller base of investment, the *proportionate* damage is about twice as great to investment as to consumption. In most of the major categories of public social "investment," nevertheless, the record is creditable. Despite a rise from 7.6 to 9.1 percent in the defense share between 1965 and 1967, the total public education and health and hospitals expenditure shares went up 4.5 to 5.3 percent and from 1.17 to 1.23 percent respectively. And even federal spending for education and health, though not hospitals, rose. There are of course other costs involved in the inability to *initiate* needed programs — massive aid to the cities is the obvious example. But on maintaining or expanding established patterns of expenditure the score is not bad at all.

The pattern of federal expenditures for *research and development* indicates some recent but partially hidden costs to education and medicine. From 1955 through 1966 R & D expenditures rose spectacularly and steadily from $3.3 billion to $14.9 billion. Obviously such a skyrocketing growth could not continue indefinitely; not even most of the beneficiary scientists expected it to do so, and in fact the rate of increase of expenditures fell sharply as early as 1966—the first year since 1961 when the defense share of G.N.P. showed any notable increase.

Finally, we must note a very important sense in which many of these cost estimates are substantially underestimated. My entire analysis has necessarily been done with expenditure data in current prices; that is, not adjusted for inflation. Since we have been dividing each expenditure category by G.N.P. in current dollars that would not matter *providing that price increases were uniform throughout the economy.* But if prices increased faster in say, education or health, than did prices across the board, the *real* level of expenditure would be exaggerated. And as anyone who has recently paid a hospital bill or college tuition bill knows, some prices have increased faster than others. From 1950 through 1967 the cost of medical care, as registered in the consumer price index, rose by 86.2 percent. Thus even though the health and hospital share of public expenditure rose in *current* prices, the *real share* of national production bought by that spending *fell* slightly, from one percent to about .99 percent. Presumably the difference has been made up in the private sector, and benefits have been heavily dependent upon ability to pay. Comparable data on educational expenses are less easy to obtain, but we do know that the average tuition in private colleges and universities rose 39 percent, and in public institutions 32 percent, over the years 1957–67. This too is faster than the cost of living increase over those years (not more than 20 percent), but not enough to wipe out a gain for government education expenditures in their share of real G.N.P.

In evaluating the desirability of an expanded defense effort, policy-makers must bear in mind the opportunity costs of defense, the kinds and amounts of expenditures that will be foregone. The relationships we have discovered in past American experience suggest what the costs of future military efforts may be, although these relationships are not of course immutable. Should it be concluded that certain new defense needs must be met, it is possible by careful choice and control to distribute the burdens somewhat differently. If costs cannot be avoided, perhaps they can be borne in such a way as to better protect the nation's future.

Money, Gold, Inflation

20. What The Vietnam War Has Cost
Terence McCarthy

Since the United States entered in force into Vietnam, through the fiscal year ended June 30, 1968, the war in Vietnam will have cost the United States $54 billion in

Reprinted from *New University Thought*, Vol. 6, No. 4, Summer 1968. Copyright © *New University Thought.* Reprinted by permission.

direct military costs plus billions of dollars of sales of government assets and rundown of military inventories; raised the annual rate of Vietnam war expenditures to $29 billion in calendar 1968; reduced the purchasing power of the consumer's dollar by almost 9 per cent; distorted the economy by adding only 1.6 million production workers to manufacturing payrolls compared with 2.3 million to government payrolls; caused a loss in housing construction of at least 750,000 dwelling units; raised interest rates to the highest levels in a century; deepened the poverty of the poor by increasing food prices 10 per cent; raised the interest-bearing federal debt by $23 billion; produced a $20 billion federal deficit in fiscal 1968 even assuming a tax increase; rendered impossible required expenditures on renovation of America's decaying cities; increased the adverse balance of payments insupportably; cost the nation the gold cover of its dollar; forced the establishing of a two-tier price for gold throughout the world; generated the greatest threat of inflation since the Civil War; and has cost Mr. Lyndon Johnson the Presidency of the United States.

These are among the visible consequences of the war, or more properly, of a war whose ferocity and cost have been underestimated by an Administration self-deceived as to the efficacy of military solution to social problems in foreign lands.

The invisible costs are at least as great. Most immediate is emergence of the Soviet Union as a Mediterranean power despite the presence of the U.S. 6th Fleet in those waters. The Vietnam war, in fact, has increased Soviet influence—economic, diplomatic, military, and political—in Europe, North Africa, India, Pakistan, and South-East Asia—a development which, whether desirable or undesirable from the viewpoint of the United States and the world at large, might not have occurred, and could not have occurred with such extraordinary ease, had the United States not become constrained as to action by its concentration upon Vietnam.

It is not too much to say that the entire world position of the United States has been weakened as its inability has been demonstrated to control the conduct of a foreign people, numerically and industrially weak, and isolated in a mere corner of South East Asia, resolved not to be controlled from abroad. . . .

Increased trade between the United States and Russia, however desirable on other grounds, has now become essential to stability of the exchange value of the dollar. Russia is the sole remaining source of potential large inflows of gold to the United States at $35 per ounce. It is by no means certain that the Soviet Union may prove willing, except sporadically, to barter her newly-mined gold at $35 an ounce for American capital equipment. It is certain that only such trade can help, at today's official price for gold, replenish America's gold stock, badly depleted by the Vietnam war.

GOLD

On the question of gold—as on many other issues—the American people are puzzled. Over the years they have been assured, successively, that (1) the gold stock of the United States was impregnable; (2) threats to the gold stock could be fended off with ease by voluntary constraints upon the movement of long- and short-term capital abroad; (3) conservation of the gold stock was critical to stability of the dollar; (4) gold is a barbarous metal unrelated to stability of the dollar; and (5) strength and stability of the dollar are functions not of gold reserves but of expansion of the domestic economy and of America's industrial productivity.

With all these protestations, including pronouncements by President Johnson that the dollar would be maintained "as good as or better than gold," expenditures on the war in Vietnam have compelled the United States in association with West Germany, England, Italy, Switzerland, Belgium, the Netherlands, the International Monetary Fund, and the Bank for International Settlements to free newly mined gold, and all gold not in the hands of the Central Banks as of March 17, 1968, to seek its own price level outside the world monetary system.

Two prices now exist for gold. One, a fixed, official price of $35 per ounce among Central Banks, the other a free market price fluctuating in some unknown range from $35 an ounce upwards or downwards. What gold is worth, i.e., what the dollar is worth in terms of gold, is the imponderable of the weeks and months ahead.

To understand the meaning, both long- and short-term, of the gold drain upon the people of the United States, it is necessary to recapitulate how America got its gold stock and what has happened to diminish it.

First, let there be demonstrated the falsity of the widely held view that acquisition of its enormous stock of gold (almost $25 billion in 1949) somehow resulted from this country's industrial superiority. It is important that one be free of this illusion in order to think objectively about the gold question. For if gold inflow is primarily a function of industrial costs relative to those of other countries, solution of the gold problem presents no insuperable difficulties. But America's gold stock did not accumulate from industrial activity nor from comparative cost advantages. It resulted from a combination of excessive devaluation in January, 1934, and the flight to this country of refugee capital in the 1930's from Europe and Asia as the probability of war grew increasingly apparent.

During the 20 years 1914–1933, the United States gold stock increased by only $4.4 billion (measured at $35 per ounce) even though domestic production of newly mined gold in the same years totalled more than $1.9 billion. In 20 years of commercial activity the United States earned only $2.5 billion of gold on international account, net of domestic output. But in 1934, with the U.S. economy still close to the bottom of the depression, the gold stock, at $35 per ounce, increased in that single year by $1.4 billion, as a result of raising the price from $20.67 per ounce, from $6.8 billion to $8.2 billion. In the seven years which followed, through 1941, the gold stock grew by $14.5 billion to $22.7 billion without a corresponding increase in exports of goods and services. As a matter of fact, in 1938 the United States suffered the severest and most rapid decline it had ever experienced in industrial output in a brief period, with a 23 per cent decline in industrial activity compared with 1937. Yet the gold stock grew by $1.7 billion.

Clearly, it was neither industrial production nor foreign commerce which brought the massive gold stock to the shores. It was war.

Equally, it is not a failure in production nor even in the visible balance of payments on commodity account which caused $925 million of gold to flee this country in the single month of December, 1967, and $2.5 billion from November, 1967, to mid-March, 1968. It was war. And the decline of the gold stock from $24.6 billion in 1949 to $10.5 billion at March 27, 1968, a fall of more than $14 billion, equal to the whole flight of refugee capital to this country during January, 1935–April, 1941, was in major part caused by United States military expenditures overseas of more than $18 billion during 1961–1966, an annual average of $3 billion rising to an annual rate of $4.3 billion in 1967. As a result, the gold stock, $10.5 billion as of late March, 1968, was actually lower than at any time since May, 1935.

War and preparation for war by Europe and Asia permitted accumulation of this nation's gold reserve. War and preparation for war by the United States have caused that gold reserve to drain away.

What the world has experienced in March of 1968 is less a raid upon the dollar than a flight from paper currencies, i.e., a flight from misgovernment and its economic results.

The world has grown convinced that the dollar is inherently unstable. It is because of this that world monetary reserves of gold, long before the panic set in, began to fall short of their norm. During 1961–1964, some 47 per cent of the $5.3 billion of free world production of gold went to monetary uses. During 1965–1967 *no* additions were made to the world's monetary gold supply although world output approximated $4.3 billion. In 1966–1967, world monetary stocks of gold declined. The monetary crisis of 1968 was precipitated by increase in mistrust of paper money, a mistrust whose start coincided with the beginning of the Vietnam war. Faith in paper currencies is a casualty of that war.

THE VIETNAM WAR IN MORE MEANINGFUL ECONOMIC PERSPECTIVE

The President's 1968 Economic Report emphasises one dimension of the Vietnam war which, factually correct, is functionally a myth. It reads, "Today the war in Vietnam is costing us 3 per cent of our total production. That is a burden a wealthy people can bear. It represents less than one year's growth in our total output."

These three sentences can hold true only if the terms "production," "growth," and "output" are semantically distorted. They can hold true only if $100 of haircuts, or $100 of carwashes, or of any other simultaneous production-consumption function is treated as equivalent to $100 of capital goods production in the system of national accounts, or if a $1 billion increase in military expenditures is treated as functionally identical to a $1 billion increase in wages paid to production workers for increased output equivalent to or greater than the increase in production workers' take-home pay.

It follows, if the President's interpretation of growth in national wealth is accepted on face, that if, say, 40 million families of four persons each were to shine, reciprocally, each neighbor's shoes each day at 25 cents per shoeshine, then, assuming each person to own four pairs of shoes, there would be an increase in Gross National Product of $40 million per day or $14.6 billion per year. If each shoe were to be shined twice a day, the increase in GNP would approximate $29 billion per year, the smallest reasonable estimate of what the war in Vietnam will cost in calendar 1968 if the fighting continues through that period.

We can, in short, pay for the Vietnam war by shining shoes, provided all of us get paid for doing so. Absurd? Of course it is, but it is no more absurd than the belief that the cost of the war is no actual burden because it approximates in dollars something euphemistically called growth in the economy in a year when industrial output did not grow at all.

Let us put the cost of the war in more meaningful perspective. Preliminary estimates indicate that industrial production in 1967, at an index number of 157.3, was virtually unchanged from the index number 156.3 of 1966, an increase of a mere 0.6 per cent. Yet the estimated Gross National Product rose to $785 billion in 1967, some $42 billion or 5.5 per cent over the 1966 figure.

Even the 0.6 per cent increase in industrial output is, from the civilian point of view, misleading. The January, 1968, Survey of Current Business tells us "Procurement costs climbed rapidly from 1966 to 1967. The increase in deliveries in 1967 for ordnance and aircraft was especially pronounced. New and more expensive types of ammunition played an increasing role in Vietnam. The growth in purchases of helicopters and tactical fixed wing aircraft continued, both for replacement and to augment existing air strength. In addition, operation and maintenance expenditures exceeded earlier estimates, largely as a result of deployment costs of the increasing numbers of troops in Vietnam. In contrast, expenditures for guided missiles and ships showed little change and military construction was down." The result was that production of equipment, including defense items, increased in 1967 by 3.8 per cent over 1966, 21.8 per cent over 1965, and 35.7 per cent over 1964. Production of consumer goods, in contrast, in 1967 was less than two tenths of one per cent higher than in 1966, 5.3 per cent higher than in 1965, and 12.5 per cent higher than in 1964.

What has occurred, it is manifest, is a shift in the direction of change of the economy with physical growth of output in the military sector and price growth in the civilian sector. Shipments of consumer home goods and apparel approximated $49.6 billion in 1967, no different from the shipments in 1966 and about $4.7 billion or 10.5 per cent higher than in 1965. Shipments of consumer staples in 1967 approximated $117.4 billion, some 6.3 per cent over 1966 represented largely by price increases. Shipments of defense products in 1967, on the other hand, totalled about $38.3 billion, some $5.1 billion or 15.2 per cent higher than in 1966 and 36.9 per cent higher than in 1965. Shipments of defense items and equipment (excluding automobiles) in 1967 totalled about $73 billion, some $5.1 billion more than in 1966. That is, substantially, the whole of the 1967 increase which occured in shipments of equipment and defense items, excluding automobiles, was in the defense area. To put the matter another way, the 1967 increase in final sales of defense items, unadjusted for price changes, approximated 12.4 per cent of the total increase in Gross National Product unadjusted for price changes. Total government purchases for defense equalled 29 per cent of the change in GNP.

In fact, more than half of the increase in GNP in 1967 was ascribable to increases of $22.1 billion in Federal, State and local government purchases. The total increase in defense expenditures, at current prices, was $12.1 billion or 55 per cent of the aggregate increase in government expenditures. Federal non-defense purchases, by comparison, rose by only $1 billion.

The state and local government sectors contributed through their purchases $86.5 billion to GNP in 1967, about $9 billion higher than in 1966. Much of this increase was caused by a rise of 500,000 in employment by State and local governments, of which about 400,000 was in increased personnel in schools, in some areas signifying an enlargement of the ratio of teachers to students as local educational efforts were intensified. In addition, wage and salary increases in these areas advanced by 4 per cent.

The crisis in America's schools needs no discussion here. But to suggest that, because GNP is enlarged by injecting money into the educational system, the cost of the war is made easier to bear, strains credulity. Equally, to claim that because the Government spends an additional $12.1 billion on defense the nation's ability to spend this added $12.1 billion is somehow increased is economic nonsense. To make this claim while industrial production fails to rise is to suggest that whatever a government spends costs a nation nothing because government purchases pay for themselves.

SELF-DECEPTION OVER THE COST OF THE WAR

Statistical juggling to minimize the cost of the war deceives the Administration more than it does the people. Let us examine the internal structure of the increase in "output" which occured in 1967.

Inventories of defense products were about $1.7 billion higher at the close of

1967 than one year earlier; of equipment and defense products about $2.5 billion. Pre-tax wages and salaries of government employees rose by $23.3 billion and in the service and distributive industries by $12.9 billion, for a total of about $36 billion.

Can one seriously suggest that the joint sum of $38–39 billion of inventory accumulations in defense-related industries and increased wage and salary disbursements in non-commodity producing industries, amounting to about 92 per cent of the 1967 increase in GNP, may in any meaningful way be related to increased ability to pay for the war? Increase in the output of physical goods, measured in constant (1958) dollars, was only $7.8 billion, a bare 2.2 per cent increase, and of this some $7.3 billion was non-durable goods, a mere $0.5 billion increase or three-tenths of 1 per cent occurring in durable goods output despite the increase in defense production. An actual decline of $1.6 billion of constant dollars output occurred in building and structures — but consumer and government demand for services, in constant dollars, increased aggregate services output (intake, perhaps, is a more appropriate term) by $10.4 billion.

One is surely staggered by the complacency of the Economic Report in its claim that the Vietnam War is costing less than one year's increase in output. That increase, as defined in the Department of Defense concept of GNP in 1967 was 2.5 per cent in constant dollars and increased sales in the service industries accounted for 63 per cent of this.

What the Economic Report does not say is that the war in Vietnam is today costing the *whole* of the constant dollar increase in real output of products every year. If further escalation should occur, the war in Vietnam would cost far more each year even than the statistical illusion of growth in national output.

The GNP illusion of growth, in a year when commodity production did not advance at all despite the growth in output of defense items, was the statistical expression of the cost of the war. Cash incomes increased, it is true. Output of goods available for purchase did not. Statistically, in constant 1958 dollars, GNP rose about

$16.6 billion but increased government purchases totalled $14.1 billion of this. Domestic investment, in constant dollars, declined by $8.7 billion, net exports of goods and services by $0.6 billion. Personal consumption expenditures other than for services increased by less than one-half of 1 per cent while population increased at more than twice this rate. Expenditures on services in constant dollars increased by 3.6 per cent, but price increases in this sector approximated 4.5 per cent with the price index of medical services rising about 8.75 per cent.

Obviously, there is something wrong with a system of national accounting which, despite these facts, can virtually dismiss the cost of war by reference to an increase of income flow of which the very cost of the war is the principal ingredient.

COST OF THE WAR IN LOSS OF NEW HOUSING

It became obvious in late 1965 that the war had set in motion so strong a competition for capital funds that capital markets were threatened with chaos. The rise in interest rates—Moody's Aaa domestic corporate bond yields rose from a 1964 average of 4.4 per cent to 4.68 per cent in December, 1965, and to 5.49 per cent in September, 1966; Baa bond yields, regarded by many as the basic price of loan capital, rose from a 1964 average of 4.83 per cent to 5.02 per cent in December, 1965, and to 6.18 per cent in December, 1966; U.S. Treasury bonds due or callable in 10 years or more rose in yield from 4.15 per cent in 1964 to 4.43 per cent in 1965 and 4.80 per cent in August, 1966—caused a flight of deposits from Savings and Loan Associations to higher yielding Certificates of Deposit which yielded 5 per cent and in some cases 5.5 per cent as commercial banks scrambled to add to their loanable reserves. Instances were not unknown of U.S. Government Participation Certificates selling in secondary markets at yields above 7 per cent. Yields on FHA new mortgages on new homes rose from 5.5 per cent in November, 1965, to 6.8 per cent one year later.

The first effect, predictable before the end of 1965, was a crash in home building in 1966 as mortgage institutions found themselves squeezed between the withdrawal of deposits and higher building costs. Private non-farm housing starts declined from 1,450,000 in 1965 to 1,142,000 in 1966, reaching a seasonally adjusted annual rate as low as 828,000 in October, 1966, compared with almost 1,380,000 in October, 1965.

The actual loss in new private dwelling units may be much greater than the 1965–1966 statistics suggest. Extrapolation of new private housing starts during the 5 years 1960–1964 — not the most reliable of procedures, be it conceded—suggests that continuance of the trend would have caused 5,300,000 new private dwelling units to have been erected in the three years 1965–1967. Instead, some 3,900,000 units were built, for a fall-short of 1,400,-000. One must not, however, assume from this that had there been no war in Vietnam 1,400,000 more new houses would have been built. But the condition of America's cities proves conclusively that at least 1,400,000 more new housing units were needed if slum conditions were to be ameliorated even partially. . . .

Had the 1964 rate of construction of 1,530,000 new private dwelling units continued through 1967, about 4,600,000 units would have been erected during 1965–1967. The actual number fell short of this by 900,000 units. The annual rate of unit construction in 1965, before the capital and interest squeeze was felt by the housing industry, was 1,500,000; the annual rate during 1966–1967 was about 1,200,000. The 1966–1967 loss in new housing construction was thus in the range 600,000-900,000, depending upon what standards are employed. The loss was closer to 1,500,000 measured against social requirements.

IMPAIRMENT OF THE CREDIT STRUCTURE

Capital resources are not infinitely expansible despite the ability of the Federal Reserve Board to expand or contract the nation's credit base. In 1966, the Federal Reserve pursued a generally restrictive credit policy and was accused—wrongly—of being responsible for the fall in housing starts. Actually, a number of structural defects in the credit structure were uncovered during the credit squeeze and were corrected, including the competition for savers' deposits as commercial banks raised their interest rates on Certificates of Deposit, drawing funds away from the housing market.

Despite the correction of this defect, the credit squeeze is far from over. Corporate bond issues during January–November, 1967, were at an annual rate of $21.7 billion compared with $15.6 billion in 1966 and $13.7 billion in 1965. New corporate securities issues in 1967 for plant and equipment were at an estimated annual rate of $16 billion compared with $12.4 billion in 1966 and $7.7 billion in 1965. New issues for working capital purposes in 1967 were at an estimated annual rate of $5.8 billion compared with $3.4 billion in 1966 and $5.4 billion in 1965. State and municipal long-term bond issues in 1967 approximated $14.2 billion compared with $11.1 billion in each of 1966 and 1965; short-term state and municipal issues totalled $8 billion in 1967 and $6.5 billion in each of 1966 and 1965. U.S. Government issues in 1967 were at an annual rate of about $14.8 billion compared with $8.2 billion in 1966 and $9.3 billion in 1965; this despite the speedup of corporate tax payments and the running down of Treasury cash balances in the first half of 1967.

What happened was a shift from corporate demand for bank loans to financing by bonds and equity issues. Commercial and industrial loans of large commercial banks rose in 1967 by $5.5 billion, far smaller than the $7.8 billion increase in 1966 and $10.9 billion increase in 1965. The shift of borrowing from bank loans to the new issues market unquestionably was more orderly than the scramble for bank loans of 1966. The effects on interest rates, however, were no less marked. Moody's Aaa bond yields had moved down to 5.03 per cent in February, 1967, only to rise progressively to 6.19 per cent in December, 1967; Baa bond yields rose from 5.82 per cent in February to 6.93 per cent in December, 1967. U.S. Treasury bonds due or callable in 10 years or more rose in yield from 4.40 per cent in January, 1967, to 5.36 per cent in December.

Thus, despite elimination of a structural defect in the nation's credit system, there still remains a threat that Savings and Loan Associations may find their ability to lend for new housing construction impaired by higher competitive yields than they can afford to pay their depositors. In an important sense, this is a quite different condition from that of late 1966–early 1967. The competition then was between two liquid forms of savings, between deposits in S & L's and Certificates of Deposit in commercial banks, neither being subject to fluctuations in value as interest rates gyrated. Competition between high-grade industrial bonds and S & L deposits is between securities whose market values can and do fluctuate and guaranteed principal sums—within the limits of federal deposit insurance. The extent to which higher yields available in industrial bonds than in S & L's will inhibit growth in deposits is a matter for conjecture, but the January, 1968, inflow of S & L deposits was $500 million less than in January, 1967.

War has thus caused a fundamental distortion in the economy's interest rate structure. Security of principal or no, S & L's are disadvantaged. Housing starts can be expected to remain at a lower level as a result. The housing industry has been impaired by the war—and this impairment will persist even after war is over if, as is probable, a high level of interest rates becomes a long-term feature of the economy.

CONFLICT BETWEEN DOMESTIC POLICIES AND INTERNATIONAL REQUIREMENTS

The unfortunate position of the housing industry typifies a dichotomy between social requirements for increased capital investments caused by the war and constraints upon capital availability imposed by the war. Domestically, this dichotomy expresses itself in the effective choice which has been made over priorities by the flow of capital from the social purpose of housing towards the political purpose of defense production. In international respects the dichotomy is even more marked.

Just as increased trade with the Soviet Union is essential to additions to America's gold supply, so a high level of interest rates is now essential to stabilization or improvement of the balance of payments. Or, a greater reduction in European interest rates than in American rates is required if foreign short-term funds are to be attracted towards or induced to remain in this country.

The difficulty is that foreign interest rates are not controllable by this country while maintenance or increase in domestic interest rates must at some point limit industrial output by rendering it unprofitable for marginal firms to borrow on short term and ill-advised for successful firms to borrow up to their needs on long term. The theory, expressed in Britain's Radcliffe Report, that increases in interest rates do not deter borrowing if lenders can utilize the borrowed funds at profit margins higher than the interest charges, holds true only in conditions approximating certainty of the excess of marginal profit over marginal interest. Risk in industrial investment increases with time. Therefore, the probability that returns on the use of borrowed capital will sufficiently exceed the interest rate thereon grows smaller the longer the debt issue.

The tendency, on the part of borrower and lender alike, is thus towards shortening of debt maturities as borrowing costs increase beyond some point. Borrowers cannot afford to take for granted that incremental profit margins earned on borrowed capital will, over extended periods, exceed the given rate of interest on borrowings. An added difficulty is that, from the viewpoint of future availability of funds for expansion of activities, the interest factor is not the only one to take into account. Critical to investment decision is the anticipated annual excess of earnings on borrowed funds over the sum of annual interest charges and debt retirement requirements. Consequently, shortening of debt maturities, i.e., increase in annual debt repayments, plus elevation of interest rates raise the required rate of return on new investment above that dictated by the interest component alone.

In this context, the extreme increase in new corporate bond issues in 1967 may represent, at least in part, anticipatory borrowings in expectation that interest rates during 1968–1969 will continue their upward move and that new bond issues will tend to be of shorter maturity.

If this is correct, one can expect a shift back from bond offerings to borrowings from banks. The probability of this occuring is enlarged by the $16 billion of new corporate issues for plant and equipment expansion in 1967. As these new installations come onstream, increased working capital needs will be felt, leading to a swing back to borrowing from banks. Upward pressures on interest rates are thus in prospect—attracting short-term funds from abroad but increasing the difficulties of small and marginal firms and of interest-sensitive industries in this country.

AN ECONOMY AT ITS LIMITS

At the beginning of 1968 unemployment among married men was a bare 1.7 per cent, including temporary layoffs; of the total labor force unemployment was about 3.7 per cent. In comparison, estimated unemployment at America's entry into World War II was about 10 per cent of the labor force with, in addition, underemployment of women and veiled unemployment of a large proportion of the 10,800,000 people employed on farms. Agricultural employment at 1967 year-end had declined to 3,500,000, eliminating the availability of manpower from substantial veiled unemployment. In fact, the long-term downtrend in agricultural employment may now be approaching its limit and a gradual increase in farm employment—of skills and sophistication inconceivable to previous generations of farmers—may be in prospect. The point is, of course, that there is little manpower slack in the economy unless one designates university students and young people engaged in the service industries as veiled unemployment.

Moreover, both the absolute number and the proportion of women of working age actually in employment has so increased that deficiencies in manpower cannot readily be made up by increased employment of females. In 1950, in contrast, when the Korean buildup was in process, females represented 29 per cent of all employed persons and 39 per cent of white collar workers; as of March, 1966, females represented 36 per cent of all employed persons and 45 per cent of white collar workers. They constituted 59 per cent of all service workers in 1950 and 65 per cent in 1966. The resulting squeeze on available labor supply is self-evident. . . .

As a result of failure by Washington to perceive in time that real limits exist in the economy—and were visibly approached in 1966—the Administration has permitted, without even a murmur of concern, and in a time of war, growth in employment outside the areas of commodity production sufficient to press hard against the limits of labor supply. The resulting generation of Personal Income uncompensated by commodity production is the real basis of the war-induced inflation. . . .

Wages and salary disbursements in distributive industries, service industries, and government have, in the same period, increased by $58 billion, or two-thirds of the total increase in wages and salaries paid.

A structural deformity has thus been brought about in the economy, and this deformity is in part a product of the war, in greater part a product of federal ineptness in management of a war economy.

Since May, 1965, through 1967, the Administration and its Council of Economic Advisers have displayed no awareness whatever that, in the absence of necessary deployment of the labor force, manpower would become a critically scarce and therefore limiting factor in the economy. Repeatedly the President has stated that he would avoid controls over the economy. This very avoidance, because it has encouraged injurious allocation of scarce capital and manpower to functions inflationary by their very nature, is the inflation engine now rolling over all of us.

In short, the American economy is now pressing against three constraints: balance of payments difficulties, the competitive scramble for scarce investment capital, and effective full employment of manpower resources. Belatedly, the Administration has grown aware, it seems, that these problems exist and are, in fact, separate facets of a single problem. Its response to them, however, is hopelessly inadequate. What

the Administration has said is that the federal sector account in the economy in calendar 1967 was $12.5 billion in deficit and, therefore, a $12–13 billion increase in taxes on personal and corporate income would bring about a balanced budget and pay for the war in Vietnam without inflation. The President stated this expressly in his 1968 Economic Report by saying, "Federal spending has not been growing rapidly since mid-1967, nor will it increase rapidly in the next year and a half. But because of the already high level of defense outlays, total federal expenditures are too large to be piled on top of *normal* private demand without overheating our economy. It is because private demand has now returned to normal after its temporary weakness that we now need new measures of fiscal restraint."

Several things are to be noted here. First is the very careful use in the Economic Report of the term *spending,* a quite different matter from *payments.* Expenditures did level off in the closing half of 1967 but the excess of federal government payments to the public over receipts from the public during July-November, 1967, totalled $19.4 billion or $16.5 billion higher than during the first six months and $7.7 billion higher than during the corresponding months of 1966. In addition, the federal interest bearing debt to the public at 1967 year-end totalled $284 billion for an increase of $11 billion in 1967 compared with an increase of $2.8 billion in each of 1966 and 1965.

Second, the assurance that federal spending "will not increase rapidly in the next year and a half" is, to say the least, optimistic unless the war is halted. What was not factored into this opinion was that the intensity of the war in Vietnam, and consequent manpower and material requirements, are not, in the course of the war, wholly autonomous American decisions. The Tet offensive of 1968 amply demonstrates this—and has led to military demands for enlargement of U.S. forces in Vietnam. The minimum expectation is that the *average* number of American troops in Vietnam during 1968 will be no less than 540,000. It is, therefore, a fair estimate that the Vietnam war will cost the United States $29 billion in 1968.

The 1968 cost increase of the war in Vietnam, assuming fighting to continue throughout the year, is thus about $5 billion higher than in 1967 at lowest estimates. How high it might rise is as much a function of NLF strategy and tactics as it is of autonomous United States decision. The situation has so altered, however, that major increases in federal spending seem certain if the war continues through the year.

The lesson is plain to see. No amount of politically acceptable tax increase, in the absence of a formal declaration of war, can halt the inflation caused by the war. Given declaration of a state of emergency, one could expect wage and price controls and a 16–17 per cent tax surcharge. A tax increase of only $10 billion would not prevent the addition of a further increase of $17 billion to Disposable Personal Income in 1968, accelerating the inflation despite the tax boost.

Formal declaration of a state of emergency, or imposition of equivalent wartime controls, might stem the inflation for the duration of the emergency, but would store it up to explode in the post-war period. But wage controls over production workers could not appreciably deter inflation because the inflation is not in production workers' wage rates. Nor can increases in income taxes deflate a nation suffering from inflation of Disposable Personal Income unless the tax increase equals the whole increase in Personal Income, i.e., $40 billion in 1968 alone. But without such controls or income deflation the dollar cannot survive international doubts as to its value—and if the dollar goes so goes America's world position.

IN CONCLUSION

The conclusion is obvious that the ultimate cost of the Vietnam war to the United States is loss of its world position. By the time this war is over the United States will be left with little but brute military force with which to conduct foreign affairs vis-à-vis friend and foe alike with enemies strengthened in their military, economic, and diplomatic positions; and with friends dubious and fearful over future actions by this country.

None of this need have been. Disregarding the moral issues, the price of Vietnam is infinitely greater than was foreseen in 1965. An error—a critical, disastrous error—was made in 1965. Those who committed this error have shown themselves to possess neither the courage to concede error, the wit to perceive it, nor the capacity to correct it.

Public Debt, Social Cost

21. Vietnam: The 200-Year Mortgage

James L. Clayton

The war in Vietnam is now the longest war in American history. Taking the date the first U.S. troops were killed in combat as the beginning (July 8, 1959), it is now nearing its tenth year. Even if the most optimistic forecasts come true, and a cease-fire is achieved this year, the Vietnamese

Reprinted from *The Nation*, May 26, 1969. Copyright © May 1969 by *The Nation*. Reprinted by permission.

conflict will have lasted two years longer than the American Revolution and more than twice as long as the Civil War.

Except for World War II, Vietnam has been by far the most expensive war in American history. In initial dollar costs, according to official figures, it will have cost $110 billion by the end of the next fiscal year. This figure is already double the initial cost of the Korean War and more than three times higher than the original cost of World War I. If the war continues for another ten months, it will also surpass World War I in the total number of casualties (already more men have been wounded than in World War I) and become our third most costly war in the number of men killed and wounded in action.

But the most striking thing about the price of the war in Vietnam is that the *greatest costs are yet to come.* If history is an accurate guide in these matters—and we have no other—the expenditures for veterans' benefits over the next century will be at least 50 per cent more than the initial cost of the war itself. Twenty per cent of the adult population are veterans, and one in every seven is receiving some kind of compensation. Their support now costs the nation almost twice as much as federal public welfare assistance. When one adds to these veteran costs the annual interest payments on debt incurred because of the Vietnamese War, the ultimate cost becomes at least *three times* its initial cost. This kind of accounting is seldom if ever mentioned in debates about the war.

It is extremely difficult to measure the monetary costs of any war. The Executive office of the President has, however, made a valiant attempt to ascertain the costs of the war in Vietnam since 1965. Its findings are printed in the 1970 *Budget of the United States Government* (p. 74). According to these, in fiscal 1970 the war will eat up 13 per cent of all federal expenditures, and will have cost a total of $108.5 billion since 1965. But these figures do not tell the whole story. Actually, only about $100 billion of the federal budget is relatively controllable; the remainder is already committed or in trust funds. Of this $100 billion, no less than 80 per cent is accounted for by national defense. Vietnam accounts for 32 per cent of the 1970 defense budget, and in terms of what the government can actually decide to spend in that year, the war is really costing us 25 per cent of all expenditures, not the 13 per cent that official figures indicate. This percentage, it should be noted, is based on a projected reduction of $5 billion from 1969 costs of the war. It is further assumed that the big increases are over. But that is what we were told in 1968 and costs *increased* by $2 billion. If the war in fact continues at its present rate, almost a third of the disposable federal budget will be committed to Southeast

Asia. If the war escalates, the ratio could easily go to one-half.

Official figures also underestimate the costs of the war in other ways. Only American personnel actually stationed in South Vietnam, now approximately 532,500, are generally counted. Since 1967, however, at least 77,000 Americans have been stationed in Thailand or serving off-shore as support forces. They would bring the total in the *immediate* zone to 634,000. In addition, more than 250,000 "back-up" men in the United States and elsewhere are probably not counted in cost estimates, and they would raise the total number of men committed to the war closer to 884,000. These additional personnel obviously add to the costs.

Moreover, for reasons that have not been made clear, the official figures measure costs only since 1965. But Americans have been stationed in Vietnam since 1954, and combat troops have been killed there since July 1959. Between 1954 and 1964, 58,885 men served a year apiece and the cost of their support is also omitted from the official estimates. At $25,000 per man year—a figure suggested in 1967 by Robert Anthony, formerly Assistant Secretary of Defense—this would increase the overall war costs by $1.5 billion.

In figuring the costs of war, however, short-run outlays are not nearly so informative as long-term. The pattern of long-term costs indicates that the bulk of the money is spent long after the fighting stops. The basic reason is that veterans' benefits for our major wars during the past century have averaged 1.8 times the original cost of those wars. The estimated original cost of the Civil War is $3.07 billion (Union forces only). Veterans' benefits by 1967 had amounted to $8.57 billion, or an increase over the original cost of 280 per cent. Projected veterans' benefits for World War I, World War II and the Korean War will increase the original cost 155 per cent, 125 per cent, and 170 per cent respectively. History, therefore, is a better guide to the real cost of war than contemporary official figures.

If one measures the original cost of our

three earliest wars—the American Revolution, the War of 1812 and the Mexican War—as the amount spent by the Departments of the Army and Navy during the war years, one finds that each of these wars cost roughly $100 million. Veterans' benefits then began to be paid out and climbed steadily, peaking in the case of the War of 1812 some sixty-eight years later. These benefits continued to be paid for the War of 1812 until 1946, 131 years after that war ended. Veterans' benefits for the Mexican War did not drop below $1 million per year until this decade, more than a century later. These benefits have increased the original cost of the first three wars by 68 per cent, 44 per cent, and 65 per cent, respectively.

The reason why veterans' costs do not peak until at least two generations *after* the fighting has terminated, and do not stop until well over a century later, is best explained by an example. Suppose a drummer boy, age 14, became a soldier in 1861 and was disabled in that war. Suppose also that he married, had children, his wife died, and he remarried late in life, at say age 60 in 1907. Suppose further that his second wife was 25 years old at marriage and that at age 30 she bore him a child who was mentally or physically incapable of supporting himself. That child would be 57 years old today and still drawing benefits—more than a century after the war ended. The example is not farfetched: in 1967, 1,353 such dependents of Civil War veterans were still drawing benefits that amounted to more than $1 million annually.

Veterans' benefits projected for more recent wars are also instructive. Up to 1967, veterans' benefits for the Spanish-American War had amounted to $5.3 billion, or *twelve times* the original cost of that war! Moreover, the peak of these payments did not come until fifty-one years after the war ended. World War I veterans' benefits probably peaked three years ago or forty-nine years after that war was over. World War II veterans' benefits will probably peak at the turn of this century, and dependents of Vietnamese veterans will be drawing benefits until the 22nd century!

After veterans' benefits, the interest on money borrowed to fight our major wars is the heaviest long-range cost. Again, any attempt to reach precise figures is extremely difficult, but the pattern is not hard to determine. Before World War I, interest costs probably ranged from one-fifth to three-fourths the original cost of a given war. These are conservatively estimated as follows: Most of the national debt during the early years of the Republic were Revolutionary War debts. If only two-thirds of the interest on that debt between 1790 and 1800 is taken as a fair estimate, the cost of the Revolutionary War is raised by about one-fifth. The increase in interest payments on the national debt from 1816 to 1836, when the debt was paid out, adds about one-third to the 1812 war costs. Prior to the Civil War, interest on the public debt was less than $4 million. During that war it jumped from that figure in 1861 to 144 million in 1867. Interest payments fell gradually over the next twenty-five years and then leveled off at about $30 million annually. Since very few federal programs that would add to the deficit were undertaken during those laissez-faire years, one may attribute the greater part of the interest payments to the Civil War.

Interest costs for World War I have been much more carefully figured. Some years ago, John M. Clark, in *The Costs of the World War to the American People*, calculated the original cost to be $33 billion. The U.S. Treasury figured the interest to 1929 at $9.5 billion. Total interest amounted to about $15 billion, or approximately 46 per cent of the original cost.

Henry C. Murphy, in *National Debt in War and Transition*, shows that the government borrowed about $215 billion at 2.5 per cent interest to finance World War II. That debt has not been paid off. Indeed, at no time since 1946 has the gross public debt fallen below $252 billion, and it has been increasing rapidly in recent years because of Great Society programs and Vietnam. Assuming that it takes *only* as long to pay off this war debt as it did the Civil War debt—say thirty years—interest payments will amount to approximately $200 billion. That is 53 per cent of the original cost and quite in line with the 46 per cent figure for World War I.

In 1951, the gross public debt was $255 billion; in 1955 it was almost $275 billion. If one-half of that increase is attributable to the Korean War, then in 25 years at 4 per cent the interest costs on the Korean War will have amounted to $10 billion.

The purpose of this exercise in figures is to give some idea of what we may reasonably expect the war in Vietnam to cost. Using the pattern of veterans' benefits paid out for World War I, World War II and the Korean War as a guide, we may anticipate that the Vietnamese conflict will eventually cost about 150 per cent of its original cost. This figure is conservative, however, because a much higher percentage of GIs now use their educational benefits, and life expectancy is increasing. Benefits also tend to be more inclusive with time and rise with the cost of living.

Using the Civil War, World War I, World War II and the Korean War as guidelines, we may fairly expect interest costs of the Vietnamese War to be roughly half again as much as the original cost. In short, even assuming a major de-escalation at the end of this year and a total withdrawal next year, the final bill for Vietnam will be about $330 billion.

It should be emphasized that this is a conservative figure, taking account of only the direct major monetary outlays. It does not include war-caused inflation, the loss of services and earnings by the 33,000 men killed in the war to date, the cost of resentment abroad, the depletion of natural resources, the postponement of critical domestic programs, the arrested training and education of our youth, the suspended cultural progress of our nation—and, of course, no price on the death and destruction suffered by the South Vietnamese civilians in the war zone itself.

The estimated ultimate cost of the Vietnamese War is so high that it boggles the mind unless placed in perspective. How much money is $330 billion? Compared with other federal expenditures during the same period (fiscal years 1960–70), the war in Vietnam has cost ten times more than Medicare and medical assistance, sixteen times more than support for education, and thirty-three times more than was spent for housing and community development. We have spent ten times more money on Vietnam in ten years than we have spent in our entire history for public higher education or for police protection. Put another way, the war has cost us one-fifth of the value of current personal financial assets of all living Americans, a third again as much as all outstanding home mortgages, and six times the total U.S. money now in circulation.

When one looks back over the cost of wars in American history, an evil nemesis seems to dog our destiny. Each of the major wars in the past century (the Civil War, World War I and World War II) has cost initially about ten times more than the previous war. The Civil War initially cost $3 billion, World War I $33 billion and World War II $381 billion. Since World War II, our major conflicts have tended to *double* in price. Korea cost $54 billion and Vietnam to date has cost $110 billion. Total federal expenditures, moreover, have tended to increase four to five times after each major war. In the case of Vietnam, government expenditures to date (1960–69) have doubled. If this trend continues, wars may soon be simply too expensive to contemplate, and governments too cumbersome to endure.

Money and Gold

22. American Dollar in Jeopardy: Can Flight of Gold Be Halted?

Terence McCarthy

The claim is made that the enormous annual expenditure on armaments and the military establishment in this country is vitally essential to the maintenance of America's world position. It is nearer the truth to say that without a shot being fired, without United States armies once engaging the enemy, her world position is being frittered away, irretrievably, by America's tacit repudiation of the basic value of her currency.

It is true that gold is still exchanged for dollars and dollars for gold at $35 per ounce. But the ability to continue doing so grows less and less as the months pass. The accumulation of foreign short-term claims upon U.S. gold reserves, despite the willingness of foreign central banks to help alleviate temporary difficulties, will undermine the employment of the dollar as the banking currency of the world. This is precisely how sterling was undermined as a world currency in 1931.

However she may try to escape this trap of her own making America cannot remedy the situation until government expenditures are brought within reasonable bounds. And this cannot be done so long as almost 10% of the gross national product is allocated in military expenditures financed by debt.

The purpose of this paper is briefly to review the embarrassing erosion of U.S. gold reserves and to suggest reasonable and prudent action to curb this erosion.

U.S. gold stocks lowest since 1939

From the end of 1949 to February, 1963, the monetary gold stock of the U.S. Treasury shrank by $8.7 billions—from $24.6

Reprinted from Seymour Melman (ed.), *A Strategy for American Security*, New York, 1963. Copyright © 1963 by Seymour Melman. Reprinted by permission.

billions down to $15.9 billions. The February balance was the lowest figure for the nation's gold reserves since May 10, 1939. The loss in gold was $100 million in the first two months of 1963 alone. This drain occurred despite reciprocal currency arrangements with leading foreign banks and the Bank for International Settlements, designed to counter speculative attacks on the dollar and to avoid hemorrhage of gold reserves when foreign central banks accumulate dollars in excess of amounts they deem prudent.

This drainage of U.S. gold stock is not some short-term phenomenon caused by malproportions which will correct themselves in the natural course of events. It is a persistent problem, arising from sales of gold to foreign governments and central banks in settlement of continuing U.S. deficits in the balance of international payments. In 1962 the overall deficit on international account totalled $2.2 billions, and the drain on U.S. gold was $912 millions. In 1961 the deficit was $2.5 billions and the loss of gold was $877 millions. In the three years 1958–1960, the U.S. experienced deficits in its balance of payments averaging $3.7 billions per year. The total adverse balance in the five years ending in 1962 approximated $15.8 billions.

Deficits persist despite favorable trade balance

The most significant aspect of the balance of payments deficits is that they have occurred in the face of a very large excess of merchandise exports over merchandise imports. During 1955–1961, U.S. exports of merchandise to all the world totalled $122.9 billions and the merchandise imports totalled $95.1 billions—giving a net balance in America's favor of $27.8 billions. Yet the loss of gold in these seven years amounted to $4.8 billions. The stock of monetary gold shrank 22%, even though U.S. commercial sales of merchandise abroad far exceeded purchases from other countries.

For years past it has been a feature of

U.S. national policy that a favorable balance of trade on merchandise account has financed government expenditures overseas. During 1955–1961, net exports by the U.S. Government totalled $28.1 billions, consisting of $14.8 billions in military supplies and services abroad, and $13.3 billions in other exports, including all kinds of non-military services abroad, grants, credits, aid and assistance programs. Government net exports during those six years were almost exactly equivalent to the favorable net balance of trade on merchandise account — $28.1 billions in government exports, $27.8 billions in merchandise trade.

To put the matter another way, 53 per cent of the gain in international merchandise transactions had been spent or dissipated in all sorts of military ventures overseas. The balance has been used up in equally costly although, in some instances, both unavoidable and constructive, expenditures by the U.S. Government in all areas of the Free World.

If there were no greatly complicating factors beyond this equation of net merchant gain and government spending abroad, there might be no real cause for concern. One could question whether U.S. resources in all cases were being employed in ways beneficial or detrimental to the national and the world's best interests. But there would be no need to fear erosion of the foundations of the economy by constant pressures against the dollar.

U.S. role in world monetary system is jeopardized

However, the matter is much more complicated. The role which the United States has assumed in world affairs, specifically its role in the world's monetary system, does not permit this fair equality between a favorable merchandise trade balance and overseas expenditures to harmonize international payments and international receipts. U.S. international deficits persist, and the national currency is increasingly jeopardized in spite of the continued excess of commercial exports over imports.

Nor, for that matter, does the continued movement away from the dollar reflect a weakening of America's position as a credi-

tor nation. In 1940 the U.S. was a debtor nation; long-term assets and investments held by foreigners in the United States in that year totalled $13.5 billions — almost $1.3 billions greater than American investments abroad. This debtor status persisted through 1945. But by 1950, America had become a massive creditor with $32.8 billions of investment assets abroad, compared with $19.5 billions of foreign investment assets in the U.S. This position of $13.3 billions of creditor status in 1950 grew enormously, so that by 1961 the U.S. had become a creditor on long-term account to the tune of $27.3 billions.

Yet gold has continued to seep out of the country. This happens, not because governments and business organizations overseas mistrust the basic credit standing of the United States, but because they have come to mistrust profoundly the ability of the dollar to continue to serve as the foundation currency of the world's monetary system, in view of the fiscal policies consistently pursued by this country.

The situation is classic. For just as U.S. Government expenditures in foreign countries are offset by a favorable balance of merchandise trade, so the massive creditor status of the U.S. on long-term investment account is offset by her debtor status on short-term account. Short-term liabilities to foreigners reported by banks in the U.S. as of December, 1962 amounted to $25 billions, of which $12.3 billions consisted of U.S. Treasury bills and certificates. Short-term claims on foreigners reported by banks in the U.S. totalled only $5.1 billions, leaving the U.S. a net debtor on these short-term accounts to the extent of $19.9 billions. Here is where the difficulties lie.

The situation resembles that of Great Britain. That once-dominant nation was forced off the gold standard in 1929–1931 because of her inability to realize her long-term foreign investments in time to stem the flight of gold as short-term liabilities were pressed upon her for payment.

The United States today is in much the same position. Rising costs-of-living, increased production prices, unsatisfactory returns upon industrial investment, and resulting industrial stagnation — inescapable accompaniments of persisting inflation induced by fantastically costly arms expenditures financed by debt increases — have caused American capital to seek more profitable and more secure investment opportunities abroad. Hence the $27 billions of net credit on long-term investments overseas. The selfsame factors have caused foreigners to keep their dollar holdings in short-term forms, and not to convert them into long-term investments in the U.S. These foreigners are understandably fearful that the decline of the dollar cannot be arrested while the U.S. national debt continues to mount and the foreign exchange earned from trade is prevented, by fiscal and military policies, extravagance abroad and at home, from being converted into Treasury balances.

The solution lies in curbing military spending

The gold problem is of America's own making. The solution must be of her own finding. Prompt and major reduction of arms budgets for both home and overseas forces, with the bulk of the savings going to bolster U.S. gold reserves, are prerequisites to remedying the situation. Or, such expenditures must be paid out of current taxation, not out of debt increases,

no matter how unpalatable a rise in taxation may be.

Whoever fears that the adoption of such a drastic surgical policy toward the national budget may weaken U.S. influence in the world, might reflect on the British experience. The decline in England's position as a great power dates, not from the end of World War II, but from the time the international financial community recognized that England could no longer meet her short-term obligations with assurance, and that sterling could no longer serve as the base of the international monetary order.

Once thoroughly weakened, world financial power cannot easily be regained. The U.S. has attained a world position through the integrity of her currency. She will lose this, together with the ability to shape much of the world's political future, if the flight of gold is not soon halted. This can be done only by curbing the extraordinary extravagance in the military area, and by strengthening the U.S. fiscal position so that short-term claims upon her gold reserves will be transformed into long-term foreign investments in the American industrial system.

Statistical data sources: *Federal Reserve Bulletin* (monthly); *Statistical Abstract of the United States* (annual).

Social Cost, Inflation, and International Disequilibrium

23. Statement to the U.S. Senate, Committee on Foreign Relations
Louis B. Lundborg

My name is Louis B. Lundborg. I am Chairman of the Board of BankAmerica Corporation and of the Bank of America N.T. & S.A. I am pleased to respond to your request that I testify here today.

Testimony by Louis B. Lundborg, speaking as Chairman of the Board, Bank of America N.T. & S.A., before the Senate Committee on Foreign Relations, Washington, D.C., April 15, 1970. Reprinted by permission.

My testimony this morning will be on some of the economic aspects of the war in Vietnam. In preparing this testimony I have had the benefit of the best thinking of the staff of the bank's Economics Department, as well as that of many other officers of our bank, on the economic impact of the war.

In this testimony I will confine my remarks to the economic impact of the war. While I have strongly-held personal feelings on other aspects of the war, I do not feel it is appropriate or proper to express these views as Chairman of the Board of Bank of America.

The thrust of my testimony will be that the war in Vietnam distorts the American economy. The war is a major contributor to inflation—our most crucial domestic economic problem. It draws off resources that could be put to work towards solving imperative problems facing this nation at home. And despite the protestations of the new left to the contrary, the fact is that an end to the war would be good, not bad, for American business.

There is, I think, a pernicious but widely-held belief that war generally has been an agent for economic growth, and therefore good for business. My plan this morning is to spend a few minutes discussing that belief and then to move on to the specifics of Vietnam where it is possible to speak, not only in general terms, but to back up our conclusions with specific economic statistics and indicators.

First, therefore, let's look at the general proposition that war has been an engine for rapid economic growth. While it is difficult, if not impossible, to prove conclusively that on balance war has not been an agent for rapid economic growth, there are a number of carefully reasoned investigations into this subject supporting the position that peace is far better for economic development. Although these careful analyses tend to reject the assumption that war is a boon to the economy, the public is generally unaware of this and continues to believe that war contributes positively to economic development. It is time to set this record straight. Mr. John U. Nef's book, *War and Human Progress,* systematically examines the interrelations of war and economic growth from 1494 down to 1950. His analysis indicates that the industrial revolutions of both the Elizabethan and Napoleonic periods were developed not in warring Europe, but in peaceful England; that the invention of gunpowder and of many other weapons of war was a by-product, not of military need but of peaceful industry, and that, certainly, pure and possibly even applied science has flourished most in peace and least in war.

Dr. John J. Clark, Dean of the College of Business Administration at St. John's University in New York, in his book, *The New Economics of National Defense,* reviews the impact of war on economic development. In summary, he states, "The preponderance of evidence supports the judgment that war, on balance, does not correlate positively with economic progress. Settlement by arms not only causes a great net waste of resources: it also retards industrial development and the division of labor."

Other authorities have shown (1) that rising expenditures for research and development may actually be reducing the rate of economic growth in the United States, and (2) that the process of transferring scientific and technological advances in space and military R and D is becoming increasingly difficult. To the extent that it can be shown that war in general is not good for economic progress, then it should be equally obvious that war is not good for business.

I could go on citing other expert testimony that war in general is not an engine of economic progress—but let me move on to the real issue—the war in Vietnam.

As you probably know, Mr. A.W.Clausen, the President of the Bank of America, specifically rejected the charge that we as an institution support and profit from the war in Vietnam. He further stated, "this bank has consistently pointed out that an end to the war in Vietnam would be good, not bad, for American business." I would like to elaborate on this point.

There have been reckless and often deliberately malicious charges that the U.S. business community has supported the Vietnam war in an effort to reap huge profits. Let's look at the record. In a very narrow sense, it is certainly true that individual firms which supply material and services to the military have made profits. In our market economy, the Federal Government purchases most of the goods and services it requires from private firms, and those firms must be profitable in order to survive. This is true whether the firm is contracted to build a highway, produce a postal delivery truck, construct a school, improve a slum or produce a military aircraft. But as Mr. Hudson B. Drake pointed out in the January-February 1970 *Harvard Business Review,* the Government has established elaborate procedures to assure that profits on government contracts are not excessive. And in general these procedures have been effective.

I recognize that it is statistically impossible with the data available to calculate what portion of various firms' profits are generated by demands for goods and services needed to prosecute the Vietnam war. In an effort to get some rough approximation of the profitability of corporations doing substantial business with the Government, I did some checking on the corporations receiving the largest amounts of funds from government contracts. Actually, I took the list from a publication of a "peace group" who proclaimed these firms to be war profiteers. The top ten firms for which we had data had a pattern of profits after taxes per dollar of sales quite similar to the national average. This means that the firms did better in the 1962–1965 period than in the post-escalation years. It is also interesting to note that except for 1962 the average profit after taxes per dollar of sales for the ten firms was below the comparable national average for all manufacturing industries or durable goods industries. When I checked the twenty-five largest firms their profits after taxes per dollar of sales figure was also below the national average.

I realize, as I said before, that these figures are inadequate to prove any case conclusively. They do, however, cast serious doubt on the extravagant claims we have heard about war profiteering.

We do have more than adequate data to demonstrate that the escalation of the war in Vietnam has seriously distorted the American economy, has inflamed inflationary pressures, has drained resources that are desperately needed to overcome serious domestic problems confronting our country, and has dampened the rate of growth in profits on both a *before* and *after* tax basis. In the middle of 1964 when the Vietnam escalation began, the economy was in quite good shape. We had at that time an uninterrupted economic advance of fifty-two months—a peacetime record—unemployment averaged 4.5 per cent, the consumer price index had increased only 1.2 per cent during the first six months of 1965, and the average operating rate of industrial capacity was at 90 per cent. There had been considerable success in maintaining Federal expenditures for goods and services below 11 per cent of GNP

from 1960 through mid-1965. In fact, the Government had even been able to change the composition of its spending by deliberately shifting emphasis from defense to non-defense spending.

The expenditures related to the Vietnam war, added to the near-full employment economy that existed in mid-1965, generated severe inflationary pressures. Consumer prices began increasing rapidly as the federal deficit grew. While there is room for a wide range of opinion covering proper tax policies during this period, especially over the timing and magnitude of tax increases, and the proper role of monetary policy, the basic cause of the inflationary forces was a sharp increase in federal spending associated with the escalation of the conflict in Vietnam.

The inflation, the growth in inflationary psychology, and the very stringent anti-inflationary monetary policies have combined to produce serious distortions in the United States financial markets and resulting distortion in the economy. These distortions include the sharp drop in residential construction and the sharp growth in investment spending.

The facts clearly show that the Vietnam war has not been good for business profits. During the four years prior to the escalation of the conflict in Vietnam, corporate profits after taxes rose 71.0 per cent. From 1966 through 1969 corporate profits after taxes rose only 9.2 per cent.

To avoid any thought that the recent tax increase may have fudged the figures, I also have similar corporate profit figures on a before tax and inventory adjustment basis. These figures show corporate profits rose 51.3 per cent from 1962 through 1965 but the gains in profits were dampened to a 16.6 per cent increase during the post-escalation 1966–1969 period. It should be clear from these figures that what is good for the economy is good for business.

Most of the concern about the upward pressures on prices and costs originating in expenditures associated with the Vietnam war arise from recognition of the damaging effects of inflation on the domestic economy. This should not lead us to neglect the important impact on our position in international markets and the balance of payments. This is not to lay the blame for our balance-of-payments problems on the recent period of inflation or on the Vietnam war. Inflation and the war-associated expenditures, however, have made the problem more intractable and solutions more difficult. These difficulties with our balance of payments have postponed indefinitely any relaxation of the restraints and controls under which international business has been forced to operate for the past several years in particular.

It is important, therefore, to comment briefly on what has happened to the U.S. balance of payments in the past few years, specifically with reference to the impact of the Vietnam war. Perhaps the first point that should be made is that the official measures of the balance-of-payments deficit have been misleading. The view, for example, that the balance of payments in 1968 was satisfactory because there was a surplus of $168 million and that the balance of payments in 1969 was very unsatisfactory because the deficit exceeded $7 billion is unacceptable. In fact, the greatest deterioration in the payments position in recent years occurred in 1968. The difference between the two years may be accounted for largely by massive flows of foreign funds in opposite directions which had very little to do with the basic balance-of-payments position.

The best measure of what happened to the long-run position is the balance on current account, that is goods and services plus private remittances and payments of U.S. Government pensions. This balance declined from a surplus of $7.8 billion in 1964 to about $4 billion in 1967 and $1.4 billion in 1968 and less than $1 billion in 1969.

A good part of the progressive deterioration in this position over the years since 1964, the year before the major acceleration of the Vietnam war, may be accounted for by the large increase in foreign exchange outflows associated with military expenditures. These rose from less than $3 billion in 1964 to nearly $5 billion in 1969. This, however, is not the only measure of the impact of the war and the subsequent inflation on the balance of payments. The more important impact and the one which is likely to have the most long lasting effects is on our competitive position in international and domestic markets, reflected in the rapid rise in the rate of importing of goods and services. In 1964 merchandise exports exceeded merchandise imports by nearly $7 billion. By 1968 this excess of exports over imports had declined to less than half a billion dollars. With moderation in the rate of inflation and inflation-induced expenditures our trade balance may be expected to improve this year and in subsequent years.

It is too early to tell, however, what permanent damage to our international competitive position the recent period of inflation has induced. It generally takes several years, perhaps four or five, before the full effects of excessive increases in price and costs show up in the competitive position and the effects are not confined to world markets where our products compete with that of other nations, but also in the United States where foreign products compete directly with U.S. products.

So much for balance-of-payments considerations. Let us return to the domestic scene.

I do not think there is any doubt that the resources used towards the Vietnam war effort could have been put to work towards solving imperative problems facing this nation at home. In the five-year period prior to the Vietnam escalation, defense spending in the United States averaged $50 billion per year. If we assume that this level would have been maintained over the most recent five-year period in the absence of escalation, the increase in actual spending totaled $118 billion. During the past four years, total spending for residential construction in the United States totaled only $112 billion.

When we survey the very real needs in our economy in the areas of housing, urban transit, environmental pollution, etc., it is clearly evident that we do not need to create war-related demand for resources in order to maintain full employment. Our problem now is one of establishing meaningful priorities to meet the quality-of-life demands of our citizenry. We obviously cannot do everything at once; we need to start strategic planning and action now if we hope to resolve these demands.

There is another point that at first blush might not appear to be an economic issue. But it is in real fact a very basic one: The war has divided, confused and bewildered Americans. Some Americans are strongly in favor of the continued prosecution of the war. Others are strongly opposed. But for many, the war and the issues surrounding the war are a source of confusion and bewilderment. As a result of this confusion and bewilderment, many people are losing trust in the institutions, public and private, through which we govern ourselves and run our economy. Such loss of trust is destructive of the cohesion necessary for an economy's ability to function at maximum effectiveness. To the degree banks, industrial firms, corporations, state and local governments, federal government agencies and universities are under attack or suspicion for their alleged part in the war in Vietnam, they lose some of their effectiveness as institutions that can provide for the common good. In the case of Vietnam it is my belief that the sum total of such loss of effectiveness is very great indeed and, while unmeasurable by any known economic indicator, this loss of effectiveness produces a very real drag on the economy.

Gentlemen, I deeply regret that the frustrations and misunderstandings arising from this conflict make it necessary to testify that overall war is not a stimulator of economic development nor is the war in Vietnam good for U.S. business. I find it repugnant, even if necessary, to have to add that I would not support our role in the war in Vietnam even if it could somehow be made profitable for American firms.

The thought that war would be initiated or sustained for a single day because it might stimulate the economy should be abhorrent to any decent human being. And yet there are those who say that American business is helping to do just that.

We do know that aggressive war has been waged, all through history, to gain territory. Certainly that was war for economic gain. But even that kind of war, that purpose for war, has been so outmoded by the experience of this century that I would like to be able to say to potential aggressors all over the world, "If you want to profit, if you want to own the world, don't dissipate your energies in wasteful warfare—follow the example of Japan and Germany since World War II and be economically aggressive."

War is, as we would say in business, a low-yield operation.

I think from all this it is obvious that Vietnam is a negative influence on our economy. Let me conclude by restating my initial premise. The war in Vietnam distorts the American economy. It is a major contributor to inflation—our most crucial domestic economic problem. It draws off resources that could be put to work towards solving imperative problems facing this nation at home. And despite the protestations of the new left to the contrary, the fact is that an end to the war would be good, not bad, for American business.

Changing Functions of Government

24. The Garrison Society
Vernon K. Dibble

The brazen disregard of law in the Korean enterprise and in the setting up of an international army in Europe is further evi-

Reprinted from *New University Thought*, Vol. 5, Nos. 1 and 2, Special Issue 66/67. Copyright © 1967, *New University Thought.* Reprinted by permission.

dence that our State Department has long since repudiated any serious respect for law and justice . . . My own feeling is that this policy in the field of foreign affairs, unless restrained, can only lead to arbitrary and totalitarian government at home, as foreign affairs come more and more to dominate our domestic activities, and to war in the world.

—— SENATOR ROBERT A. TAFT, 1951

The United States today is a garrison society. A garrison society is one in which it makes no sense to ask whether or not civilians control the military. It is a society in which the institutions and the men who hold military, economic, and political power have become so dependent upon one another; in which their goals and interests are so complementary; and in which the traditional boundaries between military and civilian spheres have broken down to such an extent, that the very conception of civilian versus military control has no meaning.[1]

In militia societies, too, it makes no sense to talk of civilian control of the military. For in militia societies—England before the English Civil War, for example—there are few or no full-time soldiers, and no independent military establishment, for civilians to control.[2]

In a civilian society—the United States before the second World War—there are full-time soldiers and an independent military establishment. Professional soldiers live, in large measure, within their own, somewhat isolated world. Many of their values—obedience to hierarchical superiors, discipline, physical courage, military honor—are at odds with, or are at least different from, the values of the rest of the society.[3] But they remain subordinate to civil authority.

In an old-fashioned militarist society—Bismarck's Germany, in some respects—the military establishment was not subordinate to civil authority. For example, military budgets in Imperial Germany did not require the approval of the *Reichstag*. Distinctly military values and styles, of which the duels in German fraternities are the best known example, spill over into civilian society.

But these old-fashioned distinctions between civilian or militarist societies, or between civilian versus military control, have no meaning in the United States today. For example, when hundreds of civilian institutions are closely involved with the military, civilian censorship of the public utterances of officers does not prevent them from having their say in public debate, or in public indoctrination. In August 1914, President Wilson wrote to the Secretary of War as follows:[4]

My dear Secretary, I write to suggest that you request and advise all officers of the service, whether active or retired, to refrain from public comment of any kind upon the military and political situation on the other side of the water . . . It seems to me highly unwise and improper that officers of the Army and Navy of the United States should make any public utterances to which any color of political or military criticism can be given where other nations are involved.

That policy still holds. The White House or civilian secretaries censor the speeches of officers, or forbid their presentation altogether. But in a garrison society the silencing of men in uniform is irrelevant. For handmaidens of the military, out of uniform, abound in politics, in scholarship, in the mass media, and in business.

It makes little difference whether the men who make speeches are generals; or retired generals working for armaments firms; or professors whose research is paid for by the Pentagon, or by the CIA; or journalists whose bread and butter depend upon good relations with Pentagon sources; or Congressmen whose re-election may be jeopardized if the bases in their districts are shut down; or researchers in institutes and think shops that survive on military contracts; or corporate executives whose firms manufacture missiles or napalm.

Whoever makes the speeches, and whatever their disagreements with one another—missiles or manned bombers, bomb Hanoi or hold up in enclaves, get tough with Russia or try peaceful coexistence— we will hear no challenge to the basic assumptions of American foreign and domestic policy. We will hear no challenge to the false view that freedom versus communism is what our cold wars and our hot wars are all about.

The point, then, is not simply the size and power of the American military establishment. To be sure, its size and power are basic features of the garrison society. The Pentagon is the headquarters of the largest corporation in the world. As Bert Cochran describes it:[5]

The sprawling bureaucracy housed in this enormous fortress . . . controls an empire that elicits the respectful attention of any of the heads of our leading corporations. The Cordiner Report of several years ago set a valuation of $160 billion on the property owned by the Defense Department, "by any yardstick of measurement, the world's largest organization." This wealth includes weapons arsenals, air bases, naval stations, army reservations, in all, more than thirty-two million acres of land in the United States, and another two and a half million acres abroad. The total is larger than the combined area of Rhode Island, Connecticut, Massachusetts, Maryland, Vermont, and New Hampshire.
. . . The assets of the military are three times the combined assets of United States Steel, American Telephone and Telegraph, Metropolitan Life Insurance, General Motors, and Standard Oil Company of New Jersey. Its paid personnel is three times as large as that of these corporations. Of a grand total of five million federal employees, more than three and one half million are working for the Defense Department: two and a half million in the armed forces, one million civilian workers. The civilian payroll alone is $11 billion a year, equal to one and a half times the combined payrolls of the iron and steel industry and of all other basic metal producers, and equal to twice the payroll of the automobile industry. The annual military budget is larger than the annual net income of all the corporations in the country.

But these figures alone do not define the garrison society. The garrison society consists, rather, of (1) a large and powerful military that penetrates deeply into civilian life; of (2) the great importance of civilians in military affairs, the increasing resemblance between military officers and civilian executives in politics and business, and the greater contact and cooperation between officers and civilians in politics, in science, and in business; such that (3) the traditional boundaries between civilian and military society break down; and (4) the military are blended into an alliance with government and with large corporations, whose goals include (a) counter revolution and American hegemony abroad and (b) a large dose of centralized, executive control of the economy and of politics at home.

Penetration Into Civilian Life: — You cannot administer a military outfit as big as the Pentagon's without penetrating deeply into civilian society. And even if you could, the largest corporation in the world, like all large corporations, seeks to expand, and to reach out for monopoly control over its environment. It sets up or takes over subsidiary corporations like the non-profit think shops. It diversifies its products. These products now include not only weapons, strategic theories, and military skills. They also include ideological indoctrination, social research, and, in Secretary McNamara's proposal to "salvage" the rejects of the draft, social work, pedagogical theory, an implicit denunciation of the failures of the welfare state, an attack upon the teaching profession, a veiled attack upon the humanities,[6] and "advanced educational and medical techniques." If our schools have failed, the Department of Defense will rescue us.[7]

. . . the imperatives of national security in our technological age make the Defense Department the world's largest educator of highly skilled men. Those same imperatives require that it also be the world's most efficient educator.

The military penetrates into education, into research and scholarship, into labor unions, into the political decisions of Senators and Congressmen, and, most crucially, into business and the economy. In education, the use of class standing as a basis for student deferments requires every college instructor in the country to confront his students as an agent of the state. He helps to decide which of his students shall live and which shall die. The selective service system has intruded into the internal government of colleges and universities, has appropriated the ordinary relations between students and teachers for its own administrative convenience, and has transformed these relations into instruments of the garrison society.[8]

The military's penetration into research and scholarship is even more direct. "There was a period after the war," writes Louis J. Halle, "when various departments of the Government tried to marry themselves to the universities." That marriage did not work well in the case of the State Department. But it "worked in the case of the

Pentagon and the faculties of science and technology, a wartime precedent having already been established at Oak Ridge and Los Alamos."[9]

Since that time, the military has continued to purchase some of the best minds in the country. Professor Melman has described some of the consequences of that fact for civilian Research and Development, for the internal structure of American universities, and for the financially neglected fields outside the natural sciences.[10] The military provides large percentages of the annual budget of many major universities.[11] And it, along with the CIA, have transformed scholars and researchers into intelligence analysts, military technicians, and apologists. Michigan State University's fronting for the CIA in Vietnam, and the University of Pennsylvania's secret research for the Pentagon are extreme, but not unique instances. For example, at last count thirty-eight universities and institutes affiliated with universities were conducting research on chemical and biological warfare for the Department of Defense.[12]

Government money for research has consequences, in turn, for education. A professor who has research money from outside his university acquires an economic base that tends to free him from collegial and departmental control. Whether he operates alone with his assistants or in a research institute with colleagues, he is under less pressure to be concerned with all the varied tasks of a university, including the task of teaching students. He is more free, if so inclined, to regard his university as a home base for his operations elsewhere. One result, even among some teachers in undergraduate colleges, is professorial disdain for teaching and for education, as opposed to the specialized training of selected students. From the students' point of view, some of the best of them are suspicious of all scholars and of all scholarship, because they see the confusion of scholarship with military intelligence or apologetics.

In many labor unions, members and dues depend upon war plants. I doubt (as Isaac Deutscher recently expressed it) that most American workers are happy about working for death instead of for life. But a man needs a job. And a union needs members. Hence, unions help munitions firms to secure or retain military contracts, or lobby to prevent the closing down of shipyards and airplane plants. And some labor leaders are among the most chauvinistic heralds of the American counter-revolution abroad.

The no-strike pledge during the second World War is to the unions' relations with the government as Oak Ridge and Los Alamos are to the post-war marriage between the Pentagon and departments or institutes of science and technology. That is, the organizational mobilization of American society that the second World War brought about has continued ever since. For the managers of unions, business firms, research institutes, and governmental agencies find advantages—less militant unions, access to power, money for research, or whatever—in continuing cooperation with one another. These advantages are quite independent of their original military significance. Hence, the organizational coordination of the Second World War goes on, but, of course, with a new definition of the enemy.

Thus, during the Korean War the Research Director of the Textile Workers Union wrote:[13]

The present emergency found American trade-unions prepared to unite with other groups on a common program of national mobilization. They were keyed to an all-out extended battle against Communist totalitarianism, for they knew its dangers and the threat it represented to the people's well-being.

One decade later the Executive Council of the AFL-CIO declared, "The nation's defense requirements obviously have top priority."[14] And in 1963, Secretary McNamara awarded the AFL-CIO a well-deserved citation for, among other things, military propaganda. The Secretary praised the union for "utilizing extensive communications media to promote greater understanding among its millions of members and the public of the vital objectives of defense programs."[15]

In Congress, we read, many silent Senators are "concerned" about Vietnam. But only three voted against the latest Vietnam appropriation. Dozens of Congressmen signed a statement of "concern" about escalation, and proceeded to vote in favor of the appropriation. In contrast, the draft was reinstated in 1948 by a vote of 70 to 10 in the Senate and 259 to 136 in the House.[17] For (except when they want to appropriate more money than the Pentagon requests) a mere Senator or Congressman does not tangle with the largest corporation in the world, whether his state or district wants to keep the bases and war plants it already has, or feels neglected and wants to acquire some. Its economic importance stifles debate. And with most labor unions, or their leaders, committed to the garrison system, one potential source of pressure on Congressmen to behave differently is eliminated.

The acquiescence of Congress and of the labor movement has repercussions, in turn, on education. Many of the most intelligent and most serious college students today spend more time on political activity than on their studies. For as they see it, and they see it correctly, America faces desperate problems that almost no one in public life is willing to face. If a dozen silent Senators who are "concerned" about Vietnam would only speak up, political activists on college campuses would feel free to spend more time on chemistry formulae and the Greek dative.

In the economy, some 10 to 20 per cent—depending on what you include and how you measure it—of the national product depends on the military. And some 10 to 20 per cent of the labor force work at jobs that also depend upon the military. About 25,000 private industrial plants operate under systems of military security, over four million employees were required to obtain security clearance during a period of ten years, and, to be on the safe side, some firms have extended military security to all of their operations, including those which have nothing to do with military work.[18]

To be sure, many, perhaps most American firms do not benefit directly from the garrison society. If 20 per cent depend upon it, 80 per cent pay taxes to make is possible.

Nor would all munitions firms, even, be hurt seriously by sudden disarmament. And some firms, in banking and in men's clothing for example, have been hurt by the war in Vietnam. But we cannot look to businessmen who are left out of the profits of the garrison society, or to firms that are hurt by the war, to lead the way toward "dismantling the cold war institutional machine."[19] For to do so would be a basic challenge to their aerospace colleagues; to the existing system of political power; in some cases to the unions that operate in their plants; and to the entire ideology of anti-communism from which they, too, derive strength and comfort in these trying times. Terminating the war in Vietnam tomorrow would be in the economic interest of many American firms. But adherence to the reigning ideology, and class solidarity with other businessmen more directly involved in the garrison society, seem thus far to be stronger than immediate economic interests. In short, as concerns the military and the American economy, a little penetration goes a long, long way.

The Boundaries Break Down: — But, as noted in the second element in our definition of the garrison society, the penetration of the military into civilian society is only part of the story. While civilian life has become increasingly militarised, civilians have become more important in military affairs, military men have more contact with civilians, and military men come to resemble civilians more than ever before. The office of the Secretary of Defense is no longer that of a coordinator. The Secretary and his civilian aides are makers of military policy. The number and the influence of civilian military theorists, in and out of the Department of Defense, moved General Thomas D. White, former Air Force Chief of Staff, to remark, "in common with other military men I am profoundly apprehensive of the pipe-smoking, trees-full-of-owls type of so-called defense intellectuals who have been brought into this nation's capitol."[20] And no longer do armaments firms simply manufacture what the military orders. They have their own staffs to devise their own weapons systems, which they try to sell to Congress and to the Pentagon.

But the military, too, is developing its own generation of military intellectuals and technological specialists. Advanced technology and a complex, sprawling organization (no longer limited to a simple command structure plus some staff positions) make brains and managerial talent more important than old-fashioned heroism in the upper reaches of military hierarchies. And, of course, constant dealings with corporate executives, plus the prospect of a career in business after retirement from the service, reinforce tendencies within the services themselves toward making the work of military leaders increasingly similar to the work of corporate executives.[21] More generally, as Allen Guttman suggests, the end of *laissez faire* liberalism in this country—the transformation, in Guttman's words, "from an imperfect liberal democracy to an imperfect social democracy"—means that "the American soldier can for the first time in our history square the dictates of his professional ethic with the accepted values and institutions of our society."[22]

In short, the traditional social and cultural boundaries between civilian and military society have broken down. The military, civilian government, and large corporations do not form a single, monolithic ruling group. There are conflicts within, and between, each party to the alliance. But on all essentials—American world power, the Cold War and anti-communism, and the shape of our domestic economy and social structure—they are as one.

The historical origins of the garrison society are reflected in this coalescence of military and civilian executives, and in this fading away of traditional boundaries. The garrison society did not come about because a military clique imposed itself on the rest of America. It was built—base by base, contract by contract, and professor by professor—through the cooperation of military leaders, politicians, and corporate executives that began during the Second World War. Universities, labor leaders,

intellectuals, and the mass media followed along.

One of the earliest prophets of the garrison society was Charles E. Wilson, former president of General Electric. In January, 1944, in an address before the Army Ordnance Association, Wilson proposed an alliance of the military, the executive branch of the Federal Government, and large corporations in "a permanent war economy." He proposed that every large corporation have on its roster a colonel in the reserves for liaison with the military, and he spelled out the role of the Federal executive, of Congress, and of business as follows.[23]

First of all such a [preparedness] program must be the responsibility of the Federal government. It must be initiated and administered by the executive branch—by the President as Commander-in-Chief and by the War and Navy Departments. Of equal importance is the fact that this must be, once and for all, a continuing program and not the creature of an emergency. In fact one of its objects will be to eliminate emergencies so far as possible. The role of Congress will be limited to voting the needed funds. . . .

Industry's role in this program is to respond and cooperate . . . in the execution of the part allotted to it; industry must not be hampered by political witch hunts, or thrown to the fanatical isolationist figure tagged with a "merchants of death" label.

The cooperation that Wilson proposed, and that in fact came about, does not create a monolithic ruling group. But it does create a system in which each party has a great stake in the other party's interests and success. That is one of the system's strong points. If one party to the alliance were imposing itself on the other two, the whole system would be weaker than it is. The economy is dependent in an important degree on the military. But it is equally true that the military are dependent on big business. If armaments firms acted like old-fashioned entrepreneurs, keeping their capital mobile and seeking out the most profitable markets, they might go in for pea canning plants in Sicily instead of missiles. The military and the government depend upon their continued preference for government-sponsored, low-risk capitalism.

Another source of the alliance's strength is the fact that most participants—politicians, generals, corporate executives, and professors—really believe in what they are doing. They are, by their lights, patriotic servants of the public weal. And the combination of power, profits, and sincerity is more powerful than power and profits alone.

International Power and Domestic Controls: — This powerful combination, of motives and of institutions, has profound consequences for American society. The world-wide goals of the garrison society—preventing social revolution and preserving both capitalism and American world power abroad—have repercussions on domestic politics and on the domestic political economy. The preservation of the American imperial system requires economic stability and steady, manageable, predictable economic growth at home. Management and predictability are crucial.

Suppose the United States had a free market economy, subject to uncontrolled fluctuations. Think of the international consequences.[24] A big depression, a great and sudden decline in profits and in employment, would mean a great decline in Federal revenues. There would also be increased political pressure to use these declining revenues for more domestic relief of one kind or another. Foreign aid programs might be threatened. American purchases abroad, public and private, would be curtailed. American multi-national corporations might import more of their undistributed profits from abroad and engage in less foreign investment, especially if low prices in capital goods made the depression a good time to invest here. And imports of the products of other nations, including unstable and potentially revolutionary nations, would go down. Previously friendly governments and businessmen in foreign countries would have to look elsewhere for friends. And, what is more crucial, what would happen to our counter-revolution in Colombia if we could not buy Colombian coffee?

On the other hand, a boom that is too big or too sudden is no good either. For one thing, booms tend to produce their opposite. But apart from that fact, too great an increase in dividends and in corporate investment creates inflationary pressure and invites social conflict in the form of wage demands and perhaps crippling strikes. Inflation means that foreign nations have less purchasing power in the United States and would take their business elsewhere, while production at high capacity forces American business to purchase more from abroad than they otherwise would. Both developments place further strain on the balance of payments, which might require, at some later point, either great cuts in foreign purchases, or a great cut in the foreign military bases of the United States.

In short, some of the international repercussions of a big boom are identical to those of a big depression. Both must be avoided if the American imperial system is to remain intact.

Avoiding both the big boom and the big depression requires an increasingly guided economy—guidelines, dumping surplus commodities on the market to prevent an increase in price, the confrontation between President Kennedy and the steel industry, using the White House instead of old-fashioned bargaining sessions to settle strikes, and using tax policy to make investment and consumption go up or down as the moment requires. These policies, in turn, have further consequences for the society.

For example, labor leaders come under pressure to suppress any signs of an active internal life, and of mass rank-and-file involvement in labor unions. Such things are unmanageable. They have unpredictable consequences. To cite a second example, we cannot permanently abolish unemployment—the classic test of the success of the welfare state—because we must worry about attendant inflationary pressure. That fact, in turn, makes any genuine integration of the mass of Negroes into American society most unlikely, so long as the garrison system lasts.

There are, to be sure, strains in the system. The airline machinists did not go along. The guidelines are breaking down.

And there is probably an inherent contradiction between the requirements of the system and the interests of each single firm or industry. Guidelines are most advantageous to you if your firm or your union is the only one that does not go along with them.

But suppose, for the moment, that the economic management that is inherent in the garrison society works well enough for the foreseeable future. What, then, are the lessons of Vietnam? The obvious lesson is that future garrison governments, in time of peace, must always manage to keep unemployment relatively high and production well below capacity. For reasons that Professor Terence McCarthy has expounded that extra slack is needed in order to fight our next colonial war without overheating the economy. That is how you incorporate Keynesian economics and the historic achievements of the New Deal and of American liberalism into the garrison society.

---

[1] The term "garrison society" is, of course, a variation of Harold Laswell's term, "garrison state." But the two terms do not refer to the same phenomena. In Laswell's words, "The simplest version of the garrison-state hypothesis is that the arena of world politics is moving toward the domination of specialists in violence." As seen in greater detail below, the term "garrison society" refers instead to a coalescence, in various ways, of "specialists" in "The Garrison State Hypothesis Today," in Samuel P. Huntington, ed., *Changing Patterns of Military Politics*, The Free Press of Glencoe: New York, 1952, pp. 51–70.

[2] For more details about this example, see the section entitled "Lords Lieutenant And Their Deputies" in Vernon K. Dibble, "The Organization of Traditional Authority: English County Government, 1558–1640," in James G. March, ed., *Handbook of Organizations*, Rand McNally: Chicago, 1965, pp. 879–909. See also the relevant chapters in Thomas G. Barnes, *Somerset, 1625–1640: A County's Government During The Personal Rule*," Harvard University Press: Cambridge, 1961.

[3] Samuel P. Huntington, in The *Soldier and the State*, notes a number of ways in which "the military ethic" is in conflict with the liberal ideology that has been dominant in American political history. For example, "The heart of liberalism is individualism. It emphasizes the reason and moral dignity of the individual, and opposes political, economic, and social restraints upon individual liberty. In contrast, the military ethic holds that man is evil, weak, and irrational and that he must be subordinated to the group. The military man claims that the natural relation among men is conflict." Quoted in Allen Guttman, "Political Ideals And The Military Ethic," *The American Scholar*, 34:2, Spring, 1965, p. 22.

[4] Quoted in Jack Raymond, *Power At The Pentagon*, Harper and Row: New York, 1964, p. 178.

[5] Bert Cochran, *The War System*, Macmillan: New York, 1965, pp. 138–139.

[6] I take it that the Secretary's statement that "One of the department's key concepts is that traditional classroom training is often largely irrelevant to actual on-the-job performance requirements" and his reference to "pruning from existing courses all non-essential information" are veiled attacks on the humanities.

[7] The quotation which follows, the quotation in the previous sentence, and the quotation in Note 3 are from the excerpts from Secretary McNamara's address to the Veterans of Foreign Wars, *New York Times*, August 24, 1966, p. 18.

[8] The administration of a number of colleges (including Wayne State, Haverford, Cornell, and a few others) have indicated that their colleges will either submit no class standings to draft boards or will otherwise refuse to go along (for example, by refusing to compute class standings separately for male and female students). The faculties of a few other colleges, including Columbia College, have voted in favor of this position.

[9] Louis J. Halle, "On Teaching International Relations," *Virginia Quarterly Review*, 40:1, Winter, 1964, p. 13.

[10] Seymour Melman, *Our Depleted Society*, Dell Publishing Co.: New York, 1965, Chapter 4, entitled "Cold War Science and Technology."

[11] *Ibid.*, Appendix C, "Index of 500 Largest Military Prime Contractors For Experimental Development, Test and Research Work." See also Raymond, *op. cit.*, Chapter VIII, "Research and the Federal Government" and Cochran, *op. cit.*, pp. 155–161.

[12] This figure is from Carol Brightman, "The Weed Killers—A Final Word," *Viet Report*, 2:7, 1966, pp. 3–5. Miss Brightman relies on "a Pentagon spokesman" as reported in the *Washington Post*.

[13] Solomon Barkin, "American Trade-Unions In The Present Emergency," *Monthly Labor Review*, the Bureau of Labor Statistics, 73:4, October, 1951, p. 409.

[14] *Proceedings of the AFL-CIO Fourth Constitutional Convention*, 1961, Vol. II, p. 70.

[15] *Proceedings of the AFL-CIO Fifth Constitutional Convention*, 1963, Vol. I, p. 355.

[16] *New York Times*, June 11, 1948 and June 23, 1948.

[17] The information on military security in business is from Raymond, *op. cit.*, pp. 154–156. On the extent to which the economy depends upon military spending, Harry Magdoff, using the estimates of the U.S. Arms Control And Disarmament Agency in its volume, *Economic Impacts of Disarmament* (Washington, D. C., 1962), writes as follows: "The more than $55 billion spent annually on what the government agencies classify as 'national defense' has a chain-reaction effect on the rest of the economy, just as other forms of investment and spending have a 'multiplier' effect. It is estimated that for every $1 spent on 'national defense' another $1 to $1.40 of economic product is stimulated. A crude, but conservative, calculation shows that in addition to the approximately 7.4 million people engaged in some phase of 'national defense,' another 6 to 9 million are employed due to the economic stimulus of defense spending." Harry Magdoff, "Problems of United States Capitalism," in R. Miliband and J. Savile, eds., *The Socialist Register: 1965*, Monthly Review Press: New York, 1965, p. 63. See also Cochran, *op. cit.*, pp. 140–141.

[19] This phrase is the title of Chapter 12 of Melman, *op. cit.*

[20] Quoted in Raymond, *op. cit.*, p. 289. More generally, see Raymond's Chapter 16, "The 'McNamara Monarchy'."

[21] See Morris Janowitz, *The Professional Soldier: A Social And Political Portrait*, The Free Press: Glencoe, Illinois, 1960. Especially Section II, "Organizational Realities: Heroic And Managerial" and Chapter 20, "The Future of the Military Profession."
[22] Guttmann, *op. cit.*, p. 237. See note #3, above for further explanation of this point.
[23] Quoted in Fred J. Cook, *The Warfare State*, Macmillan: New York, 1962, pp. 76–77. Mr. Cook, in turn quotes from an article by John M. Swomley

in *The Progressive*, January 1959. I was unfortunately not able to locate the full text of Mr. Wilson's speech in any of the usual courses such as *Vital Speeches* or *The New York Times*. Note that this man is Wilson of G. E., not Wilson of General Motors.
[24] I am grateful to Mr. William Martin for his suggestions about the links between the current international and domestic economic policies of the Kennedy-Johnson administration.

Scarce Resource Allocation

25. Whither California?

Martin Gellen

During 1970, The Department of Defense, NASA, and the AEC will spend approximately $75 billion. This is more than any other nation spends for war, let alone "defense." In fact, this sum is larger than the total Gross National Product of all but eight nations of the world. Within the United States a similar pattern of inequity exists, for over half of that $75 billion will go to only ten states: Missouri, Georgia, Massachusetts, Virginia, Ohio, Pennsylvania, Connecticut, New York, Texas, and last but not least, California.

In terms of dollar value, California is by far the largest beneficiary of defense expenditures in the country. In 1968, with only about 10 per cent of the population of the United States, California received about 18 per cent of all defense contracts, with a worth of approximately $6.5 billion. In fiscal 1970, total defense expenditures in California will amount to $10.8 billion, with an additional $1.3 billion for NASA programs. This is almost twice the $6.2 billion which the State of California spends on everything.[1]

What these figures mean is that California plays a central role in the industrial base of the American military system. California supplies 46 per cent of all the nation's missiles and space systems, 44.3 per cent of all military building supplies, 27 per cent of all petroleum used by the Department of Defense, 23 per cent of all military subsistence (food, clothing, etc.), 20 per cent of all military construction, 21 per cent of all military electronics equip-

ment, and only 9.9 per cent of all military aircraft. In addition, California conducts over 35 per cent of all defense research and development. California is also the major supplier for NASA, and since 1965 has pocketed about 50 per cent of all its prime contract awards. Half of this share has gone to one California company: North American Rockwell.[2]

A breakdown of California defense contracts according to type reveals the true heart of military capitalism in the state. Thirty-five per cent on the total goes for missile and space systems (this portion was much larger prior to the war in Vietnam), 15 per cent for aircraft, 13 per cent for electronics and communication equipment, 6 per cent for ammunition, and 4 per cent for petroleum and fuel supplies. This means that about 65 per cent of all defense contracts are handled by California's aerospace companies. For most of these firms, defense contracts represent their major market. Moreover, one-third of all these prime contracts are for research, development, testing, and evaluation. This is the most lucrative of all defense business since costs are not strictly fixed and nothing need be actually produced. At the same time, R & D contracts are crucial for they often lead to large prime contracts for production: $20 million in R & D can pave the way for $200 million in production.[3]

The largest defense contractor in the state as well as the nation is Lockheed. Between 1961 and 1968 Lockheed has received approximately $12 billion in contracts for defense, comprising about 88 per cent of its total business. In 1967, Lockheed was awarded $709 million for R & D, of which about 80 per cent went to its five California plants (Los Angeles, Burbank, Ontario, Redlands, and Sunnyvale). Following close behind is General Dynamics, with about $200 million in R & D for its six California installations, located primarily in Pomona and San Diego. McDonnell-Douglas with six plants in the state, Hughes with eleven, North American Rockwell with five, and Aerojet-General with six each raked in over $100 million in R & D work for their California divisions. These thirty-nine plants receive most of defense contracts going to California and represent the foundation of defense industry in the state.[4]

The total capital investment in defense activities in California has never been accurately determined. Some economists believe it may be somewhere between $35 billion and $50 billion if land, buildings and equipment are included. Altogether, this would cover eighty-seven military installations and approximately ninety-nine defense plants. DOD land holdings alone are known to be extensive. According to a 1964 report by the Office of the Assistant Secretary of the Department of Defense, the United States Government owns 4.3 million acres of military landed property in California with a total worth of $4.1 billion. Both in acreage and in dollar value this is the largest military holding in any state.[5]

Defense spending is probably the single most important contributor to employment in the state. About 37.5 per cent of manufacturing employment in California is attributable to space and defense-related industries. Between 1967 and 1968, this represented about 600,000 employees. A rough estimate of total employment generated by defense spending would include both indirect employment from subcontractors and suppliers and their suppliers in turn, as well as the induced employment generated by the spending of workers in defense jobs and the 266,000 civilian and 320,000 military persons on DOD payrolls in California. The table below shows what such an estimate looks like. This is approximately 30 per cent of the state's total employment of 7.5 million people in 1968.[6]

Space & defense related industries	600,000
Indirect defense employment	120,000
Induced employment	950,000
DOD payroll—civilian	266,000
DOD payroll—military	320,000
Total	2,256,000

Estimates by the Joint Economic Conversion Committee in the state legislature are a bit more conservative but still quite dramatic. The committee attributes 946,000 jobs to defense and space activities in California and an additional million jobs indirectly dependent upon defense spending. If the families of these 1,946,000 workers are included, then "more than one-fifth of California's population depends on the flow of defense dollars into California," concludes one of the committee's consultants.[7]

Regionally within California, the proportion of total employment dependent on defense expenditures is considerably higher. About 70 per cent of all aerospace manufacturing employment in the state is situated in the Southern California region, with most of this concentrated in the Los Angeles-Long Beach area. According to Charles Tiebout, 1960 figures show that about 43.5 per cent of the employment in the area is tied in one way or another to defense monies. In San Diego, aerospace currently accounts for about 60 per cent of all manufacturing employment; for Orange County the proportion runs about 66 per cent. Moreover the Security First National Bank of Los Angeles claims that over one-third of the $30 billion Gross Regional Product of Southern California can be traced back to defense spending in the state. On the other hand, Santa Clara County in the San Francisco Bay area, receives more defense dollars per capita than any other county in the state ($1.3 billion), and recent estimates show that seven out of every ten new jobs in Santa Clara County are dependent in one form or another upon defense and space-related funds.[8]

The high proportion of R & D, as well

as contracts devoted to space, missiles, and electronics, gives the aerospace labor force a sharp trend toward white-collar and technical salaried workers. Over 52 per cent of the employees of Southern California aerospace companies, for example, consist of engineers, scientists, technicians and other salaried personnel. This same pattern is reflected in the utilization of floor space in aerospace plants where, on the average, only about 40 per cent is devoted to manufacturing, but 30 per cent is allocated for laboratories and offices and 30 per cent for storage and other purposes. A recent SRI report suggests that this trend is on the increase.[9]

It should come as no surprise, then, that California has drawn a disproportionate number of scientists to the state. The only available data on the subject, although somewhat incomplete, indicates that 27,631 scientists, or 11.4 per cent of the national total, live in California. If this number is broken down according to disciplinary categories, then California can claim 12 per cent of the nation's earth-scientists and meteorologists, 13.2 per cent of its psychologists and about 16 per cent of its mathematicians, statisticians, and physicists. Again, reliable figures are not available, but rough estimates show that California also accounts for about 20 per cent of the nation's electronic engineers and about 30 per cent of its aeronautical engineers.[10]

The fact that this large proportion of the manufacturing labor force dependent upon defense spending in the state is also highly skilled, well-educated, and well-paid means that the multiplier effect of defense spending in aerospace industries is much higher than that for military installations or large commercial factories. The consumption patterns and cultural needs of defense workers usually mean a higher standard of living for the communities which they inhabit (primarily suburban, of course). Also, the need to reproduce that labor force in terms of both its special magnitude and its composition requires large public and private expenditures for education and training. It is therefore no accident that California has the most highly capitalized university system (both public and private) in the country. Cal Tech, USC, and UCLA feed workers into the aerospace complex down in the Los Angeles-Long Beach region, on the one hand, and Stanford and Berkeley are similarly hooked into the Northern Santa Clara County space, missiles, and electronics industries.

However, the "knowledge industry" in the state is more than a source of labor and expertise. It plays a pivotal role in guiding the development of the war economy of the state. This is particularly clear with respect to the interlocking relationship between the University of California and the Pentagon, for example. Glenn Seaborg, former chancellor of Berkeley, is now head of the AEC, which is both a cause and an effect of Berkeley's control of over 90 per cent of the nuclear weapons research in the country. In addition, the past three directors of the Office of Defense Research and Engineering in the Pentagon have all come from the Lawrence Radiation Laboratory (UC). The function of the Office of DRE is to determine future armament priorities for the whole defense establishment and then to spend the money which will put those projects into motion. It should not be surprising then that California's research and educational institutions receive about 26 per cent of all the dollars which go to non-profit R & D contractors and that the state's universities (UC campuses, Stanford, Cal Tech and USC) receive about 20 per cent of all R & D money granted for defense research at universities and colleges throughout the nation. The flow of personnel which has been observed between the heavily research-oriented aerospace firms in California, the universities, and the Pentagon is therefore not accidental; it is an essential mechanism through which the defense-oriented industries of California maintain profitable operations.[11]

Considering all this, it is plain that California's growth since World War II has largely been tied to the defense-aerospace sector of the state's economy. Between 1949 and 1957 defense-related employment increased 228 per cent compared to an 81 per cent increase in non-defense employment. From 1953 to 1963 defense spending rose 57 per cent in the state while population trailed slightly behind with an increase of 50 per cent. For the first half of the sixties, approximately three out of every five new jobs added to industrial payrolls were in defense-related fields. Since 1965, almost four out of every five new manufacturing jobs are attributable to aerospace and defense. Clearly, the defense orientation of California's industrial base has grown and continues to grow. Defense has become the state's largest industry. It produces twice the revenue of the $4.3 billion cash income of agriculture and four times the total income of the construction industry, and how much of agribusiness and construction depend on the flow of defense dollars is anybody's guess.[12]

The defense industry, then, with about $50 billion in total assets, producing about $12 billion per year in income and almost $1.5 billion in profits, and employing over a million people, is the veritable backbone of the state's economy. The major consequence of this extraordinary dependency upon defense spending is that any significant change in the international military situation or a shift in American foreign policy can bring boom or bust for the state. The fate of California is therefore inextricably tied to the fortunes of American power throughout the globe.

THE SAN FRANCISCO BAY AREA

The San Francisco Bay Area, it can be said without exaggeration, is a militarized society. Federal military spending here is greater than in any other metropolitan region except Los Angeles, accounts for half of the government spending at all levels and is responsible for one-third of the area's jobs. If the Bay Area were a state, in fact, it would rank as the fourth largest recipient of defense dollars in the country, exceeded only by New York, Texas and California.

The ever-increasing amount reached a staggering $4.2 billion in 1969. Half went to buy goods and services, 28.5 per cent or $1.2 billion for payrolls, $438 million or 9.9 per cent for veterans' programs and $292 million or 6.5 per cent for atomic energy programs.

Looked at another way, about 60 per cent of the money went to supply, maintain and operate military posts and installations. The rest went into production and research, with aerospace firms on the Peninsula getting $1.289 billion or 29 per cent of all local military expenditures. On a per capita basis, this means that Federal military money is being poured into the Bay Area at a rate of about $930 for every single person.

Los Angeles draws more military dollars —36 per cent of the total spent in California as contrasted with the Bay Area's 30 per cent—but the per capita figure there is $735. For California as a whole, it is $750.

The government spends a lot less for other programs. The per capita figure for its Bay Area expenditures on education, welfare, health and culture services is $386 per person.

The military spending has its greatest impact on employment. About 217,000 jobs, or just slightly more than 11 per cent of the Bay Area's employment total, are directly dependent on the military. But that is only a small part of the picture. For the personal spending by these workers generates roughly another 434,000 jobs. This means that, directly or indirectly, the military expenditures account for 651,000 jobs—and that's 33.3 per cent of all Bay Area jobs.

Many of these workers are involved in a vast array of research and development projects in electronics, guided missiles and atomic energy.

A large portion of this work is done by the Lockheed Aircraft Corporation, the largest private corporation in California and the recipient of about half of all the Federal procurement money spent in this region. Last year, Lockheed grossed $796,379,000 in military contracts at its plants in Palo Alto, Pleasanton, Santa Cruz and Sunnyvale. Almost all the money went to the Sunnyvale plant which produces Poseidon missiles and a variety of special satellites for the space program and for counter-insurgency use in Asia.

Other important aerospace centers are at Philco-Ford in Santa Clara, which got $63,244,000 in military contracts last year, and at Sylvania in Mountain View, with $45,153,000 in contracts. Along with Stanford Research Institute, these two firms have been working on electronic battlefield programs to be used in place of the large numbers of ground troops in Southeast Asia or elsewhere as needed.

Employment has been declining in recent months. But for the past two decades the aerospace industry has been the key factor shaping the spectacular economic growth of the belt between San Francisco and San Jose. The industry has been responsible for about one-third of the jobs developed in Santa Clara County over the past decade, and at least 60 per cent of the jobs in the county today are dependent in one way or another on military spending.

Lately, the aerospace industry has been spreading to other sections of the Bay Area. Fledgling research and development complexes already exist in places like San Leandro, Richmond and Walnut Creek.

In Pleasanton, Kaiser Aluminum and Chemical Co. has opened a sprawling 80-acre Center for Technology, to replace and consolidate research facilities situated elsewhere throughout the country. Along with its valuable contributions to U.S. military technology, the Bay Area acts as a key staging area and command center for operations in the Pacific—a role it has played in every war which the country has waged around the Pacific rim.

San Francisco's Presidio, for example, is the headquarters of the Sixth Army, the third largest in the country with about 70,000 troops, 11,000 civilian employees and 40,000 reservists assigned to various units. Also situated in the city is Letterman General Hospital, with an annual patient load of more than 250,000, many of them war casualties in Vietnam.

In Oakland, there is the army base, the Western Military Traffic Management and Terminal Service and the Military Ocean Terminal.

Through these facilities move all the army personnel travelling to military bases in Southeast Asia and the entire Pacific and most of the ammunition and other supplies.

The Twelfth Naval District, which covers Northern California, Utah and Nevada and is responsible for the Naval defense of the entire Western Pacific and Western United States, also is situated in the Bay Area.

The District has more than 26,000 uniformed people, 43,000 civilian employees and a yearly payroll of nearly $400 million. (The Navy also spends about $1.3 billion a year with local firms for supplies, research and service.) District facilities include the naval shipyards at Hunters Point and Mare Island, a weapons station in Concord, a supply center at Oakland and Military Sea Transportation Service facilities.

The two shipyards alone include half the West Coast's major shipbuilding facilities. Hunters Point does conversion, overhaul and repair work, while Mare Island has been used for construction. Since 1958, the Mare Island facility has built and delivered thirteen nuclear submarines to the Pacific Fleet and currently is building three more.

The weapons station—largest of its kind —supplies ammunition for all armed forces connected with the Pacific Fleet and the supply center handles most of the other supplies—a $6 million-a-year operation.

The Sea Transportation Service, which carries all the cargo, puts about $100 million in contracts and subsidies annually into the Bay Area's maritime industry.

The Air Force also has important facilities in the area, especially at Travis Air Force Base at Fairfield just north of San Francisco.

The base is the Western Pacific Center for the Military Airlift Command, meaning it is responsible for such tasks as evacuating wounded troops by air, taking air photographs, providing weather reports and rescuing downed pilots throughout the entire Pacific region. It houses the second largest Air Force Hospital in the world.

Finally, the Army Corps of Engineers has its Northern California and South Pacific divisions situated in San Francisco. They direct all military construction in California and eight other western states, help in nuclear testing programs and secure labor and supplies for Army construction projects in several Asian areas. The Corps also acts as real estate agent for other federal agencies, military and otherwise, in buying, selling and directing the development of federal lands.

The Corps has extensive control over the bay's development, far greater than the Bay Conservation and Development Commission. It has always supported large Bay fill projects and currently wants to reclaim more than ninety acres for an aircraft carrier maintenance site near the Alameda Naval Air Station.

The role of the agencies, Army, Navy and Air Force, in planning, managing, and directing U.S. operations in Vietnam, has had a great economic impact on the area. The war alone is responsible for 21,000 new jobs in the area or 16.7 per cent of the total increase in employment since 1965. Indirectly, the war has generated another 44,000 jobs, meaning that almost half of the new jobs created were dependent in one way or another on the war in Vietnam. The center of this boom has been the water and air transportation industry, which has accounted for nearly one-third of the new war-related jobs.

Military shipments from Pacific Coast ports—about 55 per cent of all that is going to Vietnam—have more than tripled since 1965, coming close to totals recorded during the high points of World War II.

The Port of Oakland, where most of the transportation activity is centered, currently receives more than $120 million in military contracts annually. Private shipping firms that are the port's tenants also have done well. In 1969, for instance, the Sealand firm got $62,269,000 from the Defense Department and the Seatrain firm got $64,532,000. In San Francisco, States Marine Lines got $87,059,000, U.S. Lines about $20 million and American President Lines close to $25 million.

Air freight carriers have done extremely well, especially those at Oakland International Airport which have the Military Airlift Command at Travis Air Force Base as their main customer. Capitol International Airways got $16,445,000 in military contracts in 1969; Saturn got $20,057,000; Trans International Airlines $20,996,000; Universal Airlines, $23,389,000 and World Airways, $54 million. As a matter of fact, between 60 and 70 per cent of all the revenues of the five airlines comes from military business, and the five companies in turn control about four-fifths of the country's supplemental charter airlines industry.

Since the military transportation complex is a key part of the Bay Area economy, those who play the leading roles in its management also are leading figures in the regional business establishment.

The Bay Area, for example, has the country's largest chapter of the National Defense Transportation Association, a world-wide organization composed of 15,000 executives involved in civilian and military transportation. The president of the Bay Area chapter is John Wagner, a senior vice president of Pacific Far East Lines, which has received as much as $20 million since 1966 for shipping food and other perishable military cargo to the Far East. The chairman of the chapter's board is W. P. Pierce of the Kaiser Steel Corporation, a subsidiary of Kaiser Industries, which gets about 15 per cent of its revenue from military contracts. Ben E. Nutter, a vice president of the chapter, got started in professional life as an engineer building air bases in the Pacific during World War II and is executive director and chief engineer for the Port of Oakland. He is responsible for the Port of Oakland's aggressive campaign to become the chief military and commercial transportation carrier in the Western Pacific and is closely tied to the Kaiser interests.

Then of course, there's the Bank of America, the major banker for American economic development in Asia. The bank is the major financial agent for the Port of Oakland, the Kaiser empire, and holds an interest in Consolidated Freightways, which owns Pacific Far East Lines. Through its investment in the four top supplemental charter airlines, the bank also is responsible for financing arrangements of close to 40 per cent of the military airlift activities in California.

In the past couple of months, the bank's financial aid also has been one of the major factors keeping Lockheed Aircraft out of bankruptcy.

MILITARY EXPENDITURES IN 11-
COUNTY BAY AREA, 1969

Defense Department......$3,297,635,000
Veterans Administration . . .   438,501,500
AEC...................   272,549,000
Merchant Marine   99,353,000
NASA   86,411,100
Selective Service   742,400
TOTAL................$4,195,192,000

COUNTY TOTALS

Santa Clara.............$1,503,630,500
Alameda   946,805,000
San Francisco...........   428,028,435
Solano................   386,722,900
Monterey   265,884,000
Contra Costa...........   237,052,000
San Mateo   167,831,800
Marin.................   92,811,000
Sonoma...............   32,793,300
Santa Cruz   17,151,800
Napa.................   7,527,000

This is by no means a new role for the
bank. It first became a key financial force in
Bay Area war industries during World War
II, when it joined Kaiser and Standard
Oil to head the Control and Planning Division of the San Francisco Port of Embarka-
tion.

It is clear, then, that the staggering
ascent of American power in the Pacific
which began at that time has created a
highly complex network of militarized
economic and government operations
throughout the Bay Area. We have a militarized industrial base which, although
it appears separate from the civilian economy, is in reality indistinguishable from it.

In our midst, there also has developed
a superstructure of military institutions
which determine land use and health care
and consumption and production, not only
for military personnel but directly and
indirectly for a vast portion of the civilian
population as well. Under such conditions,
the foreign policy crisis over Vietnam
obviously will disrupt the Bay Area.

The failure of American intervention
in Asia can only mean failure for the war
economy at home. Inflation, rising unemployment, the deterioration of vital social
services, the increasing consolidation of
police power—all this represents the ultimate logic of this economy geared to war.

THE MILITARY INDUSTRY CRISIS AND CONVERSION

With a huge aerospace industry and a big
commitment to R & D work, California's
defense industries have not really profited
that much from the war in Vietnam or
the Kennedy-McNamara-Johnson emphasis
upon the development of tactical military
forces. Only about 15 per cent of the prime
contracts going to California involve the
production of military aircraft, and a good
portion is allocated to R & D. However,
about 37 per cent of all prime contracts
awarded to California since 1966 have gone
for items like ammunition, petroleum,
building supplies, combat vehicles, subsistence supplies, and other materials
necessary to support ground troops in a
major land war. These defense dollars tied
to Vietnam have created about 100,000
jobs in the state. With the de-escalation of
the American involvement in ground
actions in Vietnam, about half of these jobs
will be threatened. In the San Francisco-
Oakland area 26,000 jobs can be attributed
to the war in Southeast Asia. About 5000
civil service seamen have already been
laid off due to cutbacks in military shipping.
The half million employees who man the
eighty-two defense bases and installations
throughout the state may also be hard hit.
Alameda County has four, San Francisco
five, Solano four, Monterey four, San Ber-
nardino five, Orange County four, Los
Angeles nine, and San Diego seventeen.
Since many of these installations are located
in rural areas where sources of income for
the residents are more limited than in the
cities, the effects of cutbacks in the war
could be severe in these places.[13]

At the same time, the aerospace industry
is going through a major contraction partially related to the domestic economic crisis
which the war in Vietnam has spawned.
Because of weaknesses in the economy and
the political uncertainty of defense expenditures, all of aerospace markets are shrinking at the same time. Firstly, the Nixon
Administration is reducing government
contracting as a means of slowing the inflationary rise in the national economy caused
originally by deficit spending for Vietnam
operations. Unfortunately, these deflation-

ary policies and the general softness in the economy are also narrowing the civilian air transportation market on which the industry is counting as its most important source of sales next to space and missiles. Secondly, the industry is also faced with a "technological trough"; hardware of the old technology presently on production lines is about to be phased out or drastically modified (Minuteman I, Poseidon, B-52, etc.), while the new technologies are still in development cycles estimated to be about two or three years away from profitable production. However, because of reduced government expenditures, these development cycles are being extended. This means that the technological trough is widening. Part of this technological change-over, while including new production items for civilian aviation like the 747, the Douglas-11, and the Lockheed Tri-Star, also covers the development and production of a brand new "generation" of strategic weapons. There is growing indication that the Defense Department and Richard Nixon are seriously considering a return to the "fortress America" policies of the fifties and a renewal of the arms race. Nixon and Laird have talked widely of "renovating" our "outmoded Strategic systems" and President Nixon personally is promoting the ABM program through Congress. R & D for strategic forces rose by 12.5 per cent in the proposed FY1971 defense budget ($4.8 billion to $5.4 billion), expenditures for further study of the Underseas Launched Missile System went from $24 million to $40 million, the Airborne Warning and Control System climbed from $40 million to $87 million, and development expenditures for the Aegis shipboard missile increased from $35 million to $75 million. ABM expenditures almost doubled. At present, the aerospace companies have their eyes glued on the Strategic Arms Limitations Talks in Vienna, despite the fact that Nixon and Laird are already clamoring for deployment of ABM and MIRV, and the new Minuteman system. At stake in the SALT talks are weapons programs worth about $75 billion dollars, of which California plants could grab possibly as much as $30 billion or $40 billion over the next decade. But all this depends on what happens in Vienna and the United States Congress.[14]

Thirdly, it is likely that NASA's budget will be trimmed by 12 per cent in FY1971. Apollo Lunar Landing Missions, earlier planned at roughly four-month intervals, now are scheduled approximately every six months through early 1972 and will probably be suspended after Apollo 18 in 1974. Also to be cut back are the communications satellite programs and Mars explorations schedules. All of this will have a severe effect upon California aerospace, which has had a big stake in the Apollo program and manned space-flight missions. The only area in which allocations have significantly risen in the proposed budget is the R & D program for a space station and space shuttle system, all of which is tied to strategic military planning. Because of budget cuts, industrial employment for NASA will probably be cut back from 218,000 (June 1969) to 140,000 (June 1971). Almost 98 per cent of this decrease will affect contractor employees.[15]

DOD and NASA budget cuts means additional layoffs for the California defense economy on top of the Vietnam cutbacks. Between December 1967 and November 1969, employment in aerospace declined by 76,200, with 60 per cent of this decrease coming in the last year (November 1968–November 1969). In 1970, this decline is expected to accelerate with about a 10 per cent reduction in current employment levels, or 55,000 workers. At the same time, with about 128,000 jobs related to Vietnam activities, and almost 80,000 servicemen returning to the state to enter the labor market, unemployment could rise by as much as 60 per cent. The 1970 unemployment rate in the state is 6.1 per cent, by 1971 this could be close to 10 per cent. Since January 1969, North American Rockwell, for example, has laid off about 30 per cent of its aerospace workers, or 22,500 of its 70,000 employees. If the company fails to get the B-1 contract it may have to lay off another 7,000.[16]

There is more than normal attention given to aerospace layoffs partly because scientists and engineers seem to be becoming proletarianized, which is quite a new phenomenon in this society, but also because the economic impact of aerospace unemployment is greater than unemployment in other industries. Nearly 53 per cent of all space and defense workers classified as white-collar, as against an average of 28 per cent in most other industrial groups. Salaries tend to be much higher in aerospace, and the high skill requirements for production workers means that wages tend to be higher also. Thus unemployment in the defense-related industries has a greater impact on demand and indirect employment than comparable unemployment in the auto or foodprocessing industries. General consumption levels are more severely affected and recession can hit harder. Also occupational changes are more difficult because of the overspecialization on the one hand or deterioration in skills (especially for the bulk of engineers who function merely as draftsmen) on the other hand. In addition, the hundreds of engineers and scientists graduating from the colleges and universities of the state will also be in trouble.

The specter of a severe recession in the state has stimulated interest in economic conversion of the state's industrial base. Nationally, Senator McGovern has called for the creation of a National Economic Conversion Commission. Locally, Assemblyman John Burton of San Francisco has established a Joint Economic Conversion Committee in the State Legislature which expects to develop legislation modelled after and linked up to the McGovern plan. The Committee has also proposed a conversion study to (1) determine the exact extent of California's economic dependence upon defense expenditures in terms of dollars and employment, and (2) to recommend both short-term and longterm remedies which can enable the state to overcome that dependence. No such study of dependence has ever been undertaken in California; consequently most of the present data on the subject is incomplete, especially with respect to indirect and induced impacts of defense expenditures. The proposal is currently awaiting Department of Labor funding. In addition, the

Los Angeles Times and *San Francisco Chronicle* have both endorsed the Committee's activities and have called for some type of conversion planning. Support is also coming from groups like TASC in the Bay Area and the Southern California Professional Engineering Association. The latter is akin to a white-collar union which has begun organizing aerospace technical workers throughout the Los Angeles-Long Beach area along with the Scientists and Engineers Guild.

WHAT IS THE NATURE OF THE AEROSPACE FIRM?

Aerospace corporations are not really like most private corporations. They seem to resemble government agencies more than business enterprises. A fairly large portion of their assets is owned by the Federal Government and operated through leasing arrangements. This includes land, buildings and key equipment. By 1967, the Pentagon had supplied defense firms with approximately $14.7 billion worth of property. A good deal of the working capital required for production and research and development comes by way of the U.S. Treasury, so that commercial capital markets are generally bypassed in the financial plans for the defense activities of most aerospace companies. These companies generally do not generate their own capital, but are dependent for capital on both banks and the government. Because of both the large input of government capital and government procurement policies regulating profits, aerospace firms have tended to have extremely low profit margins compared to commercial companies but at the same time have produced higher investor rates of return than do commercial firms. During 1962–65 (a bad period for aerospace because of the 1964–65 decline), aerospace firms had an average capital turnover (sales per privately invested capital) of 6.8X compared to 2.3X for commercial companies, and an average rate of return of 17.5 per cent compared to 10.6 per cent for commercial companies.[17] In addition, the government determines management policies, labor policies, subcontracting arrangements, financial plans, production schedules, and quality of work.

While more or less agents of the government, the big aerospace firms act as systems engineers and technical directors for multi-billion dollar R & D and production activities involving hundreds of other corporations. Big prime contractors who, like Boeing, McDonnell-Douglas or Lockheed, organize the production of military systems or, like AT&T and General Electric, manage gigantic space facilities and military laboratories, guide along a whole host of specialized subcontractors like Northrup, Aerojet-General, Sperry Rand, Hewlett-Packard, TRW, Raytheon, etc., as well as dozens of giant corporate suppliers like Standard Oil, Dow, Ford, DuPont, AMF, Kaiser Industries, ALCOA, Singer, etc. In and out as consultors and planners move the universities, drawing the majority of their research budgets from the government and the special nonprofit outfits like Rand, SRI, and IDA conducting strategic studies and developing policy formulations. At the same time, the private contractors penetrate government at all levels, exploiting the so-called "national priorities" on space, defense and scientific progress, with an eye to aggrandizing their own power. In the process, narrow special interests become indistinguishable from the collective interests of society, and the divisions between the public and the private sectors blur.

This is the world of C. Wright Mills' "power elite," a world in which the generals, the statesmen, and the industrialists all change hats—and frequently, too. It is a world which has been held together, until recently, merely by an elite of several thousand men, mainly corporate managers and brokers, who play a wide variety of interlocking roles. They do consulting work for government agencies, hold military rank, sit on boards of directors, sometimes sit on government advisory committees, and often negotiate or supervise contracts for the government. But this is a world which is quickly changing. For what was once an informal coalition of bureaucrats, generals, politicians, and industrialists, in which the lines between all these groups were blurry,

has now become institutionalized in the form of a centralized industrial management in the Pentagon, and which is run through the Office of the Secretary of Defense in the Pentagon. This is now the formal administrative center of the military-industrial complex.[18]

It has regional offices also. In 1965, the Defense Supply Agency completed the creation of its Defense Contracts Administration Services system. This is a nationwide organization the purpose of which is to administer procurement contracts for the three military departments, for DSA, NASA, other Federal and State agencies, and, when authorized, for foreign governments. Previously, the military departments and other agencies managed their own contracts. Altogether, the eleven regional offices of the DCAS manage about $48 billion worth of production each year. This is equal to the total sales of Standard Oil, Ford, G.M. and G.E. The two largest cities on the West Coast are the regional centers for management of procurement contracts throughout the entire western half of the continent. The San Francisco office in Burlingame, California, manages 12,308 contracts throughout Northern California, Nevada (except for Clark County), Utah, Montana, Idaho, Oregon, Washington, Alaska, and Hawaii, for such items as naval guns, communications satellites, components for Polaris and Poseidon missile systems and high altitude bombers, subsistence, electronic systems and components, and ammunition. The Los Angeles office, located near Inglewood, manages 28,619 contracts worth over $8.5 billion and spread throughout Southern California, Arizona, and Clark County, Nevada. Materials for which contracts are administered are: basic and applied research, air frame, and aircraft systems, missile components, avionics systems, ammunition and weapons, computing equipment, rubber, and plastic products. Clearly, the problem is not one of converting a business enterprise but of dismantling a full-blown state capitalism which has grown up in our midst.[19] How can a state government develop a coherent and genuine economic plan when its role is merely that of providing services such as highways, police, resource development, and education for the regions over which the military-industrial complex has been flung? Moreover, is it very wise to advocate as "conversion" the movement of the industrial agents of this system into the management and control of those very local services?

Commercial diversification for aerospace companies has so far been a failure. Everything from buses, sport boats, and coin changing machines to drycleaning apparatus, hearing aids, artificial hands, and aluminum coffins has been tried. Some firms have tried to become suppliers for established companies in commercial markets. In this role, aerospace companies have built musical instrument parts, automobile components, radio cabinets, heater cases, etc. In almost all cases, the income from such ventures has been disappointing. Most of these activities have been either abandoned or sold to firms normally oriented to commercial markets.

In most cases, what happened was that the firm diversified by financial means only; that is, the aerospace company used its capital surpluses from defense profits to buy a commercial company or it has merged with a commercial firm (North American Aviation with Rockwell Standard). In either case, military production and defense research have remained untouched. Sometimes, when California-based aerospace companies have diversified, or when aerospace companies with a large number of California plants has done so, the new commercial plants have often tended to be located outside the state, unless it was a question of buying out a supplier located near a major defense plant facility. In these instances, the government has financed the purchase.

The reasons for the discouraging history of diversification are twofold. First of all, aerospace managements are reluctant to go into commercial markets; they know the defense business and declare that they have neither the time nor the energy to learn all the ins and outs of commercial marketing and production. Also, there is little indication that the Department of Defense, the financial community and the

nation's commercial manufacturers would like to see defense firms diversify into the private sector. Secondly, the specialized capabilities of these firms do not at all suit them for diversification. Compared to commercially-oriented companies these firms have relatively low capitalization levels, little if any commercial marketing abilities, no distribution systems, and practically no experience in producing at high volume and low cost. Moreover, the high concentration of technicians, scientists, and engineers does not constitute the type of labor force required for most forms of commercial production.[20]

If aerospace companies do diversify, there's only one place they can go: and that's further into the public sector in which they are already deeply entrenched. The danger of this type of diversification is that whether the aerospace companies divest themselves of military production activities *willingly* or not (and I don't think it will be *willingly*), corporations like aerospace firms taking up the planning for education, highways, transportation, housing, etc., and using aerospace methods of organization, will only introduce what has happened in the area of national security policy to other areas of government. Instead of just a military-industrial complex, there will also arise a transportation-industrial complex, or a housing-industrial complex, or an educational-industrial complex, or a pollution-industrial complex.

Since about 1964, over forty contracts for state and local planning have been awarded to aerospace companies in California. Aerojet-General, for example, used its first such contracts to produce a twenty-five-year program for waste management to be conducted by systems-engineering techniques at a cost of billions. Lockheed has formulated a similar program for schools in poverty areas, and is already penetrating the management of school districts in Northern California. Once programs like this get on the road, companies like Lockheed, Aerojet-General, and North American Rockwell would of course become the "prime contractors" who would organize a broad tier of subcontractors out of the companies and consulting firms which have already had experience in the planning field but on a fragmented, uncoordinated basis. The technical resources of state agencies will be drawn away and put in the pay of aerospace firms. In time, further planning projects in education, transportation, waste management, or law enforcement will not be possible without the help, resources, and personnel of the "systems" corporations, which will have successfully monopolized most of the skills and knowledge in these fields. In addition, these companies will control production programs and financing arrangements, which means that they will appropriate the ability to allocate the state's resources, to control the distribution of government jobs, and to manage the state budget so as to ensure investor profits through tax revenues. If a centralized management is then established to "efficiently" administer the educational-industrial complex, let us say, which has developed in the state (read: *is already developing*) then an entire new realm of state capitalism will have been established. Actually, we are moving more rapidly in this direction than most people realize. In relation to the diversification problem, Harry Biederman, Lockheed's senior economic adviser, has already pointed out how "fragmented" the markets are in environmental engineering, urban renewal, housing, and systems analysis in health and education, and has called for a "central contracting authority" to coordinate contract activities between city, state and county governments.[21]

At the same time, it is highly questionable whether the social engineering approach to the problems of poverty, crime, education, pollution, and health care will really be able to solve these problems. Calling for the application of military technologies seems to be a logical response for a society unable to face up to the moral and political origins of what is so far its deepest historical crisis. Defining poverty and pollution as technical problems soluble by a technological fix conveniently defines away the social and economic restructuring that is ultimately necessary. Our present problems are not really technological ones. The problem of education has little to do with teacher shortages, lack of facilities, and ill-

supervised classrooms. The real problem lies in what people are being educated for, the authoritarian nature of present classroom methods which destroy rather than liberate minds, and the highly stratified nature of the socialization process in our schools. Similarly, the environmental ills about which we are told so much today are not really solvable by technology, for pollution is a product of the way in which our society is organized with its massive overgrown cities, with its centralized marketing patterns, the cultural pressures to consume totally out of proportion to need or genuine desire, the mobilization of natural forces primarily in the interest of capital accumulation, and the bloated bureaucracies which overlook this whole nightmare and offer little as a solution except more of the same. In the long run, the endeavors of Lockheed, Litton Industries, and Westinghouse in the management of Job Corps Camps, Vista projects, and ghetto schools indicate nothing but how technology can be used to manage and administer an unjust and repressive society.

All this is not to say that conversion is impossible. Functionally, it can work. Seymour Melman has shown some of the ways in which technology and resources can be shifted away from military production and into areas of civilian need. Going even beyond Melman, a blueprint for the liquidation of military capital assets and a dismantling of the financial and managerial organization of the aerospace industries is not impossible to formulate. The assets can be liquidated and transferred to all sorts of other organizations: community corporations, individual voucher systems for education, community health care cooperatives, factories, etc. Scientists and engineers could undertake the planning procedures for creating decentralized communities, for developing computerized technologies for local neighborhood communications, production and distributive systems. Scaling down technological and administrative systems could be very easily planned through a systems approach, and so could broader regional development. Minicomputers do exist. Honeywell and IBM make them, but the centralization of this

Various Contracts Awarded by State & Local Governments of California to California-based Aerospace Firms During the Period 1965 to 1969.

SUBJECT	CUSTOMER	CONTRACTOR
Education		
Drug Abuse Educational Program in Grades 6–10	State of California	Lockheed
Curriculum for Schools in Poverty Areas	State of California Office of Compensatory Education	Lockheed
School Management in Poverty Areas	San Jose Unified District	Lockheed
Math & Reading Curriculum for Underprivileged Students to Develop Skills for Electronic Data Processing	San Francisco Unified School District	Lockheed
Curriculum for Electronics Manufacturing Training	Santa Clara Unified School District	Lockheed
Blueprint for Computerized Informational Network on Educational Research for Public Schools Throughout Northern Cal. and All of Nevada	Far West Laboratory for Research and Development S.F., California (U.S. Office of Education)	Lockheed
Computerized Teacher Credential Evaluation System	Cal. Dept. of Education	Aerojet-General
State-wide Computerized	Cal. Dept. of Education	Aerojet-General
Urban Problems & Transportation		
Urban Renewal Plan	Fresno	TRW
Management Operation Guide for Planning	Orange County	TRW
Waste Management	State of California	Aerojet-General
Water Treatment Systems	Los Angeles and San Diego	General Dynamics
Waste Food Conversion	State of California	North Am. Rockwell
High Speed Transit Cars	Bay Area Rapid Transit District	Rohr Corporation
Plan for State Transportation System	State of California	North Am. Rockwell
Highway Planning	State of California	General Electric
Instrumentation for California Water Plan	State of California	North American Rockwell
Computerized Management System for California Water Plan	State of California	Aerojet-General
Government and Law Enforcement		
State-wide Information System for Gov't Agencies	State of California	Lockheed
Information System	State of California Dept. of Professional and Vocational Standards	Lockheed
Computerized Criminal Record System for all State Law Enforcement Agencies	State of California	Lockheed
Information Systems	Sacramento Area Economic Council	Aerojet-General
Computer Data System for Police Communications	City of San Francisco	Sylvania, Socio-Systems
Electronic Sensors for Police Cars	City of Los Angeles	North American Rockwell

SOURCE: *Aerospace Technology* (publication of Aerospace Industries Association)

essentially social technology in the hands of these private firms represents a vested interest which prevents their broad dissemination. The problem of conversion is not just a matter of material resources and technologies from military to civilian production; we are faced in fact with altering the manner in which these resources are channelled and organized under the present mode of social organization. In a sense, conversion of the military economy would also require a basic conversion of the civilian economy as well, so as to allow the former. Politically, this means it has not simply been the generals alone who are responsible for allocation of the nation's resources into a military-industrial system; the managers of the economic realm, of the super-corporations have played a critical role here also.

[1] Lou Cannon, "Federal Spending Vital to Area," *San Jose Mercury*, March 12, 1970.

[2] *California Statistical Abstracts*, 1969.

[3] *Ibid.*

[4] Kerry Napuck, *Dependency of the California Economy on Aerospace Industry* (unpublished report). Seymour Melman, *Pentagon Capitalism, The Political Economy of War* (New York: McGraw-Hill, 1969), pp. 77–8.

[5] *Report of the Committee on Economic Impact of Defense and Disarmament*, July, 1955. U.S. Government Printing Office, p. 90.

[6] Method used here is based on analysis of Charles M. Tiebout, "Regional Impact of Defense Spending," in *Defense & Disarmament*, (Englewood Cliffs, New Jersey: Prentice-Hall, 1966), pp. 123–7. See also Roger Bolton, *Defense Purchases & Regional Growth*, (Washington D.C.: Brookings Institution, 1966), especially chaps. 3 and 4.

[7] Napuck, *Ibid,*; Tiebout, *Ibid,*; Cannon, *Ibid.*

[8] Tiebout, *Ibid.*

[9] Security First National Bank, *Monthly Bulletin*, vol. 42, no. 8.

[10] *California Statistical Abstracts*, 1969. Crocker Citizens National Bank, *California's Economic Diversity*, p. 16.

[11] James Ridgeway, *The Closed Corporation* (New York: Random House, 1968), p. 138.

[12] Security First National Bank, *Southern California Report, 1965*, p. 57.

[13] Napuck, *Ibid.*, *S.F. Chronicle*, April 26, 1970. *California Statistical Abstracts*, 1969. *California Labor Statistics Bulletin*, December 26, 1969.

[14] *Aviation Week & Space Technology*, March 9, 1970, pp. 21–25.

[15] *Space/Aeronautics*, March 1970, pp. 12–14.

[16] Harry Biederman, "Keeping California Aerospace in the Air," in *Pacific Business*, Mar-Apr. 1970, pp. 10–14.

[17] Joint Economic Committee, U.S. Congress Report of the Subcommittee on Economy in Government, *Economy in Government Procurement and Property Management*. Washington, D.C., April 1968. Murray Weidenbaum, *The Public Sector* (New York: Basic Books, 1969), p. 56.

[18] Melman, *Ibid.*, pp. 1–21.

[19] Bernard Nossiter, "Defense Firms Leery of Civilian Work," in *Washington Post*, December 19, 1968.

[20] *Ibid.*

[21] *Wall Street Journal*, May 15, 1970, p. 1.

IV. CONVERTIBILITY OF MILITARY INDUSTRY TO CIVILIAN ECONOMY

Scarce Resource Allocation, High Employment Equilibrium

26. Characteristics of the Industrial Conversion Problem

Seymour Melman

Can the United States prosper in peace? This problem has become important to many Americans as choices on war and peace and on foreign policy are considered. More than half of the federal tax dollar has recently been used for military purposes, employing about 3.5 million men in the uniformed armed forces, 1.2 million men on the civilian staff of the Department of Defense, and between 3 and 6 million persons scattered throughout the American economy devoting themselves (directly and indirectly) in large part to the service of the Department of Defense through military contracts of various sorts.

The impact of economic activity for the Department of Defense is emphasized to many Americans by the high degree of concentration of defense activity — geographic, industrial, and professional. Thus, a handful of states — California, Texas, New York, Massachusetts, Connecticut, Washington — include a lion's share of the military activity. And within these states there is concentration in particular counties and metropolitan areas. The concentration of military activities is also seen by industry; aerospace, electronics, ordnance, and shipbuilding are all focal points of military contract work. Finally, there is a major element of occupational concentration in work for the Department of Defense, highly skilled personnel being used in substantial

From *The Defense Economy*, Seymour Melman, editor, Frederick A. Praeger, Inc., New York, 1970. Copyright © 1970 by Seymour Melman. Reprinted by permission.

numbers to perform research, design, and production work for military purposes.

A high level of military-industrial activity has been sustained for so long a time in the United States that many Americans view this as a continuing and integral part of American economy and society. This perception is a valid one for the considerable number of Americans who have spent the greater part of their occupational lives in the service of military industry.

The problem of whether the American economy can prosper without military industry goes beyond the issues of the Vietnam war that have preoccupied many Americans since 1965. International peace and a deceleration and reversal of the arms race are increasingly viewed as conditions for human security. At the same time, members of the Congress generally are reluctant to vote unemployment into their districts or states. In the absence of competent conversion planning, economic upsets in the military-industry areas of the United States would probably follow military cutbacks. In sum: *Competence for industrial conversion to civilian work is a precondition for ability to consider peace or disarmament proposals on their own merits.*

OPTIONS ON PRIORITIES

The nation's ability to convert men and machines from military to civilian uses also has major bearing on the actual availability of choice with respect to national priorities.

The national priorities issue is this: The United States is rich but not indefinitely rich; the critical limits on resources are reflected in money but the limits consist basically of a finite stock of manpower available for productive work, especially skilled manpower. During the last twenty years the Federal Government has marshaled important parts of the nation's skilled manpower pool for direct and in-

201

direct service of U.S. military and allied programs. For this reason the choice of foreign policy is not only a choice between war and peace but also, automatically, a choice between functionally productive as against economically parasitic use of a part of the nation's skilled manpower.

A major effort to erase the conditions of economic underdevelopment within the United States would require a capital outlay over a period of years of about $375 billion ($30,000 for each of 7.5 million families, for "human capital" development; and $20,000 for each of 7.5 million new jobs for the unemployed, underemployed, and out-of-the-labor-force poor, for productive investments that create jobs). This investment in human and in physical productive capital is impossible if present priorities are sustained. By the same reasoning a continuation of present priorities, with their emphasis on the economically parasitic use of crucial national resources, places major constraints on the nation to cope with problems of medical care, education, deterioration of civilian industries, and the crisis in the value of the dollar.

With continued top priority to military purposes, the sort of thing that could be readily done on behalf of the economically underdeveloped population in the United States is the provision of some additional food, for the food either exists or can be readily produced with a modest increment to acreage in use.

A serious economic development program for the United States involves a cost in capital outlays equivalent to the cost of the new military programs of the Department of Defense (a major anti-ballistic-missile system with accompanying civil defense, intercontinental jets for deployment of heavy military equipment, enlargement of strategic attack forces, enlargement of conventional forces to cope with an anticipated program of Vietnam-type wars). For example, in 1962 Professor John E. Ullmann calculated the cost of a less-than-complete national shelter program as $254 to $302 billion. The military programs listed above would cost over $400 billion. Even with a gross national product of $850 billion per year, the nation could not, except

with a statist economy, sustain present and prospective military priorities and deal constructively with dangerously lingering domestic underdevelopment.

As soon as one considers the option of a shift in national priorities from military emphasis to a stress on domestic economic development, one must confront the problem of conversion from a military to a civilian economy. Such conversion in response to decisions to alter national priorities could be a major opportunity for American society and could be carried out with penalty to the men and women who have served the nation until now in military and related activities. Nevertheless, the nation's ability to have major options in national priorities is conditioned by competence or incompetence to cope with the conversion of industry and people to new work.

CONVERSION OF INDUSTRY, CONVERSION OF PEOPLE

At this time there is no firm knowledge of just how much of the military-industrial firms' operations could be converted to civilian uses. Obviously, from firm to firm there is bound to be variation in this capability, depending on the ingenuity and skill of the management and the nature of the technical equipment, skills, and adaptability of the people—individually and as organized in the enterprise.

It would be imprudent to overlook the judgment of many persons that the military-industrial firms—as organized entities —are not good prospects for civilian conversion. This is judged to be owing to the special qualities of the organizations as servants of the Department of Defense: for example, limited capability for cost-minimizing design and production; limited skills in civilian products marketing.

Insofar as this estimate is valid, it is essential that preparations for conversion include, on national and local levels, plans for facilitating the changeover of individuals. This means that the nation needs something like an economic bill of rights for veterans of military industry, covering retirement pay, separation pay, support of education for occupational retraining, a schedule of living allowances during, say, one year of occupational training, relocation allowances, and so on.

In my judgment, plans and legislation to make possible the conversion of individuals is necessary insurance against the inability of enterprises to afford gainful employment for all or part of their military-related staffs. The same preparations would also mitigate pressures for government subsidies, in the name of protecting the people involved, to former defense-industry enterprises.

Planning for the conversion in industries and enterprises is the responsibility of managers, and also of government, local and federal. The conversion of individuals also needs preparation by professional societies, educators, and trade unions. All these groups could contribute studies of what is needed to generate new productive employment, its location, and the requirements for assuring the ex-employees of military industry that they will be aided and encouraged by their professional colleagues in their turn to new work.

CONVERSION, NOT RECONVERSION

The problem of conversion from military to civilian work is fundamentally different now from the problem that existed after World War II. At that time, the issue was reconversion; the firms could and did go back to doing the work they had been involved in before the war. They could literally draw the old sets of blueprints and tools from the shelf and go to work on the old products. At the present time, the bulk of military production is concentrated in industries, firms, or plants that have been specialized for this work, and frequently have no prior history of civilian work. Therefore, the problem is one of conversion—redesigning the total operation of enterprises and parts of enterprises. Some firms are primarily or totally specialized in military work. These include firms like General Dynamics, Martin Aircraft, and other principal missile and military electronics manufacturers.

Where military production is carried on in divisions of large multiproduct firms also engaged in civilian production, military divisions tend to become specially organized and separated off from civilian activities. But the managerial and other ties to civilian divisions of the same firm can be made a source of strength, by infusing key men with civilian industry skills to help convert the defense section.

Feasibility of conversion

The feasibility of industrial conversion to civilian work has been studied in a number of industries. In the airframe industry, for example, a vigorous program of civilian product development by the private managements could be carried out, and the resulting industry could employ many of those engaged in these factories. The civilian products would include commercial aircraft, private and business aircraft, space products, rapid transit, industrially-produced homes, and sections of commercial buildings, electric power vehicles, hydrofoil boats, and ground effect machines. While the proportion of employable present employees will vary, and while it might be increased as a result of large markets generated by government and other new private investment, some considerable proportion of airframe industry employees would still have to be located elsewhere.

Aspects of markets, consumer and governments

The market demand for consumer goods, soft and hard, has been virtually saturated, as contrasted with the condition existing following World War II. The main opportunity for large expansion in civilian product markets within the United States lies in the generation of new markets and new jobs and in the enlargement of consumer purchasing power among the 20 per cent of the American population that lives in poverty.

The case of the electronics industry is also vital in this respect. The industry now manufactures about two-thirds of its products for military use. A set of alternative products could conceivably be produced, but these have the important feature of involving major dependence on new, expecially government, markets for civilian goods.

The new goods to be produced by the

electronics industry can include, for example, traffic control machines, electronic educational equipment, and medical electronic devices. The purchasers of this equipment will mainly be governments — cities and towns, states, and the Federal Government. This requires creation of a government market on the basis of capital budgeting plans by all sectors of government. The separation of capital spending plans from expense for current operations, by cities, counties, states, and the Federal Government, will create a calculable market to which firms can bid. A few electronics firms have found that the unknown size of the government market at this time deters serious production planning for this market.

Occupational retraining

A high degree of occupational specialization in management, engineering, technical, and production work has come to characterize military production. This specialization involves special orientation to meeting the quality and technical requirements of military products. Cost minimization has been a lesser consideration in military research, design, and production. The experience of several firms raises doubt as to the ability of some military-industry managers to take leadership in developing opportunities for conversion of their firms.

Occupational retraining will be an issue for many occupations whose members become substantially surplus with the diminution of military production — for whatever reason. Retraining will be essential for managers, marketing men, engineers, and skilled workers; they will all have to unlearn the habits of work that have been appropriate for the Pentagon and learn the standards of civilian design, managing, production, and selling.

Production facilities have also become highly specialized. The extreme case is to be found in certain factories, for example in poison gas factories, where equipment could not even be dismantled because of the risk of lethal effects from the materials in the chemical processing system. A lesser degree of specialization is to be found in classes of metal-working machinery. These include, for instance, the lathes designed and built to handle unusually wide diameter work pieces. While there are some requirements in civilian work for a few of these machines, the decline of missile production would surely result in a glut on the market in this class of equipment.

The criteria of civilian work are so different from those of military work that initial retraining will be required for all levels of management, technicians, and workers. One of the crucial elements here is the role of cost factors. Cost minimization must be given prominent consideration for civilian products. The men in military work have generated a trained incapacity for minimizing cost, as various performance characteristics were given first priority. Military aircraft, for example, have sometimes been built so that the finished product is worth as much as, or more than, the weight of the product in gold.

Occupational conversion

One of the features of military industry is the very high concentration of engineering and scientific talent among those employed. At the end of World War II, in one large firm about 4 per cent of the staff were engineers. By the 1960's the percentage of technical employees had risen to 15–20 per cent. There are few civilian industrial operations that require such a high proportion of technical personnel. Therefore one of the important conversion problems is that of defining useful work to which many of the technically talented men in military industry could apply themselves.

During the last decades the high schools, junior high schools, and junior colleges of the United States have been short of teachers in the mathematics and science fields. I have ascertained that it is reasonable to expect engineers or scientists who have some industrial experience and who have aptitude for teaching to be convertible into competent teachers following a one-year training program that could be operated by schools of education.

By questioning several groups of engineers now employed in military work, I have determined that about one quarter of them would give close attention to the possibility of utilizing their technical talents in the teaching field. There are programs for occupational retraining under the Labor Department which could be applied to sponsoring this transfer of technical talent from an area of manpower surplus to the schools where they are badly needed.

I have also found that the prospect of job security in the teaching field is attractive to engineers and others who have become accustomed to a semi-migrant professional pattern of employment in military industry.

Occupational conversion for the whole range of defense-industry employees would be facilitated by solid planning on behalf of production workers for occupational retraining, in parallel with enough income for a decent minimum level of living. Ben D. Segal, Director of Education of the International Union of Electrical Workers, suggests:

Another proposal that should be considered and developed is the establishment of a Readjustment Fund for workers displaced by defense phase-outs. The Fund would be set up by adding 1% to each government contract. The Fund, in turn, would be used to supplement unemployment compensation to bring the worker up to where he was drawing up to two-thirds of his regular pay for a 2-year period. The Fund would also assist in earlier retirement (such as 55 years of age) and assist in setting up retraining programs. Figuring roughly, about $35 billion is spent in government contracts including research as well as direct defense expenditures. One percent of this figure would provide about $350,000,000 a year.

Triggering contracts

One of the industrial devices that has been used by the defense agencies for converting from civilian to military work is the triggering contract. Industrial managements are invited to prepare bids for specified products. If the bids are accepted the firm is directed to set up production facilities and to train its staff for operating the new plant. The new facilities are kept in stand-by condition and they are set in motion at full capacity only when the authorities issue an order for going into full production.

The same principle can be used to facilitate conversion from defense to civilian work. In this case, defense contractors would be asked to prepare plans for civilian activity which would be set in motion when the military contract had been completed. The use of this device would remove incentives to stretch out the defense work either in time or in cost, for alternative civilian work would be waiting to be done.

Industrial reorganization as a requirement for conversion

Some industries involved in the conversion problem are characterized by depressed or partially depressed conditions. These are mainly machinery-producing industries. They include, for example, shipbuilding, machine tools, and other machinery-producing industries in the American industrial system. This means that conversion, to be carried out in these industries, will require major restructuring of the operations of the industry, in order to ensure the operation of viable firms.

In the shipbuilding industry, for example, the modernization of the industry will surely require new capital investment in modern production facilities and the introduction and training of production engineers and research and development teams. The methods of standardization, large-scale subassembly, and stable operation of production systems will have to be introduced in the shipbuilding industry in order to allow it to compete, for the first time in recent years, on the world market.

University research and development

The conversion of university facilities will present a special set of problems. In 1968 about 50 per cent of the research and development funds received by universities were from the Department of Defense and from the Atomic Energy Commission. While some of these funds surely represent basic research grants, it nevertheless remains that universities will have to make major readjustments to new sources of funds, even for basic research. In the cases of certain large technological institutes, major readjustments will have to be made to enable the conversion or dismantling of large laboratories and institutes established primarily for carrying out military development work.

Decentralization: technically essential

The treatment of the conversion problem will involve an organizational issue of wide political-economic importance for American society: What should be the scope and the limits of responsibility of federal, state, and local government? This involves the issue: How can we have large organization with freedom? If one is sensitive to these problems, there is a pressure to develop methods of decentralized operation so that the Federal Government shall not be asked to assume responsibility, by default, for the operation of Mrs. Murphy's boarding house.

Communities at military bases and communities almost wholly involved in military production present a special set of conversion problems. Conversion will in some cases involve the closing of communities and, in other cases, major conversion to other types of activity.

In the judgment of this writer, it is of the greatest importance that planning on the community level be carried out in a highly decentralized way; else the Federal Government will be involved in an unworkable problem of centralized administration over the myriad details of life in thousands of communities.

The industrial conversion process is necessarily a highly decentralized activity. The crucial activity must be the budgeting and blueprinting in each factory, industry, county, town, state, and region. There is no conceivable way to administer the infinitely complicated details of many factories, firms, industries, and communities from any central location or any federal office. Decentralization is therefore the technically essential requirement of the conversion process.

Lead time

The problem of lead time cuts through all aspects of the conversion problem. Lead time is the time span between a decision to do some work and the actual beginning of the work. This is the planning time. In industrial factories of size, the lead-time requirement extends to at least one year for preparation of a blueprint for conversion when the product is already well-defined.

NEW MARKETS AND NEW JOBS FOR AMERICANS

A nation's "needs" are given workable meaning by a plausible, socially validated shopping list of goods and services, set against the production capability of the nation. In terms of these criteria it is possible to define the following set of American needs, prepared by me in 1967 as a set of estimates on new capital-productive investments and activities in the United States (for the Conference on National Priorities at Columbia University):

About seven million American families live in dwellings that are substandard in terms of minimal requirements of health and decency. The replacement of this housing on a nationwide basis will require an annual outlay of not less than $15 billion per year over a period of five years.

In order to raise the level of health services to a reasonable standard, additional outlays of $8 billion per year are required in the nation.

In order to conduct education from the nursery school to the university at an acceptable (not goldplated) standard, the United States requires additional educational outlays of $25 billion per year.

In order to assure an adequate supply of clean drinking water, the nation requires additional outlays of $4 to $5 billion per year to develop new water resources.

Many aspects of transportation in the nation require substantial investment for acceptable performance. The railroads of the nation can be brought up to a modern standard of performance with capital investment of $1.5 billion per year over the 1967 level of investment.

The conservation of natural resources, including soil for agriculture, forests, restoration of eroded or strip-mined land, and the care of beach areas, requires additional investment by the nation of $2 billion per year.

Major water and hydroelectric power developments that would restore and improve these resources for the whole North

American continent require an annual capital outlay of $5 billion per year.

Technological and allied renewal of many depleted civilian industries, for example merchant shipbuilding and many machinery-producing industries, requires incremental investment of about $10 billion per year.

All told, this partial agenda of America's investment needs amounts to $76 billion per year. This means 9.5 million new jobs at a cost of $8,000 per man per year.

None of these estimates takes into account major upgrading of acceptable standards in the several spheres involved. Many classes of public outlays are not included: Air pollution reduction will require major investments in every large city, and these will appear increasingly urgent as the public health impact of air pollution is more widely understood; regional economic development in several parts of the United States will require major investments over a long period; upgrading the nation's poor into participation in an equal opportunity (choice availability) system will need special occupational, medical, educational, and allied investments. The omission of these and other areas of need from the present national estimates defines the figure of $76 billion per year as a minimal agenda of social investments.

These investments that could be made in American society would substantially improve our present depleted human and community resources, raising them to an acceptable American standard. The largest part of these new investments clearly belong in the public sector, and must therefore come from the tax revenue of federal and local governments. The present [1967] allocation of taxing power means that local governments will not in the immediate future have the capability for making investments of these magnitudes. New York City alone, for example, needs $4.3 billion each year for the next ten years if it is to do a serious job of replacing its abominable slum dwellings. Bringing education and health care in the city up to a reasonable standard will surely cost at least $1 billion more per year. In 1966–67 the whole city budget amounted to $4.5 billion. So New York City alone needs $5 billion more per year for the most essential needs of its people.

The Federal Government now has the largest single block of tax revenue. This is the primary capital reservoir whose allocation could have a controlling effect on the ability of the United States to fulfill a plausible set of national needs.

Imperfections in Adjustment of Resource Uses

27. U.S. Industrial Economy Unprepared for Peace

Seymour Melman

The industrial economy of the United States has not been prepared for peace. In 1969, 3.4 million Americans worked in industry on Pentagon orders, 1.1 million

Reprinted from *The New York Times*, Section 3: Business & Finance, Sunday, June 7, 1970. Copyright © 1970 by Seymour Melman. Reprinted by permission.

civilians were on the Pentagon payroll and 3.4 million Americans served in the uniformed armed forces. Adding those whose livelihood is indirectly dependent on the 7.9 million Pentagon and military-industry employees, about 20 per cent of the United States labor force of 77 million (excluding the armed forces) is economically dependent on the Department of Defense.

Until now, there has been little planning effort for converting from military to civilian work. In the military-serving factories, laboratories, and military bases, there had been no effort like the concerted 1944–45 program of conversion to civilian work.

Many thoughtful men have believed that, in a generally expanding economy, fiscal and monetary policies would suffice to facilitate a transfer of men and material from military to civilian tasks. In my judgment, it is unreasonable to expect that labor and other market mechanisms would facilitate a conversion process without substantial economic damage. This estimate is based upon:

1. The condition of concentration of military work in terms of industry, geography and occupation.

2. The institutional features that differentiate military from ordinary civilian work.

3. The consequences of long concentration of the nation's research and development capacities on military work.

In 1968, six industries had more than 25 per cent of their labor force dependent on Pentagon orders. They were: ordnance and accessories (76.8 per cent); machine shop products (27.8 per cent); electronic components and accessories (38.6 per cent); miscellaneous electrical machinery, equipment and supplies (33.8 per cent); aircraft and parts (72.4 per cent), and other transportation equipment (26.4 per cent).

A few states account for more than half of military industry—Massachusetts, Connecticut, New York, New Jersey, Texas, California and Washington. Finally, there is a concentration of certain occupations in military work. Defense workers made up 6.1 per cent of the nation's employment in 1968, but here are the percentages of certain skilled occupations in military industry:

All engineers, 20 per cent; aeronautical engineers, 59 per cent; electrical engineers, 22 per cent; mechanical and metallurgical engineers, 19 per cent; draftsmen, 14 per cent, and skilled metalworkers, 10–25 per cent.

The density of military work by industry, geography and occupation means that localized rather than average national conditions determine capability for converting from military to civilian work.

Special features of military industry are also important. In these factories, cost-minimization is of secondary importance, and there is virtually no market test of the functional adequacy and price of key products. These conditions have produced a trained incapacity in much of military industry for serving a civilian economy. This affects general management, the design of products, production engineering and the marketing function. Thus, designing for the Pentagon often means priority to esoteric requirements remote from civilian needs and selling to the Pentagon has included diplomacy and negotiation that are remote from the marketing practices of civilian industry.

More than half of the nation's research and development budgets and manpower work for the military. The combined effect includes elaborate technology for military purposes and depleted technologies in many civilian industries. Polaris submarines are produced at an acceptable cost of $12 per pound, while merchant ships must be produced at less than $1 per pound.

Air frames have been manufactured so that they cost more than their weight in gold, but these are inconceivable as design and manufacturing practices for commercial vehicles.

Electro-mechanical instruments about the size of an egg are constructed at $15,000 per unit, and that is why the electronics industry of Japan, free of military priorities, designs and produces fine, low-cost electronics products for the world market. Military industry has lost the traditional American industrial capacity for offsetting high wages with high levels of productivity.

Firms that specialize in weapons will have the greatest difficulty in attempting a conversion of facilities and organizations to civilian use. Military divisions of larger civilian firms will have the best chance for successful conversion because of the professional assistance they can get from parent enterprises.

Plans for occupational conversion are as important as the best efforts for conversion of industrial plants. While substantial lead-time is needed for planning enterprise conversion, individuals should be able, within one year, to train for substantially new occupations.

As institutions, many of the firms and laboratories in military work are not readily convertible, but there is a fine chance for retraining individuals and regrouping them in new organizations that are civilian-oriented. Occupational conversion requires imaginative support from the Federal Government in the form of a "bill of rights for military industry employees," to sustain men from military industry, laboratories, and bases for a year while they are training for new occupations. Such an investment would create important new productive assets for the whole nation.

The 600-odd major military bases within the United States and their one million employees need economic development planning, requiring, on the average, about one year of leadtime.

The market and product potentials for the veterans of military industry include the whole array of industries, services and facilities that have been allowed to deteriorate during 25 years of military priority. The agenda for public and private investments ranges from city rebuilding, housing, water supplies and medical facil-ities to reconstruction of depleted indus-tries like railroads, shipbuilding and important parts of machinery production.

If the Indochina war is ended, more than $20 billion per year will be saved, and sensible recasting of United States military security policies—to exclude overkill buildups (ABM and MIRV) and Vietnam-type wars—can yield further annual Penta-gon budget savings of as much as $30 billion.

These funds represent a vast new market potential, but will not be sufficient for an American reconstruction agenda that I judge to need not less than $70 billion per year for at least a decade. Add to this a reasonable investment for economic de-velopment of 30 million Americans in poverty and the annual new productive outlays for the nation would exceed $100 billion.

Thus, conversion of part of military in-dustry and manpower to use $50 billion of potential Pentagon budget savings would start the nation on the road to civilian priority use of public-responsibility money, in a perspective that includes a shortage especially of skilled labor for the rest of the century.

Oligopoly and Changes in Market Demand

28. Arms Firms See Postwar Spurt

Leaders show little interest in applying skills to domestic ills

Bernard D. Nossiter

The shrewd and skillful men who direct large, sophisticated defense firms look for-ward to a post-Vietnam world filled with military and space business.

Reprinted from *The Washington Post,* December 8, 1968. Copyright © 1968 *The Washington Post.* Reprinted by permission.

For them, the war's end means no un-comfortable conversion to alien civilian markets. Quite the contrary, and with no discoverable exception, they expect hand-some increases in the complex planes and missiles, rich in electronics, that are the heart of their business.

The view these firms take of their future has political significance. Some government officials and economists have been suggest-ing that the major aerospace companies are capable and ready to use their consid-erable managerial skills and engineering expertise to solve a broad array of pressing social problems. No less an authority than Defense Secretary Clark Clifford recently said:

We now have a military-industrial team with unique resources of experience, engineering talent, management and problem-solving capacities, a team that must be used to help find the answers to complex domestic problems as it has found the answers to complex weapons systems. These answers can be put to good use by our cities and our states, by our schools, by large and small business alike.

This kind of thinking raises hopes that the aerospace industry's ability and interest in domestic areas will supplant its concern with defense dollars. So, the argument runs, there need be no fear that the industrial wing of what has been called the "military-industrial complex" will remain a continuing source of pressure for ever-expanding arms budgets.

However, an extended survey of industry leaders in Dallas, Fort Worth, San Diego and Los Angeles—the heartland of the aerospace world—offers little support for this view. The great defense contractors display only a marginal interest in work outside their accustomed military-space sphere, devote only a fraction of their resources to it, and, for the foreseeable future, see no economic reason to change their ways.

Basically, we're a big systems builder for military weapons. Over 90 per cent of our business is military. We're in that business to stay.

So says Edward J. LeFevre, the canny vice president in charge of the Washington office for General Dynamics, currently the Nation's largest defense contractor.

Our future planning is based on visible contracts. One must believe in the long-term threat.

This is the view of James J. Ling, the extraordinary Texan who has put together almost overnight a $3.2-billion conglomerate with enough defense subsidiaries to make his Ling-Temco-Vought the eighth biggest military contractor.

Defense spending has to increase in our area because there's been a failure to initiate (new weapons systems)—if we're not going to be overtaken by the Soviets.

Thus John R. Moore, the handsome, white-haired president of the Aerospace and Systems Group, the military heart of North American Rockwell, the ninth ranking contractor.

On the other side of the street, a top official at the Arms Control and Disarmament Agency despairingly agrees. The official, who asked that his name not be used, says:

I'm not sanguine about any reductions in military spending, especially since the election. We are now at the edge of a precipice where we can escalate sharply. The industry thinks that agreements to limit arms are unlikely and will go all out to realize their expectations. We are at the threshhold of another round in the arms race, just as we were eight years ago when we went all out for long-range missiles.

From the "blue books"

The best way of discovering how an aerospace company sees its future is to peek at its "blue book," the loose-leaf folder that projects in voluminous detail sales, profits and other data for the next five years. These volumes are the core of any large corporation's plan and usually are kept under lock and key.

However, the LTV Aerospace Corporation, the most important defense subsidiary in the Ling empire, opened its book to a visiting reporter (appropriately, it is bound in blue plastic) and here is what it showed:

TOTAL SALES	
1968	1973
$530 Million	$1.3 billion
of which	of which
A-7 Navy Attack Plane	New Navy VSX Plane, A-7
$245 million	$322 million
F-8 Navy Fighter	F-8 Navy Fighter
$82 million	$1 million
New VFX Fighter-Bomber	VFX Fighter-Bomber
$1 million	$320 million
Missiles-Space	Missiles-Space
$70 million	$149 million
Other Military-Space	Other Military-Space
$67 million	$270 million
Non-military, Non-space	Non-military, Non-space
$65 million	$230 million

Competitors of LTV Aerospace will be struck by the firm's calm assumption that it will win the development contracts for the two new Navy planes. But more important is the company's forecast that five years hence it will earn more than 80 per cent of its dollars from military and space work, nearly the same share it is now receiving. Moreover, this slice will come from a sales total more than twice as large as the company enjoys today.

The breezy optimism of LTV Aerospace

is a special case, even in the wonderland of defense contractors. Its parent, Ling-Temco-Vought, Inc., is the unique creation of the slightly unbelievable James J. Ling.

A high school dropout at fourteen, Ling, with $3000, opened an electrical contractor's shop in Dallas after the war. Ten years later, he parlayed this into a modest equipment company and, by a series of audacious financing operations, ultimately picked up defense firms, Braniff Airways, the big Wilson Company (meat packing, sporting goods, drugs) and the substantial Jones & Laughlin steel company.

The metallic and fast-talking Ling now presides, at the age of forty-five, over a sprawling conglomerate that betrays some uncertainty about its identity. Executive suites in the new and stark thirty-two-story Ling Tower in Dallas are elaborately paneled in aged wood; neo-classical statuary and eighteenth century Italian paintings give them the air of a modest gallery or an Edwardian bordello; deep pile carpeting runs from wall to wall (chartreuse for LTV Aerospace, beige for LTV Electrosystems and gold for the parent LTV Inc.).

Change of mood and motif

In contrast, the defense divisions of North American Rockwell in Los Angeles exude an air of brisk, antiseptic, scientific competence. Doors are in bright, primary colors, trimmed with aluminum; furnishings run to the functional; impressionist reproductions hang outside the offices of lesser executives and bold, dribble-school abstractionists decorate the quarters of the upper echelon.

But whatever their differences in imagery, a common theme runs all through these firms, an almost religious belief in the efficacy of engineering logic. "The buzz word," says a bemused observer, "is systems analysis," a disciplined and systematic attack on problems that begins by determining what something is intended to do. (A systems engineer would not try to build houses; he would attempt to optimize shelter and its related sub-systems of water, sewerage, heating, power, recreation, transportation and the like.)

Solemn essays on the future

So each company begins its forecast of future sales with a solemn, schematic essay in global political projections, attempting to evaluate possible courses of action in the same way that different metals might be compared for strength, lightness and heat resistance.

For example, a study compiled last year by the Electronics Industries Association, "The Post-Vietnam Defense and Space Market Environment," attempts to measure six different ways in which the war will end. The report concludes that "U.S. Escalation" is the likeliest route; a "Soviet Diversion" in Europe or elsewhere is the second likeliest and "U.S. Compromise" from "domestic pressures," the course now being followed, is rated a weak third.

Happily for the industry's members, the document forecasts that arms control agreements "during the next decade are unlikely," the "likelihood of limited war will increase" and "thus for the electronic firms, the outlook is good in spite of (the end of hostilities in) Vietnam."

Three possibilities envisioned

At North American Rockwell, producers of electronic equipment for strategic bombers, Navy reconnaissance jets and a small family of missiles, these geopolitical scenarios are, properly enough, composed by the marketing division. In a post-Vietnam world, the company envisions three possibilities: Limited War, Cold War or Detente (with arms limiting agreements). The house judgment is that something between Cold and Limited War is the best bet.

Nonengineers might charitably regard these exercises as naive and misleading. Obviously, as in the case of the Electronics Industries Association's forecast of war's end in Vietnam, the best of computers can go wrong. But this is not the point. These forecasts govern the planning of aerospace firms and provide them with a rationale for promoting their views and wares.

Self-fulfilling prophecies

To an undetermined extent, the companies can be expected to use their influence to make their prophecies self-fulfilling. By no mean coincidence, their views of the world outlook usually coincide with conditions that would maximize their military orders.

The companies are understandably guarded in talking about the effect of more immediate political changes on their future. But they leave little doubt that an important source of their optimism lies in the departure of Defense Secretary Robert McNamara and the election of Richard Nixon.

"People are pressing for new programs more intensely than ever," says W. Paul Thayer, the quiet ex-test pilot who runs Ling's LTV Aerospace. "With McNamara stepping out, that was the turning point."

J. Leland Atwood, the low-keyed president and chief executive officer of North American Rockwell, an aviation designer for nearly 40 years, employs the cautious euphemisms of many modern corporate executives.

"A little more awareness"

"All of Mr. Nixon's statements on weapons and space are very positive," he says. "I think he has perhaps a little more awareness of these things than some people we've seen in the White House."

Samuel F. Downer, the financial vice president for LTV Aerospace, covers the walls of his sparkling new Dallas apartment with his own paintings and is proudest of a cityscape that looks west on New York's Wall Street ("because it's all there, the flag, the church and money"). For the energetic Downer, the postwar world must be bolstered with military orders.

"It's basic," he says. "Its selling appeal is defense of the home. This is one of the greatest appeals the politicians have to adjusting the system. If you're the President and you need a control factor in the economy, and you need to sell this factor, you can't sell Harlem and Watts but you can sell self-preservation, a new environment. We're going to increase defense budgets as long as those bastards in Russia are ahead of us. The American people understand this."

Richard E. Adams, the plain-spoken engineer who directs advanced projects for the Fort Worth division of General Dynamics, producer of the controversial F-111 fighter-bomber, also talks of the domestic political realities that favor expanding military business.

"Where the power is"

In any conflict between increased spending on social programs and spending on defense, he says:

"We know where the power is (on Capitol Hill and among the Executive Departments). There's going to be a lot of defense business and we're going to get our share of it."

These political estimates, global and domestic, are carefully translated by each company into dollar terms, new weapons systems and the amounts that will be spent for them. There is a standard industry view here and it runs like this:

Vietnam is eating up about $22 billion a year of the $80 billion defense outlay (the war's cost is actually about $6 billion more but this sum would be spent on repositioning American forces elsewhere if they were not in Vietnam). Only $2 billion of the Vietnam budget, however, buys the advanced weapons that the aerospace crowd makes. Thus, the war's end will do little damage to these companies: "We are little impacted by the cessation of hostilities." Military payrolls and makers of uniforms, artillery shells, C-rations and the like will bear the brunt of any cutback.

Thus the end of hostilities opens up great new opportunities for sophisticated munitions makers. They and their Pentagon colleagues will press for bigger research and development budgets, an outlay guaranteed to produce new designs that military men could find irresistible. Several new weapons already designed will be ordered for extensive production. The VFX, a new Navy fighter-bomber; the VSX, an antisubmarine plane and the AMSA or Advanced Manned Strategic Aircraft, a new bomber, all fall in this category.

The pentagon's "wish list"

Over and above these items, each worth several billion dollars, are those on the Pentagon's "wish list" as it is known in the trade. It comprises more fighter wings; A V/STOL, or Vertical/Short Takeoff and Landing, transport; thickening the "thin" anti-ballistic-missile system so that it supposedly could shoot down Russian as well as Chinese nuclear missiles; a new fleet of submarines armed with missiles.

Also, a new intercontinental ballistic missile for the Air Force; new light attack aircraft; a new series of interceptor planes and a new generation of MIRV, the Multiple Independently Targeted Re-entry Vehicle, a missile with several warheads, each capable of being electronically guided to a different target.

Looking at this shopping list, some knowledgeable Pentagon officials see post-Vietnam defense budgets conceivably rising to $100 billion a year in dollars of present purchasing power.

The aerospace executives are more modest. They think defense budgets will fall by $5 to $10 billion after the war, but then begin to grow at some constant percentage of an expanding gross national product. Space budgets, it is thought, will be held on their current plateau a bit longer, but in time will gently start climbing again, too.

Again, a table of some representative firms reflects the industry's view of the near future. What follows is very unofficial. Some parts of the table are based on percentages provided by the companies and from inferences drawn from them. Few companies are as open with their books as LTV Aerospace. Percentages represent military-space sales.

(If Convair fails to win the big new contracts for which it is now competing, its military-space business will drop in 1973 to 60 per cent of total sales.)

(Electrosystems expect $140 million in additional sales from new civilian companies it intends to acquire.)

No major shift seen

The point again is that everybody expects a brisk rise in business and no substantial change in the dominant share bought by the Defense Department and NASA.

To be sure, this is not the whole story. Ling has bought up a string of nondefense companies that turn out steel sheets, tennis rackets and packaged hamburgers among other things. Combined, they dwarf his sizeable defense subsidiaries.

North American, the big plane and missile maker, merged last year with Rockwell, a conventional producer of parts for trucks, autos, and heavy construction equipment as well as textile looms. Five years hence, the company expects its commercial products to be generating more sales than its defense orders.

Even General Dynamics, which was frightened away from civilian business after a disastrous experience with jet airliners a few years ago, expects to work on parts for other companies' commercial planes if it loses too many military contracts.

Moreover, the very corporate divisions that focus on Pentagon business have all made some cautious stabs at nonmilitary markets.

None of this, however, detracts from the central theme: The great aerospace firms have a strong appetite for military business. They look forward to expanding, not contracting, their sales in this sphere.

Which comes first?

To what extent are these expectations self-fulfilling? Do new weapons systems originate in the fertile design shops of the companies, then to be sold to the Pentagon? Or are the firms simply passive contractors, responding to what the trade calls a "military requirement?" In sum, is it an

	1968 Sales	1973 Sales
General Dynamics		
Fort Worth:	$800 mill. 95%	$1.4 bill. 95%
Corvair Div.	$300 mill. 95%	(Unavail.) 95%
North American Rockwell		
Aerospace and systems		
Group:	$1.9 mill. 95%	$2.4 bill. 95%
Ling-Temco-Vought		
LTV Electrosystems:	$220 mill. 87%	$400 mill. 81%
LTV Aero-Space:	$530 mill. 88%	$1.3 bill. 82%

industrial military or a military-industrial establishment?

There is no simple answer to this question. Indeed, some authorities think it should more properly be called a military-industrial-political complex to account for the influential Congressmen who press requirements on the Pentagon and contracts on their constituents.

There are differences even within the same division of a single firm.

For example, John W. Bessire, the manager for pricing at General Dynamics' Fort Worth Division, says:

"We try to foresee the requirements the military is going to have three years off. We work with their requirements people and therefore get new business."

But a few doors away, in the enormous plant where a dozen or so of the swing-wing F-111s are quietly produced each month, the advanced projects director, Richard Adams, takes a different view:

"Things are too systematized at the Pentagon to invent weapons systems and sell them on a need. Even if you invent one, all you do is give the military an idea and you'll end up in a competition (with another firm for the production contract)."

President Moore of North American Rockwell's Aerospace and Systems Group, sees the process as one of joint parenthood.

"People getting together"

"A new system usually starts," he says, "with a couple of military and industry people getting together to discuss common problems. By far the largest part of the business comes from requirements established by the Defense Department or NASA."

"But it isn't a case of industry here" (gesturing with one arm outstretched to the ground) "and the Government here" (pointing with the other to the air). "They are interacting continuously at the engineering level."

One of the shrewdest and most important civilian officials at the Pentagon also sees the initiating process as a seamless web. "Pressures to spend more are going to be there," he says. In part, they come from the industry selling new weapons ideas, he thinks, "and in part from the military here."

"Each (military) guy has his own piece, tactical, antisubmarine, strategic. Each guy gets where he is by pushing his own particular thing. Don't forget, too, part of it is based on the perception of needs by people in Congress."

If the origins of increased defense spending can't be isolated surgically, talks with the men in the industry make it clear that they are expecting enough to go around in the years after Vietnam. This is one important reason why Secretary Clifford's proposal that they turn their talents to social problems as well is regarded as unnecessary and unwise.

In fact, one of the industry's most sophisticated men, President Atwood off North American Rockwell, remains convinced that Clifford's speech "was aimed at his own department, at small business firms — but not really at us."

Comparative Advantage

29. Conversion and the Import Problem

John E. Ullmann

One important problem is conversion—the task of finding commercial or other nonmilitary tasks for the large sector of the industry that now does defense work. A second problem is competition from other countries. Although it has not been extensively noted, the two actually are quite closely linked in at least three ways. First, it will not be easy to find new nonmilitary markets for electronics, and those that do seem promising will prove illusory if they are taken over by imported items. Second, the ability of U.S. industry to respond to international competition depends on its cost structure and the quality and variety of research talent it brings to bear on these new areas; both of these factors are critically affected by the extent of its defense concentration. Third, the changes necessary for success in the coming years must be made against a background of a crisis of confidence in product quality, of which the monumental cost overruns and performance deficiencies of military systems on one hand, and inferior electronic consumer products on the other, are prominent symptoms.

These problems, of course, are not peculiar to U.S. industry; the question of quality in consumer items, for example, is obviously as international as the manufacturers themselves. However, the simultaneous occurrence of all three factors is perhaps more pronounced in the United States than anywhere else. No discussion of the future of U.S. industry, therefore, can properly fail to take them into account. . . .

THE CONVERSION PROBLEM

The existence of a conversion problem is generally conceded, at least in the sense that manufacturers of military equipment have to find other work when their contracts expire. However, as a practical matter, so far there has not been much need for planning and implementation of this kind, mainly because no sustained cuts in defense spending have been made in at least the last eight years. Market planning by defense contractors could thus look forward in general to an expanding overall market, or in any case to another contract once a first one was completed or irretrievably bungled. Contracts were "slots," and surely the ratchet mechanism that defense budgeting had exhibited would assure that nothing drastic would happen. . . .

Developments over the past year suggest that strong concern with the conversion problem is again warranted. For the first time since 1961, there has been a fundamental change in the nation's strategic planning, involving a cut in combat readiness from "two and a half wars" to "one and a half wars."[1] The implications are that the coming years will include a 40 percent manpower cut in the armed forces[2] and a cut in expenditures for fiscal 1971 of some $5 billion, which in turn will mean the loss of some 212,000 defense-related jobs. Three hundred DOD installations will also be closed, with the loss of a further 70,000 jobs, some of them technical.[3] Recent estimates have put the total effect at close to 1.25 megajobs. Moreover, these reductions are coming at a time when increased unemployment is being expected as a side effect of anti-inflation medicine. Finally, the space program is suffering from what might be called a *postpartum* depression; many of its more talented executives and engineers have left and various facilities have been closed.[4] Cape Kennedy has become a distressed area.

It has been argued, of course, that all these cutbacks are only temporary, and that in a few years the defense budget will be back at the $80 billion level even without a Vietnam-type enterprise. It is pointed out that weapons inventories have been depleted because of the war, that some

Reprinted from *IEEE Spectrum*, April 1970. Copyright © 1970 by the Institute of Electrical and Electronics Engineers, Inc. Reprinted with permission.

projects have been deferred, and that, because of inflation, everything will cost more. Again, it is said, there is not really much to worry about. Disarmament seems more remote than ever, since the SALT talks appear designed more to keep Russo-American weapons preeminent than to lead to any real reduction. . . .

It is not the purpose of this article to discuss conversion in terms of a "wishing list." Alternative products for the defense industry have been extensively reviewed in the literature, including works pertaining particularly to the defense electronics industry.[5] In general, new products can be classified as (1) those that derive from what might be called "natural" markets — i.e., the array of actual and potential consumer products that the industry might produce and would be bought by customers without government intervention or subsidy (computer systems, industrial controls, such new consumer products as television tape units); and (2) those that would require government stimulation for the markets to become realities. . . .

There have been extensive proposals, for example, for new approaches to air transportation. Thanks to ground and air congestion, the chant of the witches of *Macbeth*, "Fair is foul and foul is fair. Hover through the fog and filthy air," accurately describes the situation at our major airports. In many of the areas subsumed under this second category — transportation, housing, education, pollution control, oceanography — the role of the electronics industry, though important, depends on satisfactory performance by others. In transportation, for instance, pollution abatement is not specifically an electronics problem, although its measurement is, and certain new forms of electric power transmission may be. Other areas require technical and cost breakthroughs, as in structural design; or new knowledge, as in ecology; or extensive software, as in educational systems.

Unfortunately, there is doubt within the industry that conversion actually is the best solution to its future business problems. Many major defense electronics firms are parts of conglomerates, or are divisions

of old, established nondefense firms that could close the plants concerned, or at least consolidate them in the area with the lowest labor costs, taxes, etc., and spend their resources where more immediate profits can be realized. . . .

The implications are plain that little will be done to find alternative work within the present firms and localities, which is, of course, the only nonconvulsive way of solving the problem. Such efforts as appear to be in hand would not be nearly enough, even for the limited cutbacks now decided upon. Finally, whatever new plans the industry chooses to make can no longer be carried out independently of the non-U.S. producers of comparable equipment. The days when the industry could expect to solve its problems *in vacuo* are over.

The objective of conversion must not be only that of corporate survival, which would be the typical first priority of management. Rather, conversion also must concern itself with the accommodation of the engineers and scientists who have long made their professional home in the military electronics industry. These have generally been considered as consisting of two groups: those in the thick of technology as such — in research, development, testing, and manufacturing — whose work content is still very much involved with theory, new products, and technical minutiae; and those for whom the technical content of the work has virtually vanished beneath a mountain of paper. It is the first group that may be quite difficult to transfer in sufficient numbers, and it is one of the objectives of this article to propose a scheme for solving the problem. Alternative employment for the latter group is more closely related to the transferability of management talent and has been discussed at length elsewhere.[6]

FOREIGN COMPETITION

The United States' strong role in international trade in machinery and other durables has long been a fact of history, and so it is not surprising that the continuation of that role should be assumed with quite a bit of complacency. American know-how, inventive genius, etc., have been

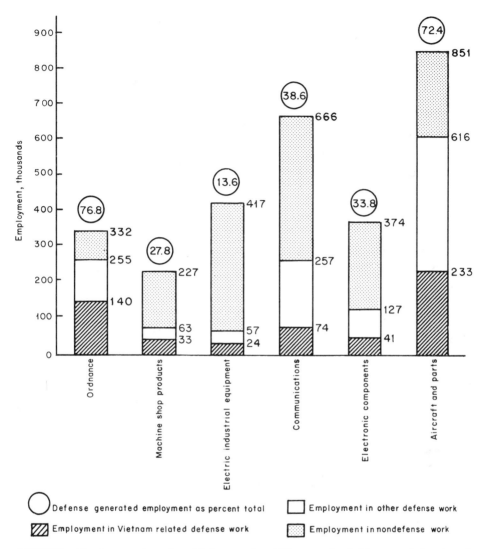

FIGURE 1. *Employment share of total defense work and Vietnam-related defense work for selected industries, 1968. Each bar gives the number of jobs resulting from total defense work and the extra employment due to the Vietnam war. In addition to the industries shown, 165,700 more workers are employed on defense work in other parts of the electrical-electronic industry.* (*Source: R. P. Oliver, "Increase in defense-related employment during Viet Nam buildup," Monthly Labor Rev., vol. 93, pp. 3–10, Feb. 1970)*

around for a long time and have made us what we are today. This is not to say, of course, that we "invented" everything; all industrial societies have pseudo-histori-cal publicity agents to make that claim on their behalf. Rather, the particular con-tribution of U.S. industry has been to take

a device, wherever "invented," and by successfully organizing its production, transform it from a laboratory curiosity or highly specialized item into something that can be used in households, offices, or factories with high efficiency and at rela-tively low cost. Since the days of the treadle-operated sewing machine, there has not been an appliance that was not first developed into a commercially viable product in the United States—until the past decade, that is. Nor is this record confined to consumer durables. Diesel locomotives had long been manufactured in relatively small numbers both in the United States and elsewhere. It remained for U.S. firms to develop modular arrangements and standardization to the point where these machines could be virtually mass-produced.

All this is far from arguing that some "manifest destiny" ordains continued U.S. superiority in machinery and consumer durables. But the fact remains that the kinds of developments just described have been the principal basis for U.S. competitiveness in international markets and must be considered a point of departure when the present situation is examined. . . .

The impact of foreign trade on the electronics industry tends to be concentrated in certain specific areas—components, radio, tape recorders, electronic desk calculators. Of radios, 85 percent are now imported; in its newspaper campaign in connection with the 1969–1970 strike, General Electric noted that its Utica radio receiver plant was the last significant one left in the United States. Some 90 percent of tape recorders are imported; nearly all small television sets are imported. It is noteworthy that these items were first created as viable commercial products by Japan—a break in the U.S. record described earlier. In fact, imports of electronic items are so predominantly Japanese that to the U.S. electronics industry "foreign competition" really means Japanese competition.[7] This competition already promises to be a serious factor in what appears to be the only major new consumer product, the television tape recorder.

Experience with desk calculators is especially interesting, not only because it reflects some highly sophisticated and successful product developments, but also because it illustrates a marketing strategy likely to lead to greater penetration of a wider market.

The desk calculator–computer spectrum may be divided into (1) simple four-rule

calculators, (2) more elaborate calculators, (3) programmable desk calculators, (4) minicomputers, (5) large computers, (6) sophisticated subsystems for large computers, and (7) novel software. The conventional U.S. view of non-U.S. competition is that the latter might be conceded the simpler end of the line, leaving U.S. industry in charge of the "high-technology" end. If there is to be competition, it will have to be on a price basis and U.S. firms will not enter that particular field of battle. But this in turn implies a rather basic change in the orientation of one of our most important manufacturing industries. It is quite true, of course, that purely on the basis of manufacturing costs, plus high administrative overhead and marketing costs, the U.S. electronics industry finds it difficult to compete for many markets. However, the great strength of technologically-oriented industries in the United States has always been in the development of sophisticated production systems, often suiting design to the exigencies of turning a product out in large quantities. In a real sense, industrial excellence must rely on the ability to keep the production line going simultaneously with research on the product itself and on manufacturing methods. It is this ability that has made "American mass production" a byword and example in all industrial countries.

A concentration on high technology means a different product strategy entirely. As a long-term strategy, moreover, it suffers from several basic drawbacks. It ignores the fact (1) that pioneering is risky and does not enjoy a reputation for profitability; (2) that such arrangements are necessarily unstable; (3) that there is nothing disreputable about price competition, which most consumers tend to regard as the stuff bargains are made of; and, perhaps most important, (4) that such arrangements are impossible to impose unilaterally.

If one applies the "high-technology" preemption to the desk calculator and computer products, then clearly the four-rule machines ought to be solidly foreign by now. A visit to the 1969 Business Equipment Manufacturers Association trade show in New York demonstrated that this has indeed happened. There was nothing to compare to the offerings of Hayakawa-Sharp, Toshiba, Canon, and Sony, the Japanese firms that dominated that product completely. Minicomputers (and larger ones) included Japanese models, the Dutch Phillips, and the Italian Olivetti and Montecatini-Edison.

This does not mean that imports were as dominant in advanced fields as in the simpler ones, but the evidence was clear that non-U.S. producers had imposed no lines of demarcation on themselves. Moreover, capability in advanced computers is a principal objective of modern industrial nations. In addition to the widespread international operations of IBM, most countries seek national systems of their own. The efforts of France through Machines Bull and others are well known. In the case of Japan, a singularly comprehensive and effective arrangement has been made, which, by uniting industry, government, and the universities, has been able to circumvent the normally rather compartmentalized structure of Japanese business. The Japanese Electronic Industry Development Association,[8] together with the Agency for Industrial Science and Technology, is currently sponsoring a major computer development consortium. It seems highly probable that Japanese producers such as Fujitsu, one of the participants, will become significant in the field of large computers.

This sort of government-sponsored research effort on behalf of ultimately commercial products extends to components. Japanese firms that have been so successful in making transistors producable by the millions are now on the way to doing this with integrated circuits as well, including large-scale types (LSI) and metal oxide semiconductors (MOS). Some important theoretical work in the field is being carried out by the Kansai Electronic Industry Development Center, which is supported by the Ministry of International Trade and Industry (MITI) and includes among its participants Osaka University, Hayakawa Sharp, Matsushita - Panasonic, and other large firms.[9] Indeed, Japanese

IC industry has proceeded to the stage at which its entry into the export field is imminent.[10]

In all these developments Japanese research has complemented and implemented U.S. research, and many of the developments have taken place in cooperation with U.S. firms. Joint working agreements, patent cross-licensing, and, most important, offshore manufacturing arrangements, have been concluded between Friden and Hitachi, American Microsystems and Ricoh, Monroe and Canon, Honeywell and Nippon Electric, and Autonetics and Hayakawa, to name a few. Of course, such arrangements are not Japanese alone; "American" television sets and other appliances are being, or shortly will be, made in Hong Kong, South Korea, or in that most recent accession to the ranks of industrial boom areas, Singapore.[11] Japanese industry is now supplying components to other manufacturing countries such as Germany, but as labor costs and labor shortages increase, Japanese industry has begun to import components, parts, and subsystems from its Far Eastern neighbors.

Electronics virtually is emulating the migratory habits of a much older industry, textiles. This industry moved from England to Rumania and Russia in Europe; to India, China, and Japan within Asia; and, within the United States, from New England to the Piedmont, then to the Deep South, to Puerto Rico, and to reliance on Far Eastern imports. It does not require clairvoyance to envisage the typical reaction of management to conversion: Move to cheaper plants within the U.S., resort to joint manufacturing abroad, or move the commercial products out altogether. The Grumman Aircraft Engineering Corporation illustrates the point. Its only significant civilian aircraft is the Gulfstream executive turboprop, which was designed in Bethpage, N.Y., at the company's principal plant, but is manufactured in Savannah, Ga.; a recent report has the company looking into the possibility of assembly in Singapore.[12] Obviously, as cutbacks become a reality, such stratagems do little for the employment prospects of those now in the defense industry. Thus, it is necessary to examine the shortcomings of the present technical achievements of the electronics industry and to find ways in which defense-related talents might be converted to their solution.

THE QUALITY PROBLEM

There can be little doubt that in electronics, as well as in most other industries, defects in quality constitute a major problem. "They just don't make 'em like they used to" may once have been a bit of nostalgia best ignored, but this no longer is true. Sloppiness in automobile manufacture has been amply documented, to say nothing of safety defects. Repair facilities for automobiles are likely to reach a point of critical shortage and, of course, the television repair area has long been scandal-ridden. Difficulties with warranties and guarantees, the inability of manufacturers to secure product liability insurance, the replacement of the legal doctrine of caveat emptor with that of merchantability and implied warranty, and extensive government intervention in product design itself have all drawn attention to the manufacturers' responsibility. This concern has been produced by exactly the kind of massive popular dissatisfaction with product quality to which we have just referred; the U.S. Federal Trade Commission finds itself bombarded by consumer complaints as never before, and, in fact, the political constituency subsumed under "consumerism" has become a strong force.

From a technical viewpoint, the chief culprits are probably cost cutting (i.e., corner cutting) and the pushing of technology beyond its reasonable limits for robust and reliable apparatus. Both of these, in turn, reflect inadequacies in manufacturing and quality control, but also, and more basically, a failure to understand fully the capabilities of modern products and processes. They also are linked to the basic cost structure of the industry and to its ability (and lack thereof) to meet foreign competition. In the present inflationary period, wages and salaries are rising much faster than productivity, which, in turn, is a function of product and process design. Something manifestly has gone wrong when there are so many complaints at the same time that

U.S. industry is also being systematically bested by its competitors.

These developments strongly suggest that the scientific resources of the U.S. electronics industry are not being used to best advantage to solve these problems. This misapplication has three aspects. The first, perhaps most important, is the diversion of industry talent to weaponry. Some 80 percent of electronics engineers, according to EIA statistics, are supported by weapons or space contracts. They are channeled there by wage differentials of as much as a third or more, which effectively constitutes rationing by the purse.

The second aspect is related to the first. Responding to various fashionable "gaps," U.S. engineering schools have tended to phase out instruction in producibility and manufacturing in general. As a result of the "applied science" binge of many of the schools, such knowledge is rare indeed among young engineers and most of them have been successfully brainwashed out of the field. As a teacher of both operations research and manufacturing processes, the writer can only note somewhat ruefully that at a time when the mathematical models of production systems become ever more elegant, and operations research taxes the greatest capabilities of our computers, such relatively simple and classical subjects have been neglected in the curriculums. In part as a result of this development, other countries are either abreast of what the U.S. is doing, or are even ahead. There may be a momentary out-of-phase situation but it does not last and is not, in any event, necessarily in "our" favor. If it is true, for instance, that some electronic manufacturing methods still elude the Japanese at this point, it is also true that their steel industry utilized oxygen lances and continuous casting more rapidly than the U.S. did.

The third element in the crisis is simply that the "fallout" of military technology has failed to materialize to the extent claimed or hoped for. But what should one have expected? Surely no industry can seriously rely on such a circuitous route to the future. A nonelectronic example will illustrate the point: Heart valves are made

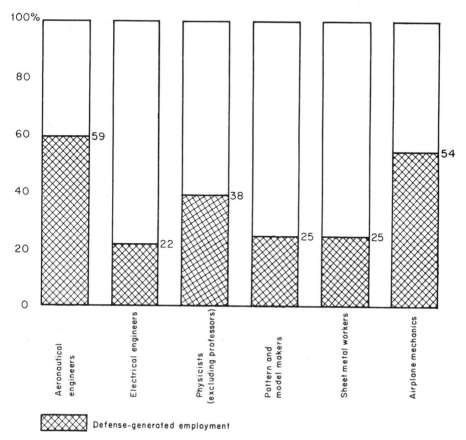

FIGURE 2.   *Proportion of selected occupations in defense-generated jobs, 1968. The chart shows the six occupations most extensively involved in defense work and related to electrical/electronic engineering. Engineers as a whole have 20 percent of their number in defense work and most technically related craftsmen are similarly affected. (Source: M. A. Rutzick, "Skills and locations of defense-related workers,"* Monthly Labor Rev., *vol. 93, pp. 11–16, Feb. 1970)*

of a raw material similar to that used for ladies' girdles, but nobody argues that the way to get better heart valves is to do more girdle research.

We have thus identified (1) the conversion problem as a need for U.S. electronics firms to consider new products and market strategies, (2) the foreign competition problem in terms of a loss of technical and managerial strength in a once highly successful industry, and (3) a quality problem to which the resources of the industry should be able to respond. Clearly, the effective implementation of conversion can free exactly those resources required to come to grips with the other two problems. The mechan-

ics for doing that will be discussed in the following.

ORGANIZING A SOLUTION

To coordinate and, in part, finance the kind of technological operation called for, it is proposed to establish a National Technology Foundation, which would act as a sponsoring agency for research on raw materials, design methodology, and applications, and would also assume that portion of "pure" research now sponsored by the Department of Defense that does not properly belong with the National Science Foundation. Its work agenda could tentatively cover the following, much of which is directly applicable to the electronics industry and, indeed, to all electrical manufacturing:

1. Material and product design studies with special reference to
   (a) Economics and cost effectiveness of materials, including substitutability.
   (b) Design methodology, e.g., stress analysis in products in which it is not now widely used, such as enclosures of equipment; circuit analysis and development, including the use of computers.
   (c) Systematic application studies of new materials and methods to replace the present random and inefficient technological fallout, e.g., integrated and molecular circuits.
   (d) Reliability and robustness studies based on the kinds of test programs proposed but seldom fully carried out on materials of all kinds;[12] applications to electronic circuitry.
2. Standardization and simplification
   (a) Feasibility studies of modularization in producer and consumer durables.
   (b) Cost studies, e.g., on economy of scale.
   (c) Organizational studies for the systematic manufacture of modules, including the legal environment.
3. Processes
   (a) Automation systems for manufacturing and service industries.
   (b) Maintenance and safety problems, including new automation systems justifiable mainly for safety reasons.
   (c) Productivity and producibility studies, both intra-industry and international.
   (d) Capacity studies on machine tools and metal-working machinery and on electronic component/circuit manufacture, including new material–machine configurations.
   (e) Rationalization and reduction of job shop manufacturing; development of versatile small-quantity production systems, "group technology"[13] (the use of common physical characteristics in order to group

the products into manufacturing subsystems; e.g., all shafts are made on one group of machines).

4. Information gathering and processing
   (a) Information systems on design.
   (b) Cost-effectiveness registry of materials, subsystems, components, etc.
   (c) Operating models for businesses, including inventory, market studies, etc.

This list is not meant to be exhaustive, but it does provide a useful beginning. Several of the items specified are likely to become of greater interest in the near future. For example, safety on the job promises to be the focus of some major legal initiatives, including a new Federal safety law complete with standards. Obviously, one way of solving safety problems is by reducing the number of people doing the jobs concerned, i.e., by automating. Another solution lies in the improvement of reliability. All these should be issues within the purview of the NTF.

The actual work could be done by qualified defense contractors, but the NRF's purpose would lie in finding jobs for people rather than assuring the survival of corporations, which, as has been noted, have numerous ways of staying afloat. Certain universities, as well as research institutes (including some new ones), would qualify. Such organized research is in line with the Japanese examples mentioned earlier as well as with similar efforts in various branches of industry in Great Britain, the Netherlands, and West Germany. The communist countries have long used such forms of research organization and these efforts are in part responsible for the formidable Soviet machine tool industry, which makes extensive use of standardization, modularization, and cost-effectiveness studies. Further expansion of such efforts was proposed in a recent study,[14] the general findings of which are worthy of careful consideration in other industries.

The results of NTF's work would be freely accessible, with patents available to everyone for licensing at low rates, and all receipts going into a special NTF trust fund. This may sound somewhat self-defeating in the sense that the whole scheme is designed to solve problems first of all for U.S. industry, but, actually, the argument for exclusiveness does not have much merit in view of the extensive international cross-licensing and information exchange that is already extant. In any event, such arrangements tend to be two-way streets. Further, many of the technical–economic findings of the NTF would necessarily be based on U.S. costs and other conditions and thus would have limited usefulness elsewhere.

The employment that NTF contracts would provide to (hopefully) some of the better-qualified defense scientists and engineers might be only temporary. Certainly, those involved should be encouraged to seek permanent jobs among organizations with whom they deal while working on an NTF research project. This situation is not dissimilar to that of industrial consultants who regularly find executive positions with their clients. And at least the NTF assignments should provide on-the-job training in a context of technical progress, especially with respect to commercial producibility. If, as a result of such efforts, cost consciousness is raised from the image of sordid money grubbing that it now has among many "sophisticated" engineers, so much the better. In fact, it will be quite essential for this to happen because, in large measure, indifference to costs lies at the root of our product and trade problems.

As to the financing of the effort, patent license fees should help, but some direct governmental support, at the beginning at least, will be necessary. Contributions by defense firms or transfer payments by the Department of Defense should be considered as additional sources of funds. During hearings on Sen. George McGovern's proposed National Conversion Act (S.1285) on December 1 and 2, 1969, Walter Reuther proposed that one quarter of all profits of defense contractors should be earmarked for conversion planning. A levy on defense contractors is thus not a new idea.

The concept of the NTF as outlined here differs from various proposals for information systems and studies to deal with the general impact of technological progress.

One such proposal, also by Walter Reuther, is for an "early warning system" to "gather information on a continuing basis [on] automation, atomic and solar energy, new materials, new products and other technological innovations." The areas of special interest would be the impact on employment, industrial location, industrial trends, educational needs, and international trade.[15] The NTF proposal goes much further, however. It suggests the actual implementation of technological needs as perceived, rather than as a response to existing problems, supplemented by such technological forecasting as may be feasible. The NTF also would be a contracting agency, doing the jobs for which firms or other institutions, acting singly, do not have the resources. Some of the clearinghouse functions of the agency that Reuther proposes (and which the NTF would also have to encompass) already exist in the Business and Defense Services Administration of the U.S. Department of Commerce.

Obviously, the NTF and similar concepts are not the only answer to the problem of conversion. Some firms will speedily change to commercial production, although whether in sufficient volume may be doubted. Individuals now in the defense industries may be able to find other jobs; this applies, for instance, to some skilled workers and to much of the clerical force. Others, in administrative tasks, may be able to participate in urban–surburban–rural planning and reconstruction. Finally, if a missile engineer should wish to become a medical doctor, for example, he should be encouraged to study for this, if otherwise qualified, with such scholarship support as may be required. The present article thus limits itself to only one of several possible modes of solution, which are by no means mutually exclusive.

CAVEATS AND DANGERS

The problems and remedies discussed here have been identified before and the response to them has often been a mixture of cynicism, indifference, and defeatism that has made concerted action unusually difficult. This is quite apart from ideological "gut reactions," which, on many occasions, have inhibited even a discussion of the problems. Firms, unions, and communities have rarely put forward responsible plans, and, since they felt they had nothing to contribute, have refused even to attend conferences on these subjects, particularly on conversion. When there is nothing to show, such gatherings tend to become, in the sense of Hans Christian Andersen, emperors' fashion shows.

One aspect of the defeatism extends throughout the spectrum of problems discussed here: It is that U.S. costs and general business profligacy are so ingrained and out of line that nothing can be done. Of course, it is quite true that the defense industry has shown a conspicuous inability to meet limitations of time and budgets.[16] It is not unreasonable to view with suspicion the creators of the B-58, the F-111, the XB-70, the C-5A, and all the other weapons that failed to work properly, cost too much, and took too long; but that is the basic dimension of the conversion job, and the technical resource that we must now direct to other urgent tasks.

Finally, one can respond to an attitude of helplessness by considering the alternatives—and these are unpleasant indeed. Conversion could be handled simply by firing those affected and accepting the the monumental dislocations this would entail. With the multiplier effects of such changes, many communities would be especially hard hit because conversion and the competition problem share the characteristic of attacking specific products and localities. It is easy to visualize political pressures against any defense cuts, and further growth in domestic extremism. It will be particularly necessary to guard against the kind of product change *within* defense work that would use up even more technical and research resources. It is in precisely that area that the shortage of talent is greatest and nothing can be done about international competition without investing exactly that kind of resource.

The more particular and immediate response to an import problem is, of course, protectionism. It has taken more than a generation to reduce the tariff and autarchy walls of the 1920s and 1930s to the more manageable scale of the General Agreements on Tariff and Trade (GATT). In any event, the U.S. electronics industry does not speak with a united voice on the subject because so much of it already makes use of plants outside the country; even component manufacturers, who are normally the most protectionist sector of the industry, have begun to "follow their markets abroad." Besides, protectionism would do nothing to help U.S. electronic exports; on the contrary, by sheltering domestic inefficiencies, it would soon reduce exports to the vanishing point, except for a few special products. And even these may be expected to decline as we become ever less able to cope with the quality problem. On that issue one can also envisage a future full of litigation (including soldiers suing the manufacturers of defective weapons!) and legal controversy, in the absence of technical efforts of the kind discussed here.

Clearly, there are major planning and action problems ahead, but, as shown here, it is possible to have the problem of conversion provide at least a partial answer to the problems of meeting foreign competition and of quality control. As Shakespeare says in *As You Like It*:

Sweet are the uses of adversity:
Which, like the toad, ugly and venomous,
Wears yet a precious jewel in its head.

---

[1] For a report on this development, including its political implications, see Rovere, R. H., "Letter from Washington," *New Yorker*, pp. 169–177, Nov. 1, 1969.

[2] Albright, J., "Laird plans a 40% troop cut," *Newsday*, p. 4, Dec. 22, 1969.

[3] "Military markets start to sag," *Business Week*, p. 140, Oct. 25, 1969; see also *New York Times*, p. 1, Oct. 27, 1969, and p. 1, Oct. 22, 1969.

[4] "Budget knives are nicking NASA," *Business Week*, pp. 21–22, Jan. 3, 1970.

[5] See, for example, Melman, S., *The Depleted Society*, New York: Holt, 1967. See also the series of studies done by the U.S. Arms Control and Disarmament Agency: *Defense Industry Diversification*, 1966; *The Implications of Reduced Defense for the Electronics Industry*, 1965; *The Transferability and Retraining of Defense Engineers*, 1967. The studies are of uneven merit and, in the view of the writer, tend to minimize the problems involved.

[6] Berkowitz, M., *Conversion of Military Oriented Research and Development to Civilian Uses*; Melman, S. (ed.), *The Defense Economy*; Ullmann, J.E. (ed.), *Potential Civilian Markets for the Military Electronics Industry*. New York: Praeger, 1970. These are three of five volumes in a series, *Con-*

version of Industry from a Military to a Civilian Economy.

[7]*Electronic Trends International,* vol. 3, May 1969 (pt. II) and July 1969.

[8]Japan Electronic Industry Development Assoc., *Annual Report 1968.* Tokyo: Kikai Shinko Kaikan, 1969.

[9]Sugata, E., and Namekawa, T., "Integrated circuits for television receivers," *IEEE Spectrum,* vol. 6, pp. 64–74, May 1969.

[10]"Now Japan discovers IC," *Business Week,* p. 39, Dec. 13, 1969.

[11]"Singapore: the robust waif," *Business Week,* pp. 66–67, Dec. 6, 1969.

[12]Freudenthal, A. M., and Gumbel, E. J. "Minimum life in fatigue," *J. Am. Statist. Assoc.,* vol. 49, pp. 575–597, 1954. Much of the extensive work on this subject relies on a few limited series of experiments.

[13]"A way to make diversity pay off." *Business Week,* p. 152, Oct. 18, 1969.

[14]L'vov, D. S., *Principles of Engineering Design Economics.* Boston Spa, England: National Lending Library for Science and Technology, 1968.

[15]Testimony of Walter Reuther before the U.S. Congress Joint Economic Committee, "The military budget and national priorities," 91st Congress, 1st Session, vol. 1, p. 438, June 1969.

[16]For an early review, see Scherer, W., and Peck, M. J., *The Weapons Acquisition Process.* Cambridge Mass.: Harvard University Graduate School of Business, 1960, chap. 3. For a recent critique see Stubbing, R. A., *Improving the Acquisition Process for High Risk Electronics Systems.* Distributed by U.S. Dept. of Commerce, Clearinghouse for Federal and Technical Information, Springfield, Va., No. AD 681 518, 1969.

Resource Allocation

30. Economic and Social Consequences of Disarmament

United Nations

SUMMARY AND CONCLUSIONS

166. The present level of military expenditure not only represents a grave political danger but also imposes a heavy economic and social burden on most countries. It absorbs a large volume of human and material resources of all kinds, which could be used to increase economic and social welfare throughout the world—both in the highly industrialized countries, which at the present time incur the bulk of the world's military expenditures, and in the less developed areas.

Resources devoted to military purposes

167. There appears to be general agreement that the world is spending roughly $120 billion annually on military account at the present time. This corresponds to about one-half of the total gross capital formation throughout the world. It is at least two-thirds of—and according to some

Reprinted from *Economic and Social Consequences of Disarmament,* United Nations, Department of Economic and Social Affairs (New York, 1962). Reprinted with permission.

estimates, of the same order of magnitude as—the entire national income of all the under-developed countries.

168. It is important that countries, in preparing to disarm, should take stock of the various resources that disarmament would release for peaceful uses. In the major military powers, military production is highly concentrated in a few industry groups. In those countries that rely upon imports for their supplies of military goods or in which the major part of military expenditure is for the pay and subsistence of the armed forces, rather than for their equipment, the resources devoted to military purposes consist essentially of manpower and foreign exchange.

The peaceful use of released resources

169. There are so many competing claims for usefully employing the resources released by disarmament that the real problem is to establish a scale of priorities. The most urgent of these claims would undoubtedly already have been largely satisfied were it not for the armaments race.

170. Increased personal consumption might well absorb a large share of the released resources. A substantial portion of them, however, would be used for expansion of productive capacities because only such expansion can provide a firm basis for further increases in consump-

tion. In the less developed countries, the utilization of released resources for capital formation must be considered vitally important.

171. Social investment is an important alternative both to private consumption and to industrial and agricultural investment. Its claims rest partly upon the clear urgency of the direct need for improved social amenities, and partly upon the fact that growth of industrial and agricultural productivity is dependent upon developments in education, housing, health, and other fields.

172. The release of scientific and technical manpower would make it possible to encourage programmes of basic scientific research in fields which have hitherto been neglected. Disarmament would also open up possibilities for joint international ventures of an ambitious kind, such as the utilization of atomic energy for peaceful purposes, space research, the exploration of the Arctic and Antarctic for the benefit of mankind and projects to change the climates of large areas of the world.

173. Thus, though it would take active decisions by Governments in the light of national and international needs to set in motion the necessary programmes for employing the released resources, it seems abundantly clear that no country need fear a lack of useful employment opportunities for the resources that would become available to it through disarmament.

Impact on national production and employment

174. Disarmament would raise both general problems of maintaining the over-all level of economic activity and employment and specific problems in so far as manpower or productive capacity might require adaptation to non-military needs. In the economic life of all countries, shifts in the pattern of demand and in the allocation of productive resources are continually occurring. The reallocation of productive resources which would accompany disarmament is in many respects merely a special case of the phenomenon of economic growth.

175. The post-war conversion was a much larger one and involved a more rapid transfer of resources than total disarmament would require at present. Nevertheless, huge armies were quickly demobilized without a significant rise in unemployment in most countries. The pace of recovery, particularly of industrial output, was impressively rapid. During the post-war conversion, however, the major concern of economic policy was to restrain, rather than to maintain, over-all demand.

176. Much attention has already been given in the industrialized private enterprise economies to the methods by which total effective demand can be maintained. Monetary and fiscal policy could be used to offset the effect of a shortfall in total demand that might result from a decline in military expenditure to the extent that it were not offset by a rise in civil government expenditure. Bearing in mind that a substantial part of military expenditure would probably be replaced by other government expenditure in most countries, it may be concluded that the maintenance of effective demand in the face of disarmament should not prove difficult.

177. For many under-developed countries, the effect of disarmament upon the industrial countries' demands for primary products, and thus on the export earnings of the primary producing countries, would be of great importance. So would the methods of dealing with the liquidation of strategic stockpiles.

178. In the centrally planned economies, the maintenance of effective demand while reducing military expenditure would be simply a matter of the efficiency of planning techniques. In consequence, effective demand could be readily maintained, and the principal problems of conversion would concern the physical adaptation of plants producing armaments to the production of goods for civilian use.

Structural problems of conversion

179. Even with the successful maintenance of total effective demand during a period of disarmament, significant problems of adjustment would remain in specific sectors and areas of the economy. The resources now supplying military

requirements could be adapted to peace-time needs partly by shifts within industries and plants. This might be a relatively easy procedure, in many cases involving little more than changes in designs, retooling, and minor adaptations of skills, particularly in plants and enterprises which already produce both military and civilian goods. Shifts between industries would necessitate new investment and acquisition of different types of skill by the working force. In the longer run disarmament would allow each country to raise the rate of investment and to adapt productive capacity more adequately to the needs of the population and to the requirements of economic growth, both in the private enterprise and the centrally planned economies.

180. Hypothetical studies on the assumption that military expenditure is replaced wholly by increases in expenditure on other kinds of goods and services suggest that in the event of very rapid disarmament some 6 or 7 per cent (including the armed forces) of the total labour force in the United States and 3½ to 4 per cent in the United Kingdom would have to find civilian instead of military employment or change their employment from one industry group to another. These shifts would be small if spread out over a number of years and would be greatly facilitated by the normal process of turnover. The higher the rate of growth of the economy, the easier the process of adaptation.

181. Under-developed countries generally have been meeting their requirements for military goods and services by imports, so that their disarmament would release foreign exchange rather than industrial workers. It would also free members of the forces, many with useful skills and training. Some of these could be usefully employed in the development of social capital. In some of the semi-industrialized countries, newly started basic industries could concentrate, without any transitional difficulty, on the manufacture of capital goods.

182. In the centrally planned economies, where productive capacity is usually fully utilized, it would be necessary to convert plants producing military equipment to production of durable consumer goods and of such investment goods as can be produced in them with only minor retooling. This could be done rapidly.

183. Some special problems would arise with regard to re-employment and training of manpower and reorientation of scientific research. While most members of the armed forces have received training that would fit them easily for civilian life, a special effort would have to be made to find suitable employment for the rest. The demobilization of the non-professional members of the armed forces would imply only that the number of new entrants for that period would be augmented by this special factor.

184. In industries depending heavily on military orders, many of the employees possess a level of skill that should find gainful employment in other branches of production, so long as over-all effective demand is rising. Even so, there might be some special cases which would require special assistance to encourage the adaptation of skills to new jobs. The uneven geographical distribution of the activity based on military expenditure would give rise to a need for various forms of public and other assistance to facilitate readjustment.

185. The task of shifting scientific and technical personnel to non-military fields of research in some countries would be considerable. No reduction in the actual employment of scientific and technical personnel need be feared, however, because the demand for civilian research would increase rapidly.

Impact on international economic relations

186. Disarmament would be bound to have favourable effects on the development of international relations. The political *détente* that would accompany an international disarmament programme would in itself imply that nations were willing to reconsider their economic relations with one another. The relaxation of international tensions would provide a sound basis for reduction of trade barriers and for modification of existing trade agreements and

trading practices. An important consequence of this would be a substantial increase in trade between the centrally
planned economies and the rest of the
world.

187. Since disarmament may be expected
to result in an acceleration of economic
growth, it should stimulate the growth
of demand for primary production in general. Accelerated economic growth would
be still more powerful in increasing total
demand for manufacturers. The over-all
impact of disarmament on the trade of
under-developed countries is likely to be
favourable, not only because of the acceleration of economic growth but also because of the greatly expanded aid to be
expected from the more advanced countries.

188. Some exports of primary products,
such as petroleum, rubber and most metallic ores, depend significantly at present
on direct and indirect demand generated
by military purchases. Provided, however,
that military expenditure were fully replaced by public and private non-military
spending, the impact on over-all demand
for these commodities would be only minor.
There might, however, be instances in
which declines in demand for particular
commodities would cause appreciable
difficulties. In these cases consideration
should be given to special aid for the countries concerned, in the same way as for
particular industries or areas within the
principal disarming countries. For most
other primary commodities, the reallocation
of military expenditure to civilian use would
probably bring about a net increase in
demand.

189. During the conversion period
changes in the level of aggregate economic
activity associated with disarmament in
the major industrial countries would be a
major determinant of the level of international trade. It is believed that significant
fluctuations in the general level of international trade could be avoided, but it
should nevertheless be realized that any
failure to achieve this goal could have
serious consequences. Regardless of the
technique employed, no country should be

allowed to suffer a disruption to its economic life, even temporarily, as a result
of disarmament.

Effects on the volume and framework of aid for economic development

190. National efforts and international
co-operation in the development of the
under-developed countries have so far not
brought about the desired acceleration of
economic growth. A much larger volume of
resources could be allocated to investment
for productive development in these countries even if only a fraction of the resources
currently devoted to military purposes
were used in this way. Disarmament could
thus bring about a marked increase in the
rate of growth of real income in the poorer
parts of the world.

191. Bilateral and multilateral programmes of aid each have their own particular advantages and disadvantages, but in
so far as political circumstances have had
any weight in determining the direction
and form of aid, effective disarmament
and the related lessening of international
tensions should improve the prospects for
more co-operative international action.
Since repayment of loans granted on commercial terms may impose heavy burdens
on the balances of payments of the underdeveloped countries, as large a proportion
of economic aid as possible should take the
form of grants or "soft" loans.

192. Because the competing claims in
developed countries are also urgent there
is a serious possibility that the financial
resources released by disarmament might
be rapidly absorbed by purely national
aims. It is therefore desirable that an
appropriate proportion of these resources
should be allocated to international aid
in its various forms simultaneously with
their use for domestic purposes.

193. Foreign aid, however, can play only
a supplementary role in the development
of these countries and the responsibility
for initiation and intensification of development efforts would continue to lie entirely
with the Governments and peoples concerned.

Some social consequences

194. In a disarmed world, a general improvement could be expected in the level of living, including an increase in leisure. With the end of the armaments race, Governments would accord social objectives a higher priority. The psychological, moral and material evils of compulsory military service and of stationing troops away from their homes would be avoided; so would the danger that security considerations and the armed forces might play an extensive role in forming the values of the community. Scientific co-operation and the arts would benefit from an extension of international exchanges.

Conclusion

195. The Consultative Group is unanimously of the opinion that all the problems and difficulties of transition connected with disarmament could be met by appropriate national and international measures. There should thus be no doubt that the diversion to peaceful purposes of the resources now in military use could be accomplished to the benefit of all countries and lead to the improvement of world economic and social conditions. The achievement of general and complete disarmament would be an unqualified blessing to all mankind.

Opportunity Cost

31. Economic Report of the President, 1969

Illustrative New Programs or Expansions of Existing Federal Programs, Fiscal Year 1972

PROGRAM	HYPOTHETICAL EXPENDITURES (BILLIONS OF DOLLARS)
Total expenditures	39.7
Education	7.0
Preschool	1.0
Elementary and secondary	2.5
Higher	3.0
Vocational	.5
Health	3.8
Kiddie-care	.5
Medicare for disabled	1.8
Comprehensive health centers	1.0
Hospital construction and modernization	.5
Nutrition	1.0
Community service programs	.8
Jobs and manpower	2.5
Public jobs	1.8
Manpower Development Training Act	.5
Employment service	.2
Social security and income support	9.5
Unemployment insurance	2.0
Public assistance	4.0
Social security improvements	3.5
Veterans	.3
Economic, area, and other special development programs	2.2
Entrepreneurial aid	.5

PROGRAM *(Con't)*	HYPOTHETICAL EXPENDITURES
Area redevelopment	.5
Rural development	1.0
Indian assistance.	.2
Crime, delinquency, and riots.	1.0
Violence and riot prevention.	.1
Safe streets programs.	.3
Rehabilitation of offenders and delinquents.	.3
Prevention of delinquency and crime by special measures for delinquency-prone youth.	.3
Quality of environment.	1.7
Air pollution prevention and control	.1
Public water supply construction programs	.3
Water pollution control and sewage treatment	1.0
Solid waste disposal	.1
Natural beautification, environmental protection, and recreational development	.2
Natural resource development and utilization	1.4
Land and forest conservation	.2
Water resources and related programs.	.5
Mineral and energy (excluding hydroelectric) development	.2
Natural environmental development.	.5
Urban development	5.5
New cities.	.5
Land acquisition and financial planning (suburban)	.5
Urban mass transportation	.5
Model cities.	2.0
Other urban facilities and renewal	2.0
Transportation	1.0
Airway and airport modernization	.4
Rapid interurban ground transit	.1
Modernization of merchant marine.	.2
Motor vehicle and transportation safety research and safety grants.	.3
Science and space exploration	1.0
Post-Apollo space program.	.5
Scientific research in oceanography, communications, social and behavioral sciences, and natural sciences	.5
Foreign economic aid.	1.0

SOURCE: Bureau of the Budget and *Economic Report of the President,* 1969 (Table 1-4).

Imperfections in Labor Markets

32. Impact of Deep Cuts in Defense

ECONOMIES IN ARMS MEAN LEANER TIMES FOR MANY WORKERS, INDUSTRIES, CITIES. HERE ARE THE PROSPECTS —PLUS A LOOK AT PLANS TO EASE THE BLOW.

Effects of massive reductions in defense spending now are spreading across the U.S., with these results:

Workers are being laid off by the thousands. Many small cities and towns that depend heavily on military spending are in trouble. One defense contractor after another reports profits are heading downward.

In the last six months, 40,000 workers have lost their jobs at defense plants, and 600,000 more are scheduled to be laid off in the next 18 months.

More than 400,000 servicemen will be leaving the armed forces in the next year or so, many coming on the job market at a time when unemployment is rising in a succession of areas.

All told, more than 1.3 million Americans—civilians and men in uniform—will lose their jobs in the two-year period to end June 30, 1971.

Reductions in military procurement, planned by the Pentagon, promise hard times for many companies in the fields of aerospace, munitions, tanks and other vehicles, electronics, communications, shipbuildings.

Nearly every State will be affected one way or another.

Civilian and military jobs generated by defense and space spending account for these percentages of total work force in the States listed:

STATE:	PERCENT
Alaska	31.6
Hawaii	18.8
District of Columbia	15.6
Virginia	14.1
Maryland	9.9
Utah	9.9
Georgia	9.7
Colorado	9.6
California	9.3
Connecticut	9.2
Arizona	9.0
South Carolina	8.8
Texas	8.4
New Mexico	8.3
Oklahoma	8.1
Washington	8.1
New Hampshire	7.8
Mississippi	7.3

Note: Figures are as of June 30, 1968, the latest available.
SOURCE: U.S. Department of Labor; U.S. Department of Defense.

Counteraction

Now the Nixon Administration, getting worried, is stepping up plans to cope with the economic impact of the defense cutbacks.

From the President's Council of Economic Advisers, in its annual report late in January, came this pledge:

"The Federal Government, in action co-ordinated by the President's office, will assist the workers and communities directly affected to make the smoothest possible transition to other activities."

A deputy assistant to the President, Edward L. Morgan, has been given the job of co-ordinating the work of Government agencies.

The Pentagon is involved in a big way, as plans are now laid. So are the Labor and Commerce Departments, as well as the Veterans Administration.

There are special programs to train and find work for returning veterans and civilians who lose jobs, to provide special loans to hard-hit communities, and to transfer abandoned military bases to nondefense use.

Behind the prospects for leaner times in defense industries is the biggest slash in military spending in 16 years.

Down 5 billions

President Nixon's military budget for the year starting next July 1 calls for outlays of 71.8 billion dollars, down 5.2 billion from this year and nearly 7 billion from the war-peak year, ended last June 30.

At the same time, spending for space programs in the coming fiscal year is also budgeted for pruning. The planned cutback is nearly half a billion, to a total of 3.4 billion next year.

Officials of the National Aeronautics and Space Administration say the reduction will eliminate 45,000 jobs.

California, with 16,000 jobs, is slated to suffer the biggest drop. An additional 11,400 people working on space projects in the Northeast will lose their jobs, as well as 7,000 in the "space crescent" which lies along the Gulf Coast, and 4,600 in Colorado.

The Michoud Assembly Facility, near New Orleans, and the Mississippi Test Facility, in Hancock County, in particular, will be hard hit.

Details on just where the drop in military spending will hurt most have not yet been fully disclosed. But you get an idea of where the impact is likely to be most severe from the charts on these pages and from a special study by the Economic Unit of "U.S. News & World Report."

Nearly 1 in every 3 jobs in Alaska is generated by defense outlays. The importance of military spending in producing is great, too, in Hawaii and Virginia.

California leads

Measured by sheer numbers, California leads the way in defense-generated jobs with 767,400, at latest official count. Generally, states of the Far West and the South are most dependent on defense for jobs.

The chart [below] . . . tells, by broad categories, how different industries will be affected by changes in buying of military goods.

To show where cuts in spending on military and space hardware can have the deepest impact —

Aircraft: Eleven states handle 90 per cent of prime contracts awarded for aircraft. Plants in Texas, Connecticut, California, Ohio, Georgia and Missouri get considerable business.

Reductions appear on the way, for example, for the F-111 fighter-bomber, made near Fort Worth, Tex., and the C-5A cargo plane, made in Marietta, Ga. But sharp increases in funds are earmarked in the new budget for the F-14A fighter, made on Long Island, New York, and for the F-15 fighter, made in St. Louis.

Spending on missiles is heading higher, too. That could offset some losses in aerospace activity in California. Other possible gainers: Massachusetts, Washington, Colorado.

Shipbuilding: New York gets more money in prime-contract awards for ships than any other state. For Virginia and Mississippi, shipbuilding makes up a large part of total defense business. A Nixon plan to build more merchant ships, however, could partly offset reductions in naval construction.

Tanks, trucks: Michigan stands to be the big loser as a result of plans for reduced buying of tanks and other vehicles. Vermont, Ohio and Indiana could suffer, too.

Munitions: Substantially less spending for ammunition will have a widespread effect. Many small towns and cities in the South and Midwest are likely to be hurt. Some areas of Pennsylvania, Texas, California, Minnesota, Illinois and Tennessee may be in for economic trouble.

Electronics: Sizable cuts are also in store for spending on electronic and communications gears — items that make up a significant portion of defense business in Maryland, New Jersey, Massachusetts, New York and California.

Clothing: Reductions in the size of the armed forces are expected to cut orders for textiles. The Carolinas and New Jersey are major suppliers.

Just what is being done to meet the growing impact on workers, businesses and local communities? Here is a look at key programs being counted on by the Administration —

Economic adjustment

The Pentagon has assigned a group of experts to assist communities hit by base closings or cuts in defense contracts.

The Sag in Buying of Arms

[In millions of dollars]

	YEARS ENDING JUNE 30		
	1969	1970 (OFFICIAL ESTIMATE)	1971 (OFFICIAL ESTIMATE)
Total military procurement	23,988	21,550	18,799
Aircraft.	9,177	7,645	6,608
Missiles	2,509	2,919	3,203
Ships	1,949	1,900	1,630
Tanks, armored vehicles, weapons	508	385	353
Ordnance, vehicles	6,590	5,603	4,389
Electronics, communication.	1,409	1,188	986
Construction and engineering equipment, other procurement	1,846	1,910	1,630
Research and development	7,457	7,300	7,382
Total, procurement and research	31,445	28,850	26,181

Note: If war in Vietnam ends, spending for arms may be reduced below the official plans reflected in the figures given here.

Plans to shut or trim down some 280 military bases within the U.S. have more than doubled, just in recent weeks, the number of communities involved in this program. Each case is handled differently. But the technique of the Pentagon's Office of Economic Adjustment is to meet with community leaders, examine the local prospects, then help channel in other federal resources to meet the problem.

In 17 recent cases, this Pentagon group arranged to set up technical institutes that use facilities of former military bases. In other cases, the abandoned bases have been sold or given to local groups for the development of colleges, civilian airports, warehouses or industrial parks.

Right now 23 small cities and towns scattered across the country are being helped—such as Newburgh, N.Y., where Stewart Air Force Base has been closed; Topsham, Me., where a 900-man radar installation has been shut down; Smyrna, Tenn., which just lost a 5,000-employee air base; Sault Sainte Marie, Mich., which lost the nearby 10,000-man Kincheloe Air Base, and Corvallis, Ore., which lost a 900-man radar station.

Job layoffs

A standby program has been established by the Labor Department for handling possible mass layoffs resulting from defense cutbacks.

In areas where unemployment soars, temporary employment offices are to be set up, to augment the 2,100 State employment offices throughout the nation. Their aim: to provide information on job opportunities in other areas.

Meanwhile, the impact of defense layoffs is expected to be eased by the Department's new "job banks"—which are already operating in 10 cities and expected to be set up in 45 more by June. Each will contain computerized job information for referring. applicants to openings in the area.

Job training is to be offered on an expanding scale, too. Last year, about 1 million people received such training, at a cost of 2 billion dollars. Most were "disadvantaged" workers or hard-core unemployed. It is believed veterans and laid-off defense workers now will participate on a growing scale.

New industry

The Department of Commerce is expanding its long-established Economic Development Administration to help hardhit areas attract new industry, create new jobs.

The case of Springfield, Mass., shows how EDA plans to help ease the impact of defense cuts. When the big Springfield armory was closed, a payroll of about 2,900 was lost.

An EDA study of the area indicated that 3,000 jobs could be created to replace those lost by the shutdown. So, guided by a technical assistance team, the city converted the armory into a regional technical institute, museum complex, and industrial park.

By last November, 1,600 new jobs had been created with these facilities, and the rest appeared to be within reach.

Work for veterans

A series of programs has been established to help more than half a million present GI's locate civilian jobs, or go back to school, in the year ahead. These are operated by the Pentagon, Labor Department and the VA.

At the nation's 304 military separation points, VA officials now lecture all departing veterans on the assistance available. Specialists conduct interviews with those needing help, with a follow-up in the veteran's home town. "Veterans Assistance Centers" are being set up in most of the larger U.S. cities, some of the smaller ones.

Even before today's GI's near the end of their military tours, a job-training program is offered. During the last six months of active duty, "Project Transition" helps servicemen who have no civilian job skills.

Classes are held, on and off military bases, to teach GI's such skills as postal work, data processing and auto repair. In some cases, private companies send in experts to train soldiers for later jobs in fields such as gasoline-station management and parcel delivery service.

Project Transition follows up with placement as well, through private firms who participate in the training programs, and State employment agencies. Municipal police departments are now recruiting.

Specialized programs for Negroes also are to be available. One such program, set up by the Commerce Department, is the Office of Minority Business Enterprise. Its aim is to establish blacks in businesses of their own. If a Negro veteran can show he has the skills and inclination to become an entrepreneur, this agency can arrange necessary loans and provide technical assistance.

The Labor Department is exploring, with VA, other ways of interesting black veterans in becoming small businessmen. New programs are expected to result. The best prospects are believed to be in such fields as electronics, auto and truck repair, and maintenance.

The programs are being relied on by the Nixon Administration to ease the pain of deep cuts in defense.

Employment and Investment

33. How to Give Up the Economy of Death and Keep Prosperity
Richard J. Barnet

When it comes to conversion, most Americans are Marxists. They do not believe that the present levels of prosperity or employment can be maintained except by

From *The Economy of Death*, by Richard J. Barnet. Copyright © 1969 by Richard J. Barnet. Reprinted by permission of Atheneum Publishers.

a war economy. They do not see or will not admit the revolutionary implications of their belief. An economic system that works only by turning out products that endanger itself and the planet is literally suicidal. If it is true that American capitalism cannot function without military socialism, then anyone who cares about survival cannot be a capitalist. But is it true?

A central problem concerns unemployment. According to the University of California sociologist Jeffrey Schevitz, one in five jobs in the United States depends directly or indirectly upon the Department of Defense. The Pentagon has 3.4 million members in the armed forces and 1.3 million civilian workers spread across seventy countries. There are 3.8 million industrial workers whose lives are wholly tied to war production. Millions more are indirectly dependent upon the defense budget. Twenty-one percent of skilled blue-collar workers are on military payrolls. Schevitz notes that nearly half of all scientists and engineers in private industry work in the aerospace and defense fields.

These figures give an inadequate picture of the extent to which the nation is addicted to the Economy of Death. Junction City, Kansas, is in the Fort Riley business. It is typical of numerous Pentagon company towns spread across the country. According to *Time* Magazine, when one Army division left Fort Riley in 1965, business fell off 30 percent. Fayetteville, North Carolina, is another string of used-car lots, army-surplus stores, drive-in movies, and more ancient forms of Army entertainment for the diversion of thousands of paratroopers. Without Fort Bragg, Fayetteville would face bankruptcy. Sunnyvale, California, is typical of numerous communities throughout the United States which have become addicted to the war business. From a population in 1940 of 4373 the town has grown to 95,000. Twenty-one thousand work in the Lockheed plant, 3000 for Westinghouse, and 1400 for a division of United Aircraft Corporation. Thousands more work for smaller subcontractors. "If the government says OK, we're not building any more Polaris or Poseidon missiles, and everybody at Lockheed was sitting on the streets, it would hurt real bad," Dan Wood, a Sunnyvale Lockheed employee who averages $10,000 a year helping to build missiles, observed to a reporter from *Newsweek*. Defense contracts and Defense Department payrolls account for more than 20 percent of the entire personal income of such states as Alaska, Connecticut, and Idaho, and the District of Columbia. In California, Kansas, Arizona, and New Mexico between 20 and 30 percent of the industrial employees work for the Pentagon. In Utah the military is the state's number-one employer. When the Army killed 6400 sheep at Skull Valley in 1968 by accidentally spraying them with VX, a deadly nerve gas, the state veterinarian, D. Avaron Osguthorpe, observed, "We've got a defense business bringing in $35 million a year into the state; sheep bring in one thirty-fifth that amount. Which is more important for Utah?"

In its approach to conversion, the federal government has specialized in positive thinking and minimal action. The President's Committee on the Economic Impact of Defense and Disarmament, created in 1965 as a response to rising Congressional concern about conversion, concluded that "even general and complete disarmament would pose no insuperable problems." The Report painted a rosy picture of defense plants as "gigantic job shops" which could easily compete for and fulfill "large-scale non-defense research and development projects." The reality has been less rosy. A few years ago Edmund "Pat" Brown, Governor of California, the number-one state in defense contracts, encouraged aerospace companies to go into research in the fields of transportation, air pollution, and communications. The results were not encouraging. The companies did not have the right skills or adequate incentive. When North American Rockwell is asked to develop a new plane, the Pentagon advances the company enough cash to hire from 70 to 100 professionals. The same company received a contract for a transport study with money for 3 to 5 professionals.

Unlike war work, contracts in the Economy of Life are not riskless, and they do not hold out the promise of big profits for sophisticated hardware. "If the Government provided the risk capital and if the vehicle contained enough technology or patentable elements so that we could close out other producers and if we could market it, then it would be viable," John R. Moore, the president of North American Rockwell's Aerospace and Systems Group, recently laid down as his conditions for a serious commitment to production for peace. Only when making high-speed transport systems is as profitable as making missiles will the weapons-makers voluntarily move out of the death business.

Because of the resistance of aerospace companies to conversion and other factors, official optimism about unemployment has proved to be unfounded. Over 290,000 engineers and scientists work directly in war industries. In 1963-64 because of the completion of a number of military programs more than 30,000 of them lost their jobs. On an average they remained jobless for more than three months. Between April 1963 and December 1964 the Republic Aviation Corporation's Long Island plant laid off 13,600 employees because of a cut-back in the F-105 fighter-bomber. About 16 percent of the men and 36 percent of the women who stayed in the community had yet to find a job more than a year later when the U.S. Arms Control and Disarmament Agency conducted a survey. Of those who did find work, 21 percent of the men and 41 percent of the women were jobless for six months or more. The Boeing Company laid off 5000 workers between December 1963 and March 1964. Despite the fact that these workers were younger and better educated than average, 22 percent of the men and 59 percent of the women were still unemployed in August 1964. According to Schevitz's calculations. new jobs in war industries accounted for 44 percent of the over-all increase in employment in the year 1965. Thus the economy is even less able to absorb defense workers in civilian production that it was five years ago. Each year the problem gets worse. There are two reasons for this. First, salaries payable in defense industries are substantially higher because the firms are able to pass the cost along to the taxpayer. Paying a premium to recruit and keep the best scientific talent in war work has been an explicit national policy. As a result, government-subsidized salaries have risen sharply. Second, military research and development on the "frontier of knowledge" tends to be more challenging professionally than much civilian technology which has not been pushed to the frontier for lack of money and energy. With billions to spend, the Defense Department can set engineers and scientists to exciting tasks that no civilian industry can match.

Most engineers and scientists would be able to find work in America's still booming economy, but they are not likely to find work at the same pay or with equivalent challenge. Unless the federal government will subsidize the technology of peace as it has subsidized the technology of war, we face the prospect of a new class of $200,000-a-year hard-core unemployed.

What can the federal government do about unemployment once it is decided to convert the economy from war preparation? The question is central, for unless there is a program instead of platitudes for dealing with this problem, the resistance to conversion will be too strong to overcome.

A national conversion program should be established which operates on the basic principle that the community, not the individual war worker or soldier, must pay the costs of conversion. Like the GI Bill of Rights, such a program would ease the transition for persons whose jobs are destroyed as a result of government policy. Government and a specialized industry have placed millions of workers in a position of dependence on the Economy of Death. They must now bear the responsibility for easing the pain of withdrawal.

Such a program should be administered by a National Conversion Commission with broad powers. A principal job of the Commission would be to assist the retraining and relocation of people released from war research and war production. Under the Manpower and Development Training Act of 1962, limited funds are presently available for "brief refresher or reorientation educational courses in order to become qualified for other employment" to assist people "who have become unemployed because of the specialized nature of their former employment." This program in greatly expanded form should become a major instrument of conversion. In accordance with the national conversion plan, the Commission should award substantial grants to scientific and technical personnel to encourage them to apply their talents to priority problems. The manpower specialist Herbert Striner of the Upjohn Institute estimates that it would take no more than three or four months to train most scientists and engineers now in war work for useful alternative jobs. For example, an engineer who specializes in the miniaturization of electronic components for a missile might be given a federal grant of up to a half-year's salary to study the technology of mass transportation, pollution, or low-cost housing. Another might be given a grant to design an experimental school.

The training programs could be carried out in several different ways. One possibility would be to subsidize on-the-job training programs in civilian plants for former war technologists. The federal government might supplement the salaries of scientists and engineers in non-defense industry to bring them somewhat more in line with the salary scales prevailing in war industry. Firms which have been found to have made excessive profits on defense contracts should be required to set up retraining programs without additional federal subsidy, for they have already received it. Another approach would be to sponsor a program of research and training in technical innovation for the civilian economy at universities. The program would be specifically designed to stimulate innovation in the civilian economy, and technologists from war industries would be given first chance to participate. The universities could run a series of programs ranging from brief refresher coursés to full-scale professional schools for new careers. The Commission should also have substantial funds rescued from the defense budget for scholarship grants. Engineers and scientists who make use of these programs should receive tax relief and outright subsidies where necessary. Some scientists and engineers released from defense plants should be encouraged to take federally subsidized sabbatical leaves in which to think about useful alternative ways to spend their lives. For example, some might receive a grant to enable them to teach science in public schools or to set up experimental teaching programs to acquaint adults as well as high school students with technical and social problems of science. In Washington, the Institute for Policy Studies has sponsored a Neighborhood Science Center that makes it possible for boys and girls in a ghetto area

to walk off the street and conduct simple scientific experiments with the help of a skilled scientist. The Commission should make it possible for persons released from the Economy of Death to try similar experiments and to invent others. Such investment in human resources would pay dividends for the whole society.

The same programs should be available for nonskilled workers. In some respects their problem is easier than that of the scientific and technical people. In others it is more difficult. Leonard A. Lecht of the National Planning Association estimates that if $20 billion were cut from the defense budget, half of which went to social programs and half into private pockets through tax reduction, new job openings would exceed jobs lost through defense cutbacks by 325,000. But the new jobs would demand different skills—fewer mahine operators and engineers, and more service personnel, craftsmen, and laborers to work in the building trades. The Commission should have a nation-wide program of job placement, retraining programs for unskilled workers, and the power to operate public-works programs with former defense workers.

The Commission should adopt an explicit policy of minimizing relocation to the greatest possible extent. Today it is common for workers laid off in one defense plant to move to a similar job in another city. However, some relocation will obviously be necessary, and the Commission should have funds to purchase houses of defense workers who cannot otherwise sell them at a fair market price. It should also pay travel costs and other relocation expenses. Britain has had a comprehensive program since 1909 to help its workers relocate to find suitable jobs. There should also be an income-maintenance program for defense workers to supplement normal unemployment benefits. Defense plants should be required to contribute to such a program by establishing insurance funds out of excess profits.

Communities that are dependent upon war industries or military installations should be eligible for special assistance. In a real sense they are "disaster areas" and should be eligible for the sort of extraordinary relief that is given to communities stricken by flood or tornado. When the Studebaker plant in South Bend, Indiana, closed in 1964, resulting in the layoff of 8700 workers, a coordinated federal program of assistance was undertaken. However, the principal instrument used to rescue the community was the defense budget. The Department of Defense arranged for the sale of the Studebaker plant to other defense firms. The Commission should stimulate non-defense production on a crash basis by making low-interest loans and emergency grants to affected communities. It could turn over federally-owned military installations to the local community at nominal cost upon receipt of a community plan for the utilization of the property. In some cases an emergency negative income tax or other income-maintenance program would be necessary.

The costs of these and other programs that might be developed by the Commission would be considerable, but they would be nowhere near the savings that could be realized by a substantial cut of the defense budget. Further, every dollar spent to stimulate useful production of goods and services needed to prevent social decay and to remove the injustices that lead to violence contributes to the real wealth of the nation as weapons stockpiles do not.

PLANNING AN ECONOMY OF LIFE

The major task of the National Conversion Commission would be to prepare a national conversion plan. For a generation, military spending has fulfilled three social purposes in America quite apart from defense. First, it has served to distract us from domestic problems. In the 1950's, according to the standard rhetoric, the nation could afford a military force "second to none" and do everything that needed to be done at home. (The unstated premise was, of course, that there wasn't much to be done.) In the 1960's, when it was no longer possible to deny the problems of the cities, the response was to blame unavoidably high defense costs for the national failure to meet the crisis. Second, military spending has satisfied the Keynesian economists' demand for a high level of government spending to stimulate growth. Third, by

having $45 billion a year to spend in the economy, the Pentagon has become the principal planner in American society.

If the federal government is to take the lead in reordering national priorities, it will have to exercise openly and rationally two functions that it now exercises covertly and irrationally. The first is subsidization, and the second is planning. A widely believed economic fairytale has it that there is an invisible wall separating the public government and private enterprise, that men get rich in spite of the government and not because of it. The reality is otherwise. The United States is a highly subsidized society. Not only defense contractors but oil interests, construction interests, shipping interests, and many others receive billions of dollars' worth of subsidies funded by the taxpayer in the form of depletion allowances, administered prices, and cash benefits. There is nothing wrong in principle with subsidies. The American system probably could not function without them. The important political questions are: Who gets subsidized? What national purpose is served? Are the taxpayers' interests protected?

There are strong traditions in America against using the federal budget to subsidize the public sector of the civilian economy. To take tax dollars to buy schools, hospitals, or food within the United States in adequate amounts is enormously difficult under our system. To buy weapons to fight an external enemy, on the other hand, is easy to understand and, until recently, almost impossible to oppose. It was not hard to find $687 million for germ warfare or $70.8 million for defoliating Vietnam in 1968, but it took a major struggle to obtain $100,000 to find out who goes to bed hungry in America. As one top weapons manufacturer put it recently, "We have the politically saleable animal—much easier than Watts."

To invest in the reconstruction of American society means redistribution of wealth and power, while military socialism for the most part means subsidizing the rich. Spending a billion dollars in the defense economy can be done with a few telephone calls and lunches involving a small number of people with an almost classic harmony of interests. Spending a billion dollars to stop pollution in New York or to fight poverty, on the other hand, involves a collision with entrenched political forces interested in the status quo. It is even easier to spend a dollar on the moon or on the bottom of the sea than on the poor, the hungry, the sick, or the old in America's cities or on her farms. Under the Puritan ethic, the government, like God, helps those who have helped themselves. For a politician, investing in the Economy of Death is bipartisan statesmanship. Investing in the Economy of Life involves a near-certainty of making at least one political enemy. To survive without civil war, however, America must now subsidize the "losers" instead of the "winners" in the national success race. Only a just society can dispense with violence.

To subsidize the Economy of Life would take some fundamental changes in American political attitudes. How these changes might come about will be discussed below. It will also take planning. This is another concept that traditionally has been greeted with great suspicion in American life. Much of what happens in our society is the result of private decisions and public non-decisions. It is clear, however, that if the society is to shift a substantial portion of its investment in military socialism to other public purposes, the reallocation of those resources cannot happen without some fundamental decisions of a public character. The problem is not finding things on which to spend the money. More than six years ago, even before the nation had discovered the true dimensions of poverty in America or the environmental crisis, the Columbia University economist Emile Benoit calculated that the nation needed to spend between $65 billion and $77.4 billion a year on itself to assure a decent society. The costs for the 1970's will be substantially higher than this. The problem is the lack of effective institutions for investing well in American society. High military spending has diverted attention from this problem for a generation.

The National Conversion Commission should have the responsibility to prepare a national conversion plan. As a first step it would, in cooperation with other domestic agencies and departments, put together an inventory of national needs. How many units of housing? How many medical schools? How much of an investment in air-traffic safety? What would it take to clean the nation's rivers? What would it take to feed the hungry? What would it take to make black people in the ghetto economically independent? What would it cost to purify the air? The Commission would attempt to determine what was needed for these tasks in manpower, facilities, and money. Each year the Commission would publish a State of the Union message on national needs and how far the nation was from meeting them.

Next, the Commission would request each community in the United States to prepare its own "wish list" or inventory of local needs. How many new beds for the hospital? How many schoolrooms? How many new jobs are needed for the rising population and what kind? What would the people of the community like to make? What would they like to do? Every community in the United States with a substantial dependence on military spending would be required to prepare a local reconversion plan as a condition of receiving further federal grants of any kind. Each defense contractor would be required to list the number and types of jobs presently dependent upon defense work and to submit a conversion schedule. The schedule would show what alternative products the contractor was prepared to make, what percentage of his present labor force he could employ, and what federal aid, if any, he would need to assist in training or relocating his employees. Defense plants would be given economic incentives to shift to the production of items listed on the local "wish list."

The National Conversion Commission would face one major dilemma. While a national plan and inventory of needs is essential, centralized administration of the conversion program would be a disaster. To replace the Pentagon bureaucracy with a pollution-control bureaucracy of similar size and character would increase the chances of survival but not the prospects for freedom. A major source of the public unhappiness is frustration with elephantine bureaucracies that literally crush the programs they supposedly administer. It has become a cliche to observe that people want greater participation in making the basic decisions that affect their lives, but the objective has seldom been realized. The conversion process should be regarded as an opportunity to experiment with new political forms for making decisions about allocating resources. Town meetings and city councils should debate the national conversion plan as well as the inventory of local needs. The National Conversion Commission should have the power to direct grants to units modeled on the "ward republics" proposed by Thomas Jefferson or the ECCO project developed by Milton Kotler in Columbus, Ohio, in which the neighborhood elects a government to look after local interest. Neighborhood health clinics, development banks for ghetto industry, local cooperatives, and other experimental structures for the society should be tried. Programs for economic development, agricultural reconstruction, and combating water pollution may need to be carried out on a multi-state basis, and the Commission's powers should be broad enough to encourage such regional structures.

Utility-Maximizing

34. Non-violent Economics: Next Task For Mankind

E. F. Schumacher

Some of mankind's greatest thinkers have seen life as a school, and history as the education of the human race. If this be so, it appears that Man has recently been put into a higher form where he is expected to learn to cope with two very difficult problems. These problems are not exactly new; but it had previously been permissible for Man to evade them; now it is no longer permissible.

The first problem, of course, is how to conduct international affairs in such a manner that there is never again a resort to large-scale violence. Just as little schoolboys are allowed to fight while grown men are not, because they are too powerful and would do too much damage to each other, so now, with the atom bomb, we have to behave as grown men. Our chances of coping successfully with the new situation are enhanced by the fact that at least everybody understands and accepts it. International "non-violence"

Reprinted from *The Observer*, London, August 21, 1960. Reprinted with permission.

is no longer merely the fond hope of a few imaginative or saintly cranks; it has become generally understood as an iron necessity for survival.

The second problem is how to conduct "economic" affairs in a manner that is compatible with both permanence and peace. It is also a problem of "non-violence," but a much more subtle one than the first. Luckily, we have still a bit of time to learn to cope with it, but considering that at present only very few people are even aware of the problem, the time is short. The problem gains real urgency from the strenuous attempts all over the world to "develop" the underdeveloped countries.

This development is generally conceived along Western lines, even in the Communist world. Yet it is easy to see that the Western way of life cannot be permanent, and will be incompatible with peace if it spreads to all mankind. It is based on non-renewable resources and rejects any idea of voluntary self-limitation.

Fossil fuels are limited

The Western way of life, even in a much more modest form than its American model, requires the annual use of several tons of fossil fuel per person. But the world's resources of fossil fuels, obtainable at a "reasonable" cost, are strictly limited. It follows that a civilization based on fossil fuels can be only an episode in the history of man — and when measured against the life of nations, a very short episode. (The present glut of fuel throughout the world is, of course, irrelevant to this argument; it merely serves as a temptation to disregard the basic predicament.)

By using coal and oil, we live on "capital" instead of income. This is quite legitimate, under certain conditions. Many a young man has his education financed out of capital funds, but if he is wise he does two things: (a) he voluntarily limits his annual drafts on capital so that it will last at least until he no longer needs it, and (b) he never loses sight of the fact that he must quickly learn to subsist on income, without further substantial drafts on capital. His principal task is to find a way of life that is self-supporting. And that, precisely that, is also the major task of modern man.

Nuclear contribution will be minute

It is a fatal error to assume that this task has already been accomplished through the discovery of nuclear energy. The experts now agree that the contribution of nuclear energy to the world's fuel supplies over the next ten years will be minute, and that it will probably still be negligible in twenty years' time. If this is so, it is practically certain that its contribution by the year 2000, reckoned as a proportion of the total, will still be very modest indeed.

By that time, the world's population will have doubled, and it is being assumed by those who favor a Western-type development in the underdeveloped countries that the average use of fuel "per head" will be then have doubled or even trebled. This would mean a world fuel requirement equivalent to something like 20,000 million tons of coal a year. For nuclear energy to provide even 15 per cent of this total would require the erection of nuclear plants during the eighties and nineties at a rate that is well-nigh unthinkable.

Be that as it may, it is certainly unthinkable that poor countries, undernourished, technically backward, and without a large "middle-class" of technologists and technicians — countries which hitherto have been unable to develop even their

potential of water power (hydro-electricity) — could benefit substantially from a process that represents the height of technical achievement, requires the maximum of technical discipline, and involves capital outlays of a size to embarrass even the wealthiest.

What is more, it must be feared that the task of finding a way of economic life based on income rather than capital can never be satisfactorily solved by nuclear energy. If we consider the magnitude of the world's use of non-renewable fuels and its rate of growth, we are forced to conclude that the price to be paid for such a "solution" would be the total enslavement of man to his machines. This has been clearly seen and graphically described by Professor Harrison Brown, of the California Institute of Technology (in *The Challenge of Man's Future*), but unfortunately by few others. Our scientific Utopians, who purport to believe that "Science" will find the answer to all questions, fail to recognize that there are limits to the complexity of life beyond which human existence becomes unendurable.

A way of life that ever more rapidly depletes the power of the earth to sustain it and piles up ever more insoluble problems for each succeeding generation can only be called "violent." It is not a way of life that one would like to see exported to countries not yet committed to it. Of course, it has its attractions. But this is not an argument in its favour any more than an individual's enjoyment of lavish living justifies him in squandering his own and other people's capital.

In short, man's urgent task is to discover a non-violent way in his economic as well as in his political life. It is obvious that the two are closely related. Both represent very great challenges to human good will, patience, and rationality. The real pessimists are those who declare it impossible even to make a start.

Problem not of man's choosing

Why should it be impossible? There have been periods of great popular well-being and high culture in nearly all countries, based on economic methods that did not significantly deplete the resources of the earth. Why should this not be possible again, with so much added knowledge of the laws of nature? In any case, let us not forget that the problem is not of man's choosing: It is being imposed by the nature of things.

The difficulties must, of course, appear greatest to those who are furthest removed from the traditional way of life—that is, to the "developed" countries. But the underdeveloped countries should not find it so difficult. To achieve development along Western lines may appear to them today, after more than ten years of almost desperate effort, as really impossible. Maybe they have reason to be grateful for their lack of success. Maybe the road of Westernization which they are attempting to travel, and which certainly cannot lead to success in the long run, cannot even take them to anything satisfactory in the short run.

Less than a penny a day

Let us resort to the simplest arithmetic. The three eminent bankers who have recently reported on the needs of India and Pakistan suggest that these two countries require Western aid amounting to £ 3,000 million to carry out their next five-year development plans. Per head of the populations concerned as beneficiaries, this means rather less than a penny a day. Without denying the possible usefulness of less than a penny a day and without wishing to discourage in the slightest the noble impulse of generosity, we surely must realize—and so must the Indians and Pakistanis—that aid in any form or feasible size cannot be the crux of the matter.

If these countries have programmes of development which, being of Western inspiration, depend primarily on Western aid, then, quite clearly, they have the wrong kind of programmes. Any worthwhile development in countries of ancient culture and hallowed tradition must be based primarily on what they can do themselves, in accordance with the best that is existent in their own souls.

One can of course do the one and not leave the other—what the Chinese call "walking on both feet." But the two feet are not of equal strength. The labour power of the indigenous population is an infinitely greater potential than foreign aid could ever be. Yet this latent labour power, so it would seem, will not become actual as long as alien methods and conceptions dominate the scene—methods and conceptions which, quite apart from being alien, are characterised by a peculiar impatience and violence, whereas the real task of the present age is to evolve a dignified and non-violent way of life.

Non-violence must permeate the whole of man's activities, if mankind is to be secure against a war of annihilation. Economics, like politics, must be led back to an acceptable philosophical base. Present-day economics, while claiming to be ethically neutral, in fact propagates a philosophy of unlimited expansionism. without any regard to the true and genuine needs of man, which are limited.

"Withering touch" of the west

It is this that gives the Western way of life that destructive and paralysing effect upon the so-called "underdeveloped" countries which has been rightly called the "withering touch." To recognise this fatal weakness does not mean underestimating the stupendous achievements of the West. In the great school of life they have their legitimate place and function. They need not be abandoned and they will not get lost, merely because new tasks have been set in the higher form.

The West can indeed help the others, as the rich can always help the poor. But it is not an easy matter, expressible in terms of money alone. It demands a deep respect for the indigenous culture of those that are to be helped—maybe even a deeper respect than is possessed by many of them themselves. Above all, it would seem, it must be based on a clear understanding that the present situation of mankind demands the evolution of a non-violent way of political and economic life.

Bibliography

The following bibliographies and readings are to supplement the materials in this reader. The additional titles are organized according to the principal categories of the reader.

Bibliographies: The following bibliographies contain extensive listings on military economy:

Geraldine P. Sica, *A Preliminary Bibliography of Studies of the Economic Effects of Defense Policies and Expenditures,* Research Analysis Corporation, McLean, Virginia, October 1968. Available to the public at $3 per copy from Clearinghouse, Springfield, Virginia, 22151. Specify document number AD 679038. (This bibliography is reproduced in full in S. Melman (Ed.), *The Defense Economy,* Praeger Publishers, New York, 1970.)

"National Security and the Military-Industrial Complex," a reading list based on a semester course offered at the University of Maryland, Spring, 1970. Reproduced in full in L. S. Rodberg and D. Shearer (Eds.), *The Pentagon Watchers,* Doubleday, New York, 1970, Appendix.

James Kuhn, "Business in the Military Industrial Complex," a bibliography and course outline at the Graduate School of Business, Columbia University. This bibliography is available on request from Professor James Kuhn at Graduate School of Business, Columbia University, New York, N.Y. 10027.

S. Melman, "The Military-Industrial Complex and American Society," course outline and bibliography. Available on request from S. Melman, Department of Industrial Engineering, Room 320, S.W. Mudd Building, Columbia University, New York, N.Y. 10027.

Extensive bibliographic listings on U.S. war economy appear in the Appendixes to S. Melman, *Our Depleted Society* and *Pentagon Capitalism.*

THE SCALE OF MILITARY ECONOMY

Stockholm International Peace Research Institute, *Sipri Yearbook of World Arma-*

ments and Disarmament, Humanities Press, New York, 1969.

Emile Benoit, "The Monetary and Real Costs of National Defense," *American Economic Review,* Proceedings of the Annual Meeting, 1968.

Michael Klare, "The University-Military-Police Complex, A Directory and Related Documents," North American Congress on Latin America, P.O. Box 57, Cathedral Park Station, New York, N.Y. 10025.

THE MILITARY-INDUSTRIAL FIRM

Walter Adams, "The Military-Industrial Complex and the New Industrial State," *American Economic Review,* May 1968.

NACLA Research Methodology Guide, North American Congress on Latin America, P.O. Box 57, Cathedral Park Station, New York, N.Y. 10025

Merton J. Peck and Fredric M. Scherer, *The Weapons Acquisition Process—An Economic Analysis,* Division of Research, Graduate School of Business Administration, Harvard University, Boston, 1962.

Fredric M. Scherer, *The Weapons Acquisition Process,* Division of Research, Graduate School of Business Administration, Harvard University, Boston, 1964.

Rodberg and Shearer, *The Pentagon Watchers.*

Clark R. Mollenhoff, *The Pentagon,* Putnam, New York, 1967.

William Proxmire, *Report From Wasteland,* Praeger Publishers, New York, 1970.

Sidney Lens, *The Military-Industrial Complex,* Pilgrim Press, Philadelphia, 1970.

John Stanley Baumgartner, *The Lonely Warriors,* Nash Publishing, Los Angeles, 1970.

H. L. Nieburg, *In The Name of Science,* Quadrangle Books, Chicago, 1966.

Comptroller General of the United States, "Status of the Acquisition of Selected Major Weapon Systems." Report to the Congress, U.S. General Accounting Office, February, 1970.

The Council on Economic Priorities, *Efficiency in Death, The Manufacturers of Anti-Personnel Weapons,* Harper and Row, New York, 1970.

ECONOMIC CONSEQUENCES OF MILITARY INDUSTRY

Barry Goldwater, "An Address in Support of the Military-Industrial Complex," *Congressional Record,* April 15, 1969, Reprinted in *Barron's,* April 21, 1969.

U.S. Congress, Joint Economic Committee, "Economic Effect of Vietnam Spending." Hearings before the Joint Economic Committee, 90th Congress, 1st Session, April 24th–27th, 1967, Volumes I and II, Washington, D.C., 1967.

Robert A. Solo, "Gearing Military R and D to Economic Growth," *Harvard Business Review,* November–December 1962.

James L. Clayton, *The Economic Impact of the Cold War, Sources and Readings,* Harcourt, Brace, and World, New York, 1970.

William N. Leonard, "Research and Development in Industrial Growth," *The Journal of Political Economy,* March–April 1971.

Bruce M. Russett, *What Price Vigilance? The Burdens of National Defense,* Yale University Press, New Haven, 1970.

Conversion from military to civilian economy

U.S. Senate, Committee on Labor and Public Welfare, "Postwar Economic Conversion." Hearings, 91st Congress, 2nd Session, Parts I and II, Washington, D.C., 1970.

U.S. Senate, Committee on Government Operations, Subcommittee on Executive Reorganization and Government Research, *National Economic Conversion Commission, Responses to Subcommittee Questionnaire,* Washington, D.C., September, 1967.

Leslie Fishman, "A Note on Disarmament and Effective Demand," *The Journal of Political Economy,* April 1962.

"Plans for New York State to Meet the Economic Consequences of Peace." Report of the Post-Vietnam Committee, to the Governor of the State of New York, The Governor of the State of New York, Albany, New York, 12224.

Emile Benoit and Kenneth E. Boulding (Eds.), *Disarmament and the Economy,* Harper and Row, New York, 1963.

Emile Benoit (Ed.), *Disarmament and World Economic Interdependence,* Columbia University Press, New York, 1967.

Seymour Melman (Ed.), *Disarmament, Its Politics and Economics,* The American Academy of Arts and Sciences, Boston, 1962.

Juan Cameron, "The Case for Cutting Defense Spending," *Fortune,* August 1, 1969.

Robert S. Benson, "How the Pentagon Can Save $9 Billion," *The Washington Monthly,* March, 1969.

U.S. Senate, Committee on Labor and Public Welfare, Subcommittee on Employment and Manpower, *Convertibility of Space and Defense Resources to Civilian Needs: A Search for New Employment Potentials,* Volumes I and II, Washington, D.C., 1964.

U.S. Arms Control and Disarmament Agency, *The Economic and Social Consequences of Disarmament,* Washington, D.C., June, 1964.

Seymour Melman (Ed.), Conversion of Industry From a Military to Civilian Economy, A Series of Studies, published by Praeger, 1970. This series includes: Marvin Berkowitz, *The Conversion of Military-Oriented Research and Development to Civilian Uses;* Aris P. Christodoulou, *Conversion of Nuclear Facilities From Military to Civilian Uses;* Daniel M. Mack-Forlist and Arthur Newman, *The Conversion of Shipbuilding from Military to Civilian Markets;* Seymour Melman (Ed.), *The Defense Economy;* John E. Ullmann (Ed.), *Potential Civilian Markets for the Military-Electronics Industry;* John E. Lynch, *Local Economic Development After Military Base Closures.*

INDEX

Armed forces, 1, 7, 20, 114, 153, 170, 201, 207, 227, 231, 234–235
Arms race, 34, 36, 40–42, 116, 120, 121, 148, 153, 154, 194, 201, 210
    See also Overkill; Competition
Arms sales, 34–43
Atomic Energy Commission, 89, 114, 117, 124, 136, 187, 189, 205

Balance of payments, 36, 113, 151, 157, 161–62, 167–68, 173, 178, 185, 227, 228
Balance of trade, 4, 53, 103–04, 157, 162, 165, 173–74, 178, 185

Capital, 55–59, 67, 72, 87, 88, 95, 113, 115, 123, 131, 148, 155–57, 165–68, 184, 197, 225–26, 235, 241
    See also Property
Capitalism, 54–55, 185, 234
    state, 2, 7–8, 54–59, 118, 124, 197–98, 240
    See also Pentagon capitalism
Chemical and biological warfare, 182, 239
Comparative advantage, 5, 36–37, 40–41, 83–84, 104, 122–32, 139, 162, 215–25
    See also Competition
Competition, 40–41, 45, 49, 62, 66, 75, 80, 82, 86–87, 97, 103, 106, 115, 116, 118, 120, 122, 178, 215, 218, 220, 224
    See also Comparative advantage
Consumption, private, 155–56, 165, 168, 185, 195, 203, 225–26
Contractors; *See* Military-industrial firm
Conversion, 7, 50, 54, 72, 119–20, 126, 150, 195–200, 201–25, 226, 232–33, 234–40
Cost, 3, 46, 51–52, 72–74, 80, 86, 89, 91–95, 102, 120, 122 passim, 129, 131, 148, 169–72, 215, 220, 224
Cost-benefit analysis, 152–60
Cost control, 23–24, 29–33, 57, 85–87, 92–95, 98–100, 101, 115, 120, 124, 215
Cost effectiveness, 25, 45, 46, 47, 91, 121, 139 passim, 151, 152–60

Decision-making, 1, 2, 25–27, 29, 31–33, 39–40, 49–50, 60–71, 72–79, 90, 93, 100, 106, 112, 118, 120, 139 passim, 147–51, 180, 183, 201, 239–40, 240–43
Defense, 30, 34–36, 40, 44–45, 47, 83, 103, 104, 109, 111, 116, 120, 121, 148, 161, 169, 173, 187, 201, 212
Defense projects, 3, 23–33, 45, 47–48, 50–52, 82, 93, 97–100, 101–06, 106–10, 120, 184, 187, 194, 202, 212–14
Defense strategies, 7, 22–23, 30, 33, 47, 49, 120, 183, 194, 215
Demand, 66, 72, 80, 113, 153, 194, 209–14, 226, 227–28
Department of Defense, 1, 2, 24–25, 44, 61–62, 66, 72, 73, 85, 97, 101, 117, 124, 136–37, 148, 181, 187, 188, 196–97, 205, 207–09, 214, 234–35

Depletion, 5, 83–84, 103–04, 114–15, 121, 122–32, 136, 149–50, 161, 172, 177, 193, 198, 202, 205–08, 220, 226
Depression, 53, 55, 79, 153, 185, 195
Dollar, value of, 4, 36, 113, 151, 160–62, 169, 173–75, 202
    See also Money

Economic development, 6, 34, 42, 150–51, 176, 190–93, 198, 202, 209, 226, 228, 233, 240, 242
Economic equilibrium, 56–59, 104, 201–07
Economies, foreign, 11–12, 19, 34, 40–42, 58, 120, 122 passim, 187
Economizing, 24, 29, 30–32, 44, 60–71, 73, 83, 85, 87, 91, 93–94, 100–01, 102, 113, 124 passim, 202, 204, 208, 220, 222–23
Economy
    California, 187–200, 232
    regional, 6, 77–79, 118, 120, 137–47, 187–200, 201, 232, 240
    U.S., 6, 53–59, 83–84, 104, 112, 115–16, 118, 119, 122–32, 148, 152–53, 156, 167–69, 175–79, 193, 201, 207–09, 234, 238–39
Education, 12, 14–22, 70, 81, 111, 114, 115–17, 151, 154, 157–60, 181–82, 189, 197–99, 205–06, 220, 223, 226–27, 229
Efficiency; *See* Productivity
Employment; *See* Labor markets; Unemployment
Enterprise, private, 1–7, 24, 25, 30, 60–76, 76–84, 87, 99, 184
    See also Firm; Mixed Economy
Entrepreneurship; *See* Enterprise, private
Expenditures
    government, 19–20, 26, 28, 55, 85, 86, 111–21, 155, 157–60, 164–65, 169–72, 173–74, 177, 189, 226
    military, 3, 4, 9–22, 23–24, 83–84, 85, 86, 91, 93, 100–01, 111–21, 132, 137–47, 152–60, 162, 173, 175–76, 178, 190, 201, 209–14, 215, 225, 231–34, 238
    See also Vietnam war

Finance, 38–39, 67, 82, 86, 88, 112, 160, 165–67, 192, 235
    international, 38–39
Firm, 60–62, 69, 180–81
    See also Enterprise, private; Management
Fiscal policy, 59, 112, 120, 156, 165–66, 168, 174–75, 208, 215, 226
Foreign assistance
    economic, 20, 21, 34, 36, 40, 228, 242
    military, 34–35
Foreign investments, 5, 122, 124, 127, 174–75, 185
Foreign trade, 5, 34–43, 53, 103–04, 126–27, 131–32, 155, 157, 161, 166–67, 178, 215–25, 227–28
Freedom, 116–19, 121, 150, 180–87, 193, 206

Gold, 4, 113, 151, 160–69, 173–75
Government
controls, 2–3, 54–59; 62–68, 71–76,
76–84, 90–94, 113, 116–18, 131, 168–69,
178, 220
federal, 22, 24, 39, 43, 104–05, 116, 124,
147, 148, 150–51, 168–69, 179–87, 203–
04, 206, 231–34, 235
Gross National Product, 3, 21, 55, 84, 86,
112, 121, 132, 133, 149, 152, 155 passim,
163–64, 226
Growth, 3–5, 11, 19, 22–33, 44–50, 57–58,
77–78, 84, 94, 98–100, 111, 115, 120,
126–28, 132–37, 148, 152–60, 161–69,
176–77, 185, 208, 226–28, 238, 240–43

Imperialism, 53–54, 185
Industry
aerospace, 209–14
agriculture, 131
airframe, 203
automobile, 126, 220
electronics, 203–04, 211, 215–25
fishing, 130–31
machine tool, 123–24
railroad, 124–25
sewing machine, 126–28
shipbuilding, 128–30, 205
shipping, 128–30
typewriter, 122–23
Inflation, 4, 26, 99, 103, 112–14, 119, 157,
160–69, 172, 175–79, 185, 193
See also Dollar, value of; Money
Information, 87, 90–94, 97, 98–100, 118, 182
Input-output, regional, 137–47, 187–200
International disequilibrium, 175–79
Investment, 1, 6, 45, 46, 57, 67–68, 75, 88,
95–96, 113, 115, 122 passim, 132–33,
150, 154, 155–59, 165–68, 174, 177,
185, 202, 206–07, 209, 226–27, 228,
234–40
See also Foreign investment

Labor markets, 1, 5, 6, 45, 55–57, 77, 101,
114, 116, 133, 136, 149–50, 153–54,
160, 164, 167–68, 182–83, 188–90, 201,
207–09, 227, 231–34, 234–36

Management, 1, 60–68, 72–79, 100–01,
103–04, 115, 125–26, 129, 131, 148,
150, 181, 185, 203
labor relations, 65–66, 74–76, 77, 100–01,
103, 105–06, 116–17, 182–83, 216 passim
product description, 62, 70, 72, 80, 92–93,
97–100, 148, 208, 214, 220
production function, 64–66, 73–75, 94,
123–32, 148, 150, 223
quality of product, 24, 31–33, 40, 49,
62–63, 65, 80, 85–87, 98–100, 103,
106–10, 124–25, 148, 215, 220–21, 224
quantity produced, 63, 74, 80, 127, 131,
148, 186

Market forecast, 24–25, 30–33, 50–59, 62–63,
71–72, 77–78, 82, 115, 119–20, 124,
184, 194, 197, 204, 209–14
Market organization, 1–8, 61–76, 79, 85–101,
102, 106, 124, 131, 183–84, 187, 204,
209–14
Markets
commercial, 196–97, 202–04, 208–14,
215–25, 235
foreign, 3, 9–22, 34–36, 124, 127, 177–78,
185, 224
Military-industrial complex, 2, 25, 80, 82–83,
105, 110, 116, 120–21, 139, 210, 214
Military-industrial firm, 1, 2, 7–8, 24, 30, 45,
49, 60–71, 71–76, 76–84, 85–101, 137,
150, 184, 187–88, 195–97, 199, 202–03,
208–09, 209–14, 224, 235
Military industry, 1, 86–87, 109, 114, 133,
149–50, 176, 183, 190, 201 passim, 212
Military service, 116, 118, 183
See also Armed forces
Mixed economy, 24–25, 30–31, 54–59, 78,
81–83, 87, 99, 102–03, 109, 111–21,
129, 180–87, 187–200, 238
Monetary policy, 112, 177, 208, 226
Money, 4, 5, 149, 160–69, 173–75
See also Dollar, value of
Monopoly, 85–101
Monopsony, 1–8, 61–76, 85–101, 124, 131, 187

National Aeronautics and Space Administration, 70, 71, 89, 114, 117, 133–37, 187–
88, 194, 214, 215, 232
Nuclear warfare, 111, 116, 151

Occupation mix, 189, 195, 201, 204
Oligopoly, 79, 89–90, 102, 106–07, 184,
209–14
Opportunity cost, 4, 5, 45–46, 105, 113–16,
152–60, 172, 178, 202, 225, 229–30,
238–39
Overkill, 45, 47–48, 53, 148, 151, 209

Pentagon capitalism, 1, 2, 7–8, 36, 43, 50,
61–71, 73–79, 83, 100–02, 148, 180–87,
196, 238, 240
See also Capitalism, state
Price, 1, 2, 3, 24, 66, 70, 72, 74, 80, 87, 89,
92, 94, 98–100, 102, 112, 123 passim,
148, 152, 160, 169, 177, 218
Product quality; See Management, quality of
product
Productivity, 5, 45, 82, 85–86, 94–95,
100–01, 101–06, 115, 122–32, 133,
150–51, 154, 161, 174, 208, 220
Profit, 1, 2–3, 60, 66, 68, 73–74, 77, 79,
82, 85–97, 106, 109, 126, 152, 174–75,
176–79, 184–85, 189, 235
Property, 67, 72, 86–89
See also Capital
Public debt, 26, 111, 154, 161, 169–72, 173,
175

Research and development, 1, 5, 27, 30, 61, 70, 72–73, 84, 89, 114–15, 117, 120, 122, 130, 132–37, 149–50, 154, 160, 176, 181–82, 187, 189–90, 194, 205–06, 208, 215, 219, 220–21, 226–27

Resource allocation, 5, 11, 31, 34, 46, 54–55, 113–14, 119, 120, 121, 132, 133–37, 149–51, 152–60, 166, 176, 187–200, 201–07, 207–09, 212, 216, 224, 225–32, 237, 240–43

Scarcity; *See* Resource allocation

Secrecy, 76–77, 117, 118, 183

Selling, 70, 74, 80, 87, 110, 115, 126, 184, 208, 212

Social consequences, 198–200, 206, 229, 238, 240–43
See also Freedom

Social cost; *See* Opportunity cost

State-management; *See* Capitalism, state; Pentagon capitalism

Sub-firms; *See* Military-industrial firm

Subsidy, 88, 102–05, 128–29, 137, 203, 236–38

Taxes, 103, 105, 112, 137–47, 152, 168–69, 175, 177, 183, 185, 236

Technology, 5, 48, 49–50, 59, 71–73, 80, 83–84, 87, 120, 122–32, 133–37, 147–51, 198–200, 218, 220, 221–23, 235–36
military, 70, 72–73, 87, 106–10, 114, 120, 135–37, 149–51, 154, 176, 198, 208, 220–21, 236
See also Research and development

Unemployment, 54–57, 102, 104, 111, 122–32, 150, 153, 158, 167–68, 177–78, 185–86, 188, 193–95, 201–07, 215, 219, 226–27, 231–40

Universities, 70, 81, 116–17, 151, 159, 181–82, 189, 196, 205–06, 220

Utility, 25, 30–31, 56–59, 240–43

Value, 4, 45–46, 98–100, 103, 180

Vietnam war, 26–28, 48–49, 112–13, 116 passim, 151, 152, 157, 159, 160–69, 169–72, 175–79, 182–83, 186, 191–93, 201, 209, 211

Wage rates, 131, 152, 164, 169, 185, 208, 220, 236

World market; *See* Markets, foreign